More-with-Less Cookbook

●●●●●●●●●●●●●●●●●●●●●●●●●●
Doris Janzen Longacre

Commissioned by
Mennonite Central Committee,
Akron, Pennsylvania,
in response to
world food needs.

Foreword by
Mary Emma Showalter Eby

Foreword to Anniversary Edition by
Mary Beth Lind

25th anniversary edition

Herald
Press

Scottdale, Pennsylvania
Waterloo, Ontario

Library of Congress Cataloging-in-Publication Data

Longacre, Doris Janzen.
   More-with-less cookbook / Doris Janzen Longacre ; foreword to the Anniversary
edition by Mary Beth Lind.—25th anniversary ed.
      p. cm.
   "Commissioned by Mennonite Central Committee, Akron, Pennsylvania."
   ISBN 0-8361-9103-X
   1. Cookery, Mennonite. I. Title.

TX715 .L822 2000
641.5'66—dc21   00-33473

The paper used in this publication is recycled and meets the minimum requirements of American
National Standard for Information Sciences—Permanence of Paper for Printed Library Materials,
ANSI Z39.48-1984.

Photographs pp. 2, 6, 11, 22, 25, 26, 44, and 316 from MCC files; front and back cover, 12, 53ff.,
Ken Hiebert; inside front cover and inside back cover, Foodpix.

MORE-WITH-LESS COOKBOOK (25th Anniversary Edition)
Copyright © 2000 by Herald Press, Scottdale, Pa. 15683
   Released simultaneously in Canada by Herald Press,
   Waterloo, Ont. N2L 6H7. All rights reserved
Library of Congress Catalog Card Number: 00-33473
International Standard Book Number: 0-8361-9103-X
Printed in the United States of America
Design for anniversary edition by Merrill R. Miller

First edition © 1976 by Herald Press, Scottdale, Pa. 15683
   Forty-seven printings (642,500 copies). More than 847,000
   worldwide, including Bantam Press, British, and German editions.
Design for first edition by Ken Hiebert

To order or request information, please call: 1-800-759-4447 (individuals); 1-800-245-7894 (trade).
Website: www.mph.org

●●●●●●●●●●●●●●●●●●●●●●●●

A full stomach says:
   A ripe guava has worms.
An empty stomach says:
   Let me see.
—Creole Proverb

An empty sack cannot stand up.
   A starving belly
      doesn't listen to explanations.
—Creole Proverb

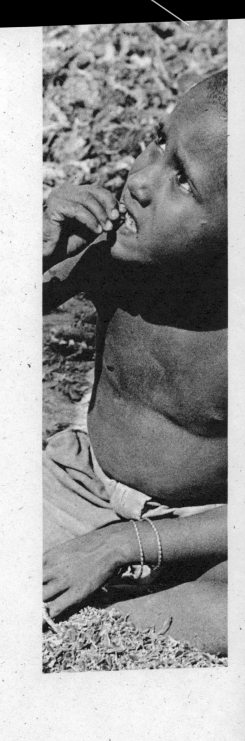

You are what you eat

"You are what you eat," cautions the old adage. We tend to think of it in a physical sense, but Doris Longacre in *More-with-Less Cookbook* raises the question on a different level. Does what you eat affect who you are spiritually? Does your belief in God affect your way of living?

In the Old Testament, the prophet Daniel's theology influenced his lifestyle and eating habits. In the New Testament, Jesus performed miracles to provide adequate food for all—turning water into wine to assure enough for the wedding guests at Cana and feeding the crowd of five thousand. In Matthew 25, Jesus says we will be judged more by our sharing of food than by our creeds.

The early Anabaptists, forebears of today's Mennonites, recognized that "to know Christ we must follow him in our lives" (Denck), a fleshed-out theology. Yes, we are what we eat, and what we eat shows our theology. This is the appeal of *More-with-Less Cookbook*. The book speaks, not only to our physical bodies, but also to our souls. It is soul food, and we need it more than ever.

Twenty-five years later: When will we ever learn?

When *More-with-Less Cookbook* was first published in 1976, Doris Longacre wrote of world shortages of food and of North Americans consuming too much of the world's resources—money, calories, protein, sugar, and processed foods. We have not learned.

Today, in spite of or because of the Green Revolution, globalization of trade, genetically engineered seeds, and high technology in farm equipment, food shortages still plague our world:

- Shortages caused by "acts of nature" (or humanity's misuse of the earth?), drought and floods, heat and frost.
- Shortages caused by political and economic sanctions.
- Shortages caused by sheer numbers—now more than six billion people on this planet.
- Shortages caused by wars and governments' inability or unwillingness to address problems of refugees and the displaced.

According to Worldwatch Institute, one in five people is chronically hungry. Christians' response to such shortages reveals our theology.

Meanwhile, North Americans are encouraged to consume. We've seen an explosion of new artificial fats and sweeteners and products made with them, yet we suffer from obesity. The nutritional supplement industry encourages us to take vitamin, mineral, and herbal supplements to be healthy and happy. We no longer see food as good, providing nutrients and needed fuel. It is either a splurge or a scourge.

More-with-Less Cookbook can help recapture the joy of preparing and eating adequate and appropriate food.

Twenty-five years later: What's the good news?

There is hope for us. Community-Supported Agriculture (CSA) and local farmers' markets now help connect people with their food source. Most CSAs and many farmers' markets sell organically grown foods. Thus, they are good for the soil, the consumer, and the community. These endeavors practice the more-with-less principle of "think globally but act locally."

More men cook—another positive sign. Men are sharing household tasks and finding creative fulfillment in the kitchen. Bread machines and other tools attract men with mechanical interests and give them a natural reason to help prepare food. Other men eagerly try new things and experiment with cooking.

In the past 25 years, vegetarian and cultural foods have become more available and more accepted. Restaurants, grocery stores, and even fast-food restaurant chains now offer alternative food selections and dishes from many cultures.

More people are eating fruits and vegetables, partly because of medical recommendations to eat five fruits and vegetables a day. We can pick up ready-to-eat produce such as mixed salads and baby carrots at the grocery store. More soy products are available—texturized vegetable protein, meat substitutes, tofu, soymilk, and cheeses. Tomatoes and peppers have found a ready market as salsa, exceeding sales of catsup.

Twenty-five years later: What's new?

Most food products now carry a Nutrition Facts label. The top section includes categories such as calories, fats, saturated fats, cholesterol, and sodium. For healthier eating, use sparingly foods that have more than 10 percent of the DV (daily value) for any of these categories. The lower section includes information on fiber, vitamins A and C, iron, and calcium—important for our diets. Choose foods that have 10 percent DV or more of these items.

Microwave cooking makes food preparation easier, safer, more nutritious, and more efficient. A cartoon from the 1970s stated, "Microwaves frizz your heirs." Today we have moved from fear and caution to acceptance; we use more microwaves than conventional ranges and ovens. Ninety-two percent of our homes have at least one microwave, although most people use the microwave only for reheating and defrosting.

Some new developments need discernment. Genetically engineered foods are designed to meet farmers' needs for disease and pest resistance. They provide longer shelf life, slower ripening, and enhanced nutrients. However, they may cause environmental, economic, or theological problems. Food safety with or without irradiation is a hot topic. Are we moving from being co-creators with God to being "gods unto ourselves"?

As Christian stewards, we need to treat all things with care and respect, including our food. Caring for animals in a humane way, treating farm workers as brothers and sisters, and caring for our soil instead of polluting it—all forge a connection between the soil and our souls.

Food: Reclaiming its spirituality

When we cultivate food in our backyards, we nurture it; in return, it nourishes us. Food is an integral part of our lives—not just at mealtime. Food is natural and unaffected.

In contrast, modern North America reduces food to a commodity that is manipulated, genetically engineered, irradiated, manufactured, or enriched and fortified. Food is fast—fast-food restaurants, meals in minutes, instant this and instant that. We fill our physical fuel tanks with as much abandon as we fill our car fuel tanks—fast and full—and sometimes at the same stations.

When we make food an integral part of our lives and our homes, it becomes part of our theology. We are connected to our food—cultivating it, preserving it, and preparing it. We are nurturers instead of consumers. This shift affects our relationship to the Giver of our daily bread. We become co-creators with God and stewards of God's garden. *More-with-Less Cookbook* invites us to recognize and remember this connection.

We are what we eat—physically and spiritually. Doris Longacre states that "change is an act of faith." Our interaction with food will express our faith.

—*Mary Beth Lind, Registered Dietitian, Harman, W.Va.*

The cross emptying into
action in the form of
a dove of peace
visually identifies the
Mennonite Central
Committee (MCC),
"a Christian resource
for meeting human need."

As used on the front cover,
the symbol will help
you remember that
combinations of grains
and dairy products
or grains and legumes
form complete protein.

More-with-Less Cookbook
emphasizes the worldwide
perspective of MCC.

Acknowledgments

This book is not a personal production, but a blend of the gifts and ideas of many. Therefore the list of acknowledgments is long.

Special thanks to:

—Karin and Walton Hackman, former neighbors, who first said, "Someone should write a cookbook."
—Hundreds of men and women who responded to Mennonite Central Committee's call for recipes.
—William T. Snyder, Edgar Stoesz, and other Mennonite Central Committee staff persons for warm encouragement and helpful criticism.
—Marjorie Ruth for competent secretarial assistance and typing the manuscript.
—Bonnie Zook for directing the recipe-testing procedure and other staff assistance.
—Helen Janzen, former Supervisor of Home Economics for the Department of Education in Manitoba, for reading and criticizing the manuscript.
—Kenton K. Brubaker, Professor of Biology, Eastern Mennonite College, and David Leaman, Assistant Professor of Medicine, Hershey Medical Center, for reading and criticizing Part One of the manuscript.
—Don Ziegler and Sarah Ann Eby for editing the manuscript.
—My husband, Paul, and our daughters, Cara Sue and Marta Joy, for their wealth of good ideas and cheerful willingness to try new dishes month after month.

—The following home economists and their families who voluntarily tested the recipes:

Ruth Alderfer, Hatfield, Pa.
Linda Baer, Hagerstown, Md.
Ann Dumper, Grantham, Pa.
Beth Frey, Conestoga, Pa.
Carol Friesen, Fresno, Calif.
Sandy Goritz, Boiling Springs, Pa.
Karen Harvey, Leola, Pa.
Mary Jane Hershey, Harleysville, Pa.
Alta Hertzler, Goshen, Ind.
Kathy Histand, Sellersville, Pa.
Betty Hochstetler, Elkhart, Ind.
Nancy Horning, Leola, Pa.
Louetta Hurst, Lancaster, Pa.
Margaret Ingold, Goshen, Ind.
Debbie Jennings, Grantham, Pa.
Sheila Jones, York, Pa.
Marlene Kaufman, Mt. Gretna, Pa.
Kate Kooker, Ardmore, Pa.
Louise Leatherman, Akron, Pa.
Ellen Longacre, Bally, Pa.
Mary Martin, Hagerstown, Md.
Jean Miller, Akron, Pa.
Mary Jo Oswald, Hagerstown, Md.
LaVonne Platt, Newton, Kan.
Doris Risser, Harrisonburg, Va.
JoAnn Siegrist, Lancaster, Pa.
June Suderman, Hillsboro, Kan.
Sharon Swartzendruber, Pekin, Ill.
Lois Weaver, Lansdale, Pa.
Erma Weaver, Manheim, Pa.
Lucy Weber, Mohnton, Pa.
Olive Wyse, Goshen, Ind.
Lillian Yoder, Goshen, Ind.
Bonnie Zook, Leola, Pa.
Catherine Mumaw, Goshen College Home Economics Department, and students of Goshen College foods classes

—these persons for additional special testing:

students in Goshen College Peace Society who arranged for alternate cafeteria meals
Ruth Detweiler, Akron, Pa.
Marian Franz, Washington, D.C.
Miriam LeFever, East Petersburg, Pa.
Kamala Platt, Newton, Kan.
Gladys Stoesz, Akron, Pa.
Don and Priscilla Ziegler, Lancaster, Pa.

Dedicated to
Helene Claassen Janzen
and
Edna Mowere Longacre

●●●●●●●●●●●●●●●●●●●●●●●●●●

two cooks who are
traditional but creative
thrifty but generous

Mennonites are widely recognized as good cooks. But Mennonites are also a people who care about the world's hungry.

Mennonite Central Committee (MCC), the cooperative relief and service agency of seventeen North American Mennonite and Brethren in Christ churches, has called for a major focus on the world food crisis by Mennonites within the next five to ten years. It is providing leadership in working at long-range solutions by broadening and strengthening rural development and family planning programs around the world.

In addition, for the first time in its 55-year history, MCC has asked each constituent household to look at its lifestyle, particularly food habits. Noting the relationship between North American overconsumption and world need, a goal has been set to eat and spend 10 percent less.

In Mennonite communities across North America, people are responding with a kind of holy frustration. "We want to use less," they say. "How do we begin? How do we maintain motivation in our affluent society? How do we help each other?" From questions like these the idea of compiling a cookbook was born.

Mennonite and Brethren in Christ periodicals carried the request for recipes, hints, and inspirational material. Within weeks, letters from men and women, from students and grandparents filled my box. Thousands of recipes arrived from around the world.

Those with whom I counseled agreed that every recipe used should first be tested. More than

4

We are prepared
with all our hearts
to share our possessions,
gold,
and all that we have,
however little it may be;

to sweat and labor
to meet the needs
of the poor,
as the Spirit
and Word of the Lord
and true brotherly love
teach and imply.
—Menno Simons

thirty home economists tried the recipes and evaluated them in their homes. I searched out resources on nutrition and world food supply.

All the recipes I received were carefully read. Over a thousand were tested. Many were adjusted according to suggestions from testers. Some are a composite of similar recipes. Many excellent recipes could not be used because of limited space.

Although the book is finished, the holy frustration goes on. Do not approach this book as a set of answers for responsible change. At its best, it tells us that Mennonites—a people who care about the hungry—are on a search. We are looking for ways to live more simply and joyfully, ways that grow out of our tradition but take their shape from living faith and the demands of our hungry world.

There is not just one way to respond, nor is there a single answer to the world's food problem. It may not be within our capacity to effect an answer. But it is within our capacity to search for a faithful response.

—Doris Janzen Longacre

Doris Janzen Longacre of Akron, Pennsylvania, was associated with the Mennonite Central Committee (MCC) and its worldwide ministries "In the Name of Christ." Doris grew up in Elbing, Kansas, and Tucson, Arizona. She attended Bethel College, North Newton, Kansas, received her BA in home economics from Goshen College, Goshen, Indiana, in 1961, and studied at Goshen Biblical Seminary.

She served as dietitian of Hesston College from 1961-1963, as MCC hostess of the Language Study Center in Vietnam from 1964-1967, and in another MCC assignment in Indonesia in 1971-1972.

Doris was chairperson of the Akron Mennonite Church from 1973-1976, member of the Board of Overseers of Goshen Biblical Seminary, Elkhart, Indiana, 1976-1979, and a frequent speaker and workshop leader at church conferences in Canada and the United States.

Doris was married to Paul Longacre. Their two daughters, now adults, are Cara Longacre Hurst and Marta van Zanten.

Just prior to the completion of her second book on simple living, Living More with Less, *Doris passed away after a 39-month battle with cancer.*

She said, "I have always liked to cook, particularly experimenting, developing a recipe. I seldom make a recipe twice the same way. I also find satisfaction in cooking and serving foods from other cultures."

Why another cookbook when the market is flooded? Paradoxically cookbooks are best sellers despite the fact that convenience foods and eating out have become big business. Put a cookbook on the market with a unique and creative idea, an attractive format, and explicit directions for using the recipes and it sells.

The *More-with-Less Cookbook* has all of the earmarks of a best seller. First of all, it is a creative idea. It was born from the compulsion that someone, somehow must prod us over-fed North Americans to do something about our over-abundance in relation to the world food crisis. It implores us to begin *today* on a program of responsible eating. Secondly, the book demonstrates clearly how we may enjoy more while eating less. "There is a way of wasting less, eating less, and spending less which gives not less but more," the author says.

This cookbook is not just another collection of favorite recipes. It is more. The recipe section, which includes about two-thirds of the total space, features recipes of a special kind. The author's call for low-cost, low-fat, low-sugar, and less expensive protein recipes within the Mennonite constituency brought in thousands of responses. She and her assistants selected and tested those which appear in the twelve recipe chapters.

As one would expect, in a collection of recipes based on economy of money, time, and energy as well as foods related to good health, the emphasis is away from expensive packaged goods to dishes prepared from simple, basic ingredients. The book includes many recipes for meat extender dishes such as soups, stews, and casseroles using vegetable proteins. It places less emphasis on the roasting and broiling of chunk meats. It encourages eating more nutrition-rich fruits and vegetables and less rich, sugary desserts.

The author's years of living abroad, plus world-wide travel on the part of numerous contributors, is reflected in the international recipes that are included. These add variety to the menu, contributing color, flavor, and nutritional value at low cost.

The one-third of the book not devoted to recipes contains valuable information which required many hours of research on the part of the author. Useful tables detail daily food requirements, the nutritive content of commonly used foods, and the comparative costs of foods. Suggestions for careful shopping appear along with suggested menus.

The *More-with-Less Cookbook* includes a number of unique features. Interspersed throughout the text are inspirational inserts and interesting personal remarks about certain recipes. Options for changing recipes allow the cook to be creative while "stirring up her own." Recipes which merit the label of Time Saving are identified with a large TS in bold face type. Each chapter contains a special feature, "Gather Up the Fragments," a clever way of presenting ideas for using leftovers.

to young homemakers whose lifestyles are more open to change, and whose desire for variety and creativity will lend enchantment for trying new recipes. Perhaps this is as it should be since they are most responsible for the food habits of the next generation.

The *More-with-Less Cookbook* will best reach its goal of helping Christians respond in a caring-sharing way in a world with limited food resources when placed in full view of family members rather than simply adding it to the collection on the kitchen shelf. It can constantly remind your family of its central theme, "There is a way which gives not less but more." More joy, more peace, less guilt; more physical stamina, less overweight and obesity; more to share and less to hoard for ourselves.
          —*Mary Emma Showalter Eby,*
            Author,
          **Mennonite Community
          Cookbook**

Substitutions

For	Use
*1 t. baking powder	⅓ t. baking soda plus ½ t. cream of tartar
	or ¼ t. baking soda plus ⅓ c. sour milk, buttermilk, or yogurt
1 T. cornstarch	2 T. flour
2 T. tapioca	3 T. flour
2 egg yolks	1 whole egg
1 c. whole fresh milk	½ c. evaporated milk plus ½ c. water
	or ⅓ c. dry milk solids plus 1 c. water
1 c. sour milk	1 c. buttermilk
	or 1 c. yogurt
	or 1⅓ T. vinegar or lemon juice plus milk to make 1 c.
*1 c. sour cream (in baking)	⅞ c. buttermilk, sour milk, or yogurt plus 3 T. margarine
1 c. sour cream (in casseroles, salad dressings, desserts)	1 c. yogurt
*1 c. sugar	¾ c. honey, molasses, or corn syrup; reduce liquid in recipe by ¼ c., add ¼ t. soda, and reduce oven temperature by 25°
1 c. brown sugar	see p. 270
1 c. confectioners sugar	see p. 269
*1 c. margarine, butter or shortening	¾ c. bacon fat
	or ¾ c. chicken fat
	or ⅞ c. lard
	or ⅞ c. oil
1 square (1 oz.) unsweetened chocolate	3 T. cocoa

*May not yield perfect results
in products of fine texture
such as light cakes; generally
acceptable in breads, many cookies,
and moist cakes.

Commercial Container Sizes

When recipes in other books call for
commercially canned or frozen foods
and you want to use home-preserved
food, use this chart to determine quantity
needed.

	Weight	Size	Approx. Measure
Can Sizes	**6 oz.**	frozen juice, tomato paste	**¾ c.**
	8 oz.		**1 c.**
	10½ oz.	No. 1 or picnic	**1¼ c.**
	14½ oz.	evaporated milk	**1⅔ c.**
	15 oz.	sweetened condensed milk	**1⅓ c.**
	15½ oz.	No. 300	**1¾ c.**
	1 lb.	No. 303	**2 c.**
	1 lb. 4 oz.	No. 2	**2½ c.**
	46 oz.	juices and fruit drinks	**5¾ c.**
	6 lb. 9 oz.	No. 10	**3 qt.**
Frozen Food	**6 oz.**	frozen juice concentrate	**¾ c.**
Containers	**10 oz.**	box of vegetables	**2 c.**
	20 oz.	bag of vegetables	**4 c.**

You have heard it said
   that because of hunger in Third World countries
   we should not overeat.
But I say unto you
   that the abuse of your body, mind, and soul
   is never justified.

You have heard it said
   conserve for the sake of the crisis
   because of limited amounts available to us.
But I say unto you
   the only wise use
   is that which brings glory to God.

Let not your hearts be troubled by this kingdom
   but let your bodies and energies be dedicated
   in service to God and man.
Surely you will find
   the future kingdom
   already being fulfilled in your life.

   —Martin Penner, Recife, Brazil

Since meeting Mennonites in the pages of More-with-Less, I have served four terms with Mennonite Central Committee, become a Mennonite, studied in Mennonite seminaries, written for Mennonite periodicals, pastored Mennonite congregations. . . . I still use the cookbook. I still measure my rice according to directions on page 125. I still see the future reign of God already being fulfilled in our lives as we dedicate our bodies and energies in service.
—Carol Rose, Wichita, Kan.

More
with Less

1

●●●●●●●●●●●●●●●●●●●●●●●●●●

Less with More

The bright sun shines unblinkingly. Wind sweeps the land. No rain. Old people shake their heads. Little children and women move to the food camps. Already there are more than 200,000 in camps. We all pray for rain.

    In the towns and cities people stand in line. As sugar, cornmeal, flour, and oil decrease, tensions in the lines increase. Lean years are upon us.

Teach us to care, O God,
  In the Somali-Muslim way
    Which does not hoard
      Nor store for the future
        But shares gladly
          Regardless of how little.

  —Bertha Beachy
    Mogadiscio
    Somali Democratic Republic

Cutting back sounds like a dismal prospect. "Let's splurge, just this once," appeals more to North American ears.

Put dismal thoughts aside then, because this book is not about cutting back. This book is about living joyfully, richly, and creatively.

When Mennonite Central Committee put out a call in church papers to find out how people were cutting back, letters poured in. "Simplifying meals to reduce food expenditures has been a joyous experiment," said one. "We are in no way deprived of tasty, nutritious food," wrote another. A third recalled "memorably delicious feasts."

As I read the daily mail, searched through nutrition texts, and pored over the writings of world food supply experts, pieces began to fall in place. There is a way, I discovered, of wasting less, eating less, and spending less which gives not less, but more. The gain is so great that the phrase "cutting back" doesn't fit at all.

But before we can understand how much there is to gain, we need to look at world food supply and North American eating habits.

World Shortages
Imagine our planet as a giant puzzle color-coded according to food supply. Throughout history, the colors would have shown hungry people somewhere. In the early seventies, however, the pieces put together make a new picture.

More people on the planet, more floods, more droughts, and a larger affluent population demanding rich diets have driven world food reserves to a precarious low. The world price of wheat tripled between late 1972 and the end of 1973. Rice followed. Soybean prices doubled within two years.[1] Between 1972 and the end of 1973, petroleum, a vital resource to modern agriculture, quadrupled in price. Poorer countries, which must often import both food and oil, suffered most.

For the first time, the world faced shortages in each of the four basic agricultural resources—land, water, energy, and fertilizer.[2] "If all the food in the world were equally distributed, and each human received identical quantities, we would all be malnourished,"[3] wrote Georg A. Borgstrom, nutritionist and geographer of Michigan State University.

From an almost overnight awareness of diminishing world food reserves came the 1974 term "food crisis." A crisis comes and goes. The hard facts give us no comfort, however, that this one will go away.

As North Americans, most of us grew up believing we were born into an era of abundance. The ability to buy something has meant the right to have it. Christian discipleship now calls us to turn around.

North America: Five Times as Much

Overpopulation and rising affluence are two main reasons for world food shortages. We North Americans are among the affluent.

The average North American uses five times as much grain per person yearly as does one of the two billion persons living in poor countries. We use about two thousand pounds each. All but 150 pounds of this we consume indirectly in meat, milk, eggs, and alcoholic beverages. But the poor Asian eats less than 400 pounds a year, most of it directly as rice or wheat. It may surprise us to realize that in Europe, where many of us have our roots and where people generally enjoy an adequate diet, each person consumes about 1000 pounds of grain a year, half of what a North American eats.[4]

People who live on only 400 pounds of grain a year are deficient in both calories and protein. But much of the 1000 pounds North

Americans consume above European levels must be called excess, both for health's sake and from a caring Christian stance. Global resources can never allow the rest of the world to approach North American levels of consumption.

North Americans have not always eaten this way, so possibly there is hope for change. Our grandparents, despite our references to their "meat 'n' potatoes," and "seven sweets and seven sours," did not eat nearly as heavily of meats or sweets as we do. Our annual consumption of beef rose from 55 pounds for each person in 1940, to 116 pounds in 1972. Poultry consumption rose from 18 to 51 pounds during the same time.[5] United States sugar consumption levels have doubled since the turn of the century.[6]

Here is an example of how rising affluence over the years changes our kitchen habits. My grandmother iced cakes only for birthdays. My mother iced most of her cakes, but thinly and only between the layers and on top—not on the sides. Until recently I stirred up an ample bowlful of frosting that covered everything and left plenty of finger-lickin's.

But most of our excesses are more complicated than this, and they mesh into each other. We are overspending money. We are overeating calories, protein, fats, sugar, superprocessed foods. We are overcomplicating our lives.

Overspending Money

Lamenting the size of a grocery bill is easy. Lowering it is not. One family wrote me that after the recent call from Mennonite church leaders to reduce food expenditures by 10 percent, they made an honest effort to cut back. They found by year's end, however, that their grocery bill was up 6 percent. With food costs inflating at a rate of 12 to 15 percent, they had of course, been partly successful.

North Americans spend a far lower percentage of their income for food than do most people in the world. Edgar Stoesz, Mennonite Central Committee's food resource person, writes:

> **Although North Americans complain loudly about the increase in food prices, we are probably the least affected. Over the past fifteen years, the average American family has spent sixteen to eighteen percent of its take-home pay for food. People in Third World countries like India, Ethiopia, and Haiti where food is always in short supply spend from seventy to eighty percent in normal times. When times are bad, all the family's earnings go for food, and still hunger stalks.[7]**

Yet in dollars and cents our diets are expensive. Food prices should have come down during this century, for we have improved land and labor productivity, higher crop yields, better fertilizers, and more efficient food-processing methods. We should be getting more with less, reaping the advantages of our efficiency. For the consumer, however, the financial advantages of our agricultural productivity are wiped out by a food-processing system that conditions us to eat fewer real foods. We are trained to look for convenience and variety, not for nutrition. We are taken in by advertising and by alluring packaging.

Instead of buying rolled oats at thirty cents a pound, we use puffed, colored, sweetened, vitamin-enriched, foil-and-cardboard-packaged dry cereal at $1.12 a pound. Instead of cornmeal at twenty cents a pound,

we buy an equal amount of corn in chips at $1.10. Soybean steaks are now on the grocery shelves. They are a more efficient protein source than meat, but cost about seven times more than the equivalent protein in home-baked soybeans.

We pay for the endless variety in our supermarkets, and for the continual development of new products. My local store carries twenty brands of detergent powder, any one of which does an adequate job of washing clothes. But the fact that I can choose means that the box I carry home is more expensive than it might be if I were offered fewer options. If I use the coupons that come in the mail for new products, I really am not saving seven cents, but paying ten or fifteen cents for the developing, testing, designing, and marketing of another food variation no one needs.

Our diet is expensive also because we get many of our daily calories from animal protein. Canadians get 34 percent of their calories from animal products.[8] In the United States the figure is several points higher.[9] Meat, milk, and eggs are nutritionally valuable, but expensive because of the resources required to produce them. We waste resources when we use more than we need.

Caroline Ackerman of Winnipeg, author of *The No Fad Good Food $5 a Week Cookbook,* says, "In comparison to what most of the people of the world pay for food, and to what we need to nourish ourselves, we spend a fortune."[10]

Overeating Calories
You have only to stand on a North American street corner and watch the world go by to be assured that we overeat. The scene in an Asian city is far different, even in an industrialized country such as Japan, where most people now eat a nutritionally adequate diet.

We were conscious of being surrounded by overweight bodies after returning to the United States from three years in Vietnam. People here looked cumbersome, ungainly, plodding. We missed the lithe grace of the Asians.

The American Medical Association says 40 percent of Americans are overweight.[11] For those of us concerned about world hunger as well as our own health, being overweight has many implications.

Overeating wastes food. It wastes money and human resources when we require medical help to reduce. Insurance premiums go up, while life expectancy and job opportunities go down for overweight people. When we overeat calories, we get less with more.

Loneliness, anxiety, boredom, and meaninglessness undoubtedly contribute to our high rate of obesity. But people in other parts of the world have their problems too. Somehow theirs do not result in national obesity. Our wrong diet must play a significant role.

Most North Americans have sedentary occupations. We live in comfort-controlled temperatures. Our calorie needs are therefore significantly lower than they were several decades ago. We fail to adjust our eating habits to these conditions.

Our bodies still require a diet heavy in cellulose waste (fiber or roughage) such as that found in whole grains, leafy vegetables, and unpeeled fruit. Cellulose helps the stomach feel full and the bowels function smoothly. "Appetite is regulated in part by a full stomach, and the human stomach is big enough to hold enough high-waste, low-nutrient food to carry the organism through the day. Fill the stomach with low-waste, high-nutrient food, and trouble is on the way in the form of various diseases associated with obesity," says The Intelligent Consumer.[12]

The food industry has conditioned us to diets high in sugars, fats, and refined flours. These foods are virtually empty of nutrients other than calories. But because they are cheap, readily available, and can be turned into all kinds of attractive snacks, the food industry produces them. Because they are quick and convenient, we eat them.

Increasing numbers of children influenced by advertising are growing up overweight. "Most nutritionists agree that the worst influence on a child's eating habits is television," wrote Sarah Eby in a series of newspaper articles on North American nutrition.[13] Breakfast cereals, cookies, candy, gum, snacks, tarts, and frozen waffles make up about two thirds of the televised food advertising directed at children, according to a study done at Columbia University in 1972. These advertisements have subtle ways of leading children to believe that the product is not only delicious and fun to eat, but even good for them. From an early age, calorie waste is built into our food habits.

Overeating Protein
Much of the what's-wrong-with-us material relating to world food needs centers on overconsumption of protein. Lester Brown calls protein the "key quality indicator" for adequate diets. Any significant lack of it has immediate dire consequences for health. But while protein is so widely lacking in poorer countries, North Americans eat twice the recommended daily allowance.[14]

A second reason why protein has received so much attention at a time of world food shortage is that much of the protein North Americans eat, in contrast to poorer nations, comes from meat, milk, and eggs.

How much grain an animal needs to produce a pound of protein for human consumption is a question that sparks wide controversy. Farmers, government officials, homemakers, church leaders, and newspaper reporters are engaged in a continuing debate.

Numbers aside, a few principles seem clear. Beef cattle are relatively poor converters of grain to food protein. As ruminant animals, however, they are very efficient at turning forage and roughage into food protein. Broiler-fryers (chickens) and dairy cows are efficient converters of feed grain to food protein. In most sources of information, hogs and turkeys rank somewhere in the middle. But no matter which animal source is most efficient, the fact stands that North Americans eat far more meat than is needed for good health.

Beef figures prominently in the discussion not only because it may or may not convert feed efficiently, but because it is our most popular meat. United States beef consumption has doubled since 1940. It hit an all-time high in 1974 of 116.3 pounds for each person.[15]

Beef can be raised entirely on the range, without grain, producing food from land otherwise not suited to agriculture. Longhorn cattle of Wild West fame were raised this way. The contemporary range, roughage, and feedlot combination has resulted in recent years in an average use of four pounds of grain for every pound of beef produced in the United States. In heavy feedlot activity, eight, ten, or more pounds of grain can be consumed for every pound of meat produced.[16]

The trend toward heavy feedlot production of beef is already reversing because of fluctuating grain costs. New feeding methods being researched promise wide use of food and industry by-products in future beef production.

North American range areas must be used to the fullest advantage. Consumers must reeducate their tastes toward a leaner, possibly even a tougher quality of beef. Range-grown meat, with more protein, fewer calories, and less high-cholesterol fat, can give us more with less, both in health and world food resources.

We must also realize that beef and other meats are on the list of commodities which are not unlimited. Suggestions that North Americans should keep on eating more beef are irresponsible—as irresponsible as condemning all beef production out of hand. We cannot keep on using more water, more fuel, more wood, more paper. Neither can we keep on eating more hamburgers, roasts, and steaks.

The crucial point, says Lester Brown, is that "once grazing areas are . . . fully utilized, it becomes very costly in resource terms to satisfy additional growth in consumer demand, requiring the use of crop lands and grains that could otherwise be used to meet human needs directly. Additional beef production in the developed countries is likely to occur in feedlots."[17]

Closely related to high protein consumption in North America is our heavy intake of saturated fats. Not all protein foods yield saturated fat. But North American favorites such as well-marbled beef, pork, eggs, and whole milk contain large amounts.

A diet high in saturated fats and cholesterol contributes to our number-one health problem—coronary atherosclerosis. This disease, which is an accumulation of fatty materials on artery walls, must be considered a disease of civilization, according to Dr. Jean Mayer, Harvard nutritionist.[18] Mayer blames eating foods high in saturated fats, lack of physical activity, and heavy cigarette smoking as contributing factors.

Our North American habit of eating a half pound of beef or pork daily contributes to high-cholesterol levels. So does the fried-chicken-hamburger-French fry-milkshake syndrome. Autopsy studies done on American casualties of the Korean War showed that many young men had the heart and arteries typical of old people. Growing up at the fast food stands was considered part of the problem.[19]

High animal-protein diets present other problems as well. *Consumer Reports* offers these cautions: Too much beef (or other meat) can mean too little calcium. A high protein intake increases the need for calcium and can deplete the body's calcium resources. Much meat and little roughage is bad for the bowel. The National Cancer Institute has suggested possible association between diets high in meat and colon cancer, the second most prevalent form of cancer in North America. Other diseases of the bowel such as diverticulosis are definitely related to high-meat, low-roughage diets.[20]

Overeating Sugar

"Sugar consumption!" writes Helen Janzen, formerly head of the Home Economics Department in the Department of Education in Manitoba. "Every day at a little grocery store at noon I see files of elementary pupils stocking up on candy—twenty-five to thirty-five cents worth apiece. It's crazy! Only calories, and acid forming for the teeth. If we could get rid of the sweet and rich dessert habit we would be better off."[21]

Much of the land now used for sugar beets and cane could produce crops far more beneficial to a hungry world. Sugar provides only calories, not a smidgen of protein, vitamins, or minerals. Especially in children, sugar can replace healthful foods like fruits, vegetables, grains, and meats. Handing out sugar-filled snack foods and drinks is like giving a stone when your child asks for bread. Sadly, once a child gets used to sugary snacks he may no longer ask for bread.

North Americans eat over 120 pounds of sugar and other refined sweeteners yearly.[22] This translates to roughly 32 teaspoons daily. Whenever I use this figure, heads begin to shake and people protest "but that's not me. I never eat that much." Here's how it can happen:

Typical menu

Breakfast:

4	Tang or other sweetened breakfast drink, ½ c.
3	Pre-sweetened cereal, 1 oz.
2	Toast, 1 slice, with 1 T. jam (or pancakes with syrup)
1	Coffee, sweetened

Lunch:

	Sandwich
	Chips
3	Pudding, ½ c.

Afternoon snack:

5	1 candy bar OR 3 cookies

Dinner:

	Roast beef
	Mashed potatoes
	Buttered carrots
2	Gelatin salad, ½ c.
2	1 roll with 1 T. jelly
2	Canned fruit, ½ c.
7	Iced cake, 1 slice
1	Coffee, sweetened

32	**Teaspoons of Sugar**

This menu counts no sugar in bread. Some commercial bread is heavily sweetened. It includes no carbonated drinks, Kool-Aid, or punch, the form in which we consume at least one fourth of our sugar. It assumes no second helpings, no ice cream, and only one snack throughout the day. Few of us have trouble living up to this level of sugar consumption.

Many people are unaware that excessive use of sugar can lead to premature atherosclerosis.[23] Most of us have known since elementary school health courses that too much sugar causes or aggravates tooth decay, obesity, vitamin deficiency, and diabetes. But few people translate this knowledge into menu-planning.

Overeating Processed Foods

A health-promoting diet calls for less meat; less white bread and other refined grain products; less of the sugar-filled soda pops, candy, breakfast cereals, and snack foods; more whole-grain foods, beans, fruits, vegetables, and nuts. If Americans adopted a diet of this type, the food industry would encounter massive dislocation.[24]

Many of the boxes and bottles on our kitchen shelves today were unknown thirty years ago. We call these newcomers convenience foods. Food processors glory publicly in the progress they represent, and more privately in the profits. Convenience foods almost always mean less with more in our diets. They are part of the cause of world hunger.

Farmers are all too aware that marketing basic foods does not yield large profits. But in turning a cheap, healthy, basic food into a convenience package, plenty of profit (and plenty of waste) can result.

Convenience foods, more than anything else, have contributed to the prosperity of corporate food systems, says a brief from the Inter-Church Center in New York City.[25] Sixteen of the twenty most profitable corporations in the United States in 1973 were involved in food and the basic components of agriculture.[26]

We pay more for convenience foods. This raises our food bills and uses funds that could help feed the hungry. But the problem does not stop there. We get less because nutrients are lost in processing, while chemicals of questionable safety are added. The corporation's concern is with what sells, not with what is good for us.

Dr. Ross Hume Hall, biochemist from Ontario with extensive experience in the biology of growth and development and cancer research, recently wrote a book detailing how inadequate is the testing on approximately 7500 new food products introduced yearly by the food industry.[27] One of Hall's central concerns is that even though food processors are required to show that chemical additives are safe, these chemicals are tested selectively on healthy laboratory animals within a given time frame. We humans eat chemical additives in endless combinations over periods of years, and our individual makeup varies widely. Eighteen hundred chemicals are added routinely to manufactured food. Little is being done to determine how they affect us in combination.

In our culture, technological possibility and economic profitability have become reasons in themselves for doing something. Production of winter tomatoes is a good example. Anybody who raises their own tomatoes knows that something strange goes on with those sold fresh in winter. *The Corporate Examiner* tells what it is:

The tomato [is] a typical product of the technological revolution in agriculture. Genetically tailored to be thick-walled, firm-fleshed, and uniformly round, these tomatoes are mechanically harvested when still green. They are then chemically ripened with ethylene gas, electronically sorted and, finally, mechanically wrapped in cellophane.

Ethylene gas, when used to speed up the ripening process in tomatoes, has been shown to provide lower quality with less vitamin A and C and inferior taste, color, and firmness. Nevertheless, it continues to be used. When consumer groups protested the loss of quality and flavor in this new "Red Rock" tomato, they were reassured that seventy chemicals that produce tomato flavor had been isolated and could be artificially reintroduced into the product.[28]

Our snow-white baked goods tell the same story. Since Roman times bakers have been aware that flour stored for a few months becomes whiter and has improved baking qualities. But storage time increases manufacturing costs. Around the beginning of this century, millers discovered they could get these same effects instantly by blowing nitrogen trichloride (agene) or chlorine gas into the flour as it descended the chute into bags. Agene was used for 41 years, but discontinued after a 1945 study showed that dogs fed the agene-treated flour developed hysteria. Chemical bleaching and maturing of flour continues in many places. Germany, where mechanical bread is resisted and small bakeries still flourish, banned the use of chemical bleaching agents in 1958.[29]

In the refining process, the most valuable parts of the wheat kernel, the bran and germ, are removed. Some of our flour is then artificially enriched, but never to the original level of whole wheat. Not only nutrients, but also much-needed fiber is lost. The uniform, tasteless white bread that results is best described as edible styrofoam.

My mother raised us on wonderful, solid, homemade loaves of Prussian Mennonite "Ruggenbrot" (rye bread). But once in awhile the supply ran out before baking day, and store-bought white bread came to the table. I remember my teenage brother once took such a slice, squashed it into a small soggy ball, and pitched it across the room in front of Mother to express his disdain. Mother accepted this as a compliment.

Sitting in a restaurant recently, I picked up one of those half-ounce plastic containers of nondairy cream substitutes used in coffee. I looked closely at the small print around the lid: "Ingredients: pasteurized blend of water, corn syrup solids, coconut oil, sodium caseinate, disodium phosphate, carrageenan, guargum, polysorbate 60, sorbitan monostearate, potassium sorbate, artificial color."

A United States Food and Drug Administration booklet extolling the safety of food additives says they are needed for color, hardening, drying, leavening, antifoaming, firming, crisping, antisticking, whipping, creaming, clarifying, and sterilizing. The brochure wraps up the subject by saying, "Without these many aids to food processing, today's grocery stores would need a lot less room to sell what foods would be left."[30]

What a saving of time, energy, money, nutrients, and food that would be! May the day come soon!

Superprocessed foods come superpackaged. Both the processing and the packaging

19

contribute to food shortages by wasting resources. Few things still come in simple paper bags. One more often finds an inner foil liner "to preserve freshness," enclosing a product laced with preservatives.

Overcomplicating Our Lives

Last week my mail brought a gorgeous multicolor foldout advertising a new recipe card set. "Makes cooking easier and more exciting than ever before," it promised. Twenty-four separate batches of cards would be sent, providing recipes on Saturday Night Parties, Sundays at Home, Children's Favorites, Cooking with Wine, Cooking with Herbs, Memorable Summer Meals, and on and on. Each card would contain "a stunning, full-color photograph of the dish, just as it will appear on your table."

The ad stunned me sufficiently that I did not need the 576 recipes, especially at the price of thirty dollars. The pitch indicates again how we try to turn eating into a superexperience.

Serving guests becomes an ego trip, rather than a relaxed meeting of friends around that most common everyday experience of sharing food. Gathering around the table in fellowship turns into entertaining. We eat out for something to do, not because we find ourselves on the road at mealtime.

Our bodily needs are real and important, and meeting them is as important as meeting any need of a whole, integrated personality. Feeding a hungry stomach is in no way less honorable than thinking lofty spiritual thoughts. But when we invest too much in feeding ourselves, and want too much in return, something goes wrong.

We work hard to make eating more exciting. We satiate our taste buds and stomachs. But something in us is not satisfied. We have gotten

less with more. Timothy's words, "If we have food and clothing, with these we shall be content," have no meaning for us.

In Asia my husband and I observed people eating a standard, repetitive diet. Asians depend on rice, Africans on a mush of corn or manioc, Latin Americans on rice and beans, Europeans on bread or potatoes. Sometimes these diets are too monotonous for good health. Eat a variety of foods, say the nutritionists, to get an adequate supply of vitamins and minerals. Our North American variety, on the other hand, too often has not been in simple fresh vegetables or grains, but in rich meats and desserts.

Time and energy are needed to keep this variety on our tables. We need several hours a week to shop and plan for it, bags for carrying it home, large cupboards, refrigerators, and freezers in which to store it. Cooking it requires four burners, an oven, a toaster, mixer, blender, coffee maker, pressure cooker, deep-fat fryer, fondue pot, electric fry pan, waffle iron, crock pot, electric knife, and electric can opener. If your menu—but not your kitchen—goes Asian, you may add an electric wok and rice cooker. You need an array of dishes and silverware to serve it. You need correspondingly shaped plastic containers with lids that burp to hold the leftovers, a garbage disposal and a crusher to handle the waste. A dishwasher and a vacuum cleaner for the kitchen carpet finish things off until mealtime comes again.

Notes

1.
Lester Brown, *By Bread Alone* (New York: Praeger Publishers, 1974), p. 4.
2.
Ibid., p. 7.

3.
The Handwriting On The Wall: A World Development Primer (Oklahoma City: World Neighbors), p. 26.

4.
Lester Brown, *World Without Borders* (New York: Random House, 1972), pp. 95-96.

5.
Lester Brown, *In The Human Interest* (New York: W. W. Norton & Co., Inc., 1974), p. 44.

6.
"The Sugar Content of Fabricated Foods," Center for Science in the Public Interest, Washington, D.C., Source: U.S.D.A.

7.
Edgar Stoesz, "Global Food Supply: Can It Stretch with the People?" Akron, Pa.: MCC Hunger Packet.

8.
Caroline Ackerman, *The No Fad Good Food $5 a Week Cookbook* (New York: Dodd, Mead, and Co., 1974). Source: Apparent Per Capita Domestic Disappearance of Food in Canada, Ottawa, 1972.

9.
Dietary Levels of Households in the United States, Seasons and Year 1965-66. U.S. Department of Agriculture, Agricultural Research Service, Household Food Consumption Survey, 1965-66, Report No. 18.

10.
Ackerman, *The No Fad Cookbook*, p. 15.

11.
"Malnutrition and Hunger in the United States," *American Medical Journal*, Vol. 213, No. 2, July 13, 1970, pp. 272-275.

12.
Christopher and Bonnie Weathersbee, *The Intelligent Consumer* (New York: E. P. Dutton and Co., Inc., 1973), p. 23.

13.
Sarah Eby, "Underlying Causes," Nutrition—Part III.

14.
Dietary Levels of Households in the U.S., U.S.D.A., Household Food Consumption Survey, Report No. 18, pp. 15-17, and Food and Agriculture Organization of the United Nations (FAO) Food Balance Sheets for 1957-59.

15.
Lancaster Farming, Feb. 22, 1975. Source, U.S.D.A.

16.
Brown, *By Bread Alone*, pp. 206-207.

17.
Ibid.

18.
Jean Mayer, "Heart Disease: Plans for Action," *U.S. Nutrition Policies in the Seventies* (San Francisco: W. H. Freeman and Co., 1973), p. 44.

19.
William Enos, Robert H. Holmes, James Beyer, "Coronary Disease Among U.S. Soldiers Killed in Action in Korea," *Journal of the American Medical Association*, Vol. 152, 1953, p. 1090.

20.
"How Much Is Enough?" *Consumer Reports*, Vol. 38, No. 9, Sept. 1974, p. 668.

21.
Letter from Helen Janzen, January 1974.

22.
Michael Jacobson, *Nutrition Scoreboard*. Washington, D.C., Center for Science in the Public Interest, 1973, p. 96.

23.
Letter from David M. Leaman, MD, Hershey Medical Center, April 1975.

24.
Testimony of Michael Jacobson, Director, Center for Science in the Public Interest, before Massachusetts Consumer Council, July 15, 1974.

25.
CIC Brief, *The Corporate Examiner*, November 1974 (New York: Corporate Information Center, Inter-Church Center, 475 Riverside Dr.), pp. 3A-3B.

26.
Ibid.

27.
Ross Hume Hall, *Food For Nought: The Decline in Nutrition* (New York: Harper and Row, 1974), p. 43.

28.
CIC Brief, *The Corporate Examiner*, p. 3.

29.
Hall, *Food For Nought*, pp. 14-17.

30.
Edward G. Damon, "Primer on Food Additives," Department of Health, Education, and Welfare Publication, No. 74-2002.

●●●●●●●●●●●●●●●●●●●●●●●●●
Change—an Act of Faith

The regenerate use
eating, drinking
clothing and shelter
with thanksgiving
to support their own lives
and to the free service
of their neighbor
according to the
Word of the Lord.
—Menno Simons

Does It Really Help Anyone If I Cut Back?

Many are saying that it does not really matter whether we eat more or less in North America. The line of reasoning may go like this: Just because we eat less meat this week is no assurance that more grain will be available in Bangladesh next year. If we stop buying sugared cereals and TV dinners, the food industry will come out with something even worse. We may stop eating out every Friday evening, but our friends will go without us, so what do we expect to prove? The problem is first with poor government policy and import-export agreements, or with snail-pace family-planning programs and corrupt governments in Third World countries.

All these arguments have elements of truth. But this thinking smacks heavily of a common human attitude—that it doesn't really matter what one person does, or that what one household can do is so small that it has no effect on the overall picture.

In our complex world, it is hard to visualize how the struggles of a few families to save food will help. Channels to the needy are long and circuitous. Yet deconsumption is an obvious first step. The very complexity that frustrates easy answers also means that our decisions in the global family are interrelated. "Life is like a huge spider web so that if you touch it anywhere you set the whole thing trembling," says Frederick Buechner in *The Hungering Dark*.

Communications in our world are good. How can we continue overeating in the face of starvation, and be at peace with ourselves and our neighbors? "The destitute suffer physically, the overindulged morally," writes one Mennonite Central Committee relief administrator. Jesus recognized the desire to get more and more as a destructive force when He asked, "What shall it profit a man if he gain the whole world and lose his own soul?" (Matthew 16:26).

When we begin eating less, the job is not finished. It is only beginning. If we expect North American food conservation to totally solve world hunger, with good reason we sound naive and even paternalistic. Concerned Christians will move on to initiate food production and distribution programs. They will challenge oppressive government policy. But these broad areas are being dealt with in other settings. The scope of this book is necessarily limited to what some older preachers called "putting our own house in order."

It Seemed Inadequate

As Christians dealing with human hurts, we have to remind ourselves again and again that we are not called to be successful, but to be faithful. Our first directions come from the way Jesus told us to live, not from what we think will work.

Wayne North, a Mennonite pastor from Ohio, makes this point in an editorial entitled "Can We Really Help Hunger?" He compares our present reaction to world food needs with the feelings of the disciples when they were surrounded by 5000 hungry people. Jesus commanded the disciples to see that all were fed. North says, "The obvious answers certainly were not going to do the trick. But what follows may be instructive for us. For, however they may have felt, the disciples responded in obedience. They shared what was available. Though it seemed totally inadequate, they brought the little lunch for distribution. Their act of faith was to share and let God take responsibility for the rest."[1]

This does not mean we are blind to realities. We must keep in touch with suffering people. Our response is to live the reality that the kingdom of God is already here. In this kingdom to which Jesus calls us, valleys will be filled and hills made low. In the last quarter of our century, this means less food for us but more for the rest of the world.

If others alone stood to gain from our changes, hopefully the motivation of Christ-inspired sharing would see us through. But we also stand to gain. Happily, the whole grains, legumes, vegetables, fruits, and moderate amounts of animal products that make sense in light of world food needs are also the best for our health. With a few exceptions, these are also the cheapest. When we reduce our need for heavily grain-fed meat, the superprocessed, the sugary, we not only release resources for the hungry, but also protect our own health and pocketbooks.

We Liked It Better
The Second Time

"It's a long road to freedom, a winding steep and high . . ." goes a Medical Mission Sisters' tune. Many cooks sending recipes to this book affirm that fact. It is a long road to freedom from pop and chips, freedom from 32 teaspoons of sugar a day, freedom from society as master.

"Our family has been working at this for several years now" was a typical opening comment above recipes we received. These families have more than a food crisis mentality. They are serious about change. We must be committed to living responsibly in a world where food shortages are not going to be solved easily. The process takes as long as it takes to raise children who know how to survive on less.

"You can't make the soufflé rise twice" was the comment of one experienced church leader reflecting on the difference between fads and convictions. If we are people of a soufflé mentality who get carried to great heights over an issue, we will probably fall flat six months later when the media moves on to other subjects. Maybe the image of sourdough is a better one. One always keeps a little dough in reserve to leaven loaves in an ongoing supply. The starter can be shared with friends. It can be stored and revived as needed. If we do not expect instant solutions, our changes are more likely to be long-lasting. People committed to eating responsibly have provided the following ideas on changing food habits:

1. Keep the basic commitment strong. Study the Bible to see what Jesus and early church writers said about living in Christ's kingdom, about sharing. Study world food needs and solutions from the perspective of farm papers, news media, Third World development experts, church periodicals. But keep in mind that our direction does not come from how society operates, but from Jesus who said, "Give to him who begs from you," "Give as freely as you have received!" "You give them something to eat," "Give, and it will be given to you."[2]

2. Expect eating habits to change slowly. At the bottom of a soybean recipe, Eleanor Kaufman from Newton, Kansas, added, "Our children have discovered this to be a tasty dish after two or three exposures." My own experience with soybeans was the same. The first time they simmered all morning on my stove I found their odor a little objectionable. The next few times I did not mind it. Now when I return from outdoors to the kitchen aroma of cooking soybeans, I respond unconsciously with the same good feeling I have for any food smell that signals mealtime. Trying to change too many things at once will only make a household defensive. A slower approach which gives people time to adjust their tastes goes more smoothly.

3. Be honest about reasons for change. One of the most unpleasant cookbooks I've read is one in which the author gives endless ideas for improving a family's nutrition without letting them know it. She even suggests cover-up things to say if anyone should suspect carrots in the meat loaf or wheat germ in the cookies. Why not simply offer matter-of-fact explanations that reflect an honest desire to share with the hungry? Often children are willing to go further than we realize if they understand our reasons and are involved in decisions.

4. Let children help plan. One mother told me her fourteen-year-old son was unhappy with her menus. He complained about cutting down on meat and other foods he enjoyed. When she allowed him to set the family menus for a week, she was surprised to see how economically he planned. She found he shared her motivation. What they ate was not really very different when he planned. But he felt better about the meals and he realized his concerns were heard.

Children can rise to the occasion in an amazing way if they are given honest explanations and time to adjust to new foods. There are days when they complain and reject any changes outright. But in the end, children's food habits are set by example. If parents are open to changes, children will be, too.

Suggestions on how to cut food costs usually include, "Don't take children along shopping." Stores display candy and cookies at knee-level up one aisle and down the next. On the other hand, why not at least occasionally discuss the week's menus with children before a shopping trip and take them along to help look for the best buys. Our children were fascinated by unit pricing signs when I explained them.

5. Be willing to celebrate. Around the world people who must live on monotonous diets still manage an occasional celebration. Undoubtedly their celebrations bring enjoyment in proportion to how much they vary from the daily routine.

The four Gospels show Jesus entering wholeheartedly into times of joy and feasting. We celebrate with family and friends when a holiday or special occasion brings us together. But the fact that in North America we tend to feast nonstop can dull our festive joy. We feel guilty about a Thanksgiving turkey and trimmings when we have not lived responsibly in the weeks preceding it. We require more and more trimmings to turn any celebration into a meal distinguishable from our daily diet.

A wedding, a son or daughter's homecoming from far away, an aged parent's birthday, Christmas or Easter—food can help express what these days mean to us. But there are simple ways to turn meals into celebrations. Hold in clear perspective the reason for celebrating. Don't expect food to be the total experience. More with less means affirming faith and relationships as the basis for celebrating, and letting food play a complementary role.

*One who is full tramples
   on virgin honey,
      but to the man who is hungry,
         any bitter thing is sweet.*
—*Proverbs 27:7*
   New American Bible

Notes
   1.
Wayne North, "Can We Really Help Hunger?" *The Ohio Evangel,* Vol. XXVIII, No. 6, Nov.-Dec., 1974, p. 4.
   2.
Matthew 5:42 (RSV); Matthew 10:8 (NEB); Matthew 14:16 (RSV); Luke 6:38 (RSV).

●●●●●●●●●●●●●●●●●●●●●●●●●
Building
a Simpler Diet

God's people wander
in the supermarket
among chemical frozen pies
overprocessed skillet dinners
nutritionless snack foods
soft drinks in throwaway bottles.
Like manna in the wilderness
hold fast
vegetables from
sun-warmed gardens
protein-rich beans
oven-fresh whole-grain breads
home-canned fruit in Mason jars.
—Idea from Jane Short
Elkhart, Indiana

Note: Some charts and information
have been revised for this 25th
anniversary edition of More-with-
Less Cookbook. *Sections with shad-*
ed area in margins reflect updated
information.

The question begins to focus: What
should we eat and what should we
not eat to free resources for hungry
people and to improve our own
health? General guidelines which
take into account world food and
energy needs, good nutrition, and
food costs can be summarized this
way:

1. Eat more
whole grains—
    rice
    wheat
    barley
    rye
    oats
    corn
    millet
legumes—
    dried beans including soybeans
    dried peas
    lentils
    peanuts
vegetables and fruits—
    inexpensive
    locally grown varieties
    or homegrown
    and preserved
nuts and seeds—
    inexpensive
    locally grown varieties
2. Use carefully
eggs
milk, cheeses, yogurt
seafoods
poultry
meats
3. Avoid
superprocessed and convenience foods
superpackaged foods
foods shipped long distances
    especially under refrigeration
foods heavy in refined sugar and
    saturated fats

How much of various foods is
enough? Not everyone in North
America eats the same. The Food
Guide Pyramid (United States) and
the Rainbow Food Guide to
Healthy Eating (Canada) are popular guides for making sure we get
an adequate diet.

Food Guide Pyramid[1]

Fats, Oils & Sweets

Meat & Meat Alternatives Group

Milk, Yogurt, & Cheese Group

Fruit Group

Vegetable Group

Bread, Cereals, Rice, & Pasta Group

Rainbow Food Guide to Healthy Eating[2]

Enjoy a variety of foods from each group every day.

Choose lower-fat foods more often.

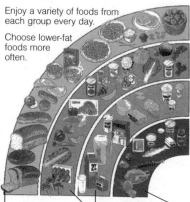

Grain Products Choose whole-grain and enriched products

Milk Products Choose lower-fat milk products more often

Vegetables & Fruits Choose dark green and orange fruits more often

Meat & Alternatives Choose leaner meats, poultry, and fish as well as dried peas, beans, and lentils more often

When *More-with-Less Cookbook* was first published in 1976, nutrition education in Canada and the United States was based on the Basic Four Food Groups guide. Now nutrition plans follow the Food Guide Pyramid and the Rainbow Food Guide to Healthy Eating. These charts reflect the importance of restricting fat and eating more whole foods such as fruits, vegetables, and whole grains.

A range of servings is recommended for each food group. **But what is one serving?**

Milk, Yogurt, & Cheese *2-3 Servings*
1 cup (8 oz.) milk or yogurt
2 slices cheese, 1/8" thick (1½ oz.)
2 cups cottage cheese
1½ cups ice milk, ice cream, or frozen yogurt

Meat & Meat Alternatives *2-3 Servings*
2 oz. to 3 oz. cooked lean meat, poultry, or fish
2 eggs
7 oz. tofu
1 cup cooked dry beans
4 tablespoons peanut butter
½ cup nuts or seeds

Vegetables *3-5 Servings*
½ cup cooked vegetables
½ cup raw chopped vegetables
1 cup raw leafy vegetables
½ to ¾ cup vegetable juice

Fruits *2-4 Servings*
1 medium apple, banana, or orange
1 melon wedge
½ cup chopped fruit or berries
¼ cup dried fruit
½ cup canned fruit
½ to ¾ cup fruit juice

Breads, Cereal, Rice, & Pasta *6-11 Servings*
1 slice bread
1 medium muffin
1 ounce ready-to-eat cereal
½ cup cooked cereal, rice, or pasta
½ bagel or English muffin
4 small crackers
1 tortilla

The number of servings for each person depends on calorie needs, based on age, sex, size, and amount of physical activity. (Serving sizes listed here are for an adult. A child's serving would be smaller.)

Dietary guidelines in both Canada[3] and the U.S.[4] recommend limiting fat to 30 percent of calories. This amounts to 60 grams of fat in a 2000-calorie diet.

Dietary guidelines recommend limiting saturated fat to less than 10 percent of calories, or about one-third of total fat intake.

The Protein Question

Getting Enough

As we noted in Chapter 1, protein is an important factor in planning a diet that gives us more with less. How much is really enough?

The recommended daily allowance for protein in the U.S. varies according to gender and age (see Chart B on page 33). The amount of protein for adult males is 58 to 63 grams (2.2 oz.); for adult females, 46 to 50 grams (1.75 oz.), or about .8 grams of protein per kilogram of body weight. Recommended Nutrient Intakes for Canadians[5] suggest a slightly higher amount.

Most people's minimum need for protein is about half the recommended daily allowances. But adjustments are made to cover individual differences and the fact that not all protein we eat is complete in essential amino acids.[6] Allowances include an adequate margin of safety.

Physically active people need no more protein per kilogram of body weight than do the sedentary. A *Consumer Reports* article on meat consumption titled "How Much Is Enough?" says protein needs go up when the body is rebuilding tissue after severe illness, or developing muscles rapidly as at the beginning of a more physically demanding job. But once tissue is replaced, or muscles are built, "the 150-pound laborer or athlete has the same protein needs as the 150-pound desk worker."[7] See the chart on page 33.

The active person needs more calories. Carbohydrates provide these additional calories more efficiently than do proteins. The excess protein we eat is broken down by the liver into nitrogen, which we excrete, and into energy molecules the same as carbohydrates. Eating protein to meet energy at a time when food is in short supply represents a waste like burning furniture for heat when firewood is available.

What Is Complete Protein?

We hear it said that the quality of protein in meat is higher than in vegetable sources, or that meat contains complete protein whereas plants do not. What is meant by these terms?

Twenty amino acids make up the proteins our bodies use. Of these twenty, eight must come directly from the food we eat. These eight are called the essential amino acids. The rest our bodies can synthesize.

All the essential amino acids must be present simultaneously and in proper proportions for our bodies to utilize them. If one is lacking, even temporarily, the body's ability to use protein will fall accordingly.

Complete protein foods contain all eight essential amino acids. Animal products—eggs, milk, and meat—provide all eight amino acids in the proportions our bodies require. Eggs most nearly match the ideal pattern. Milk is a close second, and meats follow. Soybeans and whole rice come close to meats in protein quality. Other grains, the legumes, seeds, and nuts are also good sources of protein but each lacks one or more of the essential amino acids.

Amino Acid Teamwork

The amino acid deficiency in plant proteins does not mean that we must rely on animal products only for a complete protein supply. The amino acids lacking in one plant source can be made up in another. Plant proteins complement each other.

But how do we know what complements what? Actually the relationships are not hard to remember. Food habits from all over the world reflect an intuitive skill in combining complementary amino acids. Chart A on page 32 shows how it works.

In terms of specific amino acids, milk contains protein rich in lysine; legumes generally are low in tryptophan and sulfur-containing amino acids and, like milk, high in lysine. Grains are low in isoleucine and lysine. Thus milk and/or legumes complement grains.[8]

Seeds such as sunflower and sesame could be listed with grains since they are also complemented by milk and legumes. Most people, however, do not eat enough seeds to consider them an important source of protein.

Diet for a Small Planet, a book focusing on the age-old practice of complementing proteins, says: "Eating a mixture of protein sources can increase the protein value of the meal; here's a case where the whole is greater than the sum of its parts. . . . Such mixes do not result in a perfect protein that is fully utilizable by the body (remember that only egg is near perfect). But combinations can increase the protein quality as much as fifty percent above the average of the items eaten separately."[9] In our terms, this means getting more with less as we plan menus involving plant protein.

Chart A on page 32 gives menu combinations that show proteins in a complementary relationship. Some of our most common are cereal with milk, cheese sandwiches, and bread with milk. These are typical of a European background where grains and dairy products make up an important part of the diet. Other parts of the world have prepared nutritious combinations for centuries. Latin Americans eat rice with beans or beans with corn. In India a pea or lentil puree (dhal) is eaten over rice. In Indonesia fermented soybean cakes (tempe) go with the rice meal. A mung bean-rice cereal is a popular Vietnamese breakfast. The Chinese and Japanese use bean noodles, bean curd, and bean sprouts with rice. Rice-lentil mixtures complemented by yogurt are common in the Middle East. Cornmeal mush eaten with beans is a staple in many African countries. We can keep using our own well-known cereal-milk combination and borrow from other traditions for a more interesting and responsible diet.

Complementary foods, to provide maximum usable protein, must be eaten together at the same meal. Chart A on page 32 shows complementary proportions that result in efficient use of plant proteins.[10] These proportions do not have to be followed slavishly in cooking. They are given to show that good proportions are realistic for the way we prepare food.

No-Meat, Low-Meat, And Which Meat

For centuries some persons and groups have lived on meatless (vegetarian) diets. We who are used to a four-ounce serving of meat at least once a day wonder how vegetarians can possibly keep up in sports or heavy physical work.

In 1974 the National Academy of Sciences (which sets United States recommended daily allowances) reported studies comparing the health of persons eating meat to those who did not. "No evidence of deficiency was found and the intake of nutrients by each group equaled or exceeded the Recommended Dietary Allowances . . . with the exception of Vitamin B_{12} which was low in the total vegetarian (not even milk or eggs) diet."[11] Vegetarians who included milk and eggs got all the essential nutrients. The report says that individual pure vegetarians from many populations of the world have maintained seemingly excellent health.

It is possible to get along without meat. Recognizing North American food habits and resources, however, we expect that most people will continue eating meat. We want to make best use of grazing land, forages, and roughage to produce protein for human consumption. We will slaughter for food the hen that stopped laying and the cow that no longer gives milk.

29

But we are clearly calling for lower-meat diets. In 1997, U.S. red meat consumption (beef, veal, pork, and mutton) was just under one-third pound per person daily.[12] Red meat consumption steadily dropped in the past 25 years. By any good nutritional standard, though, one-fourth pound of red meat, or preferably its equivalent in poultry or vegetable protein, is adequate. What is consumed above that, given the limited resources of our planet, has to be called waste.

Below are four days' menus, with protein grams given for each food containing a significant amount. We can aim for fifty grams a day and get enough. Day One and Two show how it is possible to get the protein requirement on meatless days. Day Three and Four use moderate amounts of meat.

In these menus below, protein could be increased for any day by adding another glass of milk, peanut butter on bread, or by using small amounts of soy flour or dry milk in baked goods.

Day One, Meatless	gr. of protein
Breakfast:*	
juice	
¾ c. cooked oatmeal	4
1 slice whole wheat toast	2.4
1 c. milk	8.8
Lunch:*	
1 c. bean soup	8
cheese sandwich	
(2 slices bread,	4.8
1 slice cheese)	7
carrot sticks	
fruit	
Dinner:*	
fried rice	10.3
(1 egg per serving)	
green beans	1
salad	
bread pudding	8.9
	55.2

Day Two, Meatless	
Breakfast:*	
fruit	
2/5″ waffles	14
1 c. milk	8.8
Lunch:	
½ c. cottage cheese	15
on tomato	
3 crackers	1
Dinner:*	
1 c. lentil casserole	12
broccoli	3
1 whole grain muffin	4
fruit	
	57.8

Day Three, Some Meat	gr. of protein
Breakfast:*	
fruit	
1 c. dry oat cereal	3.4
1 slice toast	2.4
1 c. milk	8.8
Lunch:	
ham sandwich	
(2 slices bread,	4.8
2 oz. ham)	9
raw vegetables	
fruit	
Dinner:*	
8 oz. pizza with cheese	
and 2 oz. ground beef	30
green salad	
¾ c. ice cream	4
	62.4

Day Four, Some Meat	
Breakfast:*	
juice	
1 egg	6.2
1 slice toast	2.4
1 c. milk	8.8
Lunch:*	
¾ c. baked beans	11
1 slice whole wheat bread	2.4
1½ T. peanut butter	5.2
fruit salad	
Dinner:*	
1 c. macaroni casserole	4
with 2 oz. chicken	11
and ½ oz. cheese	3
carrots	1
green salad	
2 cookies	1.5
	56.5

*Includes a complementary protein relationship which would increase protein quality.

The following ways to increase protein in various dishes should be used only by households making a serious attempt to cut down on meat consumption. There is no point in using bread containing soy flour to make a meat sandwich, for example.

Increasing Protein Content in Foods

In baked goods:
use part or all whole wheat flour
add wheat germ—2 T. per cup of flour
add dry milk powder
use soy flour—replace 2 or more T. per cup of all-purpose flour with soy flour
(2 T. low-fat soy flour has 14 gr. protein)

In vegetables, casseroles, soups, main dishes:
add cheese
use a sauce made with milk
add extra dry milk powder
use soybeans
use ground soybeans as extender
add hard-cooked eggs
add nuts

In salads:
add grated cheese, cottage cheese
add chilled marinated soybeans
sprinkle with roasted sunflower seeds or nuts
whip cottage cheese or yogurt into dressings
add hard-cooked eggs

In desserts:
use yogurt, milk, eggs, cottage cheese
add extra dry milk powder
add soy flour
add nuts
sprinkle with granola

Which meat one chooses is important along with how much meat. Cheaper grades contain just as much and often more protein than expensive marbled grades.

The top three grades of beef in the United States are prime, choice, and good. Prime, usually reserved for restaurant use, is well marbled. Choice, containing less fat, is the grade commonly sold in supermarkets. Good is acceptable for braised and stewed dishes but may be hard to find on meat counters.

In Canada, beef from youthful animals is graded A or B. A contains fat marbling, while B has no minimum marbling standards. Within both A and B are four fat levels numbered from one (lowest) to four (highest). Grades C and D are from older animals.

Check the grade of meat your store carries. If you find a butcher who sells a lower grade, it should be cheaper and may represent less grain in production. It will be a bit tougher, but when braised slowly can yield delicious dishes likely to be higher in protein than those made from expensive cuts.

Use more variety and organ meats. Why eat only roasts, steaks, and hamburgers, neglecting liver, kidneys, tongue, tripe, brains, and heart? *The Intelligent Consumer*, a gold mine of information on responsible living, calls this "our purely cultural squeamishness."[13] These meats are usually made into hot dogs laced with coloring and sodium nitrate, or they are turned into pet food. Some of the world's tastiest dishes are made from variety meats.

Chicken is one of the most efficient converters of plant to animal protein, and one of the cheapest meats. Fish is an even more efficient converter. One can not recommend growing dependence on fish as a protein source, however, because the world fish catch is declining due to decades of wanton exploitation. Even that old economy standby, tuna, is heavily overfished all over the world.[14]

a

Milk Products
should always be served with **Grains**

cereal with milk
  bread and milk
    cheese sandwiches
      macaroni with cheese
        rice-cheese casserole
          lasagne (pasta and cheese)
            pizza (crust and cheese)
              cheese fondue
                granola or grape nuts made with milk
                baked goods containing milk
              rice pudding (rice and milk)

1 c. skim milk	complements	¾ c. rice
¼ c. grated cheese	complements	¾ c. rice
½ c. skim milk	complements	1 c. whole wheat flour
3 T. dry milk powder	complements	1 c. whole wheat flour
1 c. milk	complements	5 slices bread
1 c. milk	complements	1 c. dry macaroni
⅓ c. grated cheese	complements	1 c. dry macaroni

Legumes
should always be served with **Grains**

peanut-butter sandwiches
  soybean salad with bread
    bread containing soy flour
      lentil soup and muffins
        lentils or split peas (dhal) with rice
          rice-bean casserole
            Boston baked beans with brown bread
              beans and tortillas
                refried beans and rice
                beans and corn bread
              bean soup and bread

1 c. beans	complements	2⅔ c. rice
¼ c. soybeans	complements	2½ c. rice
½ c. beans	complements	3 c. whole wheat flour
¼ c. soy flour	complements	1 c. whole wheat flour
¼ c. beans	complements	1 c. cornmeal or 6 tortillas

b

Adapted from
Recommended Dietary Allowances
Tenth Edition © 1989
National Academy of Sciences
National Academy Press, Washington,
D.C.

	Age (years)	Weight (pounds)	**Energy (calories)**	**Protein (grams)**
Children	1-3	29	**1300**	**16**
	4-6	44	**1800**	**24**
	7-10	62	**2000**	**28**
Males	11-14	99	**2500**	**45**
	15-18	145	**3000**	**59**
	19-24	160	**2900**	**58**
	25-50	174	**2900**	**63**
	51+	170	**2300**	**63**
Females	11-14	101	**2200**	**46**
	15-18	120	**2200**	**44**
	19-24	128	**2200**	**46**
	25-50	138	**2200**	**50**
	51+	143	**1900**	**50**
Pregnant			**+300**	**60**
Lactating	*1st 6 months*		**+500**	**65**
	2nd 6 months		**+500**	**62**

The following chart (based on .8 grams protein per kilogram of body weight) shows how calorie needs, but not protein needs, vary according to level of physical activity.* (Some sources suggest that protein needs increase slightly for the most strenuous forms of exercise, such as intense athletic training.) The male is 5 feet, 10 inches tall; the female is 5 feet, 4 inches. Both are 35 years old. (Calorie needs decrease with age, but protein needs do not.)

* *Calorie needs based on Harris-Benedict Formula of Basal Energy Expenditure*

Activity categories are as follows:

Basic
Represents energy required for basic life processes. It is calculated differently for males and females.
A
Sedentary (desk work, reading, watching TV, spectator at games)
B
Moderately active (household chores, gardening, walking, dancing)
C
Very active (heavy housecleaning, digging, moving or lifting heavy packages, active sports)

	Weight (pounds)	Activity Category	Calories	Protein (grams)
Male	170	Basic	1800	61
		A	2340	61
		B	2520	61
		C	3060	61
Female	135	Basic	1370	49
		A	1780	49
		B	1920	49
		C	2330	49

33

**Protein and Calorie Content
of Some Common Protein Foods**

		Portion Size	Calories	Protein (Grams)
Cereals	All-Bran	1/3 c.	70	3
	Cheerios	1 c.	102	3.4
	cornflakes	1 c.	95	2.1
	cream of wheat, cooked	1 c.	130.	4.4
	oatmeal, cooked	1 c.	148	5.4
	oatmeal, dry	1 c.	312	11.4
	Special K	1 c.	60	3.2
	wheat germ	1/4 c.	103	7.5
	Wheaties	1 c.	104	2.8
Dairy Products and Eggs	eggs, large	1 egg	88	7.0
	cottage cheese	1/2 c.	120	15.3
	natural cheddar cheese	1 oz.	115	7.2
	natural Swiss cheese	1 oz.	106	7.7
	process American cheese	1 oz.	107	6.5
	milk, whole, fresh	1 c.	162	8.6
	milk, skim	1 c.	88	8.8
	(same as buttermilk from skim milk or reconstituted nonfat dry milk)			
	nonfat dry milk solids	1 c.	215	21.4
	ice cream	1/6 qt.	186	3.6
	ice milk	1/6 qt.	137	4.3
	yogurt, from skim milk	1 c.	122	8.3
	yogurt, from whole milk	1 c.	151	7.3
Flours	soy, low fat	1 c.	356	43.4
	white, all-purpose	1 c.	400	11.6
	whole wheat	1 c.	400	16.0
	rye	1 c.	268	7.5
Grains and Pasta	barley, pearled, dry	1/4 c.	196	4.6
	cornmeal, dry	1/4 c.	135	2.9
	rice, white, dry	1/4 c.	178	3.3
	brown rice, dry	1/4 c.	176	3.7
	egg noodles, dry	1/4 c.	70	2.3
	macaroni, dry	1/4 c.	101	3.4
	spaghetti, dry	1/4 c.	140	4.8
Legumes	kidney beans, dry	1/2 c.	343	22.5
	lentils, dry	1/2 c.	340	24.7
	limas, dry	1/2 c.	345	20.4
	navy beans, dry	1/2 c.	340	22.3
	pinto beans, dry	1/2 c.	349	22.9
	split peas, dry	1/2 c.	348	24.2
	peanut butter	1 T.	86	3.9
	peanuts, shelled	1 T.	86	4.0
	soybeans, dry	1/2 c.	403	34.1
	soybeans, immature, cooked	1/2 c.	88	7.4
	soybeans, mature, cooked	1/2 c.	130	11.0

Meats and Fish	beef:			
	ground beef	¼ lb., raw	304	20.3
	ground beef, lean	¼ lb., raw	203	23.4
	chuck roast, choice grade	¼ lb., raw	337	15.5
	chuck roast, good grade	¼ lb., raw	288	16.7
	sirloin steak, choice grade	¼ lb., raw	229	17.8
	round steak, choice grade	¼ lb., raw	216	22.1
	liver	¼ lb., raw	159	22.6
	chicken fryers:			
	whole, ready-to-cook	½ lb., raw	191	28.7
	breasts	½ lb., raw	197	37.3
	drumsticks	½ lb., raw	157	25.6
	thighs	½ lb., raw	218	30.8
	livers	¼ lb., raw	146	22.4
	fish:			
	cod, flesh only	¼ lb., raw	89	20.0
	flounder, flesh only	¼ lb., raw	90	19.0
	haddock, flesh only	¼ lb., raw	89	20.8
	mackerel, canned	¼ lb.	208	21.9
	perch, flesh only	¼ lb., raw	108	21.6
	salmon, canned	¼ lb.	160	27.0
	tuna, canned in water	¼ lb.	144	32.0
	pork:			
	bacon	¼ lb., raw	667	9.3
	ham, picnic	¼ lb., raw	265	15.6
	ham, canned boneless	¼ lb.	189	20.9
	loin chops	¼ lb., raw	266	15.3
	sausage, links or bulk	¼ lb., raw	565	10:7
	miscellaneous meats:			
	bologna	¼ lb.	345	13.7
	frankfurters, all-meat	¼ lb.	361	14.9
	luncheon meat, canned	¼ lb.	334	17.0
	salami	¼ lb.	352	19.9
	scrapple	¼ lb.	194	10.0

Comparative Costs of Protein Sources

Prices based on western Pennsylvania supermarkets, June 2000

Prices change, but you can easily adapt this chart to meet contemporary needs. Put the revised price per pound in the first column; divide it by the figure in the second column to obtain the price per gram; move decimal point two places to the right to obtain price per 100 grams. This gives you the revised figure for the third column.

		Typical price per pound	Grams of protein per pound	Cost of 100 grams of protein
Beef	liver	.98	90.3	1.09
	hamburger	1.43	81.2	1.76
	ground chuck	2.03	93.9	2.16
	chuck roast, bone-in	2.38	71.6	3.32
	sirloin steak	3.09	71.1	4.34
	round steak	2.89	88.5	3.26
Pork	ham, smoked picnic	1.35	68.3	1.97
	pork chops, loin	3.23	72.2	4.47
	ham, canned	3.44	83.0	4.09
	bulk sausage	2.93	53.0	5.53
	link sausage	4.11	53.4	7.70
	boiled ham, sliced	3.63	103.5	3.51
	bacon	3.09	38.1	8.11
Chicken	whole	1.04	57.4	1.81
	cut-up	1.59	57.4	2.77
	breasts	1.94	74.5	2.60
	thighs	.99	61.6	1.61
	legs	.78	51.2	1.52
	canned white meat	3.97	98.9	4.01
Turkey	turkey, young whole	.99	65.9	1.50
	ground turkey	1.28	79.6	1.61
Fish	perch, frozen	3.98	87.5	4.55
	cod, frozen	4.69	79.8	5.88
	fish sticks	3.42	74.7	4.58
	haddock, frozen	5.54	83.0	6.67
	flounder, frozen	5.49	75.8	7.24
	mackerel, canned	.90	87.5	1.03
	sardines, canned	2.82	89.3	3.16
	tuna, canned	2.32	109.8	2.11
	salmon, canned	1.55	93.0	1.67
Misc. Meats	frankfurters, all meat	1.91	59.4	3.22
	salami	2.63	79.4	3.31
	luncheon meat, canned	2.71	68.0	3.99
	bologna, sliced	2.73	62.4	4.38
Legumes	navy beans, dry	.79	101.2	.78
	lentils, dry	.63	112.0	.56
	split peas, dry	.54	109.3	.49
	baby limas, dry	.89	92.5	.96
	kidney beans, dry	.84	103.9	.81

	pinto beans, dry	.59	103.9	.57
	black-eyed peas	.88	101.2	.87
	large limas, dry	1.09	92.5	1.18
	baked beans, canned	.76	27.7	2.74
	soybeans, dry	1.22	154.7	.78
	vegetable burger patties	2.98	99.6	2.99
	meatless breakfast links	5.01	80.0	6.26
	tofu, firm	2.40	36.6	6.56
	peanut butter	1.68	115.2	1.46
	peanuts, dry roasted	3.31	107.2	3.08
Grains and Pasta	spaghetti	.99	56.7	1.75
	egg noodles	.91	58.1	1.57
	rice	.51	30.4	1.68
	brown rice	.81	34.0	2.38
	cous cous	2.69	58.7	4.58
Cereals	wheat germ, toasted	4.64	144.0	3.22
	oatmeal	1.72	73.1	2.35
	Cream of Wheat	2.07	54.4	3.81
	Special K	4.55	93.7	4.86
	Cheerios	3.19	64.0	4.98
	All-Bran	2.75	48.0	5.73
	Wheaties	2.99	48.0	6.23
	Great Grains (pecan)	3.08	45.0	6.84
	cornflakes	2.63	32.0	8.22
	Golden Crisp	2.25	25.0	9.00
Flours	soy	1.28	196.9	.65
	white	.28	47.6	.59
	whole wheat	.51	60.3	.85
Dairy Products and Eggs	2% milk, one pint	.32	17.2	1.86
	nonfat dry milk powder	4.43	162.4	2.73
	soy milk, one pint	.75	13.4	5.60
	cottage cheese	1.69	61.7	2.74
	process American cheese	3.34	105.2	3.17
	cheddar cheese	3.67	113.4	3.24
	Swiss cheese	3.95	124.7	3.17
	eggs, large (dozen)	.98	58.2	1.68
	yogurt, plain low fat	1.28	24.0	5.33
Misc.	pizza, frozen pepperoni	2.85	50.3	5.56

10 **expensive** sources of protein	Cost of 100 grams of protein		10 **economical** sources of protein	Cost of 100 grams of protein
bulk pork sausage	5.53		split peas, purchased dry	.49
pizza, frozen pepperoni	5.56		lentils, purchased dry	.56
meatless breakfast links	6.26		pinto beans, purchased dry	.57
tofu, firm	6.56		soybeans, purchased dry	.78
haddock, frozen	6.67		mackerel, canned	1.03
flounder, frozen	7.24		beef liver	1.09
pork link sausage	7.70		peanut butter	1.47
bacon	8.11		young, whole turkey	1.50
cornflakes	8.22		chicken legs	1.52
Golden Crisp cereal	9.00		eggs, large	1.68

e

General Helps

Equivalents

		Weight — yields —	Approx. Measure
Dairy Products	**nonfat dry milk solids**	1 lb.	4 c.
	cheese	1 lb.	4 c. shredded
	cottage cheese	1 lb.	2 c.
	cream cheese	8 oz.	1 c.
	butter or margarine	1 lb.	2 c.
			Approx. measure, cooked
Dried Beans	**kidney**	1 lb. (1½ c.)	6 c.
	lima	1 lb. (2⅓ c.)	6 c.
	navy	1 lb. (2⅓ c.)	6 c.
	soybeans	1 lb. (2⅓ c.)	6 c.
	split peas	1 lb. (2 c.)	5 c.
	lentils	1 lb. (2⅓ c.)	6 c.
			Approx. measure
Eggs	**7 small eggs**		1 c.
	6 medium		1 c.
	5 large		1 c.
Flour and Grains	**enriched white**	1 lb.	4 c. sifted
	enriched cake	1 lb.	4½ c. sifted
	whole wheat	1 lb.	3½ c.
	rye	1 lb.	4 c.
	soy	1 lb.	6 c.
	cornmeal	1 lb.	3 c.
	oatmeal	1 lb.	4¾ c.
Nuts	**almonds**	1 lb. in shell	1¾ c. shelled
		1 lb. shelled	3½ c.
	pecans	1 lb. in shell	2¼ c. shelled
		1 lb. shelled	4 c.
	peanuts	1 lb. in shell	2¼ c. shelled
		1 lb. shelled	3 c.
	walnuts	1 lb. in shell	1⅔ c. shelled
		1 lb. shelled	4 c.
	coconut	1 whole	2-3 c. shredded
		1 lb. shredded	5 c.
			Approx. measure, cooked
Rice and Pasta	**rice**	1 lb. (2 c.) dried	6 c.
	macaroni	1 lb. (4 c.) dried	8 c.
	spaghetti	1 lb. (5 c.) dried	9-10 c.
	noodles	1 lb. (6 c.) dried	10½ c.

		Approx. measure	
Sugar	**granulated**	1 lb.	2 c.
	brown	1 lb.	2¼ c.
	confectioners	1 lb.	3½ c.
	honey	1 lb.	1⅓ c.
	molasses	1 lb.	1⅓ c.

Misc.	**1 pkg. dry yeast**	1 T.
	1 envelope unflavored gelatin	1 T.
	(enough to jell 2 c. liquid)	
	1 lemon juice	2-3 T.
	rind, grated	1½-3 t.
	1 orange juice	⅓-½ c.
	rind, grated	1-2 T.
	1 lb. bananas (3-4)	2 c. mashed
	1 lb. dates	2½ c. pitted
	1 lb. seedless raisins	2¾ c.
	1 lb. raw potatoes	2 c. cooked and mashed

Metric Conversion Table

	when you know	you can find	if you multiply by
Weight	ounces	grams	28
measured in grams (G)	pounds	kilograms	0.45
1 gram=1/28 ounce	grams	ounces	0.035
=1/1000 kilogram	kilograms	pounds	2.2
Liquid Volume	ounces	milliliters	30
measured in liters (L)	pints	liters	0.47
1 liter=1.06 quarts	quarts	liters	0.95
	gallons	liters	3.8
	milliliters	ounces	0.034
	liters	pints	2.1
	liters	quarts	1.06
	liters	gallons	0.26

	Fahrenheit (F°)	Metric: Celcius (C°)
Temperature	32°	0°
	212°	100°
	98.6°	37°

Shorten the Shopping List

Reducing the grocery list to fewer, more basic foods and buying these in quantity will almost always save money. It also lessens the likelihood of running out of vital ingredients when cooking. It means fewer trips to the supermarket and fewer searches up and down its aisles. It means less checkout, bagging, and home storage time. It means fewer containers to open and discard, fewer loaded wastebaskets to empty. The current practice of marketing everything in ten-ounce containers necessitates a thousand small motions. Small containers and vast variety run us in circles.

Dry milk is a good example. For several years I bought a certain brand because we liked its taste. One day I could find it only in boxes of ten pre-measured foil packets. I picked up a couple of these every other time I went shopping, and often ran out of milk anyway. I could have bought ten at a time, but the boxes were twice as bulky as their actual contents. Ten would have filled my shopping cart and my cupboard. Empty boxes and foil packets jammed our wastebasket. When the milk began to cost 35 cents a box more than other brands, I quit buying it.

One recipe contributer wrote that she buys a fifty-pound container of dry milk at a local dairy. It is much cheaper. It takes room to store it, but not the room its equivalent in foil packets and boxes would take. Leaving a cup in it makes measuring easier and eliminates throw-away. When are we going to stop putting up with the inconvenience of convenience foods?

Stores are not designed for people who want a cheap, sensible system of getting food into their homes. We have to look hard to find beans or dry milk in a ten-pound bag, or yeast in anything but micro-mini envelopes.

In every community it takes time and energy to ferret out places where bulk quantities of food are sold. Local feed mills are good places to look for straight-run whole wheat flour, white flour, cornmeal, rolled oats, wheat germ, bran, and soybeans. Feed mills may also be willing to grind your own wheat, corn, or soybeans.

Check local farmers for milk, eggs, wheat, animals for slaughter (ask about stewing hens), garden and orchard produce in season, honey, maple syrup, and soybeans. Many soybean varieties are available, but any field variety is edible. Farmers ask about one fifth as much for soybeans as grocery or health food stores charge. In many communities consumers and farmers are getting together again to eliminate the waste and expense of super packaging, processing, and advertising.

Community businesses, such as the dairy mentioned earlier, buy foods in quantity for their own uses and might pass on these advantages. Ask your local grocer to order for you in quantity.

Wholesale produce markets sell fresh produce by the crate. One farmer who regularly delivers potatoes to such a market, then loads his truck with crates of produce for his neighborhood.

Food co-ops usually handle staples. A co-op may already be operating in your community. Literature on how to organize a co-op is available.

Learning to buy food this way does take more time initially. Perhaps you could set aside a day or two every six months for stocking up on staples. The list could include:

white flour
whole wheat flour
wheat germ
cornmeal
rolled oats
quick oats
dry beans and peas
soybeans
shortening
oil
dry milk
honey
syrup
sugar
raisins
dried fruits
spices and herbs
nuts
potatoes
soaps
detergents
cleaning supplies

You need storage when you buy food in quantity, but this system also makes space in kitchen cupboards by reducing the number of small boxes and jars. In climates with cold winters, buy more items in quantity and store them in a dry basement, attic, porch, or garage. Transfer small amounts to kitchen canisters for daily use. Tightly covered cans or large jars (restaurants often throw them out) are good for storing staples.

Reduce your stock of flour, cornmeal, and oats or refrigerate it in warm weather. Do not try to keep twenty pounds of whole wheat flour in a warm kitchen cupboard. It may get rancid or buggy.

The art of properly storing dry food is one we need to revive. New houses usually have little provision for this kind of storage. Instead they have yards of expensive kitchen cupboards, all of them located in the warm kitchen where staples are most apt to spoil. The enclosed unheated porch of an old house is a great place in winter to line up cans of staples and baskets of fruit. In summer the porch stores garden produce. Leaving one room of a new house unheated can save energy in several ways.

The term "nonprocessed" can be misleading. Many basic foods are processed in some way. Grains may be dried at the mill. They need grinding to yield flour. Processing turns peanuts into peanut butter and cane into molasses.

"Nonprocessed" as used here means food sold as nearly as possible in its natural form. So we buy plain peanut butter. We do not need a factory to mix it with jelly or bananas for us. We can make our own puddings from eggs and milk instead of using mixes, which contain very little of either. We can get a wire whisk, learn to stir up a white sauce, and flavor it in our own way instead of dumping canned soup on every casserole.

Kool-Aid and Jello were two of our earliest convenience foods. Now they are so firmly entrenched in our menus that it is hard to imagine life without them. Both are made with artificial colorings and flavorings. They are simply a pleasant way to add more sugar to the diet. Kool-Aid, when mixed according to package directions, has six teaspoons of sugar in each cup. Gelatin salads and desserts can be made with unflavored gelatin and real fruits for more nutritious dishes.

What we drink is also a question of wise use of resources. First to be struck off the list are alcoholic beverages. Their destructive powers over health and human relationships have always been apparent. Added to this is the waste of grain in the production of some alcoholic beverages.

But we can't stop there. Per capita consumption of soft drinks in the United States has doubled in the past eleven years. Kamala Platt, a Newton, Kansas teenager, writes:

We in America are compulsive drinkers. I am not speaking of alcoholics, although they are included. I am speaking of

41

Good cold water is an amazing thirst quencher which many people overlook.

Which fruit juice to buy is one question with an easy answer. Frozen concentrated orange juice, when reconstituted, usually costs less per ounce than any of the sugary, watery, so-called fruit drinks in 46-ounce cans. One ounce of orange juice still provides more Vitamin C than an ounce of the highly advertised "high Vitamin C" drinks. Frozen concentrated juice, unsweetened, is one of very few sensible convenience foods.

The Best Food Supply of All

Early last spring I bought a packet of Big Boy Hybrid Tomato seeds for fifty cents. I planted the seeds in a small pot and, when they were one and a half inches tall transplanted them into a flat. There were fifty-four plants. When the danger of frost was over, I transplanted them deeply in the black muck at the end of North 23rd Street.

Throughout the summer we hoed and weeded. They grew profusely. When the tomatoes ripened we ate all we could. Then THE ELEVEN VARIETIES began. I canned tomato juice, whole tomatoes, tomato soup, and vegetable soup. On Labor Day I made spaghetti sauce from a new recipe sent by a sister in Ohio. It required three pecks of tomatoes, three large sweet potatoes, celery, peppers, onions, and garlic. By the time it was in the kettle the amount was so enormous that the whole family joked about it. I said, "I like to can." Barbara affirmed, "You sure must like it. Nobody

would can that much if they didn't like to do it."

I tried a new catsup recipe which the family liked—and made three batches. Later I made Thorley's Chili Sauce and Lick-Um Relish. After the first hard frost, I gathered the green tomatoes and made relish and mincemeat. The last of THE ELEVEN VARIETIES was green tomato dills using a recipe from the October Family Visitor. This winter our family will dine on the "poisonous love apple."
—Ada Beachy, Goshen, Indiana

Gardening does something for the soul. "Less mow—more hoe" is the watchword for those who want their yards to yield more than status. Turn that sod under and plant food.

Lawn gardening–
Uses land wisely in time of world food shortages
Saves power mower gas
Improves the soil
Uses composted garbage
Saves energy–no trucking from farm to factory to store to home
Provides nutrients–why buy vitamins?
Assures eating more vegetables– low-calorie vitamins and roughage
Saves shopping trips–pick fresh salad at home
Provides delicious summer meals
Provides something to share with friends
Gives good exercise–why pay to work out at a gym?
Wears you out–why buy sleeping pills?
Facilitates group endeavor–work together
Teaches life processes
Occupies children in summer
Gets you out of the house
Keeps you home on weekends– saves gas and money
Makes you feel good inside

If these factors are not enough, the final touch is that it does save on the food bill, if you know how to manage. Share expensive power tools. Use a compost heap and recycle kitchen garbage and yard

42

clippings regularly to improve the soil. This makes commercial fertilizer unnecessary, at least in smaller gardens. Plants and seeds can be shared. Take good care of tools and they will last for years.

Many apartment and city-dwellers do not have space even for leaf lettuce. Community gardens on church, school, or other institutional grounds are becoming more and more common. Organizing and setting up guidelines takes time, but there are advantages. New gardeners can learn from the more experienced. Produce is easily shared, especially at canning time, and the work is more fun when you can talk to the person in the next plot.

Home preserving which accompanies gardening is a long-standing tradition in rural Mennonite homes, but should not be rejected out-of-hand by urbanites. It also can pay off with produce purchased in season. In our community, for example, it is much cheaper to buy fresh broccoli in summer and freeze it than to depend on the ten-ounce frozen boxes of broccoli. Freezing broccoli takes little time and no special equipment.

Making pickles, canning tomato juice, canning or freezing applesauce and peaches, freezing green beans, strawberries, blueberries, and making jams and jellies are simple processes possible in any small kitchen. Apples can be dried in the oven. Chapter 11 includes some simple recipes.

Drying, the most energy-saving kind of home food preservation, is making a comeback in many homes. Detailed how-to books now available on all home-preservation methods provide the kind of help beginners need.

Home food preservation is hard work, but it can provide meaningful opportunities for family members to work together. I remember late summer evenings stuffing cucumbers into jars with Paul, my right-hand man at canning time. Some couples would not call it a romantic encounter, but we like it. Paul grew up in a family where everyone—male or female—helps cut and peel. When all help, the work is no great burden to anyone.

Recommended Resources

The American Dietetic Association's Complete Food and Nutrition Guide, by Roberta Larson Duyff, MS, RD, CFCS, © copyright 1996, Chronimed Publishing. ISBN 1-56561-098-9. (Also available in paperback.)
Dietetics hot line: 1-800-366-1655
American Dietetic Association Web site: www.eatright.com

Notes

1. The Food Guide Pyramid, Center for Nutrition Policy and Promotion, U.S. Department of Agriculture, Washington, D.C., August 1992. Revised October 1996.
2. Canada's Food Guide to Healthy Eating, published by Health Canada, Ottawa, Ontario, 1993.
3. Action Towards Healthy Eating . . . Canada's Guidelines for Healthy Eating and Strategies for Implementation, Report of the Communications/Implementation Committee, Minister of Supply and Services, Health Canada, Ottawa, Ontario, 1990.
4. Dietary Guidelines for Americans, U.S. Department of Agriculture, U.S. Department of Health and Human Services, fourth edition, 1995.
5. Recommended Nutrient Intakes, Tables 19 and 20, in Nutrition Recommendations: Report of the Scientific Review Committee, Health Canada, 1990.
6. Francis Moore Lappé, Diet for a Small Planet (New York: Ballantine Books, 1971), p. 42.
7. "How Much Is Enough?" Consumer Reports, September, 1974, p. 667.
8. Letter from Kenton K. Brubaker, PhD, Professor of Biology at Eastern Mennonite College, October 4, 1974.
9. Lappé, Diet for a Small Planet, pp. 51-52.
10. Ibid.
11. "Vegetarian Diets," A Statement of the Food and Nutrition Board, National Research Council, National Academy of Sciences, May 1974, p. 3.
12. Source: U.S.D.A./Economic Research Service.
13. Christopher and Bonnie Weathersbee, The Intelligent Consumer (New York: E. P. Dutton and Co., Inc., 1973), p. 16.
14. Ibid, p. 20.
15. Letter from Kamala Platt, Newton, Kansas, January 1975.

•••••••••••••••••••••••••

Eat with Joy

*When you are having a party
for lunch or supper, do not
invite your friends, your
brothers or other relations,
or your rich neighbours; they
will only ask you back again
and so you will be repaid.*
*But when you give a party,
    ask the poor,
      the crippled,
        the lame,
          and the blind;
            and so find happiness.*
—*Luke 14: 12, 13*
New English Bible

But I've Always Loved to Cook

North American Mennonites enjoy a tradition of creative, bountiful cooking. Some knew hard times and put rivels (little balls of moistened flour) in the soup. But when times were better and livestock, gardens, and orchards flourished, meals with two meats, three vegetables, and the traditional seven sweets and seven sours ended in four desserts.

Our grandmothers had reasons for cooking so heartily. Pies, pickles, and quilts were among their few creative expressions. Aunt Anna might not have been allowed to speak in church, but when all Uncle Jake's brothers' families came for dinner afterward, it was quite acceptable to show them what she could do. Besides, with bedrooms unheated and hard work waiting for Monday morning, extra calories would not hurt anybody.

Now a wide range of creative pursuits are open to women. Warm homes and sedentary occupations mean people need fewer calories. But some people still love to cook.

And cook we shall. For simple is not necessarily plain, dull, or unattractive. "Simplicity is the keynote to good taste," emphasized my high school home economics teacher. If this applies to architecture, painting, and music, it applies to cooking—even cheap cooking.

Could a Meal Be Like a Symphony?

Great music is characterized by a central theme on which the rest of the work is built. Give a meal a theme by making one nutritious, perfectly cooked and seasoned dish. Complement it with a few plain foods offered much as nature produced them.

An example is the curry meal. You hover over the curry, cutting, mixing, adding, tasting, simmering it long and slowly until the flavor can only be described as an experience.

But the rest of the meal can be plain steamed rice, chopped raw garden vegetables, coconut perhaps, and fruits.

Too many of our meals are tasting parties. The church potluck with twenty each of casseroles, salads, and desserts, is an extreme example. In an effort to try everything, we overeat. The variety becomes cloying. No dish gets the appreciation it deserves. An improvement on the potluck might be to ask every family to bring only one dish, but more of it.

At home we will save ourselves time, money, frustration, and fuel if we make fewer dishes at each meal. Creativity can still flourish. In fact, it is enhanced when we can concentrate, unharried, on a single dish.

Who has not had the experience of stashing an extra salad in the refrigerator for guests and forgetting it completely in the logistics of sending all four hot dishes to the table at once? And who has not watched children, with their blessed simplicity, stuff their tummies with one delicious food at a meal and refuse to confuse their taste buds with anything else?

Sara Janzen Regier, nurse and nutritionist in Zaire, wrote me that she does not make vegetable, salad, and fruit dishes all in a single meal. She selects one dish and makes plenty of it. During a furlough in North America, one of her children said at a family reunion potluck, "I sure will be glad to get back to Africa where we just have to eat manioc."

Our Family Likes
The Old Recipes

The last attitude we should take in view of world food needs is one that says because Grandma did not eat bean sprouts and soy flour she was all wrong, and that at last a few of the younger people who do not eat beef have figured it out.

Traditional cooking can be quite responsible, as long as we recognize that most of us need fewer calories than did our ancestors. Dig through old cookbooks if you want to find economical recipes. Ask Grandma what she knows about thrifty cooking, and make sure you are settled for the afternoon to listen. Now more than ever we should affirm the best of old eating habits. They would take us back to meals of mush and milk more often than we suspect.

A 1912 volume, *Economical Cooking,* says on the jacket, "The simplest and cheapest can also be the best, if one knows how to buy, prepare, and serve in an economical way." The book gives sample menus:

Luncheons

Banana Salad
Crisp Rolls
Coffee

Fried Mush
Milk

Corn Bread
Blackberries
Milk

Dinners

Bluefish
Sliced Tomatoes and Cucumbers
Boiled Rice with Butter
Sliced Peaches

Meat En Casserole
Baked Sweet Potatoes
Bread Pudding

Baked Beans with Bacon
Stewed Tomatoes
Apple and Celery Salad
Coffee

Just because our North American grandmothers did not eat soybeans or bean sprouts does not mean these foods are a new invention. The Chinese were eating soybeans when Christ was born. We are fortunate enough to benefit from the traditions of many cultures. Most good ideas with food are just that—someone's tradition. Try your own. Then branch out to Russian Borsch (p. 207), Garden Vegetable Curry (p. 133), or Navajo Fry Bread (p. 83).

Every Time I Make This It Turns Out Different

While testing the recipes for this book, I realized for the first time that either in spite of or because of proper home economics training, I have trouble following a recipe exactly. I am a chronic recipe improver. But this is what makes cooking a joy!

Recipes are not sacred canon. They exist only to lure us into the kitchen. The real recipe writing begins when I check what is in our own cupboards, how much time I have, what we are prepared to spend, what we feel is responsible, and what we like. Substituting what I have on hand for a missing ingredient not only is more economical, but far more creative than running to the store. Great recipes are born this way.

Find a clever way to use what you have in cheap abundance rather than demanding variety while things go to waste. Doris Hammon, a former Mennonite Central Committee worker, wrote: "After World War II, I was sent to the Waldensian Valleys in Europe. Food was scarce and expensive, but they had a good crop of chestnuts. And chestnuts are filling." Doris sent in recipes for chestnuts roasted, boiled, glacéd, in soup, stuffing, and mashed into a fabulous dessert called Monte Bianca. Simple does not have to be plain.

Learn to handle basic foods and you can cook creatively with the plainest ingredients. A good cook knows you do not tamper with the structure of a soufflé, but varying the herbs or variety of cheese is your privilege. You measure accurately to get a light cake. But you can make a stew when the measuring cup is lost.

Many letters received for this book were from people who write their own cookbooks. A few I could not bear to standardize. They show how creative, responsible cooks operate. Here they are as I received them:

Garden Stew

I start with one pound of hamburger and one large onion fried in a little oil. Then I add five large tomatoes cut up, salt and pepper. After that, anything in the garden goes in. One great stew this summer had thirteen vegetables in it. First to go in can be a combination of coarsely shredded cabbage, sliced carrots, diced celery, corn, finely diced green or red peppers, any kind of beans, and diced potatoes.

The last fifteen minutes these can go in (they should not cook so long that they get mushy): cubed eggplant, zucchini squash, a few okra pods, brussel sprouts, broccoli, and cauliflower.

Last I check the seasoning, add some herbs and more water if I want a thin stew. I consider it one of my more creative dishes, dependent on the state of the garden.
—Helen Alderfer, Scottdale, Pa.

Chicken and Noodles

In our community the farmers who sell hatching eggs must clear their barns of one-to-two-year-old fat hens. They could be bought for forty cents this fall, so I bought ten of them. Many had partially formed eggs which can be used for making noodles. The following nutritious dish can be made very economically.

Cook hen with water to cover. For seasoning use one medium onion, some parsley, salt and pepper. Cool. Skim off fat. Bone the chicken.

Make noodles with one teaspoon salt, two eggs, and enough flour to make a stiff dough. Boil in salted water for five to seven minutes. Strain. Put noodles in with chicken and broth. Heat thoroughly. Cooking for a while improves flavor.

If you have gotten a hold of an old, tough bird, you can use the pressure cooker. But a fat hen gives better flavor.
—Mrs. Darrell Unruh, Hillsboro, Kan.

Nameless Soybeans

Soak a cup or so of dried green soybeans overnight in about two cups water. In the morning put on slow heat. We use a "crock pot." After lunch fry one-fourth to one-third pound of hamburger with one egg and several handfuls of soybean meat extender. For added flavor add half a chopped onion, or a handful of dried onion flakes. When fried, drain grease, add soybeans, and one-half teaspoon pepper, basil to taste, and a small amount of salt. Douse liberally with soy sauce. This also adds salt. I once grabbed Worcestershire sauce by accident, but it added to the flavor also.

We finished off a box of Uncle Ben's rice by adding it with water to the above. Adding one-half cup of precooked brown rice would complete a fairly tasty dish, which I haven't yet named. Feeds four to six people, depending on how hungry you are.
—Ken Gingerich, Akron, Pa.

Glazed Apples and Frankfurters

I am an old Mennonite grandmother who cooks with a pinch of this and a pinch of that. All measurements are according to taste. First I prepare a large fry pan full of cored and sliced apples with peelings left on. Then I slice about one pound of wieners in circles and spread them amongst the apples. Over this I pour about half a cup of either white or brown syrup, and sprinkle on half a cup of white or brown sugar. Then I fry until well glazed, stirring often with one stick of oleo in the bottom of the mixture.

This makes a delightful main dish, very nutritious and good enough for company. It uses economical meat, too. I serve it often to my farmer men, and they like it.
—Hilda Harms, Whitewater, Kan.

Where Do You Find the Time?

"A simpler, more responsible style of eating, going back to basic foods, will take time—something I just don't have," one person told me. "I'm not going to spend hours in the kitchen the way Grandma did."

The increased use of convenience foods, and the increasing number of women working outside their homes have gone hand in hand. Breakfasts when everyone is rushed to get to school or job preclude more than pouring milk on dry cereal. Mothers help children out the door with lunches and library books in hand, while getting themselves ready as well. They have little mental energy left to decide what to thaw for dinner. Too often the solution is a late-afternoon stop at the supermarket for something fast and convenient.

All this is not to say that women should stay at home. Housework can be shared. But if every member of a household leaves for the day, we need to plan specifically if we wish to maintain a responsible, nutritious eating style.

Superconvenience makes it hard to protect God's created world. Time is needed to prepare food for every household. Otherwise people rely on expensive foods produced through systems that waste and pollute.

During the months spent compiling this book, I worked six to ten hours daily in my office. I needed to develop time-saving cooking habits, and yet was deeply concerned that I cook responsibly. From this experience and the shared insights of other busy cooks, I offer these suggestions:

1. Share cooking and clean-up tasks within the household. No one person can do it alone while maintaining a working day elsewhere.

2. Community or close-proximity living styles offer further possibilities for shared cooking. Two families we know share a large house. One couple is responsible for meals on week nights while the other cooks on weekends. They also alternate dishwashing responsibilities.

3. Morning can be the most hectic time. If there are no outdoor chores, father and an older child might make breakfast while mother packs lunches and helps younger children get dressed. When nutritious bread and quick-cooking cereal or granola are on hand, good breakfasts are fast.

4. Simplify the menus. Make fewer dishes but larger quantities. If the family eats bedtime snacks anyway, omit desserts. One household eats desserts only on weekends.

5. Plan menus a week at a time. In the morning you can do a few things to prepare for dinner and lose no time wondering what to fix.

6. To cut down on weekly shopping time, buy in quantity staples that do not spoil. (See Chapter 3, p. 40).

7. Organize a cook-bake-freeze system. Make double or triple amounts of main dishes and baked goods on weekends. Refrigerate or freeze extra quantities in oven-proof dishes for week night dinners. If frozen, remove dish from freezer in the morning, and place in oven. Set timer to heat for dinner.

8. Bake five to six loaves of bread on the weekend and freeze. Or, using refrigerator bread recipe, mix dough one evening and bake the next.

9. Make large batches of granola for ever-ready breakfasts, lunches, and snacks.

10. To use soybeans or other legumes, soak and cook large amounts. Freeze in small containers or keep in refrigerator for quick use throughout the week.

11. Freeze meat in small amounts so it can easily be chopped and stir-fried Chinese-style with vegetables.

In the recipe section, recipes which have special time-saving advantages are identified with TS.

But Won't All That Bread Make Me Fat?

Getting more with less means eating joyfully. We can release resources for the hungry. We can gain more nutrients for ourselves. We can get more for our food dollars, and eat with more creative expression and good taste. But the joy will quickly fade if we gain weight.

This is what protein-conscious dieters fear when they hear phrases like "more bread and beans!" Popular diet plans say eating more protein will burn up fat, and that lowly carbohydrate-rich foods like bread, beans, and rice are no-nos for people trying to stay slim. But Chapter 1 pointed out that North Americans already eat more protein than needed, and still obesity is a national health problem.

A more responsible eating pattern will actually help people control their weight. A diet emphasizing more whole grains, beans, and vegetables does not have to be high in calories. Because of the things it de-emphasizes, such as high-fat animal proteins, sugars, empty processed foods, and overeating in general, it can help people lose weight. Often we turn up our noses at basic foods, but accept substitutes that are even more caloric.

We can begin by eating more moderately of all foods. This is easy to say but hard to do. In our society self-discipline is out of style, and advertising encourages us to satiate every desire. Change requires motivation and commitment. "The fat is in our head and the cure is in our soul," says Charlie Shedd, author of an inspirational book for weight-watchers, *The Fat Is in Your Head*.

Cut the intake of nutrition-empty sweets and processed foods. This includes soft drinks, candy, potato chips, sweetened dry cereals, commercially baked cookies, snack cakes, and rolls. These foods are empty of nutrients except calories. Even commercial puddings and ice cream are full of sugar and high-calorie fillers.

We can choose lower calorie protein foods to fill protein requirements. Among meats, poultry and seafood have roughly half the calories that beef, pork, and lamb have per gram of protein. Soybeans contain fewer calories than common white beans, per gram of protein. The comparison follows for nonfat and whole milk, cottage cheese and hard cheese. See Table C on p. 34.

I Need a Simpler Way To Serve Guests

Eating with joy is eating together. Jesus hallowed the common meal when He broke bread, shared wine, and said, "This do in remembrance of me." It was at mealtime that He revealed Himself as risen Lord to the two from Emmaus. He invites us to join the consummation feast, the marriage supper of the Lamb. Let us eat together in His name.

But the word *entertaining* has crept into our guest-meal vocabulary. Mennonites used to just "have you over for dinner." Now people speak as though they are about to stage a show.

What does more with less mean in a guest meal? We want more real meeting of persons, more warmth, more relaxation to enjoy guests. Sometimes we want to give our guests a homemade, personalized gift—a beautifully cooked meal—just because we love them. All this with less time and cheaper food. Can it be done?

My solution has been to focus on one nutritious, cheap, but interesting dish. I put out a few simple foods to complement it. This gives the meal a theme and builds around it. Keeping the menu simple is still the best way to make guest meals less demanding and more enjoyable.

Following are ideas collected in my kitchen and from letters received for this book. I find that guests, including children, particularly enjoy "build-your-own" meals. A relaxed spirit takes over as everyone participates. Not all the variations listed here should be offered at a single meal. Choose from what is on hand.

● Bread Meal

Theme:
— loaves of fresh homemade bread served on boards
Variations:
— butter, cheese, soybean spread, peanut butter, apple butter and cottage cheese, lettuce, tomatoes, onions, pickles, sprouts, other raw vegetables
— hot or cold drink according to season
More with less:
— guests slice and spread their own
— leftovers reusable
— inexpensive, nutritious

● Salad Meal

Theme:
— big bowl of mixed greens
Variations:
— small bowls of chopped hard-cooked eggs, marinated soy or garbanzo beans, tomatoes, slivered meats, cheeses, onions, raw vegetables, peanuts, roasted sunflower seeds, croutons
— homemade salad dressings
— breads, muffins, biscuits, breadsticks
More with less:
— guests build their own salads in bowls
— make ahead and chill
— leftovers reusable
— inexpensive for gardeners
— no cooking on a hot day

● Waffle or Pancake Meal

Theme:
— basic batter
Variations:
— add to batter berries, nuts, bacon bits, cheese
— eat with syrup, honey, fruit sauce, peanut butter and syrup, creamed meat or vegetable, thin pudding, yogurt, ice cream
More with less:
— spouse or older child in charge of baking
— make batter ahead

● Casserole Meal

Theme:
— any baked main dish
Variations:
— vegetables, salads, breads, fruits
More with less:
— make ahead
— use inexpensive ingredients

● Slow Cooker Combination Meal

Theme:
— meat, vegetables, grains, legumes layered in crock pot
Variations:
— raw vegetables, salads, breads, fruits, desserts
More with less:
— prepare meal early in the day
— conserve fuel

● Granola Meal

Theme:
— big batch of granola
Variations:
— fruits, yogurt, ice cream
More with less:
— all made ahead
— no cooking on a hot day

● Vegetable Dish Meal

Theme:
— filling vegetable main dish
(See recipes for Gado-Gado, p. 240,
Garden Stew, p. 46, Zucchini
Skillet Supper, p. 236.)
Variations:
— breads, fruits
More with less:
— use homegrown vegetables in
season, or home preserved
— high in nutrients, low in cost

● Soup Meal

Theme One:
— filling, thick soup
Variations:
— raw vegetables, breads, fruits,
desserts
More with less:
— make ahead and keep hot
— perfect in cold weather
— good reheated

Theme Two:
(inspired by Indonesian chicken
soup):
— pot of hot broth with dipper,
centered on table (serve in cooking
pot or appliance to keep hot)
Variations:
— bowls of hot rice, hot noodles,
chopped cooked meat, chopped
green onions, chopped greens,
sprouts, soy sauce, hot peppers
More with less:
— guests build their own soup in
bowls (Fill bowl with other
ingredients first, then ladle hot broth
over all.)

● Rice Meal

Theme:
— steamed or fried rice
Variations:
— meat and vegetables stir-fried,
curry, dhal, or hot chili beans
— raw chopped vegetables,
tomatoes, greens, hard-cooked
eggs, peanuts, seeds, raisins,
coconuts, chutneys, soy sauce,
fruits
More with less:
— eat lots of rice, a little meat
— stretch meat with vegetables and
spices

● Ice-Cream Meal

Theme:
— homemade ice cream
Variations:
— fruits, sweet sauces, granola,
cookies, cakes, small sandwiches,
nuts and seeds, crackers, pretzels
More with less:
— volunteers will hand-crank
— good celebration for hot day

Note:
Ice cream is not a suitable food on
which to base frequent meals
because of sugar and fat content.
But for those with a cheap source of
dairy products, it makes a good
celebration. Why not let it be the
meal instead of adding its calories
to already satisfied stomachs?

Using the Recipes

1.

T·S indicates a recipe which has time-saving advantages for busy cooks.

2.

Certain recipes call for ingredients which are cheap in one community but expensive in another. As the cook, you must make final choices about economy, depending on what is available. If possible, omit a locally expensive ingredient or use a substitute.

3.

Recipes, with a few exceptions, do not call for convenience products. In some cases you may feel their use is justified. For example, when a recipe calls for cloves of garlic, garlic salt may be used with similar results, except in stir-fried Chinese dishes. Such options could not all be given because of limited space. Experience teaches a careful cook when and how to substitute.

4.

All measurements are level and standard measuring utensils must be used.

 Many recipes have grains, legumes, and dairy products in amounts significant enough to produce, in combination, complete protein. See the charts in the colored section for detailed information concerning complementary proteins.

More-with-Less Cookbook *is more than a collection of recipes. When I was a young adult, it helped shape my worldview. The tips and suggestions taught me how to buy food and cook responsibly. It helped me realize that for Christians, even the simple act of cooking a meal can be a testimony of faithfulness.
—Marlene Harder Bogard, Newton, Kan.*

Sharing
the Recipes

2

yeast and quick breads

"Here's a new menu idea at our house—bake bread, and you've got a meal!" writes Marian Franz, Washington, D.C.

Home bread-baking is returning to popularity. Creative enjoyment and the real quality of the product are the first reasons people give for baking. The time spent becomes more of a lark than a chore.

Health-wise there are good reasons for baking bread. Increasingly, nutritionists are questioning the effects of eating year after year bread baked with over 25 different chemicals used to retard spoilage or simplify the manufacturing process. Further, they are asking whether the U.S. and Canadian practice of enriching, or putting back synthetically the vitamins and minerals lost in processing, really works. Initial reports of a recent Canadian nutrition survey show about half the population with thiamine intake below recommended levels and moderate deficiency for a substantial number of adults. These people eat thiamine-enriched bread.[1]

Home-baked bread with whole-grain flours and bran adds fiber lacking in North American diets. Specialists in diseases of the digestive tract writing in the *Journal of the American Medical Association* say many of the diseases of Western civilization have appeared only in the past century and are caused, at least in part, by removal of fiber from flour and cereal. Fiber has no calories or nutritional value, but is needed for bulk and for its effect on chemical and bacterial processes in the intestine.[2]

My cost calculations for whole wheat bread show that when you purchase flour and yeast in bulk, when you use dry milk, and when you bake three to four loaves at once to conserve heat, homemade bread costs about half as much as commercially baked bread. In terms of taste appeal, nutritional value, and creative experience the home-baked product is worth more than its dollar-and-cents value.

Baking bread, like all other worthwhile activities, takes time and a certain amount of practice. For large families, it may not be possible to bake all the bread at home. The saving factor is four or five loaves baked at once and a freezer for storing them. Bread dough can also be mixed one day and baked the next. See p. 56.

Baking Yeast Bread

Essential Equipment:
— Large metal or glass bowl
— Measuring utensils
— Wooden stirring spoon
— Large wooden board or durable surface set at comfortable height for kneading
— Bread pans or casserole dishes for baking

Ingredients:
Yeast
— Cheaper purchased in jar or can; divide with a friend
— 1 T. dry yeast is equivalent to 1 package.

— Store in refrigerator, tightly covered.
— Dissolve first in lukewarm water with pinch of sugar for speedy rising.
— Needs *warm* liquid (120-130°) for quick rising, but *hot* liquid kills it.

Liquids
— Use warm water, milk, potato or other vegetable water, or whey from making cheese.
— Scald and cool raw (unpasteurized) milk before using.
— Substitute water for milk and add dry milk powder with flour.

Sweeteners
— Use sugar, brown sugar, honey, or molasses interchangeably in most recipes.

Fat
— Yeast breads need only small amounts—use lard, shortening, oil, margarine, fresh meat drippings, or rendered chicken fat.

White flour
— Flour from hard winter wheat, sometimes called Western or Occident flour, works best.
— Unbleached flour is satisfactory.
— Most recipes call for ⅓ to ½ white flour for light texture.

Whole wheat or graham flour
— Look for straight-run whole wheat flour directly from mills.
— Hand or electric grinders are available for home use.
— Use up to ½ whole wheat flour in any baked product.
— Some heavier but delicious breads are made with all whole wheat.
— Store whole wheat flour in refrigerator or freezer in hot weather.

Soy flour
— Sold as low-fat or full-fat soy flour; interchangeable in recipes.

— Has 40-60 grams high-quality protein per cup.
— More expensive per pound than wheat flour, but one of the cheapest *protein sources* currently available (see Table D, p. 36.)
— Contains no gluten to hold gas produced by yeast; cannot be used alone to bake bread.
— Excellent for adding protein to any baked product; for each cup replace 2-4 tablespoons other flour with soy flour.
— Add to soups, stews, casseroles, hot cereals, loaves, and patties to raise protein content.

Other flours: rye, rye graham, buckwheat, corn, millet, oat
— Combine with wheat flour in breads.
— Millet, rolled oats, and wheat can be whirled in a blender to produce flours.

Wheat germ
— Buy raw or untoasted from mill or health food store; toasted is available in supermarkets at higher price. Avoid sweetened wheat germ.
— Add to baked goods to increase protein, vitamins, and minerals.

Processes:
1. Dissolve yeast in warm water with pinch of sugar. Some recipes now omit this step and combine yeast with flours.
2. Making a sponge: Most recipes omit this step but many experienced bakers still believe in it. Mix liquid, dissolved yeast, sugar, and about half the flour to a smooth batter; beat well. Allow to rise until light and bubbly. Stir down and add salt, fat, and remaining flour; proceed with kneading.

3. How much flour? Since flours vary in moisture content, experience alone tells exactly how much flour you need. Dough will be sticky at first, but as kneading progresses, add just enough flour so dough no longer sticks to hands and board.

4. To knead: Fold dough over toward you, press down with heel of hand, give a slight turn, fold over, and press again. Dust board lightly with flour as needed, and repeat process until dough is smooth, satiny, and no longer sticky.

5. Rising: Place dough in greased bowl, flop over once to grease top surface, cover with clean cloth and allow to rise at 75-80° if possible. To speed the rising process in a cool kitchen, put stopper in the sink and fill with several inches very hot water. Place an empty bowl upside down in the sink and set bowl with dough on top of empty bowl just so that bowl with dough does not touch hot water. Cover dough and entire sink with large tea towel to hold steam in. Allow dough to rise this way about 1 hour, but punch down and turn after 20-30 minutes. Allow dough to rise only until doubled in bulk before punching down or coarse, dry bread may result.

6. Forming loaves: Roll or press out each piece of dough into a rectangle, about 9x12" for a 9x5" bread pan. From 9" edge, roll up tightly and place in greased pan with seam down and ends tucked under if necessary to fit into pan. Bake bread in any oven-proof utensil—coffee cans, casseroles, round cake pans, etc. Cover with cloth and allow to rise again until doubled.

7. Baking and cooling: For a shiny crust, just before baking brush carefully with beaten egg mixed with a little water; sprinkle with sesame or poppy seed if desired. See recipe instructions for baking.

Bread is done when it shrinks from the side of the pan, looks nicely browned, and sounds hollow when you tap the bottom of a loaf. Experience tells. Remove from pans immediately and brush with margarine for a soft crust.

To mix now, bake later
— Any yeast dough containing at least 1 T. sugar per cup of flour can be refrigerated up to 3 days. Immediately after kneading, grease top of dough and cover with waxed paper or plastic, then a damp cloth. Refrigerate until ready to use. Punch down occasionally as necessary. About 2 hours before baking, remove dough from refrigerator, shape into rolls or loaf, and let rise until doubled (1½ to 2 hours for cold dough). Bake as directed.
— White or whole wheat bread dough with less sugar can be refrigerated 2 to 24 hours. After dough is put in the pans, brush with oil and cover with plastic. Refrigerate until ready to bake. Preheat oven. Uncover dough carefully, and let stand at room temperature 10 minutes. Puncture any gas bubbles with greased toothpick. Bake as directed.
— Sunday dinner hint: Make rolls according to favorite recipe and put on pans. Cover and freeze immediately. When you leave for church, remove rolls from freezer and leave at room temperature. When you return they will have risen and be ready to bake (takes about 3 hours). Fresh rolls for dinner! Do not freeze longer than 3 weeks.
—Mary Kathryn Yoder,
  Garden City, Mo.

Notes
1.
Ross Hall, "Nutrition: An Ailing Science," *Atlas World Press Review*, Vol. 22, No. 2, February, 1975, p. 24.
2.
D. P. Burkitt, A. R. P. Walker, and N. S. Painter, "Dietary Fiber and Disease," *Journal of the American Medical Association*, Vol. 229, No. 8, Aug. 19, 1974, p. 1071.

Flours vary widely in moisture content. A good practice with any kneaded bread is to reserve the last cup to add as necessary, a little at a time, during kneading.

●●●●●●●●●●●●●●●●●●●●●●●●●

Honey
Whole Wheat Bread

Makes 2 loaves
375°
40-45 min.

Combine in mixer bowl:
3 c. whole wheat flour
½ c. nonfat dry milk
1 T. salt
2 pkg. dry yeast
Heat in saucepan until warm:
3 c. water or potato water
½ c. honey
2 T. oil
Pour warm (not hot) liquid over flour mixture. Beat with electric mixer 3 minutes. Stir in:
1 additional c. whole wheat flour
4-4½ c. white flour
Knead 5 minutes, using additional white flour if necessary. Place in greased bowl, turn, let rise until double in bulk. Punch down, divide dough in half and shape into loaves. Place in greased 9x5" bread pans. Cover and let rise 40-45 minutes. Bake at 375° for 40-45 minutes.

Options:

Replace 1 c. whole wheat flour with soy flour.

Add ¼ c. wheat germ.

Bonnie Zook, Leola, Pa.
Bob Friesen, Fresno, Calif.

●●●●●●●●●●●●●●●●●●●●●●●●●●

High Protein
Whole Wheat Bread

Makes 2 loaves
375°
35 min.

Dissolve:
2 pkg. dry yeast in
½ c. warm water
1 t. sugar
Warm in a saucepan to 130°:
1 c. water
1 c. milk
3 T. sugar
2 T. margarine
1 T. salt
Pour into large mixer bowl. Add:
yeast mixture
⅔ c. dry milk powder
⅓ c. soy flour
3 T. wheat germ
1½ c. whole wheat flour
1 c. white flour
Beat at medium speed 3 minutes. By hand stir in:
1½ c. whole wheat flour
1 c. white flour
Turn out onto floured board and knead 10 minutes, using:
1 additional c. white flour
Let rise until doubled. Punch down and knead briefly. Let rest 10 minutes. Divide dough and place in two 9x5" greased loaf pans. Let rise until almost doubled. Brush with beaten egg and sprinkle with sesame seeds. Bake at 375° for 35 minutes.

Jean Miller, Akron, Pa.

A light bread
with a lovely blend
of flavors.

●●●●●●●●●●●●●●●●●●●●●●●●●

Easy No-Knead Whole Wheat Bread

T·S

Makes 2 loaves
375°
35-40 min.

Combine in large mixer bowl:
3 c. whole wheat flour
½ c. sugar
2 T. salt
3 pkg. dry yeast
Heat in saucepan until very warm
(120-130°):
2 c. water
2 c. milk
½ c. oil
Add to dry ingredients:
warmed liquids
2 eggs
Blend at low speed until moistened. Beat
3 minutes at medium speed. Stir in by
hand:
5-6 c. white flour
Use enough flour to form a stiff batter.
Cover and let rise until double. Stir down
and spoon into 2 greased 9x5″ bread
pans. Let rise 20-30 minutes. Bake at
375° for 35-40 minutes.

Elsie Dyck, Akron, Pa.

●●●●●●●●●●●●●●●●●●●●●●●●●

Pilgrim's Bread

Makes 2 loaves
375°
45 min.

Combine in a bowl:
½ c. yellow cornmeal
⅓ c. brown sugar
1 T. salt
Stir gradually into:
2 c. boiling water
Add:
¼ c. oil
Cool to lukewarm.
Dissolve:
2 pkg. dry yeast in
½ c. warm water
Add yeast to cornmeal mixture.
Beat in:
¾ c. whole wheat flour
½ c. rye flour
By hand stir in:
4¼-4½ c. unbleached white flour
Turn onto lightly floured surface. Knead
until smooth and elastic. Place in a
lightly greased bowl, turning once to
grease surface. Cover and let rise in
warm place until double. Punch dough
down; turn out onto lightly floured
surface. Divide in half and knead a
second time for 3 minutes. Shape dough
into 2 loaves and place in greased pans.
Cover and let rise again in warm place
until double in bulk. Bake at 375° about
45 minutes.

Ruth B. Hess, Akron, Pa.

Be gentle
  when you touch bread.
    Let it not lie
      uncared for, unwanted.
        So often bread
          is taken for granted.

There is so much beauty
  in bread—
Beauty of sun and soil,
Beauty of patient toil.
Winds and rains have caressed it,
  Christ often blessed it.
Be gentle
  when you touch bread.
—Author unknown

●●●●●●●●●●●●●●●●●●●●●●●●
Ruggenbrot
(Rye Bread)

●●●●●●●●●●●●●●●●●●●●●●●●
Heidelberg
Rye Bread

Makes 2 loaves
350°
35-40 min.

Makes 2 loaves
400°
25-30 min.

Dissolve in large bowl:
  1 pkg. dry yeast in
  1 c. warm water
Add:
  1 c. scalded milk, cooled
  1 T. salt
  2 T. melted fat or oil
  2 T. molasses or brown sugar
  2 c. fine rye flour
Beat until smooth. Slowly blend in:
  4½ c. white flour
Turn dough onto floured surface. Knead
5-10 minutes. Let rest 20 minutes. Punch
down and divide dough into 2 equal
portions; shape into loaves. Place in
greased bread pans, cover and let rise
until double. Bake at 350° for 35-40
minutes. Butter tops after removing from
oven.

Lena Schmidt, Newton, Kan.

Combine in large mixer bowl:
  3 c. flour
  2 pkg. dry yeast
  ¼ c. cocoa
  1 T. caraway seeds (optional)
Heat in a saucepan until warm (120°):
  2 c. water
  ⅓ c. molasses
  2 T. margarine
  1 t. sugar
  1 t. salt
Add to dry mixture in mixer bowl, beating
at low speed ½ minute, scraping sides of
bowl constantly. Beat 3 minutes at high
speed.
Stir in by hand:
  3-3½ c. rye flour
Turn onto floured surface; knead until
smooth, about 5 minutes. Cover; let rest
20 minutes. Punch dough down; divide
in half. Shape each half into a round loaf;
place on greased baking sheets or 8" pie
plates. Brush surface of loaves with a
little oil and slash with sharp knife. Let
rise until double, 45-60 minutes. Bake at
400° for 25-30 minutes.

Kathy Hostetler, Akron, Pa.

*I have used this cookbook for
worship program ideas, especially in relation to cultures
beyond our own. In study
groups and for meditations,
I've found it an excellent
source of "nugget thoughts"
packed with "nutrition for the
soul."*
*—Lois C. Shank,
Hagerstown, Md.*

*Oatmeal bread
makes delicious
toast.*

●●●●●●●●●●●●●●●●●●●●●●●●●
Three-Flour Bread

●●●●●●●●●●●●●●●●●●●●●●●●●
Oatmeal Bread

Makes 3 loaves
450°/350°
25-30 min.

Makes 2 loaves
350°
30-40 min.

Dissolve in large bowl:
**2 pkg. dry yeast in
1 c. warm water**
Stir in:
**1 T. salt
¼ c. vegetable oil
¼ c. honey or molasses
3 c. warm water**
Mix in:
**1 c. dry milk powder
1 c. rye flour
¼ c. soy flour
¼ c. wheat germ
4 c. whole wheat or graham flour
5 or more cups white flour**
Turn out on floured surface and knead until smooth, adding more flour if needed. Place in greased bowl, turning once. Cover and put in warm place to rise until doubled, about 2 hours. Turn out onto floured surface, knead, and place in 3 greased 9x5" pans. Let rise until almost double; place in cold oven and set at 450° for 10 minutes. Turn down to 350° and bake 25-30 minutes.

*Marcia Beachy, DeKalb, Ill.
Rosemary Moyer, North Newton, Kan.*

Combine in large bowl:
**1 c. quick oats
½ c. whole wheat flour
½ c. brown sugar
1 T. salt
2 T. margarine**
Pour over:
2 c. boiling water
Stir in to combine.
Dissolve:
**1 pkg. dry yeast in
½ c. warm water**
When batter is cooled to lukewarm, add yeast.
Stir in:
5 c. white flour
When dough is stiff enough to handle, turn onto floured board and knead 5-10 minutes. Place in greased bowl, cover, and let rise until doubled. Punch down and let rise again. Shape into 2 loaves and place in greased 9x5x3" pans. Bake at 350° for 30-40 minutes. Cool on rack, brushing loaves with margarine for a soft crust.

*Ella Rohrer, Orrville, Ohio
Carol Ann Maust, Upland, Calif.*

Every year, I bake Oatmeal Bread for my children's teachers. As I share this bread with neighbors, sick families, newcomers, teachers, homes with new babies, and as we eat it daily at home, I think of the symbols that accompany it. Grains of wheat come together, just as individuals come together to make the body of Christ, forming a complete loaf or strong body. It's the joining together that brings strength. —Lori Kaufman Gant, Decorah, Iowa

*Deliciously
fragrant and moist;
slice and serve warm
with bean soup.*

●●●●●●●●●●●●●●●●●●●●●●●●●
Cornmeal
Yeast Bread

Makes 2 loaves
350°
30-45 min.

Dissolve:
   2 pkg. dry yeast in
   ½ c. lukewarm water
Combine in mixing bowl:
   ½ c. sugar
   1½ t. salt
   ⅓ c. butter or margarine
Pour over:
   ¾ c. milk, scalded
Cool to lukewarm. Stir in:
   1 egg
   1 c. white flour
   ¾ c. cornmeal
   yeast mixture
Beat well. Stir in enough additional flour
to make a soft dough:
   3-3½ c. flour
Turn dough onto lightly floured board
and knead until satiny, about 10 minutes.
Place dough in greased bowl; cover and
let rise in warm place until double in size,
about 1 hour. Punch dough down. Divide
in half and place in 2 greased 8″ loaf
pans. Brush with melted margarine.
Cover and let rise in warm place until
nearly double, about 45 minutes. Bake at
350° for 30-45 minutes or until golden
brown.

   Kathy Hostetler, Akron, Pa.

●●●●●●●●●●●●●●●●●●●●●●●●●
Round-Loaf
Herb Bread

Makes 2 loaves
350°
45 min.

Dissolve:
   2 pkg. dry yeast in
   ½ c. warm water
Sauté in small skillet until onion is
tender:
   3 T. cooking oil
   ½ c. chopped onion
Combine in mixer bowl:
   sautéed onion
   1⅔ c. evaporated milk (1 can)
      OR 1½ c. milk plus ½ c. nonfat
      dry milk powder
   ½ c. chopped parsley
   3 T. sugar
   1 t. salt
   ½ t. dried dillweed
   ¼ t. thyme
Beat in:
   yeast mixture
   1 c. cornmeal
   2 c. whole wheat flour
Stir in by hand:
   2½ c. additional whole wheat flour
Turn out on lightly floured surface. Knead
5 minutes. Place in greased bowl,
turning once to grease surface. Cover
and let rise till double, about 1 hour.
Punch down; divide in half. Place in 2
well-greased 1-pound coffee cans.
Cover and let rise until double, 30-45
minutes. Bake at 350° for 45 minutes,
covering loosely with foil if bread
becomes too brown.

   Author's Recipe

61

*I memorized the French Bread
recipe and make it at least
once a month, adding
flaxseed, wheat germ, and
soy flour.
—Beth Yoder, Lawrence, Kan.*

*When mixing baked goods, put
in the bottom of each cup of
flour called for:
1 T. soy flour
1 T. dry milk solids
1 T. wheat germ
Fill cup with flour and proceed
with recipe. OR, when pouring 5
pounds of flour into kitchen
canister stir in 1½ c. of each of
the three enriching ingredients.
—Jean Liechty Jordan,
  Goshen, Ind.*

●●●●●●●●●●●●●●●●●●●●●●●●●
Pinto Bean Bread

Makes 2 loaves
350°
50 min.

Blend in large bowl:
   **2 c. scalded milk, cooled to
      lukewarm
   2 pkg. dry yeast**
Add:
   **2 c. cooked, mashed, unseasoned
      pinto beans
   2 T. sugar
   2 t. salt
   2 T. shortening**
Stir in:
   5-6 c. flour
Add enough flour to handle dough
easily. Turn onto floured board and
knead until smooth and elastic. Place in
greased bowl, turning once. Cover and
let rise in warm place until double in size,
about 1 hour. Punch down, cover, let rise
again until almost double. Divide dough
into two portions and shape into loaves.
Place in greased pans; cover, let rise
until almost double in bulk, about 45
minutes. Bake at 350° about 50 minutes.

Elaine Schmidt, Greeley, Colo.

●●●●●●●●●●●●●●●●●●●●●●●●●
Dill Bread

Makes 1 loaf
350°
30 min.

Dissolve:
   **1 pkg. yeast in
   ¼ c. warm water**
Combine in mixing bowl:
   **1 c. cottage cheese
   2 t. dill seed
   2 t. salt
   ¼ t. soda
   1 unbeaten egg
   1 T. melted butter or margarine
   ½ T. minced onion
   2 T. sugar**
Add:
   **yeast mixture
   2¼-2½ c. sifted flour**
Stir well to combine. Let rise in greased
bowl to double in size. Punch down. Put
into two 7x3″ or one 9x5″ well-greased
bread pans. Let rise again, about 45-50
minutes. Bake at 350° about 30 minutes.
Remove from pans and brush with
melted margarine.

Option:
For a finer grain, add enough additional
flour to handle easily and knead 5-10
minutes.

*Selma Johnson, North Newton, Kan.
MCC Dining Hall, Akron, Pa.*

I ask a local mill to save clean middlings for me. Middlings are a byproduct of grinding white flour and are usually sold for animal feed. The mill sells it to me for eight cents a pound, and I use it for baking breads, cookies, and making gravy.
—Fern Hertzler, Amelia, Va.

Make hot dog buns from unsliced bread. Cut thick slices of bread, cut each slice in half, and make a slit for the hot dog.
—Gayle Gerber Koontz and Karen Harvey, Leola, Pa.

Commercial French bread is expensive. You can make 3 or 4 loaves for the price of purchasing one.

This is my basic French Bread recipe. I get the best results using a high-gluten flour. I substitute 1-2 c. whole wheat flour for some of the white flour. Or add ½ cracked wheat or bulgar for a crunchy texture. For gifts, I top loaves before baking with poppy, sesame, and fennel seeds. Tied with a colorful bow, this makes an attractive, tasty gift.
—Jocele Meyer, Fresno, Ohio

●●●●●●●●●●●●●●●●●●●●●●●●●

Easy French Bread

Makes 2 loaves
400°
20 min.

Dissolve:
2 pkg. dry yeast in
½ c. warm water
½ t. sugar
Combine:
2 T. sugar
2 T. fat
2 t. salt
2 c. boiling water
Cool to lukewarm and add yeast mixture. Stir in:
7½-8 c. flour
Knead 10 minutes, or until smooth and elastic. Place in greased bowl, turning once. Let rise until doubled. Punch down and let rest 15 minutes. Divide dough in half. On floured surface, roll each half to a 12x15″ rectangle. Roll up, starting at 15″ edge. Place loaves on greased cookie sheets and make 4 or 5 slashes diagonally across tops. Let rise until double.
Mix and brush on:
1 egg, beaten
2 T. milk
Sprinkle on, if desired:
poppy or sesame seeds
Bake at 400° for 20 minutes.

Ernestine Lehman, Akron, Pa.

●●●●●●●●●●●●●●●●●●●●●●●●●

White Bread

Makes 4 loaves
350°
30-35 min.

Dissolve:
2 pkg. dry yeast in
½ c. warm water
1½ t. sugar
Combine in large mixer bowl:
½ c. sugar
1 T. salt
¼ c. lard or shortening
3 c. warm water
yeast mixture
Add:
5 c. flour
Beat with electric mixer 3 minutes.
Stir in by hand:
6 c. flour
Turn onto floured board and knead 5 minutes. Place in greased bowl, turning once, cover and let rise ½ hour. Punch down, turn over and let rise again until double. Knead a few minutes, then shape into 4 loaves and place in greased 9x5″ loaf pans. Cover loaves with damp cloth and let rise until doubled. Bake at 350° for 30-35 minutes. Brush tops with margarine if desired.

Louetta Hurst, Lancaster, Pa.

63

We grind wheat in our blender. We put about 2 c. wheat in a glass quart jar (wheat might crack a plastic container), screw on the blender blades, and process at high speed about 4 minutes, or until all the wheat is ground up. Then we put it through a sifter or sieve. What goes through we use in baking bread; what doesn't we cook as breakfast cereal. We add raisins and eat the cereal with brown sugar. The fresh wheat flavor is wonderful!
—Martha and Walter Dyck, Danvers, Ill.

This Christmas I baked special yeast breads instead of cookies to save sugar.
—Anna Mary Brubacher, St. Jacobs, Ont.

For more nutritious cinnamon rolls I sprinkle the dough with wheat germ along with cinnamon and sugar.
—Pauline Wyse, Mt. Pleasant, Iowa

Sweet rolls made with yeast dough are economical desserts or snacks because they do not contain as much sugar as cakes and cookies—and they still satisfy the sweet tooth.
—Elsie Epp, Marion, S.D.

●●●●●●●●●●●●●●●●●●●●●●●●●
Whole Wheat Rolls

Makes 4 doz. rolls
375°
20-25 min.

Dissolve:
   2 pkg. dry yeast in
   ¾ c. lukewarm water
Combine in large bowl:
   3 c. warm water
   1 c. dry milk powder
   ½ c. soft shortening, margarine, or oil
   2 eggs
   ⅓ c. sugar
   2 t. salt
   yeast mixture
Have ready:
   6 c. white flour
   4 c. whole wheat flour
Add 5 c. flour and beat thoroughly, by hand or with electric mixer. Stir in an additional 3 c. flour. Turn dough onto floured board and use 2 more c. flour to knead until smooth and elastic. Let rise in greased bowl until doubled in bulk. Punch down and shape into dinner or cinnamon rolls. Let rise and bake 20-25 minutes at 375°.

MCC Dining Hall, Akron, Pa.

●●●●●●●●●●●●●●●●●●●●●●●●●
High-Protein Rolls

Makes 2 doz. rolls
350°
20-25 min.

Dissolve:
   2 pkg. dry yeast in
   ½ c. lukewarm water
Heat until lukewarm:
   2 c. cottage cheese
Combine in large bowl:
   cottage cheese
   ¼ c. sugar
   2 t. salt
   ½ t. baking soda
   2 eggs, slightly beaten
   yeast mixture
Gradually add:
   4-4½ c. sifted flour
Turn onto floured board and knead 5 minutes. Put dough in a greased bowl, turning once. Let rise in warm place until doubled, about 1½ hours. Punch down. Turn dough onto lightly floured surface. Divide dough into 24 equal pieces and shape into balls. Place balls in two greased 9" baking pans. Bake at 350° for 20-25 minutes or until golden.

Option:
Replace 1-2 c. white flour with whole wheat flour.

Gladys Longacre, Susquehanna, Pa.

Edna Byler, Mennonite Central Committee's Akron hostess through the early lean years, is widely known for baking classes she held teaching this master recipe. Products based on it appear annually at MCC Relief Sales.

●●●●●●●●●●●●●●●●●●●●●●●●●

Edna Ruth Byler's Potato Dough Baked Goods

100 doughnuts or rolls
375° deep fat/400° oven

Dissolve:
   3 pkg. dry yeast in
   1 c. lukewarm water
Mix in large bowl:
   1 qt. scalded milk
   2 c. mashed potatoes (no milk added)
   1 c. fat (half butter, half margarine)
   1 c. sugar
Let cool to lukewarm, then add:
   yeast mixture
   6 c. flour
Let stand until mixture foams up (about 20 minutes).
Add:
   2 eggs, beaten
   1 T. salt
   11-12 c. additional flour
A little more flour may be needed, but dough should be soft. Turn out on floured board and knead until satiny. Let raise in warm place until doubled in bulk.

Doughnuts: Roll out dough, cut doughnuts, place on trays and let raise until not quite double. Fry in hot shortening (375°). When drained and while still hot dip in glaze mixture. Insert a stick through holes and let a number of doughnuts drain over glaze bowl until next ones are ready to do.

Glaze:
Combine:
   1 lb. powdered sugar
   1 T. margarine
   1 t. vanilla
   dash of mace
   enough rich milk to make thin icing

Cinnamon buns: Prepare a mixture of butter and margarine and a mixture of sugar, brown sugar, and cinnamon. Roll a piece of dough to about 18x9″. Spread dough with butter mixture and sprinkle over some of the sugar mixture. Roll up the dough as for jelly roll. Cut 1½″ chunks and place in greased pans, pressing down lightly on each chunk. Cover and let raise in warm place until nearly double. Bake at 400° for 15-20 minutes or until browned. These may be iced with doughnut glaze as soon as they are taken from the oven.

Sticky buns: Handle dough same as for cinnamon buns, except make a mixture of brown and white sugar, cinnamon, and a little white corn syrup and water. Spread in bottom of heavily greased pans with nuts, if desired, before putting in rolls. Immediately after baking, invert pans over trays and let syrup run down before removing pans.

Dinner rolls: Shape dough as desired, place on greased pans, and bake at 400° starting on a lower rack and changing to upper rack about halfway through for 15 minutes of baking time. Brush tops lightly with butter to remove any floury appearance.

Coffee cake: A good way to use all the leftover bits of dough—put dough in greased pan, dab or punch holes in it, and spread leftover sugar, syrup, or butter mixtures over. Let raise and bake as for cinnamon buns.

To freeze: Let baked goods cool. Wrap or place in large plastic bags and freeze the same day.

   Edna Ruth Byler, Akron, Pa.

*Traditional among
Prussian Mennonites
when guests come for
Sunday afternoon coffee.
"Blech" is a large
baking pan.*

●●●●●●●●●●●●●●●●●●●●●●●●
Raised Coffee Cake
(Blechkuchen)

Makes 2 large cakes
375°
20 min.

Scald and cool to lukewarm:
  3 c. milk
Stir together to dissolve:
  2 pkg. dry yeast
  1 c. warm water
Combine in large bowl:
  lukewarm milk
  yeast mixture
  1½ c. soft shortening or lard
  ½ c. sugar
  4 t. salt
  1 egg
  6 c. flour
Beat well until dough is smooth and
satiny.
Stir in:
  1 c. raisins combined with
  ¾ c. flour
Cover and let rise in a warm place until
doubled. With back of spoon spread
dough thinly onto 2 greased 10x15"
cookie sheets. Brush generously with
melted margarine and sprinkle with
sugar.
Bake 20 minutes at 375°.

Elsie Epp, Marion, S.D.

●●●●●●●●●●●●●●●●●●●●●●●●●
Brown Breadsticks

Makes 6 doz. breadsticks
325°
30 min.

Dissolve:
  1 pkg. dry yeast in
  1 c. warm water
Mix in large bowl:
  1 c. melted shortening or oil
  3 T. honey
  2 t. salt
  1 c. boiling water
When lukewarm, add:
  2 beaten eggs
  1 t. honey
  dissolved yeast
Stir in gradually:
  6 c. whole wheat flour
Mix well, but do not knead. Place in
refrigerator to chill one hour or more.
When chilled, break off pieces of dough
with well-floured hands. Make into balls
the size of a baseball, then roll the ball
between hands to form a long roll. Divide
each roll into 8 pieces and roll each
pencil-thin. Place thin rolls on greased
cookie sheets. Let rise until double in
bulk. Bake at 325° until crisp, about 30
minutes. Serve plain or with dips.

Options:
Roll thin rolls into sesame or sunflower seeds, or sprinkle with garlic salt.
Add 1 c. shredded cheese when mixing dough.

LaVonne Platt, Newton, Kan.

•••••••••••••••••••••••••••
English Muffins

Makes 18 muffins

Heat in a saucepan until very warm
(130°):
1½ c. milk
¼ c. margarine
In large mixer bowl, combine:
2 T. sugar
1 t. salt
1 pkg. dry yeast
1½ c. flour
With mixer at low speed, gradually beat
liquid into dry ingredients. Increase
speed and beat 2 minutes, or beat
vigorously by hand.
Beat in:
1 egg
1 c. flour
With spoon, add:
**2 c. flour, or enough to make
stiff dough**
Turn dough onto lightly floured surface
and knead just until well mixed, about 2
minutes. Shape dough into a ball and
place in greased large bowl, turning
once. Cover; let rise in warm place until
doubled, about 1½ hours. Punch down.
Turn onto lightly floured surface; cover
with bowl 15 minutes, and let dough rest.
Meanwhile, place cornmeal in a pie
plate. Roll dough about ⅜" thick. Cut
dough into 3" circles; reroll scraps to
make 18 circles in all. Dip both sides of
each circle in cornmeal; place circles on
cookie sheets. Cover and let rise in warm
place until doubled, about 45 minutes.
Brush large skillet with salad oil and
heat. When medium hot, put in 6 muffins,
cook 8 minutes on each side or until
brown. Repeat until all are cooked.
To serve, split muffins horizontally with
tines of fork and toast.

Ruth Detweiler, Akron, Pa.

●●●●●●●●●●●●●●●●●●●●●●●●●
Master Baking Mix

T·S

Makes 8 or 4 lbs.

8 lbs.	4 lbs.

Sift together 3 times:
5 lbs.	10 c. flour
¾ c.	6 T. baking powder
3 T.	1½ T. salt
1 T.	1½ t. cream of tartar
½ c.	¼ c. sugar

Cut in to consistency of cornmeal:
2 lbs.	2 c. vegetable shortening

Stir in:
4 c.	2 c. dry milk powder

Store in covered container at room temperature. To measure baking mix, pile lightly into a cup and level off with spatula.

Options:

Replace ⅓ of the white flour with whole wheat flour.

Add 2 c. untoasted wheat germ to large recipe, 1 c. to small recipe.

Replace 3 c. flour in large recipe or 1½ c. flour in small recipe with soy flour.

Dry milk powder in the mix is optional, but assures higher protein products.

June Suderman, Hillsboro, Kan.
Roberta Kreider, Osceola, Ind.

▼ Recipes for Master Baking Mix

●●●●●●●●●●●●●●●●●●●●●●●●●
Corn Bread

Serves 8
400°
20-25 min.

Preheat oven to 400°.
Stir together in a bowl:
  1½ c. Master Mix
  2 T. sugar
  ½ t. salt
  ¾ c. cornmeal
  1 t. chili powder (optional)
Combine in a separate bowl:
  1 egg
  ¾ c. milk
  1 c. cream-style corn
Stir liquids into dry ingredients just until flour is all moistened. Pour into greased 9″ square pan and bake 20-25 minutes.

Options:

Add ¼ c. chopped green pepper.

For crunchy topping, sprinkle on ½ c. grated cheese and 2 T. sesame seed before baking.

Add ¼ c. bran.

●●●●●●●●●●●●●●●●●●●●●●●●●
Pancakes or Waffles

Serves 4

Beat together in a bowl:
  1 c. milk
  1 egg
Stir in:
  1½ c. Master Mix
Bake on hot griddle or waffle iron. For lighter waffles, separate egg; add yolk with milk. Beat egg white until stiff and fold into batter just before baking.
Increase milk for thinner batter if desired.

●●●●●●●●●●●●●●●●●●●●●●●●●
Biscuits

Makes 8 biscuits
450°
10 min.

Preheat oven to 450°.
Combine in bowl:
   1½ c. Master Mix
   ⅓ c. milk
Add milk all at once, stirring 25 strokes.
Knead lightly on floured board. Roll ½"
thick, cut, and place on ungreased
baking sheet. Bake 10 minutes.

Options:
Add grated cheese, chopped herbs.
Increase milk to ½ c. for drop biscuits.
Use as topping on casseroles, cobblers, meat and vegetable pies, or wherever biscuit dough is called for.

●●●●●●●●●●●●●●●●●●●●●●●●●
Coffee Cake

Serves 6
375°
25 min.

Preheat oven to 375°.
Beat together in a bowl:
   ⅓ c. milk
   1 egg
Add:
   ¼ c. sugar
   2¼ c. Master Mix
Stir until well blended (about 1 minute).
Pour into greased 8" square baking pan.
Combine and sprinkle over:
   ½ c. brown sugar
   3 T. margarine
   ½ t. cinnamon
   ¼ c. chopped nuts (optional)
Bake 25 minutes. Serve warm.

●●●●●●●●●●●●●●●●●●●●●●●●●
Muffins

Makes 12 muffins
425°
20 min.

Preheat oven to 425°.
Beat together in a bowl:
   1 egg
   1 c. milk
   2 T. sugar
Add:
   3 c. Master Mix
Stir just until dry ingredients are
moistened. Spoon into greased muffin
pans and bake 20 minutes.

Options:
Add drained fruit, chopped nuts or chopped dried fruit.
Replace one third of mix called for with quick-cooking oatmeal or all-bran cereal.
Add chopped dried fruit and/or nuts to muffin recipe and bake as a fruit bread; use greased 5x8" loaf pan and bake 40 minutes at 350°.

I received **More-with-Less Cookbook**
*at a baby shower after our oldest
son, Karl, was born. The note from
my friend Alice read, "Mothers need
gifts too." I read the cookbook while
rocking Karl and the two babies that
followed. The children grew up on
Grandma Witmer's Crumb Cake and
Vietnam Fried Rice. My margin notes
calculate the cost of Master Mix in
1983, and one of the granola pages
has fallen out entirely. Karl, now a
college student, is beginning to cook
for himself. I gave him a* **More-with-
Less Cookbook.** *Together we marked
family favorites with sticky notes.
College students need gifts too!*
—Rose Mary Stutzman, Scottdale, Pa.

*These are delicious
hot or cold.
Bake and serve as cupcakes
by adding a sprinkling
of brown sugar
and nuts or granola
before putting
in the oven.*

*An old recipe
and still perfect
to fill out a skimpy meal.*

●●●●●●●●●●●●●●●●●●●●●●●●●
Refrigerator
Bran Muffins

T·S

Makes 4-5 doz.
400°
20 min.

Place in bowl:
   2 c. ready-to-eat bran cereal
Pour over:
   2 c. boiling water
Set aside to cool.
Cream together in large mixing bowl:
   1 c. shortening or margarine
   1½ c. sugar
   4 eggs
Add and beat in:
   1 qt. buttermilk
   soaked bran mixture
Sift together:
   5 c. flour
   5 t. soda
   1 t. salt
Add dry ingredients to creamed mixture
and fold until flour is moistened.
Fold in:
   4 c. additional *dry* bran cereal
Store batter in covered containers in
refrigerator. Keeps 3-4 weeks. When
ready to bake, preheat oven to 400° and
fill well-greased muffin tins ⅔ full. Bake
20 minutes.

Option:

Add raisins and/or nuts just before
baking.

Carol Welty, Akron, Pa.
Faye Brenneman, Palmer Lake, Colo.

●●●●●●●●●●●●●●●●●●●●●●●●
Graham Gems

Makes 12 muffins
375°
15 min.

Preheat oven to 375°.
Combine in mixing bowl:
   1 c. graham or whole wheat flour
   1 c. white flour
   1 t. soda
   ¼ c. dark brown sugar
   ¼ t. salt
   ½ c. raisins (optional)
Make a well and add:
   1 egg, beaten
   1 c. buttermilk or sour milk
   3 T. melted fat
Stir only until blended. Fill greased
muffin tins half full and bake 15 minutes.
Serve hot.

Elizabeth Showalter, Waynesboro, Va.

Crumb Muffins

Makes 12 muffins
375°
25 min.

Preheat oven to 375°.
Combine in mixing bowl:
1 large egg, slightly beaten
1 c. milk
¼ c. melted margarine
1 c. dry bread crumbs
Stir and set aside.
Sift together:
1 c. flour
1 T. sugar
½ t. salt
1 T. baking powder
Fold dry ingredients into liquids. Stir just until all is moistened. Fill greased muffin tins ⅔ full. Bake 25 minutes.

Sandra Miller, Akron, Pa.

Cinnamon-Topped Oatmeal Muffins

Makes 12 muffins
425°
15 min.

Preheat oven to 425°.
Sift together into mixing bowl:
1 c. sifted flour
¼ c. sugar
3 t. baking powder
½ t. salt
Stir in:
1 c. quick or old-fashioned oats
½ c. raisins
Add:
3 T. oil
1 egg, beaten
1 c. milk
Stir only until dry ingredients are moistened. Fill greased muffin cups ⅔ full. Sprinkle with cinnamon topping:
2 T. sugar
2 t. flour
1 t. cinnamon
1 t. melted butter
Bake 15 minutes.

Anna Ens, Winnipeg, Man.

Through the wisdom and recipes of this book, I have built a foundation of good health and common sense for my family. My first year of marriage, I divided my time between doing things with my husband and reading all the helpful text in More-with-Less. We established habits of buying bulk products, unrefined flours when possible, avoiding over-packaged and over-sweetened products, always baking from scratch. Recipes from afar, such as Pakistani Kima and Tabouleh Salad, became my favorites. Now my second daughter, Constance, who is eight, is beginning to use the book to make pancakes and muffins. All my children are eager to cook, and I trust More-with-Less will guide us until it finally falls apart.
—Kellie O. McKinney, Chicago, Ill.

●●●●●●●●●●●●●●●●●●●●●●●●
Whole Wheat
Pineapple Muffins

Makes 12 muffins
400°
15-20 min.

Preheat oven to 400°.
Sift together:
1 c. white flour
1 c. whole wheat flour
3 t. baking powder
½ t. salt
Set aside.
In small bowl, cream together until fluffy:
¼ c. sugar
¼ c. margarine
Add:
1 egg
Beat well; stir in:
1 c. crushed pineapple, undrained
Add dry ingredients to creamed mixture and stir just enough to moisten flour. Fill greased muffin tins ⅔ full. Bake 15-20 minutes. Remove from tins at once. Serve hot.

Alice and Willard Roth, Elkhart, Ind.

●●●●●●●●●●●●●●●●●●●●●●●●
Basic Biscuits

Makes 18-20 biscuits
425°
10-12 min.

Preheat oven to 425°.
Sift together in a bowl:
2 c. sifted flour
3 t. baking powder
½ t. salt
Cut in:
¼ c. shortening
Add all at once, stirring until soft ball is formed:
¾ c. milk
Turn dough onto floured board; knead lightly 20 to 25 times. Roll or pat dough ½" thick. Cut with floured biscuit cutter or glass. Place on ungreased baking sheet and bake 10-12 minutes. Serve hot. Makes 18-20.

Option:

Cheese Drop Biscuits: Stir 1 c. grated cheese into flour mixture before cutting in shortening. Increase milk to 1 c. and drop onto cookie sheet by tablespoonfuls.

Miriam LeFever, East Petersburg, Pa.

My family and I had just arrived in India and had to cook from scratch. We soon began trying as many recipes as we could from More-with-Less Cookbook. The basic Pancake Mix recipe became our favorite. We would mix up the 4 lbs. and use it as we needed. Breakfast was again a time to look forward to. Without all the great recipes from scratch, we would have had a much harder time getting adjusted to a foreign culture.
—Chad Mann, Milford, Ohio

Add ½ c. applesauce and a dash
of cinnamon to 1½-2 c. pancake
batter. Decrease milk slightly.
Just delightful!
—Iona S. Weaver,
    Collegeville, Pa.

*Costs half as much
as commercial mix
and milk is included.*

●●●●●●●●●●●●●●●●●●●●●●●●●
Pancake Mix

T·S

Makes 2 or 4 lbs.

2 lbs.   4 lbs.
Combine in large bowl:
**6 c. flour   12 c. flour
1 T. salt   2 T. salt
6 T. baking   ¾ c. baking
    powder   powder
6 T. sugar   ¾ c. sugar
2 c. powdered   4 c. powdered
    milk   milk**
Mix well and store in airtight container on
cupboard shelf.

To use:
Combine in a bowl:
**1 egg (beat with fork)
1 c. water
2 T. melted fat or oil
1½ c. pancake mix**
Fry on hot ungreased griddle.
Serves 3-4.

Options:
Replace one third white flour with
buckwheat flour, whole wheat flour,
oatmeal, or rye flour and cornmeal.
Replace one sixth of the flour with soy
flour.
Add 1 c. wheat germ to small recipe, 2 c.
to large recipe.

Karen Rix, Fonda, Iowa

●●●●●●●●●●●●●●●●●●●●●●●●●
Whole Wheat
Buttermilk Pancakes

Serves 3

Combine in a bowl and mix with fork:
**1 c. buttermilk
2 T. vegetable oil
1 egg**
Add and mix only until moistened:
**½ c. whole wheat flour
½ c. unbleached, white flour
    (part soy flour and wheat germ
    can be used)
1 t. baking powder
½ t. baking soda
½ t. salt**
Fry in hot, lightly greased skillet.

Marcia Beachy, DeKalb, Ill.

*We use the Pancake Mix
almost every Sunday morning.
When we gave up all meat for
Lent the year our daughter
became a vegetarian, we hardly missed it because of the
many great alternative protein
recipes in* More-with-Less.
—Becky Horst, Goshen, Ind.

*Wheat germ adds
vitamins and protein to
pancakes without
making them heavy.*

●●●●●●●●●●●●●●●●●●●●●●●●

Wheat Germ
Griddle Cakes

Serves 6-8

Beat together at medium speed of
electric mixer for one minute, or whirl in
blender:
   1½ c. wheat germ
   2¼ c. milk
   3 eggs
   6 T. salad oil
   1¼ c. white flour
   4 t. baking powder
   1 T. sugar
   1½ t. salt
   ½ t. cinnamon
   ¼ t. ginger
   ⅛ t. mace
Bake on hot griddle.

Option:

For crispy waffles, reserve egg whites,
beat until stiff, and fold into batter just
before baking. Thin batter slightly with
milk.

Selma Johnson, North Newton, Kan.

●●●●●●●●●●●●●●●●●●●●●●●●

Apple-Walnut
Pancakes

Serves 4

Combine in bowl:
   1 c. whole wheat flour
   1 c. white flour
   1 t. salt
   2 t. baking powder
   1 T. brown sugar
Combine in separate bowl:
   2 c. milk
   2 eggs, well beaten
   2 T. oil
Add liquids to dry ingredients and stir
until just mixed.
Add:
   1 c. diced apples
   ½ c. chopped walnuts
Bake on moderately hot, lightly greased
griddle.

Options:

Use yogurt or juice in place of milk.

Substitute another whole grain flour or
cornmeal for ½ c. whole wheat flour.

Use other fruit, drained and chopped, in
place of apples.

Rosemary Nachtigall, Reedley, Calif.

Serve for dessert
or a gourmet brunch
if you live
where fresh coconuts
are cheap.

●●●●●●●●●●●●●●●●●●●●●●●●●
Grandmother's Russian Pancakes (Pflinzen)

Serves 4-5

Combine in mixing bowl:
  2 eggs, beaten
  2 c. flour
  2 c. milk
  ½ t. salt
Whirl in blender or use rotary beater.
Melt and keep hot:
  ⅓ c. fat or oil
Heat 10" skillet until medium hot. Add
approximately 1 t. hot fat to skillet and
pour in about ¼ c. pancake batter, tilting
skillet with left hand to allow batter to run
over entire surface. Turn in a minute or
two when underside is browned. Remove
to serving plate and keep warm. Repeat
with remaining batter, adding small
amount hot fat to skillet each time.
Finished pancakes should be thin and
slightly crisp on the edges. Serve
pancakes with cinnamon-sugar, honey,
syrup, applesauce or other fruit sauce.
Traditionally each person adds filling
and rolls the pancake with a fork, then
cuts into bite-size pieces.

Option:
Use this whole wheat recipe with same
method:
  3 eggs
  1½ c. milk
  ½ t. salt
  1 T. oil
  1 c. whole wheat flour
  1 T. soy flour

Helen and Adam Mueller,
* Cape Girardeau, Mo.*
Eleanor Hiebert, Elkins Park, Pa.

●●●●●●●●●●●●●●●●●●●●●●●●●
Coconut Pancakes

Serves 4-6

Combine in a bowl:
  2 c. flour
  ½ c. sugar
  2 t. baking powder
Add:
  1 egg, beaten
  ¼ fresh coconut, shredded
  ¼ t. cardamom powder
  ½ t. salt
  2½ c. milk
Stir until smooth. Prepare filling.
Combine in saucepan:
  1½ c. brown sugar
  ¾ fresh coconut, shredded
  ¾ c. milk
  ¼ c. raisins
Cook, stirring frequently, until mixture is
thick and liquid absorbed.
Heat 1 t. margarine in 9" skillet. Pour in a
small amount of batter, tilting skillet to
spread batter thinly over entire bottom.
Cook until nearly dry on top. Add a
narrow strip of filling and roll up. Repeat
with remaining batter and filling,
keeping pancakes warm in oven. Serve
hot.

LaVonne Platt, Newton, Kan.

●●●●●●●●●●●●●●●●●●●●●●●

High Protein
Pancakes or Waffles

Serves 3

Combine in a blender:
**1 c. cream-style cottage cheese
4 eggs
½ c. flour
¼ t. salt
¼ c. oil
½ c. milk
½ t. vanilla**
Whirl at high speed 1 minute. Bake on lightly greased griddle or waffle iron. Serves 3 as main dish.

Option:
Beat well with mixer or rotary beater instead of in blender.

*Danita Laskowski
Alice Lapp, Goshen, Ind.*

*One recipe we frequently use
is Whole Wheat Yeast Waffles.
Served with maple syrup,
peanut butter, and perhaps
sausage and mixed fruit, the
waffles provide nutrition for
body and soul!
—Becky Miller, Goshen, Ind.*

●●●●●●●●●●●●●●●●●●●●●●●

Whole Wheat
Yeast Waffles

Serves 6

Combine in mixing bowl:
**½ c. water
2 T. sugar
1 pkg. dry yeast**
Stir and allow to stand 5 minutes. Add to yeast mixture:
**1½ c. sweet or sour milk,
    buttermilk, or yogurt
3 egg yolks (reserve whites)
⅔ c. oil
½ c. untoasted wheat germ
    (optional)**
Sift in:
**1½ c. whole wheat flour
½ c. nonfat dry milk powder
1 t. salt**
Stir to blend. Let rise in warm place 2 hours or longer, stirring down each time batter has doubled in bulk. Just before baking, fold in:
3 egg whites, stiffly beaten
Bake on preheated waffle iron.

Option:
Mix batter in the evening, omitting eggs. Let rise once or twice, stir down and set in refrigerator overnight. Remove from refrigerator 30 minutes before baking. Stir egg yolks into batter, then fold in egg whites just before baking.

Don Ziegler, Lancaster, Pa.

●●●●●●●●●●●●●●●●●●●●●●●●●
Fruit Syrup
For Pancakes

Combine in saucepan:
  ½-¾ c. sugar
  3 T. cornstarch
Add:
  2 c. water
Bring to boil, stirring constantly.
Add:
  2 c. sliced fresh peaches
Simmer until fruit is tender. Remove from
heat and add:
  2 T. lemon juice.
Serve hot with pancakes.

___Option:___
Use mangoes, raspberries, strawberries,
blueberries, cherries, or pineapple.
Canned or frozen fruit may be
used—reduce sugar and use juice to
replace part of the water.

Norma Johnson, Lobatse, Botswana

●●●●●●●●●●●●●●●●●●●●●●●●●
Pineapple Sauce

Melt in saucepan:
  3 T. margarine
Add:
  1 c. crushed pineapple
  2 T. brown sugar
Heat 5 minutes, stirring until clear and
thick. When sauce cooks down a bit, add
dash mace or nutmeg.
Use hot or cold.
Makes about 1 cup. Serve with
pancakes, waffles, or on ice cream.

Alice and Willard Roth, Elkhart, Ind.

●●●●●●●●●●●●●●●●●●●●●●●●
Maple Syrup

Combine in saucepan:
  1¾ c. white sugar
  ¼ c. brown sugar
  1 c. water
Bring to boil, cover, and cook 1 minute.
Cool slightly.
Add:
  ½ t. vanilla
  ½ t. maple flavoring
Cover saucepan for a few minutes as
syrup cooks to melt down crystals; helps
prevent syrup from crystallizing later in
storage.

Elsie Epp, Marion, S.D.

●●●●●●●●●●●●●●●●●●●●●●●●
Economy
Pancake Syrup

Combine in saucepan:
  1 c. brown sugar, lightly packed
  3 c. water
  5 t. cornstarch
Cook until slightly thickened.
Add:
  1 t. maple flavoring
Store in refrigerator.

Lois Hess, Columbus, Ohio
Helen Burkholder, St. Catherines, Ont.

•••••••••••••••••••••••••
Indian Corn Pone

*Double the recipe
to have enough left
for Creamed Chicken and
Cornbread Stuffing, p. 187,
later in the week.*

Serves 2

Combine in a bowl:
1 c. cornmeal
½ t. salt
1 t. baking powder
Add:
2 T. fat (bacon drippings are good)
½ c. milk
Grease a large, heavy skillet with bacon drippings. Drop batter from a tablespoon, shaping into 4 pones. Brown on both sides. Serve hot with butter or margarine.

Option:
Add ¼ c. dry milk powder to increase protein content.

LaVonne Platt, Newton, Kan.

•••••••••••••••••••••••••
Basic Corn Bread

T·S

Serves 9
400°
25 min.

Preheat oven to 400°.
Mix together:
1 c. cornmeal
**1 c. flour (may use part or all
whole wheat)**
4 t. baking powder
½ t. salt
2 T. brown sugar
½ c. dry milk powder (optional)
Make a well and add:
2 beaten eggs
1 c. milk
¼ c. oil or melted shortening
Stir just until smooth. Pour into a greased 9x9" pan and bake 25 minutes. Serve hot with butter, syrup, honey or milk.

Options:
Reduce cornmeal to ¾ cup. Add 3 T. soy flour, 3 T. wheat germ, 3 T. bran.
To use sour milk in place of sweet, reduce baking powder to 2 t. and add 1 t. soda.

*Esther Landis, Lancaster, Pa.
Eleanor Hiebert, Elkins Park, Pa.*

•••••••••••••••••••••••••
Southern Spoon Bread

Serves 6-8
400°
45 min.

Preheat oven to 400°.
Combine in saucepan:
1 c. cornmeal
2 T. margarine
3 c. milk
Bring to a boil, stirring constantly. When thickened, remove from heat.
Add:
4 eggs, beaten
1 c. milk
½ t. salt
Beat well. Pour into 2 qt. greased casserole and bake 45 minutes. Serve with hot butter or margarine.

Elizabeth Showalter, Waynesboro, Va.

*Usually served by
Paraguayans
as a meat accompaniment.*

●●●●●●●●●●●●●●●●●●●●●●●●●

Sopa Paraguaya
(corn bread)

Serves 8
375°
30 min.

Heat oven to 375°.
Combine in large mixing bowl:
½ c. white flour
2¼ c. fine cornmeal
1 T. sugar
1½ t. salt
1½ t. baking powder
2½ c. grated cheese (⅔ lb.)
Set aside.
Sauté in skillet until transparent:
¼ c. oil
2 medium onions, chopped
Beat together in small bowl:
2 eggs
1½ c. milk
Add onions with oil and egg-milk mixture
to dry ingredients. Stir just until blended.
Pour into greased 9x12″ pan and bake 30
minutes.

Ruth Brown, Filadelphia, Paraguay

*Good spread with margarine
and toasted under the broiler.
Consider it a
high source of protein
at 9.5 grams protein per slice
(10 slices per loaf).*

●●●●●●●●●●●●●●●●●●●●●●●●●

Three-Grain
Peanut Bread

Makes 1 loaf
325°
1 hr., 10 min.

Preheat oven to 325°.
Combine in mixing bowl:
1 c. white flour
½ c. quick cooking oats
½ c. yellow cornmeal
½ c. dry milk powder
½ c. sugar
3 t. baking powder
1 t. salt
Cut in:
⅔ c. cream-style peanut butter
Blend and pour in:
1 egg
1½ c. milk
Mix well. Turn into greased and floured
9x5″ loaf pan. Spread batter evenly. Bake
1 hour and 10 minutes, or until cake
tester inserted in center comes out clean.
Cool 10 minutes and remove from pan.

Becky Mast, State College, Pa.

•••••••••••••••••••••••••
Whole Wheat
Orange Bread

Makes 1 loaf
350°
60-65 min.

Preheat oven to 350°.
Combine in large mixing bowl:
   1½ c. whole wheat flour
   1½ c. white flour
   ¾ c. sugar
   1-2 T. grated orange peel
   2 t. baking powder
   ½ t. salt
Add:
   **¾ c. fresh or reconstituted
      frozen orange juice**
   ½ c. milk
   ½ c. cooking oil
   1 egg, beaten
   ½ c. chopped nuts (optional)
Stir until dry particles are moistened,
about 75 strokes. Pour batter into
greased 9x5″ or 8x4″ loaf pan.
Sprinkle with mixture of:
   1 T. sugar
   ½ t. cinnamon
Bake 60-65 minutes, or until toothpick
inserted in center comes out clean.

Marjorie Ruth, Akron, Pa.

•••••••••••••••••••••••••
Carrot-Coconut
Bread

Makes 4 small loaves
350°
45-50 min.

Preheat oven to 350°.
In large bowl, sift together:
   2½ c. flour
   1 c. sugar
   1 t. baking powder
   1 t. baking soda
   1 t. cinnamon
   ½ t. salt
Combine separately and add:
   3 beaten eggs
   ½ c. cooking oil
   ½ c. milk
Stir just until dry ingredients are
moistened.
Stir in:
   2 c. shredded carrots
   1⅓ c. coconut
   ½ c. raisins
   ½ c. pecans or other nuts
Turn into 4 well-greased and floured 16
oz. fruit or vegetable cans, or two 9″
bread pans. Bake 45-50 minutes.
Remove from cans and cool thoroughly.
Wrap and refrigerate overnight or until
used.

MCC Dining Hall, Akron, Pa.

•••••••••••••••••••••••••
Heirloom
Boston Brown Bread

Makes 4 small loaves
350°
45-50 min.

Preheat oven to 350°.
Combine in mixing bowl:
   2 c. graham or whole wheat flour
   ½ c. white flour
   2 t. baking soda
   1 t. salt
Add:
   2 c. buttermilk or sour milk
   ½ c. dark molasses
   **1 c. raisins, chopped and lightly
      floured**
   ¼ c. nuts (optional)
Mix until smooth. Spoon into either 4
well-greased 1 lb. tin cans or a ring mold.
Let stand ½ hour. Bake 45-50 minutes.
Cool thoroughly on cake rack before
removing from cans. Wrap airtight and
store 24 hours before serving.

Ruth Herr, Columbus, Ohio

*Soy flour is expensive among flours,
but not as a source
of protein.
One slice has 8 grams protein
(10 slices per loaf.)*

●●●●●●●●●●●●●●●●●●●●●●●●●
Soy-Banana
Bread

Makes 1 loaf

Preheat oven to 350°.
Sift together:
    1 c. plus 2 T. soy flour
    1⅓ c. white flour
    2¾ t. baking powder
    ½ t. soda
    ¾ t. salt
    ½ c. sugar
    ⅓ c. dry milk powder
Cut into dry ingredients:
    ¼ c. shortening
Add and mix just until moistened:
    1 egg, beaten
    ⅓ c. water
    1 c. mashed bananas (2-3)
    ½ c. chopped nuts (optional)
Spread in greased 9x5x3" loaf pan. Bake
50 minutes. Remove loaf from pan to
cool. Delicious warm or toasted.

Author's Recipe

●●●●●●●●●●●●●●●●●●●●●●●●●
Dutch
Apple Bread

Makes 1 loaf
350°
55 min.

Preheat oven to 350°.
Cream together:
    ½ c. margarine
    1 c. sugar
Add and beat well:
    2 eggs
    1 t. vanilla
Combine separately:
    2 c. flour
    1 t. soda
    ½ t. salt
Add dry ingredients alternately with:
    ⅓ c. sour milk or orange juice
Fold in:
    1 c. chopped apples
    ⅓ c. chopped walnuts
Bake in greased 9x5" loaf pan for 55
minutes, or until loaf tests done.

Options:
Add ⅓ c. chopped raw cranberries.
Serve thin slices spread with whipped
cream cheese.

Sandra L. Miller, Akron, Pa.

●●●●●●●●●●●●●●●●●●●●●●●●●
Onion Cheese Loaf

Makes 1 loaf

350°

1 hr.

Preheat oven to 350°.
Combine in mixing bowl:
1 c. white flour
1 c. whole wheat flour
1 T. sugar
3 t. baking powder
1 t. dry mustard
1 t. salt
Cut in until mixture resembles coarse meal:
¼ c. margarine
Add and stir lightly:
½ c. shredded cheddar cheese
2 T. grated Parmesan cheese
Combine separately:
1 c. milk
1 egg
Add all at once to cheese mixture and mix with fork just until dry ingredients are moistened. Turn mixture into greased loaf pan. Sprinkle over batter:
½ c. finely chopped onion
paprika
Bake 1 hour.

Ruth Gish, Mt. Joy, Pa.

●●●●●●●●●●●●●●●●●●●●●●●●●
Zucchini Bread

Makes 2 loaves

350°

1 hr.

Preheat oven to 350°.
Combine in mixing bowl and beat well:
3 large eggs
¾ c. sugar
1 c. vegetable oil
2 c. raw, peeled, grated zucchini
1 T. vanilla
Sift together:
3 c. flour
1 t. salt
1 t. baking soda
1 t. baking powder
3 t. cinnamon
Add to zucchini mixture and stir until blended.
Add:
1 c. coarsely chopped nuts
Pour into 2 greased 8" bread pans. Bake 1 hour. Remove from pans and cool on rack.

Option:

Frozen zucchini may be used if pureed in blender.

Danita Laskowski, Goshen, Ind.

*Russian Mennonites
must have these
to accompany
a watermelon feast.
The salty version
also goes well with soup.*

●●●●●●●●●●●●●●●●●●●●●●●●●
Rollkuchen

●●●●●●●●●●●●●●●●●●●●●●●●●
Navajo
Fry Bread

Serves 6-8

Serves 6

Beat together:
  3 eggs
  1 c. cream, whole milk, or mixture
Sift and add:
  2 t. baking powder
  1 t. salt
  3½-4 c. flour
Add a little more flour if necessary to make a soft dough which can be rolled out. Roll on floured board to ¼" thickness. Cut in 2x4" rectangles, cut slit in each, and fry in ½" hot fat (375°) until browned, turning once. Drain on absorbent paper.

Sprinkle with powdered sugar or salt as desired.

Susan Duerksen, Killarney, Man.

Sift into a bowl:
  4½ c. flour
  ½ t. salt
  2 t. baking powder
Stir in:
  1½ c. water
  ½ c. milk
Knead with hands. Pat or roll into circles approximately 5" in diameter. With fingers make small hole in center. Fry in several inches hot oil at 400°; electric skillet is convenient. Dough will puff and bubble. Turn when golden brown. Drain on absorbent paper and serve hot with honey, or use while fresh for Navajo Tacos (see p. 146).

Options:
Use half whole wheat flour.
Add ⅓ c. dry milk powder.

*Shirley Kauffman Sager, Arriba, Colo.
Kathryn Leatherman, Goshen, Ind.*

*Indian chapatis (much like
the Mexican tortilla) are
one way people without ovens
turn flour into bread.
Traditionally they were baked on
a hot rock near an open fire.
Serve with rice and
a simple vegetable curry,
using chapatis Indian-style
to scoop up the food.*

●●●●●●●●●●●●●●●●●●●●●●●●●
Chapatis

Serves 4

Combine in a bowl:
2 c. whole wheat flour
½ t. salt
Stir in:
2 T. melted margarine
⅞ c. water (see below)
Add ¾ c. of the water, then sprinkle on an additional 2 T. as needed to make a soft dough that can be kneaded. Knead well; cover with a damp cloth and set aside for 1 hour. Knead again. Break into golf ball-sized lumps, roll into balls, and roll each out on a floured board to ¼" thick. Dust each lightly with flour.

Heat a heavy ungreased skillet. Cook each chapati 2 minutes on a side, then remove from pan, brush chapati with melted margarine, return to pan and fry until lightly browned. Or brush skillet with fat after frying each chapati. Set oven at 200° and keep chapatis warm and puffy by placing directly on lowest rack until ready to serve.

Ruth Eitzen, Barto, Pa.
Herta Janzen, Calcutta, India

●●●●●●●●●●●●●●●●●●●●●●●●●
Flour
Tortillas

Makes 8-11 tortillas

Fresh or frozen tortillas, if available, are usually cheap; canned or dry packaged varieties are much more expensive. Flour tortillas may be made at home. A properly cooked flour tortilla remains mostly white, but is flecked with brown and puffed in spots; it has a dry look but is still soft and pliable.
Combine in mixing bowl:
2 c. unsifted flour
1 t. salt
Cut in with pastry blender:
¼ c. lard or shortening
When particles are fine, add gradually:
½ c. lukewarm water
Toss with fork to make a stiff dough. Form into a ball and knead thoroughly on lightly floured board until smooth and flecked with air bubbles. To make dough easier to handle, grease surface, cover tightly, and refrigerate 4-24 hours before using. Let dough return to room temperature before rolling out.

Divide dough into 8 balls for large tortillas, or 11 balls for common 8-inch size. Roll as thin as possible on a lightly floured board, or between sheets of waxed paper. Drop onto a very hot ungreased griddle. Bake until freckled on one side. (Takes only about 20 seconds.) Lift edge, turn, and bake on second side. To serve at once, fold each limp tortilla around small lumps of margarine. Or cool tortillas, wrap airtight, and refrigerate or freeze. To serve later, place in tightly covered baking dish and warm in oven, or fry briefly in hot shallow oil.

Option:
Replace ½ c. flour with cornmeal or whole wheat flour.

Carol Friesen, Reedley, Calif.
Louise Claassen, Elkhart, Ind.

*Serve warm tortillas
with rice and beans,
or use to make a variety
of Mexican
specialties (see p. 145).*

Gather Up
the Fragments

1.

Save any leftover bread heels, stale bread, uneaten toast, dry rolls, crusts, and crumbs in a plastic bag in the freezer. When the oven is heated to 300-325° for another purpose, make crumbs or croutons:

Crumbs:

Dry bread *thoroughly* in a slow oven, turning occasionally. Eat as melba toast; let the baby chew it. Put remaining pieces in heavy plastic bag and crush with rolling pin, or whirl in a blender. Put crumbs through coarse sieve. Toss hard pieces to the birds. Dry bread crumbs keep indefinitely on the shelf in a covered container. Add herbs and seasoned salt if desired. Use to bread meat for frying, in croquettes, meat loaves and patties, or to top au gratin dishes and casseroles. Use to make Coating Mix for Oven-Fried Chicken, p. 179. Mix unseasoned crumbs half and half with graham cracker crumbs for a pie shell.

Croutons:

Spread stale bread lightly with margarine or brush with oil; dice into cubes. Sprinkle with seasoned salt, garlic or onion salt, parsley, basil, oregano, or a combination. Toast in a slow oven until thoroughly dry and crisp. Sprinkle on salads, into soup, on casseroles before baking. Use whenever recipes call for herb-seasoned croutons or stuffing mix.

2.

Dice untoasted stale bread to use in meat loaves and patties. A blender quickly turns a handful of stale bread pieces into crumbs.

3.

Dip stale bread in egg and milk and fry for French toast.

4.

Make bread pudding by pouring custard mixture over stale bread; bake at 325° until knife inserted comes out clean.

5.

Freeze leftover corn bread for use in stuffing. See Creamed Chicken with Cornbread Stuffing, p. 187.

6.

To serve leftover pancakes, place a slice of cheese on each and broil until bubbly. Makes a delicious snack or high-protein lunch entrée.

—*Flo Harnish, Akron, Pa.*

7.

Recipes using stale bread:

—Basic Burger Mix, p. 166
—Chicken Strata, p. 183
—Chicken or Turkey Loaf, p. 184
—Creamed Chicken
  with Corn Bread Stuffing, p. 187
—Tuna Soufflé Sandwiches, p. 191
—Old-Fashioned Bread Omelet, p. 150
—Oven Cheese Fondue, p. 154
—Cheese Strata, p. 155
—Scalloped Rhubarb, p. 271
—Applesauce Bread Pudding, p. 269

cereals...

Few superprocessed foods have established themselves so securely on North American tables as boxed dry cereals. At breakfast each person hides behind a favorite brand.

Controversy rages concerning which cereals are the most nutritious. Box labeling assures consumers that enough nutrients lost in processing are replaced to bring the crunchies back to where so nutritious a food as whole grain normally ought to be. Then someone does a study feeding dry cereal to laboratory animals, and the results indicate that cereals captioned most nutritious on the side of the box are not necessarily the ones that keep a living organism healthy.

A few facts about packaged dry cereals are indisputable:

1. They are a very expensive way to consume grain—more expensive than bread and far more expensive than hot cooked cereals, even instant varieties. Cereal has no magical nutritional qualities not found in bread. Dry cereal is twice as expensive as breakfast toast (three times as high for those who bake bread). Dry cereals have risen in price to the point where some are more expensive per pound than certain varieties of meat.

2. Dry cereals waste packaging materials, space on shelves, and energy as they are developed, processed, advertised, and delivered to the stores.

3. Most dry cereals are laced with dyes and preservatives of dubious safety. Many are loaded with sugar. They accustom young children to expect heavy sweetening on their foods. Cereal grains in their natural state contain much-needed fibers and are virtually free of fat; dry cereals have most fibers removed in processing and many contain added fats.

4. The dry cereal market brings people under the thumb of mass advertising—and it presses down hard. Few foods are so exploited on children's TV, through box-top games, and even in contests co-opting schools and fire stations. Parents with preschoolers in the cart find the trip down a supermarket cereal aisle the low point of the week if they're trying to save money.

Consider again the cooked cereals, standby of our grandparents. Quicker varieties can be prepared in the time it takes to set the table and fix orange juice. Beyond the usual oatmeal, all sorts of grains are available that cook up into delicious hot cereals if one searches for them. This book doesn't give many as recipes because availability and naming varies widely, but a little experimenting with amounts of water and cooking times will serve to get them onto the table. Look for:

Wheat germ meal or raw wheat germ—at feed mills or health food stores. Cook like cream of wheat or mix with cream of wheat.

Bulgur wheat—widely available.

Cracked, ground, or rolled wheat —feed mills, health food stores, or grind your own in hand mill, in blender (p. 64), or in small electric coffee grinder.

Millet—health food stores.

Rolled oats—widely available.

Barley grits or groats—mills, supermarkets, other stores.

Brown rice or cornmeal—both widely available. Cook with milk to porridge consistency.

Some of these products, if available only in specialty stores, may be expensive; in other areas they are cheap. In any case, compare prices pound for pound with dry cereals before deciding against them.

Several grains can be combined in your own hot cereal mix. Take another hint from the old cookbooks and don't limit hot cereals to breakfast. They make a good fast meal any other time of day, especially appealing topped with fresh or dried fruits, nuts, brown sugar, or honey.

Experiment with whole grains growing locally. Myrtle Hostetler, Harper, Kansas, writes:

> *I am sharing some of the fun and pleasure of experimenting in the kitchen cooking whole kernel wheat. We brought the wheat, harvested in our fields, to the house and stored it in glass jars.*
>
> *Whole kernel wheat is very nourishing, as well as economical when purchased in that form. If wheat were six dollars per bushel, this would be only ten cents per pound. Compare this to anything in the grocery stores.*
>
> *The challenge was: What length of time and what temperature would be required to change this hard winter wheat into plump kernels? This is what I did. Wash wheat in cold water, removing chaff, etc. For*

> *each cup of whole kernel wheat, add 1 cup warm water. Cook in heavy aluminum kettle on very low heat for twenty-four hours. I don't have a crock pot, but wish I could have experimented with one.*
>
> *Various ways to use plump cooked kernels:*
> *Breakfast cereal—store in refrigerator, heat amount needed.*
> *Use in meat loaf and hamburger patties.*
> *Special favorite—add to dinner roll dough.*
> *I froze some, ready-measured to use later.*

If you don't have a crock pot, save energy on the process above by soaking the wheat overnight, bringing it to a boil, and then cooking 2 hours on low heat. Or cook 35 to 40 minutes in a pressure cooker.

From a family who doesn't have a wheat field:

> *Our family and another family buy a bushel of wheat on the day it is combined and grind it for hot cereal and whole wheat bread recipes. We eat it every morning for breakfast. Add a little cocoa if the children like cocoa wheat. Keep it stored in tight container and in a cool dry place until you need to grind some more.*
> *—Pauline Wyse,*
> *Mt. Pleasant, Iowa*

Another cereal hint:

> *Because breakfast is such a hurry-up time, add instant dry milk to cooked hot cereal, stir, and serve. Good for a family with young children.*
> *—Virginia Birky, Salem, Ohio*

Probably as a reaction against the overprocessed quality of commercial cereals, homemade granola recipes are suddenly being traded everywhere. With the exception of grape nuts, few people imagined ten years ago that you could make your own dry cereals. Now the possibilities of combining and toasting grains at home seem endless.

Most of the cereal recipes given here are for granola, and these represent only a fraction of the large number received. One contributor summed it up by saying:

> *There is almost as much joy in mixing up granola as in making bread. And since you never make it exactly the same, it's always an adventure. As for eating, it is not only a breakfast cereal with milk, but can be used as a snack, on ice cream, as a topping on apple desserts or pumpkin pie, or in cookies. And there's something in granola—an old-fashioned, earthy, homemade, simple goodness that's not like any other cold cereal.*
> *—Kamala Platt, Newton, Kan.*

Making homemade granola can be expensive, depending on the sources for certain ingredients. Honey, sunflower seeds, and coconut are usually the culprits if you add up the cost of a batch and find it approaching, pound for pound, a commercial dry cereal. (Be sure to weigh the batch of granola to see how much you're getting and take into consideration ingredients left for future batches.)

Corn syrup, molasses, or brown sugar plus a few tablespoons of water can substitute for honey if the price makes honey prohibitive. But check first for honey by the gallon directly from a farmer. Using honey is a good way to please a sweet tooth while cutting down on refined sugar, and you won't need to sprinkle on additional sugar at the table. Corn syrup and molasses don't sweeten as well as honey, cup for cup.

Sunflower seeds add a delightful crunch and are a good source of protein, but aren't essential. Try to buy them in quantity or raise your own. See p. 295 for home shelling method.

To use sesame seeds in granola, purchase them by the pound in a specialty or health food store. They're far cheaper that way than in tiny spice boxes.

Coconut adds good taste but has no important nutritive value and is expensive. In tropical areas where fresh coconuts are cheap, use them but reduce liquid in honey or oil. Buy unsweetened coconut in bulk if available.

Remember that cereals should be eaten together with milk or legumes to make maximum use of the protein they contain. For breakfast this happens most naturally by pouring milk on cereal, but you can also add dry milk to granola, pancakes, muffins, coffee cakes, and breads before baking, or cook hot cereal with milk instead of water. Add soy flour, soy grits, or soybeans to granola. Use roasted soybeans or soaked beans, finely ground. For the latter, cooking is unnecessary.

●●●●●●●●●●●●●●●●●●●●●●●●●
Basic
Dry Cereal Formula

300°
30-60 min.

Preheat oven to 300°.
Combine in large bowl:
7 c. dry ingredients, including
**at least 2-3 c. rolled oats, plus
other grains and nuts as
desired:
wheat germ
whole wheat flour
wheat bran
wheat grits
cornmeal
soy flour, grits, or roasted beans
grape nuts
uncooked cereals (Ralston,
Wheatena, etc.)
sunflower seeds
sesame seeds
pumpkin seeds, roasted
fresh grated or dried coconut
dry milk solids
chopped nuts
spices—cinnamon, nutmeg, etc.**
Combine separately and pour over dry
ingredients:
1 c. liquids, including as desired:
**honey
syrup
molasses
brown sugar (use 2 T. water with
½ c. sugar)
oil
melted margarine
peanut butter
milk or cream**
Bake in large greased baking pans
30-60 minutes, stirring often. Do not
overbrown. Crunchiness depends on
proportions and baking time. For a
chunkier cereal, allow to cool
undisturbed, then break into pieces.
Add when cool, as desired:
**raisins
chopped dates
dried apples
apricots
other fruits**

●●●●●●●●●●●●●●●●●●●●●●●●●
Mother's
Grape Nuts

Makes 2½ lbs.
350°
25-30/20-30 min.

Preheat oven to 350°.
Combine in large mixing bowl:
**3 c. graham or whole wheat flour
½ c. wheat germ
1 c. brown sugar or ¾ c. corn syrup
2 c. buttermilk or sour milk
1 t. soda
pinch salt**
Beat until smooth.
Spread dough on 2 large greased cookie
sheets. Bake 25-30 minutes.
Crumble by one of these methods:
1. While still warm, break into
chunks and grate on slaw
cutter, or whirl briefly in
blender, about a cupful at a time.
2. Allow to cool thoroughly, then
put through food grinder,
coarse plate.
Crisp in 250° oven for 20-30 minutes.
Store in airtight container. Eat with milk.
No added sugar needed.

Option:
Omit wheat germ and increase flour by ½ c.

*Ada Beachey, Goshen, Ind.
Viola Dorsch, Musoma, Tanzania
Vincent Krabill, Hesston, Kan.*

*One of the simplest
and cheapest;
easy for
small children to chew.*

*Choice recipe from a
well-known Christian
community. Make up this
huge batch, fill into
peanut-butter jars, tie with
ribbon, and use for Christmas
gifts. If ingredients are
bought in bulk, cost is
about two thirds that of
commercial "natural" cereals.*

●●●●●●●●●●●●●●●●●●●●●●●●●

Simple Granola

●●●●●●●●●●●●●●●●●●●●●●●●●

Koinonia
Granola

Makes 2½-3 qts.
250°
1 hr.

Makes 5 qts.
350°
20-25 min.

Preheat oven to 250°.
Combine in large mixing bowl:
**2 c. whole wheat flour
6 c. rolled oats
1 c. coconut
1 c. wheat germ**
Blend together separately:
**½ c. water
1 c. oil
1 c. honey or corn syrup
2 t. vanilla
1 T. salt**
Add blended liquids to dry ingredients
and mix thoroughly.
Spread out on 2 greased cookie sheets
and bake 1 hour, or until dry and golden.
Store in covered containers.

Option:

With same liquids, use 4 c. quick oats, 3
c. whole wheat flour, 1 c. wheat germ, 1 c.
soy flour (optional), 1 c. coconut, 1 c.
nuts.

*Marian Zuercher, Wooster, Ohio
Anna Beth Birky, West Chicago, Ill.*

Preheat oven to 350°.
Melt in large roasting pan:
**½ c. oil
½ lb. margarine
2 T. molasses
1 T. vanilla
1 c. brown sugar
1 c. honey
½ t. salt**
When mixed, let cool slightly and add:
**2 lbs. rolled oats
½ c. sesame seeds
1 c. chopped nuts
2 c. grape nuts
1 c. wheat germ
1 lb. coconut
1 c. sunflower seeds**
Stir thoroughly. Bake in shallow pans for
20-25 minutes. Stir every 5-7 minutes.
After granola has cooled, add 1 c.
raisins.

Koinonia Farms, Americus, Ga.

Koinonia Granola – When
cool, add 2 c. raisins and 2 c.
chopped pineapple or apricots.
—*Sylvia F. Shelly,*
Telford, Pa.

●●●●●●●●●●●●●●●●●●●●●●●●
Soybean
Granola

Makes 2 qts.
325°
15 min.

Preheat oven to 325°.
Combine in large bowl:
   4 c. rolled oats
   1 c. wheat germ
   1 c. sliced almonds or other nuts
   1 c. sunflower seeds
   ½ c. whole wheat bran
   1 c. roasted soybeans (see p. 305)
Heat to boiling in saucepan:
   ¼ c. oil
   ½ c. honey
   1 t. vanilla
Pour liquids over dry ingredients and stir
thoroughly. Toast on 2 greased cookie
sheets for 15 minutes or until golden.

Jean Miller, Akron, Pa.

> *I received this book many*
> *years ago from a friend. As*
> *new wives and mothers, we*
> *focused on being "provident*
> *and resourceful." This book*
> *became a welcome resource.*
> *Recipes we have used over*
> *and over have become part*
> *of our family celebrations,*
> *hard times, and now memo-*
> *ries. We raised our children*
> *on many of the principles*
> *expressed in this book. As*
> *things come full circle, our*
> *daughter, Teresa, is now part*
> *of Mennonite Central*
> *Committee (although we are*
> *a Catholic family).*
> *—Marie Reimers,*
> *South Bend, Ind.*

●●●●●●●●●●●●●●●●●●●●●●●●
Apple Cinnamon
Crunch

Makes 2 qts.
350°
20-25 min.

Preheat oven to 350°.
Combine in large bowl:
   4 c. old-fashioned rolled oats
   ½ c. coconut
   1 c. nuts, finely chopped
   ½ c. sesame seed
   ¾ t. salt .
   1 t. cinnamon
Combine separately and add:
   ½ c. honey
   ⅓ c. vegetable oil
   ½ t. vanilla
Mix thoroughly. Spread on 2 large
greased baking pans and bake 20-25
minutes, stirring occasionally.
Add:
   8 oz. finely cut dried apples
Store in tightly covered container in
refrigerator.

Esther Deal, Ft. Wayne, Ind.

> *What do you say about a*
> *cookbook that changed your*
> *life? I was born in the year of*
> *its first printing and have been*
> *eating homemade Granola and*
> *Whole Wheat Rolls for as long*
> *as I can remember. I appreci-*
> *ate the healthy diet my mother*
> *gave us. Delayed gratitude, but*
> *a deep gratitude. Thank you,*
> *More-with-Less, and you,*
> *Mom, for 25 years of good*
> *food and the education that*
> *came with it.*
> *—Teresa Reimers,*
> *Ozamiz, Philippines*

Try this granola sprinkled generously over a bowlful of fresh sliced peaches for an outdoor summer breakfast. Some Swiss restaurants offer granola topped with fresh fruit and whipped cream as "Skiier's Breakfast."

●●●●●●●●●●●●●●●●●●●●●●●●

Crunchy Granola

Makes 2 qts.
325°
30 min.

Preheat oven to 325°.
Mix together in large bowl:
 ½-1 c. coconut
 4 c. rolled oats
 1 c. sunflower seed
 1 c. wheat germ
 ¼-½ c. sesame seed
 1 c. peanuts or chopped walnuts
Bring to a boil:
 1 c. honey or brown sugar
 ½ c. oil
 1 T. cinnamon
Pour honey mixture over dry ingredients and mix thoroughly. Spread on 2 greased cookie sheets. Bake about 30 minutes, stirring often. Watch closely at the last, not allowing granola to become too dark. Allow to cool undisturbed, then break into chunks.

Options:

If using brown sugar, increase oil to ¾ c. or add ¼ c. water.

Add 1 c. cornmeal to dry mixture. Omit cinnamon.

Pat and Earl Martin, Quang Ngai, Vietnam
Miriam Witmer, Manheim, Pa.
Dale Suderman, Newton, Kan.

●●●●●●●●●●●●●●●●●●●●●●●●

Chunky Granola

Makes 2½ qts.
350°
10-15 min.

Preheat oven to 350°.
Place in ungreased 9x13" pan:
 6 c. rolled oats
Bake 10 minutes. Remove from oven and stir in:
 ½ c. sunflower seeds or nuts
 ½ c. coconut
 ½ c. wheat germ
 ½ c. powdered milk
Add to dry mixture:
 ⅔ c. honey
 ⅔ c. oil
 1 t. vanilla
Stir until thoroughly coated. Bake 10-15 minutes, stirring every 3-5 minutes until uniformly golden. Do *not* overbake.
Let it cool in pan undisturbed, then break into chunks.

Option:

Chopped raisins, dates, or dried fruits may be added.

Granola bars: For this or other recipes containing 6 to 8 c. dry ingredients and 1 to 2 c. liquid, add to liquids: 1 beaten egg, about ⅓ c. milk. Stir liquids into dry ingredients and mix well. Press mixture firmly into 2 well-greased 10 x 15" cookie sheets. Bake at suggested temperature until nicely browned. Cut immediately into bars. Remove from pans when cool. For sweeter bars, increase honey.

Mary Lou Houser, Lancaster, Pa.

••••••••••••••••••••••••••
Peanut
Granola

Makes 5 qts.
325°
30 min.

Preheat oven to 325°.
Combine in saucepan:
   1¼ c. honey
   ⅔ c. oil
   1 c. peanut butter
   1 T. salt
   1 T. cinnamon
   ½ c. water
Stir over low heat until peanut butter melts.
Combine in large bowl:
   10 c. rolled oats
   1 c. chopped raw peanuts or other nuts
   1 c. wheat germ
   1 c. cornmeal
   1 c. coconut
Add liquids and mix well. Place in 2 large shallow greased pans and bake about 30 minutes or until crunchy and brown. Stir often to prevent overbrowning. When cool, add:
   2 c. raisins
Store in airtight container.

   Louise Leatherman, Akron, Pa.

••••••••••••••••••••••••••
Everything
Cereal

Makes 4-5 qts.
300°
45-60 min.

Preheat oven to 300°.
Combine in large heavy roasting pan:
   1 c. whole wheat or soy flour
   1½ c. dry milk powder
   1½ c. unroasted wheat germ
   ½ c. buckwheat (optional)
   1 c. sesame seeds
   6 c. rolled oats
   1 c. shelled unroasted sunflower seeds
   1 c. grape nuts
Combine in saucepan:
   1 c. oil
   ½ c. honey
   2 T. molasses
   1 t. vanilla
Warm over low heat to blend. Pour into dry mixture, stirring well.
Roast for 45-60 minutes, stirring every 15 minutes at first, then more frequently, until particles are golden (not dark) brown. After mixture has cooled, add:
   2 c. raisins
   1 c. each chopped prunes, dates, dried apricots, coconut (all optional)
   1 c. dry-roasted chopped peanuts or other nuts
Store in tightly covered containers in cool, dry place.

   Rosemary Moyer, North Newton, Kan.
   Marlin Dick, Swan Lake Christian Camp, Viborg, S.D.

●●●●●●●●●●●●●●●●●●●●●●●●●
Apple Oatmeal

Serves 4-6

Combine in saucepan:
1 c. rolled oats
2 c. cold water
½ t. salt
Cook 10 minutes on low heat.
Add:
2 chopped apples
dash nutmeg
Cook 5 minutes more, or until apples are done to desired consistency.
　　Serve with milk or yogurt and honey, brown sugar, or cinnamon-sugar.

Option:
Use raisins or dates in place of apples.

Grace Whitehead, Kokomo, Ind.

●●●●●●●●●●●●●●●●●●●●●●●●
Cornmeal Mush

Serves 4-6

Bring to a boil in heavy saucepan or top of double boiler:
3 c. water
Combine and stir in:
1 c. cold water
1 c. cornmeal
¼ c. flour
1 t. salt
Stir constantly as mush thickens. A wire whisk works well. Cook 30 minutes, covered, on very low heat or over hot water. Eat hot from the kettle with milk and sugar, or pour into loaf pan to cool and set. Slice, dust with flour if desired, and fry in well-greased skillet.

Grace Geiser, Apple Creek, Ohio

●●●●●●●●●●●●●●●●●●●●●●●●●
Ground Wheat
Breakfast Cereal

Serves 6

Bring to a boil:
3 c. water
Combine separately and add:
1 c. cold water
1 c. ground wheat
2 t. salt
Stir constantly while thickening to prevent lumps. Reduce heat and cook 15-20 minutes. Serve with milk and sugar, honey or molasses.

Grace Geiser, Apple Creek, Ohio

I was a volunteer coordinator for MCC Central States, doing More-with-Less workshops. We used the themes from the four chapters preceding the recipes in the cookbook. Although most workshop groups were Mennonite, I remember doing programs for Methodist, Lutheran, Church of Christ, Presbyterian, Christian Reformed, and other churches, and a few at women's groups and other events not church-affiliated. Sharing the philosophy of More-with-Less was a major focus of my volunteer work for five years. That philosophy has become integral to my family—who we are and how we live.
—LaVonne Platt,
Newton, Kan.

*This recipe (tropical version)
was first given
to Saigon MCC workers
by Seventh-Day Adventist
missionaries in 1966,
and has since been used
by MCCers in many countries.*

●●●●●●●●●●●●●●●●●●●●●●●●
Coconut-Oatmeal
Cereal

Makes 2 qts.
350°
45 min.

Preheat oven to 350°.
Combine in large mixing bowl:
- **3 c. white or whole wheat flour**
- **2 c. flake coconut**
- **2 c. quick oatmeal**
- **3 T. sesame seed**
- **3 T. water**
- **¾ c. sugar**
- **5 T. cooking oil**

Mix well. Bake in 2 or 3 shallow baking
pans until browned, about 45 minutes,
stirring occasionally to produce
crumbles of desired size.
Serve as cold cereal.
Serves 16 (½ c. servings).

Options:

Add for variety:
raisins
brown sugar
sunflower seeds
nuts

Tropical version: Use 1 finely grated
fresh coconut to replace flake coconut
and omit 3 T. water.

June Suderman, Hillsboro, Kan.

●●●●●●●●●●●●●●●●●●●●●●●●
Family
Familia

T·S

Place a large bowl of rolled oats in the
center of the table. All around place
small bowls of whatever is available of
the following:
- **coconut**
- **sesame seeds**
- **sunflower seeds**
- **wheat germ**
- **rolled wheat, rye, or barley**
- **sprouts**
- **nuts**
- **dates, raisins, other dried fruits**
- **fresh, frozen, or canned fruits**

Each compiles his/her own. Pass honey
and a pitcher of hot milk.

Kathy Histand, Sellersville, Pa.

beans, soybeans, and lentils......

Beans or legumes, a food of humble reputation in North America, are usually considered staple diet for the poor. Few cookbooks devote more than a couple of pages to them. Books will include a baked bean recipe or two, and possibly a soup, but that's the end of the matter.

In dismissing legumes so quickly, a whole resource of cheap plant protein is ignored. Prices have risen markedly, but pound for pound dry beans still do very well on the table of costs for 100 grams of protein. See Chart D, p. 36.

One-half cup cooked white beans has seven grams protein, the same as a whole egg. A half cup of soybeans has eleven grams. Granted the egg has higher quality protein, but by eating beans together with grains (rice or whole grain bread) the quality or usability of protein in both the beans and the grain improves significantly. For a meatless high-protein meal, baked beans and whole grain bread are an excellent choice.

Dry legumes, especially soybeans, are good sources of minerals and B vitamins. As a double bonus to heart-conscious North Americans, soybeans are one of the few high-protein foods containing *no* saturated fats. In fact, they contain lecithin, which helps in the absorption and utilization of any kind of fat, including cholesterol.

Buy legumes in their dry form, in bulk if possible. They come to the kitchen shelf with almost no backlog of energy used in processing or storage and keep well with little attention.

A row of glass jars containing a variety of dry legumes adds color and texture interest to the kitchen and makes it easy to reach for them in meal planning. Visualize the natural color tones of little green split peas, earth-brown lentils, deep-red kidney beans, and creamy-golden soybeans arranged together.

"But they take so long to soak and cook and I can't ever remember to do it ahead of time," many cooks complain. Consider these suggestions for cooking legumes:

Soaking

Presoak all dry beans and peas by one of the methods given below, except for split peas and lentils. Two to three hours soaking is enough for split peas, although longer won't matter. Lentils need no presoaking and only 30 to 40 minutes cooking time.

1. *Overnight Method:* Wash beans, sort, place in kettle in which they will be cooked, and cover with 4 cups water to 1 cup beans (or follow recipe proportions). Cover and let stand 8 hours or overnight. Use soaking water for cooking—do not discard it.

2. *Quick Method:* Follow directions for overnight method but instead of soaking, bring water and beans to a boil and cook 2 minutes. Cover, remove from heat, and let stand 1 hour. Beans are then ready to cook.

Cooking Beans

1. One cup dried beans yields about 2½ cups cooked beans. See p. 38 for more complete information.

2. Cooking time varies according to size of bean and length

of time in storage. Peas and smaller beans usually need less than an hour; larger beans 2 to 3 hours, and soybeans 3 to 4 hours. Large dry limas may tenderize in less than an hour, however. Bring beans to boiling in soaking water, cover, and reduce heat to simmer. Test for tenderness by tasting.

3. Add 1 tablespoon fat to cooking beans to control foaming.

4. Beans may be cooked 20 to 35 minutes in a pressure cooker, but some authorities warn against this because beans tend to sputter and foam which can clog the vent. Never fill pressure cooker more than three fourths full. Timetable for pressure cooking:
small beans, split peas, lentils, 20 minutes
kidney and navy beans, 35 minutes
soybeans, 40 minutes

5. Since beans require long cooking, which uses energy, cook several pounds at once and freeze them. Frozen cooked beans have almost the same convenience as canned; thaw them quickly by setting the container in hot water. Drop a frozen chunk of beans directly into boiling soup, or place chunk in casserole in hot oven and add baked bean seasonings. Stir half an hour later and continue baking.

6. Cooked beans may be canned in jars in pressure canner. See p. 299.

7. Cook beans just until they begin to tenderize, then add seasonings and liquid and bake slowly for 4 to 8 hours for wonderful browned-in flavor. Native Americans taught New England colonists how to make these famed "Boston Baked Beans" in earthen pots. Use that oven heat to good advantage. Bake rice pudding or plain rice, make granola or roast soybeans.

Soybeans

With the shortfall in world food supply, North Americans are again taking an interest in eating soybeans, the high-protein plant food already relied upon for centuries in parts of Asia. Older people remember eating soybeans during Depression days. Several have said to me, "You know, we ate soybeans when I was young. We just cooked them up, poured on a little milk or butter, and that's what we ate. But somehow we got away from it."

Eva Carper, a Mennonite schoolteacher from Virginia, wrote a food column for the *Rural New Yorker* in the mid-1930s. Here are suggestions she gave regarding soybeans:

We use soybeans any way that we use navy beans. Of course the flavor is different, because they are a protein food instead of starchy. We plant them in the corn at the edge of the field when we see the corn coming up, and they are about the last thing harvested. The beans grow along the stem and after the leaves drop off they may be stripped off the stalk. After they are dry they are put in bags and the children have a "jumping bee." We clean the pods out on a windy day by pouring from one tub to another.

For soybean soup, soak beans overnight, and boil slowly

and long to bring out their best flavor. After they have boiled a while I add salt. When soft add whole milk, season with pepper, and heat. Then pour over pieces of dry or toasted bread and pour browned butter over the soup. This is a hearty dish and not much else needs to be served with it. Also, after beans are boiled, I add molasses, mustard, tomato juice, and ham broth or bacon, and bake like baked beans.

As Mrs. Carper notes, soybeans do have a different flavor. Some describe it as bland, needing spicy seasonings. Some call it mildly objectionable and try to cover it up. Others love soybeans just as they are. A dining-hall dietitian who is experimenting with serving soybean dishes said to me recently, "Why is so much attention focused on doctoring up soybeans? The more we use them, the more I like them just as they are. I find myself snitching them out of the kettle as they cook!"

Another way soybeans can be used is as soy flour, which essentially is milled dry soybeans. Soy flour is one of the most highly concentrated protein foods available. See p. 34.

Textured vegetable protein made from soybeans is sold in supermarkets as a meat extender or substitute. If such products are not overpriced and overpackaged, give them a try. Remember, though, that a cup of leftover home-cooked soybeans, mashed or blended, will do the same thing if you're stretching ground meat.

A variety of soybean "meats" are also in your grocer's freezer. Food industry experts maintain people will never eat plant proteins in any quantity until they are flavored and processed into the form of a well-liked meat. There is some good sense in this claim, but soybean sausage should not cost $1.80 per pound (more than pork sausage) the same year that farmers receive less than 10 cents per pound for soybeans.

Using Soybeans

1. Use any field soybean for eating. Some varieties may be tastier than others, but all are edible by people. Raise your own or buy directly from a farmer or mill.

2. Immature *green* soybeans need no presoaking and only a short cooking time like that of fresh green limas. See p. 295.

3. Always presoak dry soybeans at least 8 hours or by quick method, then allow 3 to 4 hours slow cooking.

4. Soybeans will become tender though not quite as soft as other beans, and they never get mushy. The skins may separate and float as cooking begins but will dissolve later. Cooked soybeans freeze well and hold their shape when thawed.

5. Mashed soybeans or soybean paste is versatile in many dishes. Drain hot cooked beans, then mash with potato masher or back of slotted spoon, or put through a food grinder. Mashing is easier when beans are hot. Use a blender if there is liquid in the recipe which can be added to facilitate getting the mixture through the blades. One cup cooked soybeans yields ⅔ cup soybean paste. Use for sandwich spread, as ground beef extender, in loaves, patties, soufflés or casseroles.

Lentils

The convenience food among legumes, lentils cook in thirty minutes with no presoaking. Nutritionally they compare closely to dry beans and, like other legumes, are complemented by grains.

Lentils are an ancient food of the Middle East and as popular there today as they were thousands of years ago when Jacob tricked Esau out of his birthright for "bread and pottage of lentils" (Gen. 25:34). Try

Middle Eastern Lentil Soup, p. 213, or Kusherie (Egyptian Rice and Lentils), p. 108, to understand part of the reason Esau gave in.

The mild nutty flavor of lentils is generally appealing, even to people who have never tried them. What may not be so appealing at first is their brownish color in cooked dishes. Try adding tomato sauce or sliced carrots and a sprinkling of chopped scallions to lentil soup. Serve colorful vegetables or salads with lentil casseroles. Lentils are definitely worth a try if you're looking for low-cost, nutritious main dish ideas. Some of our recipe testers became true converts.

Long, slow baking develops rich flavor. Rice pudding (p. 268) bakes at the same oven temperature and complements protein in beans. Add a crunchy salad.

●●●●●●●●●●●●●●●●●●●●●●●●●
Beans with Sweet-Sour Sauce

T·S

Serves 4

TS with pressure cooker

Soak and cook until tender:
   ½ lb. white beans, such as navy or great northern
   1 qt. water
Brown lightly in skillet:
   1½ T. fat
   1½ T. flour
Gradually add:
   2 T. brown or white sugar
   2 T. corn syrup
   ¼ t. salt
   2 t. vinegar
Stir until blended. Gradually add:
   1 c. liquid (hot water or bean liquid)
Bring to a boil and cook a few minutes. Pour over hot beans.

Options:
Sauté a chopped onion in the fat before adding flour.

Cook the whole pound of beans and reserve extra for another dish later in the week.

Helen E. Regier, Newton, Kan.

●●●●●●●●●●●●●●●●●●●●●●●●●
Basic Baked Beans

T·S

Serves 6-8
275°-300°
4-8 hrs.

TS—needs time not attention

Soak overnight or by quick method:
   1 lb. navy beans
   2 qts. water
In same liquid, bring beans to boil and simmer until tender, about 1½ hours. Drain, reserving liquid.
Preheat oven to 275-300°.
Combine in 2 qt. casserole:
   cooked beans
   ½ c. molasses
   ¼ c. ketchup (optional)
   1 t. mustard
   2 t. salt
   ¼ t. pepper
   1 onion, chopped
   2 slices bacon, chopped, or ¼ lb. salt pork (optional)
   bean liquid to cover
Bake 4-8 hours, adding liquid occasionally if necessary. Cover during first half of baking time, then uncover.

Options:
Substitute soybeans or a combination of bean varieties.

Add 2-3 t. chili powder.

Sarah Grove, Markham, Ont.

Calico Baked Beans
For a Crowd

Serves 10-12
325°
1½ hrs.

Use canned beans, or soak and cook dry beans. Several varieties of dry beans may be soaked and cooked together. One cup dry beans usually yields 2½ cups cooked.

Preheat oven to 325°.
Combine in large casserole, reserving liquids:
   2 c. green limas, cooked and drained
   2 c. large dry limas, cooked and drained
   2 c. red kidney beans, cooked and drained
   1 qt. pork and beans, or leftover baked beans
Fry:
   6 slices bacon, diced
   OR 1 c. leftover ham bits
   OR ½ lb. sausage or ground beef
Pour off excess fat.
Add:
   1½ c. onions, cut up
Fry briefly.
Add:
   ¾ c. brown sugar
   2 t. salt
   1 t. dry mustard
   1 clove minced garlic
   ½ c. vinegar
   ½ c. ketchup
Cook 5 minutes and pour over beans. Add enough reserved bean liquid to barely cover beans. Bake uncovered 1½ hours, adding additional liquid if beans become too dry.

Options:
Substitute other varieties of dry beans, including soy—but keep color contrast for an attractive dish.

Omit meat altogether—still delicious!

Sharon Baker, Larkspur, Colo.
Karin Hackman, Hatfield, Pa.

---

*Serve chili beans on rice
or with corn bread
for the grain-legume
protein relationship.*

Mexican
Chili Beans

Serves 6

Soak overnight or by quick method:
   1 lb. dried red kidney beans
   2 qts. water
Bring to a boil.
Simmer just until tender, about 40 minutes.
Fry in Dutch oven:
   ¼ lb. salt pork, finely diced
When crisp, add:
   2 c. onions, finely chopped
   4 cloves garlic, finely chopped
Saute until golden. Add:
   2 t. salt
   1 t. pepper
   2-4 t. chili powder, according to taste
   1 t. dried leaf oregano
   ¼ t. cumin
   ¾ c. tomato paste
   1 c. tomato sauce
Simmer 15 minutes.
Drain beans, reserving liquid. Add beans to tomato mixture along with 2 c. reserved liquid. Cover and simmer 1 hour.

Marjorie Ropp, Montreal, Quebec

*Use as filling in tortillas,
as side dish with rice or tacos,
or on Navajo Tacos (see p. 146).*

●●●●●●●●●●●●●●●●●●●●●●●●●

Mexican
Refried Beans

Serves 5-6

Soak overnight or by quick method:
  **1 lb. dried pinto, pink, or kidney
  beans**
Add:
  **6 c. water
  2 onions, chopped (optional)**
Bring to a boil, cover and simmer slowly
until beans are tender, about 3 hours.
Mash beans with potato masher.
Add:
  **½ c. hot bacon drippings,
  margarine, or lard
  salt to taste**
Mix well; continue cooking, stirring
frequently until beans are thickened and
fat is absorbed. Serve at once or
refrigerate for later use.

Options:

Cook beans with half the onion; heat fat in
skillet, sauté remaining onion, then mash
¼ c. beans into skillet. Fry a short time
and push to side, adding more beans by
¼ cupfuls and mashing. Simmer 10
minutes to finish.

Add chili powder and/or cumin and
tomato sauce to taste. Place in greased
casserole, sprinkle with cheese, and
keep hot in oven until ready to serve.

Use soybeans or chick peas (garbonzos)
for delicious variation.

*Carol Friesen, Reedley, Calif.
Anne Rogers, East Petersburg, Pa.*

●●●●●●●●●●●●●●●●●●●●●●●●●

Crusty
Mexican Bean Bake

Serves 6
350°
30 min.

Crust:
Combine:
  **½ c. flour
  ½ t. salt
  ½ t. baking powder
  2 T. shortening or margarine
  ½ c. sour cream or yogurt
    (increase flour by 2 T. if
    using yogurt)
  1 egg, beaten**
Stir together. May be slightly lumpy.
Spread thinly with back of spoon on
bottom and sides of shallow greased
2-qt. casserole. Fill with bean mixture.
(Crust may be stirred together in
advance. Refrigerate until ready to use.)

Filling:
Brown in skillet:
  **¾ lb. ground beef
  ½ c. chopped onion**
Add:
  **1 t. salt
  2 t. chili powder
  ½ t. Tabasco sauce
  2 c. undrained cooked kidney
  beans
  ¾ c. (6 oz.) tomato paste**
Spoon into crust and bake at 350° for 30
minutes. Remove from oven. Sprinkle
over or serve alongside:
  **½ c. grated cheese
  1-2 c. shredded lettuce
  1 c. chopped raw tomatoes**

Evelyn Fisher, Akron, Pa.

101

●●●●●●●●●●●●●●●●●●●●●●●●●
Monterey Beans
And Cheese

T·S

Serves 6

Fry, drain, and break into pieces:
2 slices bacon
Set aside. Sauté in bacon fat until tender:
½ medium-sized onion, sliced
½ green pepper, diced
Add:
bacon bits
2 c. cooked kidney beans
¼-½ lb. shredded cheddar cheese
2 ripe tomatoes, diced, or
   ¾ c. tomato sauce
¼ c. beef bouillon or tomato juice
1 t. chili powder
½ t. salt
dash of pepper
Cook slowly, stirring constantly, until ingredients are blended and cheese is smooth—about 5 minutes. Serve with rice.

Mary Ella Weaver, Lititz, Pa.

●●●●●●●●●●●●●●●●●●●●●●●●●
Puerto Rican Rice
And Pigeon Peas

Serves 6-8

Soak, then cook until tender:
½ lb. pigeon peas, pinto or
   kidney beans
4 c. water
Brown in dutch oven or deep skillet:
1 lb. pork ribs or cooking ham,
   cut in 1" pieces
Measure accumulated drippings and add enough vegetable oil to make ½ c. Return fat to skillet and add:
achiote, if available, OR
   ¾ c. tomato paste
Stir to coat meat.
Add to skillet:
2 tomatoes, chopped
½ green pepper, chopped
1 large onion, chopped
2 cloves garlic, minced
2 c. cabbage, finely chopped
1 t. oregano
1 T. capers with juice
1 T. salt
Stir-fry briefly just to wilt vegetables. Add:
2 c. uncooked rice
cooked pigeon peas, drained
Stir well. Add:
6-7 c. bean liquid and water
Cook at moderate heat 15 minutes. Stir once or twice. Then reduce heat, cover, and finish cooking slowly until rice is done.

Option:
Omit meat. Begin by sautéeing vegetables in ½ c. fat, then add tomato paste and remaining ingredients.

*Maria Luisa Rivera de Snyder,
Hesston, Kan.*

*Brazilians like to accompany
this complete meal
with manioc flour
sprinkled on top.*

●●●●●●●●●●●●●●●●●●●●●●●●
Carribean Rice
And Beans

●●●●●●●●●●●●●●●●●●●●●●●●
Brazilian Rice
And Beans

Serves 6-8

Serves 8-10

Soak overnight or by quick method:
- **2 c. dry pigeon peas, pinto beans, or kidney beans**
- **6 c. water**
- **1 T. salt**

Bring to a boil, reduce heat, and simmer just until tender—about 40 minutes.
Drain beans, reserving liquid.
Heat in large covered skillet:
- **2 T. oil or margarine**

Add:
- **1 clove garlic, crushed**
- **2 green onions, chopped**
- **1 large tomato, chopped**
- **1 T. lime juice (optional)**
- **⅛ t. ground cloves**
- **1 T. chopped parsley**
- **¼ t. pepper**
- **drained beans**

Sauté about 5 minutes.
Add:
- **2 c. rice**
- **4 c. reserved bean liquid (add water if necessary)**

Bring to a boil, cover, reduce heat to simmer, and cook 20-25 minutes without stirring.

Shirley King, Grande Riviere du Nord, Haiti
Abe and Katherine Dyck, Manchester, Jamaica

Soak overnight or by quick method:
- **2 c. pinto or kidney beans**
- **6 c. water**

Cook about 2 hours or until tender.
In saucepan, cook together about 4 c. of 2-4 of the following vegetables in large pieces:
- **potato**
- **chayote**
- **cabbage**
- **pumpkin**
- **okra**
- **carrot**

Cook just until tender.
Sauté together in a skillet:
- **½ lb. ground meat (beef or pork)**
- **¼ lb. smoked meat (bacon, sausage, etc.)**
- **2 garlic cloves, minced**
- **1 medium onion, chopped**
- **½ green pepper, chopped (optional)**
- **1 t. Worcestershire sauce**
- **2 T. tomato paste**
- **1 t. coriander**
- **1 bay leaf**
- **salt and pepper to taste**

Simmer 30 minutes.
Join beans, vegetables, and meat mixture and heat together 2 minutes.
Serve with rice.

Josefa Soares, Recife, Brazil

103

●●●●●●●●●●●●●●●●●●●●●●●●●
Italian Beans
And Pasta

Serves 8

Soak overnight or by quick method:
**1 lb. dried Great Northern or
   marrow beans
4 c. water**
In large kettle, bring beans to boil, cover
and simmer 1 hour, adding water if
necessary.
Cook and drain according to package
directions:
8 oz. elbow macaroni
Brown in skillet:
**¾ lb. sausage, broken up
1 clove garlic, minced
1 onion, chopped**
Drain off excess fat. Add macaroni and
sausage mixture to bean kettle.
Add:
**4 c. cooked tomatoes
¼ c. dark corn syrup
2 T. chopped parsley
2 t. salt
2 t. dried oregano
¼ t. pepper**
Bring to boil, cover and simmer about 15
minutes, adding tomato juice if
necessary for stew consistency. Serve in
soup bowls with a green salad and whole
wheat bread.

Option:
Thin with more water or tomato juice for a
soup.

*Belmont Mennonite Church Low-Cost
Collection, Elkhart, Ind.*

---

*Serve as summertime meal
with whole grain bread
and fresh fruit.*

●●●●●●●●●●●●●●●●●●●●●●●●●
Scallions
And Beans

Serves 6

Soak overnight or by quick method:
**1 lb. dry white beans
2 qts. water**
Cook in water to cover until tender. Drain
and cool. (Reserve liquid for soup or
stew.)
Combine:
**4 scallions, chopped,
   including tops
2 cloves garlic, peeled and
   pressed
¼ c. fresh lemon juice
½ c. olive oil
salt and freshly ground pepper**
Pour dressing over beans. Sprinkle with
parsley. Chill several hours before
serving.

Option:
Other oil may replace olive oil but won't
yield the same flavor.

*Louise Claassen, Elkhart, Ind.
Gwen Peachey, Amman Jordan*

Basic Cooked
Lentils

T·S

Serves 6

Bring to a boil and simmer 20 minutes:
- **1 c. lentils**
- **2½ c. water**
- **2 beef bouillon cubes**
- **1 bay leaf**
- **1 t. salt**

Flavor options:

Curried Lentils
Sauté together:
- **¼ c. margarine**
- **1 large onion, chopped**
- **1 clove garlic, minced**
Add:
- **1 t. salt**
- **1-2 T. curry powder**
Fry briefly. Add to Basic Cooked Lentils
with:
- **2 T. lemon juice**
- **chopped parsley**
Serve over rice.

Sweet-Sour Lentils
Reduce water by ½ c. in preparing Basic
Cooked Lentils.
When lentils are cooked, add:
- **¼ c. apple or pineapple juice**
- **¼ c. cider vinegar**
- **¼ c. brown sugar**
- **1 clove garlic, crushed**
- **⅛ t. cloves**
- **sautéed onion, if desired**
Heat to bubbly. Serve over rice.

Easy Lentil Stew
Add to lentils:
- **½ lb. diced ham, browned
  sausage, or browned
  ground beef**
- **¾ c. tomato paste**
- **2 c. water**
- **¼ t. oregano**
- **1 t. salt**
- **1 onion, chopped**
- **2 stalks celery, chopped**
- **1 clove garlic, minced**
Bring to a boil, reduce heat, and simmer
20-30 minutes until vegetables are
tender. Serve plain or over rice.

Zona Galle, Madison, Wis.
Becky Mast, State College, Pa.
Marian Franz, Washington, D.C.

•••••••••••••••••••••••••••
Savory
Baked Limas

T·S

Serves 6-8
300°
About 5 hrs.

TS—Needs time not attention

Wash and soak overnight:
- **1 lb. dried baby lima beans**
- **6 c. water**
Preheat oven to 300°.
Drain beans (reserve liquid) and place in
2 qt. casserole.
Add:
- **liquid from soaking beans plus
  water to make 2 c.**
- **2 c. diced, unpeeled tart apples**
- **½ c. chopped onion**
- **¼ c. dark brown sugar**
- **2 T. Worcestershire sauce**
- **¼ c. molasses**
- **2 t. salt**
- **1 t. dry mustard**
Stir well. Score or cut up:
- **¼ lb. salt pork or slab bacon**
Bury pork deep in center of beans. Cover
and bake about 5 hours. Stir once or
twice and add water if needed.

Erma Weaver, Manheim, Pa.

Baked Lentils With Cheese

Serves 6
375°
1 hr., 15 min.

Preheat oven to 375°.
Combine in shallow 9x13″ baking dish:
  1¾ c. lentils, rinsed
  2 c. water
  1 whole bay leaf
  2 t. salt
  ¼ t. pepper
  ⅛ t. *each* **marjoram, sage, thyme**
  2 large onions, chopped
  2 cloves garlic, minced
  2 c. canned tomatoes
Cover tightly and bake 30 minutes.
Uncover and stir in:
  2 large carrots, sliced ⅛″ thick
  ½ c. thinly sliced celery
Bake covered 40 minutes until vegetables are tender. Stir in:
  1 green pepper, chopped (optional)
  2 T. finely chopped parsley
Sprinkle on top:
  3 c. shredded cheddar cheese
Bake, uncovered, 5 minutes until cheese melts.

Catherine Kornweibel, Easton, Pa.

Honey Baked Lentils

Serves 8
350°
1 hr.

Combine in a dutch oven or saucepan:
  1 lb. (2⅓ c.) lentils
  1 small bay leaf
  5 c. water
  2 t. salt
Bring to a boil. Cover tightly and reduce heat. Simmer 30 minutes. Do not drain.
Discard bay leaf.
Preheat oven to 350°.
Combine separately and add to lentils:
  1 t. dry mustard
  ¼ t. powdered ginger
  1 T. soy sauce
  ½ c. chopped onions
  1 c. water
Cut in 1″ pieces:
  4 slices bacon
Stir most of the bacon into lentils and sprinkle remainder on top.
Pour over all:
  ⅓ c. honey
Cover tightly. Bake 1 hour. Uncover last 10 minutes to brown bacon.

Options:

Bacon may be partially precooked if desired. Substitute ½ lb. browned ground beef or sausage, or omit meat completely.

Delicious served with hot baked rice. Pass soy sauce.

Replace ginger, soy sauce, and 1 c. water in second group of ingredients with 2 T. sugar, 1 t. oregano, 2 c. tomato sauce. Omit honey.

Joann Smith, Goshen, Ind.
Larry Gingrich, Monmouth, Ore.

•••••••••••••••••••••••••
Skillet Beef
With Lentils

T·S

Serves 6-8

Bring 1 qt. water to boil in saucepan.
Add:
  1½ c. lentils, rinsed
Cook 20 minutes. Drain, reserving liquid.
In deep skillet, sauté:
  2 T. margarine or butter
  2 medium onions, chopped
  1 clove garlic, minced
Stir in:
  1 lb. ground beef
Brown well. Dissolve in 2⅓ c. reserved
liquid:
  2 beef bouillon cubes
Add liquid to meat mixture; cover and
simmer 10 minutes.
Stir in:
  reserved lentils
  2 T. long-grain rice
  1 t. sugar
  1 t. salt
  1 t. ground cumin
  ½ t. pepper
Bring to boil, reduce heat, cover, and
simmer 30 minutes, or until lentils and
rice are tender and liquid is absorbed
(add more liquid if necessary). Check
seasonings and stir in:
  1 T. cider vinegar
Top with parsley sprinkle.

Ellen Longacre, Bally, Pa.

•••••••••••••••••••••••••
Lentil-Barley
Stew

Serves 6

Sauté in large pan:
  ¼ c. margarine
  ¾ c. chopped celery
  ¾ c. chopped onion
Add:
  6 c. water
  ¾ c. lentils
Cook 20 minutes. Add:
  1 qt. tomatoes, canned
  ¾ c. barley or brown rice
  2 t. salt
  ¼ t. pepper
  ½ t. rosemary
  ½ t. garlic salt
Simmer 45-60 minutes. Add:
  ½ c. shredded carrots
Cook 5 minutes, and serve.

Option:

Brown ¾ lb. boneless pork shoulder,
diced, then add celery and onion and
sauté until golden, omitting margarine.
Proceed with recipe as given.

S. V. Martin, Duchess, Alta.
Frances Lehman, Goshen, Ind.

*Although it looks
like a production,
Kusherie is surprisingly easy
to make
and contains high-quality protein.
In Egypt plain yogurt
is served as a side dish.*

●●●●●●●●●●●●●●●●●●●●●●●●●
Kusherie
(Egyptian Rice and Lentils)

Serves 6-8

Rice and Lentils:
Heat in heavy saucepan or covered skillet:
 2 T. oil
Add:
 1¼ c. lentils
Brown lentils over medium heat 5 minutes, stirring often.
Add:
 3 c. boiling water or stock
 1 t. salt
 dash pepper
Cook uncovered 10 minutes over medium heat.
Stir in:
 1½ c. rice
 1 c. boiling water or stock
Bring to boil, reduce heat to low, cover, and simmer 25 minutes without stirring.

Sauce:
In a saucepan, heat together:
 ¾ c. tomato paste
 3 c. tomato juice, tomato sauce,
  or pureed tomatoes
 1 green pepper, chopped
 chopped celery leaves
 1 T. sugar
 ½ t. salt
 1 t. cumin
 ¼ t. cayenne pepper or
  crushed chilis to taste
Bring sauce to boiling, reduce heat, and simmer 20-30 minutes.

Browned Onions:
Heat in small skillet:
 2 T. oil
Sauté over medium heat until brown:
 3 onions, sliced
 4 cloves garlic, minced
To serve, put rice-lentil mixture on a platter. Pour tomato sauce over. Top with browned onions.

Option:
Omit the sauce (but not the browned onions) and serve with plain yogurt.

Carolyn Yoder, Cairo, Egypt

Bean, Soybean, and Lentil Discoveries ▶

When our sons were teenagers, I used this book and was told I was a soybean nut. We lived on a farm and raised soybeans, so I deep-fried some and sent them along in a care package to our son at Hesston College. He was happy for the package, but his friends wondered what kind of mom would send that food in his box! We appreciate More-with-Less *for keeping us aware of ways we can help equalize the space between the haves and the have nots.*
—Gladys Sprunger, Berne, Ind.

Use soybeans in a chili recipe and reduce ground beef to just enough for flavoring, using all soybeans or half kidney and half soybeans.
—Clara Brenneman, Waynesfield, Ohio
—Virginia Birky, Salem, Ohio

●●●●●●●●●●●●●●●●●●●●●●●●●
Savory Baked Soybeans

T·S

Serves 6
300°
3 hrs.

TS—Needs time not attention

Soak overnight or by quick method:
   2 c. dry soybeans
   2 qts. water
Cook slowly 3 hours, or until tender.
Preheat oven to 300°.
Combine with beans:
   2 c. tomato sauce
   1 large onion, chopped
   1 green pepper, chopped (optional)
   1 clove garlic, minced
   1 t. dry mustard
   2 t. chili powder (optional)
   2 t. salt
   ¼ t. pepper
   2 T. dark molasses
   3 strips bacon, diced, or ¼ lb. diced smoked sausage or ham
Bake in large uncovered casserole 3 hours, adding water if necessary. Stir occasionally.

Options:

Use electric slow cooker.

Bake at 375° for 40 minutes—won't have slow-baked flavor, but still a good dish.

Mabel Kreider, Lancaster, Pa.
Estelle Krabill, Hesston, Kan.
Kathryn Seem, Emmaus, Pa.

●●●●●●●●●●●●●●●●●●●●●●●●●
Soybean Loaf

Serves 6
350°
1 hr.

Preheat oven to 350°.
Combine in large bowl:
   2½ c. soybeans, cooked and mashed
   ½ c. cottage cheese
   ½ c. fresh or cooked tomatoes, drained and chopped
   2 eggs
   2 T. oil
   1½ t. salt
   ½ c. bread crumbs
Mix well. Form into loaf and place on greased baking pan.
Pour over:
   1 10-oz. can cream of mushroom soup OR equivalent sauce, see p. 118.
Bake 1 hour.

Options:

Add herbs to taste—thyme, oregano, chopped parsley.

Add finely chopped onions and celery.

Substitute 1 c. mashed potatoes (no milk added) for 1 c. soybeans.

Use a tomato or creole sauce to replace mushroom sauce.

Goshen College Dining Hall
Alternative Line, Goshen, Ind.
Genevieve Buckwalter, Osahigawa, Japan

Cook fresh green soybeans with sautéed onion, a little bacon, and canned tomatoes for a savory vegetable dish.
—Lois Weaver, Lancaster, Pa.

Cook fresh green soybeans in the pod about 10 minutes. Give each person a plate with a generous pat of butter and dash of soy sauce. Procedure for eating: Pick up a hot soybean pod with fingers, dunk in butter and soy sauce, shell inside the mouth, then discard pod. Share this delightful finger-lickin' experience with a few other people at a picnic table to celebrate a good summer of gardening.
—Dwight Platt, Newton, Kan.

Recommended to us by William Snyder, MCC Executive Secretary, who was served this casserole in Doreen Snyder's home.

●●●●●●●●●●●●●●●●●●●●●●●●

Soybean Hamburger Casserole

Serves 6
350°
45 min.

Preheat oven to 350°.
Sauté in large heavy skillet:
2 T. cooking oil
½ c. onion, chopped
1 c. celery, chopped
¼ c. green pepper, chopped (optional)
¼-½ lb. hamburger
When meat is brown, stir in:
1 t. salt
⅛ t. pepper
½ t. seasoned salt
2½ c. cooked soybeans
1¼ c. tomato soup, tomato sauce, or stewed tomatoes
1 beef bouillon cube, dissolved in
1 c. hot water
2 c. cooked rice
Heat and simmer a few minutes. Place in greased casserole and bake 45 minutes. Remove from oven and top with:
½ c. grated cheese or cheese slices
Return to oven a few minutes until cheese has melted.

Doreen Snyder, Waterloo, Ont.

●●●●●●●●●●●●●●●●●●●●●●●●

Soybean Casserole

Serves 6
350°
45 min.

Preheat oven to 350°.
Sauté in heavy saucepan about 5 minutes:
5 T. oil
2 c. chopped celery
¼ c. chopped onion
2 T. chopped green pepper
Add:
⅓ c. flour
Cook and stir until bubbly. Add:
2 c. milk
1 t. salt
Bring to boiling point, stirring constantly. Add:
2 c. mashed or chopped cooked soybeans
Pour mixture into greased casserole. Cover with:
1 c. whole wheat bread crumbs or ¼ c. wheat germ
Bake 45 minutes or until brown.

Options:

Use fresh green soybeans instead of dried cooked beans. Leave whole or mash as desired.

Add 1 c. grated cheese to white sauce.

Eleanor Kaufman, Newton, Kan.
Irene Claassen, Holmesville, Neb.

Soybean Pie

••••••••••••••••••••••••••••
Fresh Soybean-Cheese Casserole

Serves 4-6
375°
45 min.

Preheat oven to 375°.
Sauté in heavy saucepan:
  1 medium onion, diced
  ¼ c. margarine
When onion is soft, add:
  2 c. fresh green soybeans, precooked
  1 c. evaporated milk
  ⅛ t. Tabasco sauce
  1 t. salt
Cook, stirring, until heated through.
Remove from heat and stir in:
  3 eggs, slightly beaten
Pour half of mixture into a greased casserole. Layer with half of:
  1 c. shredded cheddar cheese
Repeat with rest of beans and top with remaining cheese.
Sprinkle over all:
  12 saltines, crushed
Bake 45 minutes.

Mary Lou Houser, Lancaster, Pa.

Serves 4
350°
25 min.

Soak overnight, or by quick method:
  1 c. soybeans
  3 c. water
Cook slowly 3-4 hours. Drain beans.
Heat in skillet:
  1 T. oil
Sauté about 5 minutes:
  1 medium-size onion, chopped
  1 clove garlic, minced
  drained soybeans
Add:
  1 c. tomato sauce
  2 t. chili powder
  2 t. Worcestershire sauce
  salt and pepper to taste
Simmer mixture while preparing cornmeal crust:
Preheat oven to 350°.
Combine:
  ½ c. cornmeal
  ½ c. flour
  1 t. salt
Cut in:
  1 T. shortening
Beat together:
  1 egg
  ¼ c. water
Add to cornmeal mixture. Press into 9" pie plate.
Fill pie with soybean mixture. Top with:
  ½ c. grated cheese
Bake about 25 minutes.

Option:

Soybeans may be ground or mashed if desired.

Susan Hurst, Bowmansville, Pa.

*Beans and Toast: Butter a slice
of toast and cut in small pieces.
Heat kidney beans, sauce and
all, salt to taste, pour over and
eat. (Complementary protein.)
—Karen Roth, Wellesly, Ont.*

*Combine cooked beans,
minced watercress, sweet
pickle relish, and mayonnaise.
Spread between slices of whole
wheat toast and add a lettuce
leaf. Or add chopped onions
and diced cheese, spread
mixture on hamburger buns,
and broil until bubbly.
(Complementary protein.)
—Verna Shelly, Brewton, Ala.*

*Serve as a side dish with rice,
or fill into tortilla shells
and top with shredded lettuce,
chopped tomatoes,
and more cheese.*

●●●●●●●●●●●●●●●●●●●●●●●●

Refried
Soybeans

T·S

Serves 4

Heat in skillet:
   ¼ c. oil
Add and sauté:
   1 onion, chopped
   1 clove garlic, minced
When onion is soft, add:
   2 c. cooked soybeans, mashed
   1-2 t. chili powder
   salt to taste
Cook in oil, stirring often; when oil is
absorbed, sprinkle with:
   ¾ c. shredded cheddar or
      Jack cheese
Let stand covered until cheese is melted.

Alice and Willard Roth, Elkhart, Ind.

●●●●●●●●●●●●●●●●●●●●●●●●

Soybean
Soufflé

Serves 6
325°
45 min.

Preheat oven to 325°.
Combine in heavy saucepan:
   3 c. warm soybean pulp (drained
      cooked soybeans forced
      through food mill)
   4 egg yolks
Stir together and heat gently, until
mixture is slightly thickened. Do not
allow to boil.
Stir in:
   2 T. grated onion
   2 T. chopped parsley
   ½ t. thyme
   ¼ t. marjoram
   1 t. salt
   dash pepper
Beat until stiff but not dry:
   4 egg whites
Fold egg whites into soybean mixture.
Pour into a well-buttered 1½ qt. baking
dish. Bake 45 minutes, or until set.

Option:

Soybeans, egg yolks, onion, and herbs
may be whirled together in blender to
puree beans. Stop blender several times
and push mixture into blades.

Lois Hess, Columbus, Ohio

Make your favorite spaghetti sauce using lentils in place of ground beef. Small and dark, they're a good stand-in for meat and give the sauce a nice texture. Sauté onions and garlic in oil, then add lentils, tomato ingredients, seasonings, and cook 30 to 45 minutes until lentils are tender. Lentils will absorb some liquid so make the sauce a little thinner than usual. Serve over cooked spaghetti. (Complementary protein.)
—Bonnie Krehbiel, Madison, Wis.

Combine fresh green soybeans with corn for a new version of succotash. (Complementary protein.)

I grind soybeans to make soy flour on our hand grinder and use it for 1/6 to 1/4 of the flour in bread recipes.
—Marianne Miller, Topeka, Kan.

Not intended as a main dish— rather as a tangy sweet-sour accompaniment to an otherwise bland meal.

●●●●●●●●●●●●●●●●●●●●●●●●●
Sweet and Sour Soybeans

T·S

Serves 4

Combine in a bowl and set aside:
**1 T. cornstarch
¼ c. firmly packed brown sugar
¼ t. ground ginger
2 T. soy sauce
¼ c. vinegar
½ c. pineapple juice, drained
from chunks (see below)**
Heat in large skillet:
2 T. oil
Add:
**1 c. green pepper, cut in 1″ pieces
1 c. onion, cut in wedges
½ c. carrots, cut in ¼″ slices
1 clove garlic, mashed**
Stir-fry for about 3 minutes until tender-crisp.
Add:
**2 c. cooked soybeans, drained
1 c. pineapple chunks, drained
½ c. tomatoes, cut in 1″ cubes,
or 2 T. ketchup**
Fry a few minutes, then add sauce ingredients.
Cook and stir until mixture boils, and all ingredients are coated with sauce (about 2 minutes). Serve over hot rice. Garnish with chopped scallions if available.

*Dorothy Liechty, Berne, Ind.
David and Joanne Janzen, Newton, Kan.*

●●●●●●●●●●●●●●●●●●●●●●●●●
Marinated Soybeans

T·S

Serves 6-8

Combine in a bowl:
**¼ c. salad oil
⅓ c. cider vinegar
⅔ c. honey
salt and pepper to taste**
Add:
**3 c. cooked soybeans, drained
¼ t. basil
½ t. garlic salt
½ t. oregano
½ c. chopped dill pickles (optional)
½ c. chopped celery
½ c. chopped onion or scallions
½ c. chopped parsley
½ c. chopped green pepper
(optional)
1 clove garlic, minced**
Mix well and chill several hours before serving.

*Mary Lou Houser, Lancaster, Pa.
Anna Mary Brubacher, St. Jacobs, Ont.*

When the men combined our soybeans, I took large cans out and filled them for our eating. Lots of farm families don't know you can do this. I soak them, cook 3 to 4 hours until tender, and flavor with a little butter and milk. The boys eat them with ketchup and mustard.
—Rhoda King, Cochranville, Pa.

Add a small handful of lentils when cooking plain steamed rice–adds protein, texture, and flavor interest. Both cook in the same time. (Complementary protein.)
—Karin Hackman, Hatfield, Pa.

Musozya: Soak overnight in large kettle equal parts hominy, dried beans, and raw peanuts. Bring to boil, salt, and simmer 2 hours. Serve with fresh vegetables for a satisfying African meal. (Complementary protein.)
—Mary Olive Lady, Choma, Zambia

●●●●●●●●●●●●●●●●●●●●●●●●●
Soybean Sandwich Spread

Makes 3 c.

Combine in large mixing bowl:
- **1½ c. cooked, mashed soybeans**
- **½ c. sunflower seeds**
- **½ c. pureed tomatoes or tomato sauce**
- **½ medium onion, finely chopped**
- **1½ T. pickle relish**
- **2 T. ketchup**
- **½ c. wheat germ**
- **1 t. salt**
- **⅛ t. pepper**
- **¼ t. thyme**
- **¼ c. finely chopped celery (optional)**

Mix well. Will keep in refrigerator several days. When ready to make sandwiches, add a little mayonnaise to desired consistency and spread a thick layer on whole wheat bread.

Lois Barrett, Wichita, Kan.

●●●●●●●●●●●●●●●●●●●●●●●●●
Basic Soybean Spread or Dip

Makes 2½ c.

Sauté in small skillet:
- **2 T. margarine**
- **1 onion, finely chopped**
- **1 clove garlic, minced**
- **2 T. parsley, chopped**

Combine in a bowl:
- **2 c. cooked soybeans, ground**
- **sautéed onion mixture**
- **1 t. dried oregano**
- **1 T. soy sauce**
- **⅓ c. mayonnaise**
- **salt and pepper**

Mix well. Add further ingredients to taste:
1. **Bacon bits, chopped green pepper, chili powder.**
2. **Celery, mustard, and chopped hard-cooked eggs.**
3. **Pickle relish and ground ham or tuna.**
4. **Ground carrots and peanuts.**
5. **Grated cheese, sunflower seeds, and/or nuts.**

Spread on whole wheat bread or toast and add leaf lettuce or bean sprouts if desired. Or use as dip with crackers or raw vegetable sticks.

Lois Hess, Columbus, Ohio
LaVonne Platt, Newton, Kan.

Soybean curd (tofu) is actually cheese made from soybean milk. A common food in Asia, it is available in North America only in Chinese groceries or health food stores. Contributor says, "This is a very flexible dish; use more meat and less bean curd at first and then gradually reverse it."

●●●●●●●●●●●●●●●●●●●●●●●●●●
Soybean Curd Sauté

Serves 4

Sauté in skillet:
  1 T. oil
  ¼ c. chopped onion
  **2 fresh red chili peppers,
    finely chopped (optional)**
Add:
  **⅔ lb. fresh pork, sliced in small
    bite-sized pieces**
Stir-fry until meat is browned.
Add:
  **4 cakes (4x4") bean curd,
    cut into bite-size pieces**
Stir-fry briefly.
Add:
  1 c. tomato sauce
  ½ c. tomato paste
  2 T. soy sauce
  2 T. vinegar
  **1-2 c. water (as needed for
    gravy-like consistency)**
  **2 c. frozen or lightly precooked
    green beans**
Simmer 15 minutes. Serve over hot steamed rice.

Jean Hershey, Pleiku, Vietnam

Gather Up the Fragments

1.
Mash leftover beans and heat according to Refried Beans recipe, p. 101. Serve with rice or tortillas. (Complementary protein.)
2.
Spread Refried Beans on toast, sprinkle with cheese, and broil until bubbly. (Complementary protein.)
3.
Spoon hot leftover beans over slices of bread and top with a strip of bacon. Loved by our children as "bean bread." (Complementary protein.)
—*William Snyder, Akron, Pa.*
4.
Combine leftover baked beans, cooked rice, and drained crushed pineapple plus ketchup, maple syrup, and dry mustard for flavoring. Heat together and serve. (Complementary protein.)
—*Emma Brubaker, Harrisonburg, Va.*
5.
Add curry powder, turmeric, and cumin to leftover split pea or lentil soup, simmer until somewhat thickened, and serve over rice. (Complementary protein.)
6.
Freeze leftover bean dishes in casseroles for convenient reheating later. Bake and carry to a potluck.
7.
For a quick spicy soup, add tomato juice and chili powder to any leftover beans or lentils.
8.
Add sautéed onions and green pepper and pineapple chunks to leftover baked beans. Bake until bubbly throughout.
—*Jocele Meyer, Brooklyn, Ohio*
9.
Slice leftover soybean loaf and fry slowly in margarine until brown and crisp. Serve with ketchup.
10.
Mash leftover beans and add to meat loaf.

At home, we kept talking about how we needed to simplify our lives. Our Sunday school class told us our understanding of the Sermon on the Mount and other New Testament teachings was out of step with the rest of the church. In October 1986, my husband came across Doris Longacre's Living More with Less in a local library. We were delighted to see Scripture references in the book that supported simple living, and to find that other Christians understood the Bible as we did.

In November 1987, we began a two-year Mennonite Central Committee assignment with our three youngest children. At MCC orientation, we discovered More-with-Less Cookbook. The assignment led to nearly 12 years with MCC, and More-with-Less was my only cookbook. It is worn, but opening it is like reviving memories of people and places far from Butler, Ohio. And to think it all started with a small book in the stacks of a public library....
—Patricia Wells Burdette, Butler, Ohio

Microwave cooking makes it easier to prepare foods that normally scorch or stick. Softening or melting fats is an easy task. Meats may be partially cooked in the microwave before grilling, to increase food safety. Microwave cooking enhances color, flavor, and nutrients in vegetables.

The microwave is a valuable tool, and we need to use it wisely. Use care in choosing microwave containers. Increasing evidence suggests that in the presence of fat and heat, some plastic chemicals can migrate into food. Some safety suggestions for microwave cookery:

* Use microwaveable glass or ceramic dishes with lids.

* Use only those plastics labeled for microwave use and reuse. (Plastic trays with microwavable entrees are intended for single use.)

* Be cautious using colored paper towels or those made with recycled fibers. Waxed paper is fine.

* Avoid using Styrofoam food trays and cling wraps.

—Mary Beth Lind, Harman, W.Va.

main dishes and casseroles

Early American cookbooks devote few if any pages to main dishes and casseroles. Surely Grandmother often built meals around a kettle of beans or a hearty stew. German cooking has its homey "ein-topf" or one-pot meal. But the hamburger-noodle-mushroom soup mixtures so familiar today are newcomers on North American tables.

Main dishes and casseroles have a reputation for economy, but thrifty cooks, beware! If your so-called economy casserole uses a pound of meat for five servings plus a can of soup, sour cream, mushrooms, frozen vegetables, frozen onion rings, and grated cheese to top it off, you might fare more cheaply and nutritiously with meat loaf, baked potatoes, and buttered carrots. Nor are all casseroles a panacea for saving time. If three or more processes are to be done at stove-top before the creation goes to the oven, you may be putting in as much time as the average meat-potatoes-vegetable meal requires. Certainly you'll have as many pots to wash. Grandmother's beans or stew might have served you better.

Casserole recipes must be evaluated for what they involve. For example, some people reject old-fashioned gravy because it's too caloric but use commercial sour cream freely. Herb-seasoned stuffing mix is the latest fashionable casserole-topper, while in many homes stale heels mold in a corner of the breadbox.

Check again that casserole recipe everyone raved about at the last potluck. Does it call for several costly convenience foods? Is it loaded with empty calories or is there real nutritive value in the ingredients? Does it duplicate expensive animal protein by using meat, cottage cheese, eggs, and grated cheese all in the same dish?

But let's not throw out all the casseroles. Their biggest bonus is advance cooking. You put a casserole in the oven, clean up the kitchen, and relax until mealtime with nothing more on your mind than making a salad and setting the table. Further this advantage by preparing an extra portion for the freezer, or have the dish again later in the week. A different menu every evening is as unnecessary as a different dress every morning.

Soups and Sauces
Contemporary casserole recipes all seem to call for a can of soup. Will future cooks be born, live, and die without knowing how to stir up a smooth white sauce? Will there finally be only three flavors identified at a carry-in dinner— cream of mushroom, cream of chicken, and cream of celery?

Buy a wire whisk and break the mushroom soup cycle. Save money and cans by returning to the basic five-minute white sauce. Variations are as infinite as the herbs and seasonings on your cupboard shelf and the cheeses, broths, and vegetables in your refrigerator. Try the white sauce mix recipe on p. 118.

●●●●●●●●●●●●●●●●●●●●●●●●
Basic White Sauce

	Thin	Medium	Medium-Thick	Thick

Melt in heavy saucepan:

| **margarine** | 1 T. | 2 T. | 3 T. | 4 T. |

Blend in, cooking and stirring until bubbly:

| **flour** | 1 T. | 2 T. | 3 T. | 4 T. |
| **salt** | ¼ t. | ¼ t. | ¼ t. | ¼ t. |

Using wire whisk to prevent lumps, stir in:

milk, stock,
  or combination

| | 1 c. | 1 c. | 1 c. | 1 c. |

Cook just until smooth and thickened. Makes slightly over 1 cup. Medium-thick compares to undiluted condensed soups, and makes approximately the same amount contained in one 10-oz. can.

Options:

Cheese Sauce: Add ½ c. grated nippy cheese and ¼ t. dry mustard.

Tomato Sauce: Use tomato juice as liquid; add dash each of garlic salt, onion salt, basil, and oregano.

Mushroom Sauce: Sauté ¼ c. chopped mushrooms and 1 T. finely chopped onion in margarine before adding flour.

Celery Sauce: Sauté ½ c. chopped celery and 1 T. finely chopped onion in margarine before adding flour.

Chicken Sauce: Use chicken broth or bouillon as half the liquid. Add ¼ t. poultry seasoning or sage, and diced cooked chicken if available.

Vary flavor with the following:
 curry powder
 garlic, onion, or celery salt
 grated nutmeg
 lemon juice
 Worcestershire sauce
 chili powder
 chopped or blended
  vegetables
 chopped parsley
 chopped chives
 chopped hard-cooked eggs

●●●●●●●●●●●●●●●●●●●●●●●●
White Sauce Mix   T·S

In a bowl, stir together:
 1½ c. nonfat dry milk solids
 ¾ c. flour
 1 t. salt
Cut in until mix resembles small peas:
 ½ c. margarine
Store in refrigerator.
To make white sauce:

	Thin	Medium	Thick

Combine in saucepan:

| **white sauce mix** | ⅓ c. | ½ c. | ⅔ c. |
| **cold water** | 1 c. | 1 c. | 1 c. |

Cook and stir with wire whisk over medium heat until smooth and thickened. Vary as indicated for Basic White Sauce. Sauté onions, celery, or mushrooms in small amount margarine before adding white sauce mix and liquid. Makes slightly over 1 cup, or about 10 ounces.

Joanne Lehman, Apple Creek, Ohio
Roberta Kreider, Osceola, Ind.

*Double or triple recipe
for freezing.*

●●●●●●●●●●●●●●●●●●●●●●●●●
Basic Spaghetti
or Pizza Sauce

Makes about 1 qt.

Sauté in heavy saucepan until tender:
  2 T. oil
  2 cloves garlic, minced
  ½ green pepper, chopped
  1 onion, chopped
Add and sauté until brown:
  ¼-½ lb. ground beef (optional)
Add:
  2 c. tomato sauce
  ¾ c. tomato paste
  1 t. Worcestershire sauce
  1 c. stock, beef, broth, or bouillon
  **¼ t. *each* oregano, basil, thyme,
    and cumin**
  salt and pepper to taste
Simmer over low heat for 1 hour.
Use for spaghetti, lasagne, or pizza
sauce.

Options:
Add 1 c. cooked lentils instead of meat.
See p. 105.

If available cheaply, add sautéed fresh
mushrooms to sauce just before serving.

Linda Albert, Visalia, Calif.

> *Basic Spaghetti or Pizza
> Sauce – I put some sauce
> on a flour tortilla. That
> makes a thin crust pizza.
> On top of the sauce, I put
> one or two different
> cheeses and fresh mush-
> rooms, then put under the
> broiler to melt the cheese.
> —Esther Gamber,
> Hesston, Kan.*

●●●●●●●●●●●●●●●●●●●●●●●●●
Lasagne
Roll-Ups

Serves 7-8
350°
1 hr.

Cook and drain according to package
directions:
  10 lasagne noodles
Filling
Steam until limp:
  **2 bunches spinach, Swiss chard,
    or turnip greens, finely
    chopped**
Add and mix well:
  2 T. grated Parmesan cheese
  1 c. cottage cheese
  ½ t. nutmeg
Topping
Prepare:
  1 c. onions, sliced
  **2 c. grated Muenster or
    Jack cheese**
Sauce
Combine in a bowl:
  4 c. tomato sauce
  2 cloves garlic, minced or crushed
  ½ t. basil
  ½ t. oregano
  ½ t. marjoram
Spread noodles with filling, roll up, and
stand on end in greased 9x13" baking
pan. Sprinkle cheese and onions on top.
Pour sauce over all. Bake at 350° for 1
hour.

Anne Rogers, East Petersburg, Pa.

119

Main Dish Discoveries ▶

*Make a pie with leftover cooked
spaghetti and meat sauce as
follows: Mix spaghetti with a
little melted margarine,
Parmesan cheese, and a
beaten egg. Form into "crust" in
greased pie plate. Spread
cottage cheese or grated
cheese on crust. Pour in thick
spaghetti sauce. Sprinkle with
additional shredded cheese
and bake at 350° for 20-30
minutes.
—Marcia Beachy, DeKalb, Ill.*

●●●●●●●●●●●●●●●●●●●●●●●●

Spaghetti With
Zucchini Sauce

T·S

Serves 4-6

Sauté in large skillet:
  ¼ c. oil
  1 medium onion, sliced
Add:
  **2 medium zucchini, sliced
  (about 6 cups)**
  3 c. diced fresh tomatoes
  ½ t. salt
  1 bay leaf
  ¼ t. pepper
  ¼ t. basil leaves
  ¼ t. oregano leaves
Simmer covered for 15 minutes; uncover,
simmer 10 minutes. Discard bay leaf.
Cook according to package directions:
  8 oz. spaghetti
Serve spaghetti topped with zucchini
sauce and grated Parmesan cheese.

Eleanor Hiebert, Elkins Park, Pa.

●●●●●●●●●●●●●●●●●●●●●●●●

Spaghetti
And Cheese

Serves 4

Preheat oven to 350°.
Cook and drain as directed on package:
  8 oz. spaghetti or noodles
Place in a greased casserole dish.
Sprinkle with:
  ¾ c. grated cheese
Combine and beat together
  ½ c. milk
  1 egg, beaten
  ½ t. dry mustard
  ½ t. salt
  dash pepper
Pour over spaghetti and cheese.
Bake 25-30 minutes. Cover first 15
minutes, then uncover to brown. Garnish
with parsley. Serve with broiled tomato
halves or fresh sliced tomatoes sprinkled
with herbs.

Bobbie Wilcox, LaVeta, Colo.

Cook separately: rice, fresh or frozen peas, and cheese sauce. When cooked, combine rice and peas and serve with sauce. I remember this dish from the cafeteria at Eastern Mennonite College, but never could find it in a cookbook. That might be because it's so easy!
—Dolores Bauman, Lancaster, Pa.

Lasagne is popular but expensive since it calls for ground beef plus several cheeses. Lasagne's unique flavor is the blend of cheeses and herbs; omit ground beef from the tomato sauce and you still have a delicious high-protein Italian specialty.
—Bonnie Zook, Leola, Pa.
—Danita Laskowski, Goshen, Ind.

A program on world hunger motivated contributor to invent her own economical skillet dinner.

●●●●●●●●●●●●●●●●●●●●●●●●
Hamburger Helper— Home-Style

T·S

Serves 4

Brown in a skillet:
¾ lb. ground beef
1 t. salt
½ t. pepper
Add:
1 T. finely chopped onion
1 stalk chopped celery
¼ c. frozen or canned peas
⅔ c. fresh or canned tomatoes, chopped
While beef is browning, cook in salted water:
1 c. crinkly noodles
Drain noodles and spread over meat mixture. Sprinkle over all:
½-¾ c. shredded cheese
OR ⅓ c. grated Parmesan cheese
Simmer uncovered 15 minutes to blend flavors. Serve from skillet.

Marie L. Berg, Hillsboro, Kan.

●●●●●●●●●●●●●●●●●●●●●●●●
Spanish Noodle Skillet

T·S

Serves 3-4

Cut into 1" pieces and fry until crisp:
2 slices bacon (optional)
Set aside. Sauté in bacon drippings:
½ onion, chopped
½ green pepper, chopped
½ lb. ground beef
Pour off any excess fat. Add:
1 t. salt
dash pepper
¼ t. oregano
2 c. pureed or stewed tomatoes
¾ c. water
Cover and simmer 10 minutes. Bring to a boil and add, a few at a time:
1½ c. egg noodles
Reduce heat, cover, and simmer 10 more minutes. Stir occasionally. Top with reserved bacon and serve.

Options:

Omit bacon. Sauté vegetables with ground beef, adding a little oil if beef is dry.

Stir in ¾ c. shredded cheese with noodles. Top with ¼ c. additional cheese just before serving.

Bonnie Sharp, Lancaster, Pa.
Martha Charles, Indiana, Pa.

121

Combine cooked green beans and diced cooked chicken and bake as an au gratin dish (see p. 220) topped with buttered bread cubes and grated cheese.
—Bonnie Sharp,
*   Lancaster, Pa.*

Brown a little ground beef with onions, then add a variety of chopped fresh or frozen vegetables and tomatoes or tomato juice for liquid. Season with salt, pepper and herbs as desired. Cook just until vegetables are tender. See Garden Stew, p. 46.
—Helen Alderfer, Scottdale, Pa.
—Marcia Beachy, DeKalb, Ill.

Contributor says, "At our house this has been added to and subtracted from all down the list, but it helps with guests and we find they like it."

●●●●●●●●●●●●●●●●●●●●●●●●●
Meat and Noodle Skillet

T·S

Serves 6

In large skillet, brown lightly:
  ½ lb. ground beef
  ½ lb. pork sausage
Add:
  1 onion, sliced
  1 clove garlic, minced
  1½ t. salt
  ⅛ t. pepper
  1 t. crushed dried basil leaves
  ¾ c. tomato paste
  3 c. water
  1 can mushroom stems and pieces (undrained)
Stir well. Add:
  2 c. wide noodles
Bring to a boil; reduce heat. Cover and simmer 15 minutes or until noodles are tender, stirring gently two or three times with a fork. Before serving, stir in:
  3 T. crumbled blue cheese
  ¼ c. chopped walnuts
Serve from skillet.

Ruth Ressler, Sterling, Ohio

●●●●●●●●●●●●●●●●●●●●●●●●●
Macaroni Tomato Pie

T·S

Serves 4
350°
20 min.

Cook and drain according to package directions:
  1 c. macaroni
Grease a 9″ pie plate and line sides and bottom with macaroni. Pour into macaroni shell:
  2 c. stewed tomatoes
Season with:
  ¼ t. pepper
  dash of oregano
  1 t. salt
Sprinkle over top:
  ¼ c. shredded cheddar cheese
  ¼ c. buttered bread crumbs
Bake at 350° for 20 minutes or until crumbs are brown.

Option:
Brown and season ¼ lb. ground beef. Add to pie just before shredded cheese.

Mary Ella Weaver, Lititz, Pa.

Contains 15 grams
high-quality protein
per serving,
and is relatively low
in calories.

●●●●●●●●●●●●●●●●●●●●●●●●●
Cottage Cheese
Casserole

●●●●●●●●●●●●●●●●●●●●●●●●●
Tangy
Tuna-Mac

Serves 8
350°
40 min.

Serves 3-4
350°
30 min.

Sauté in a large skillet:
   2 T. margarine
   ½ c. chopped mushrooms
   ½ c. chopped onion
   ½ c. chopped celery
   1 clove garlic, minced
Stir in:
   ¼ t. marjoram, crushed
   4½ c. water
   ¾ c. tomato paste
   4 c. elbow macaroni
   2 t. salt
   1 t. sugar
Simmer until macaroni is tender, about
25 minutes.
Have ready:
   ¼ c. parsley, chopped
   2 c. cottage cheese
   ⅓ c. grated Parmesan cheese
Put half of the macaroni mixture in a
greased 2 qt. casserole dish. Top with 1
c. cottage cheese and ½ of Parmesan
cheese and parsley. Repeat layers.
Bake at 350° for 40 minutes.

   Selma Johnson, North Newton, Kan.

Cook and drain according to package
directions:
   1 c. elbow macaroni
Add and stir to combine:
   1 7-oz. can tuna, drained
   1 c. tomato sauce
   ½ c. cottage cheese
   ¼ c. yogurt or sour cream
   1 small onion, minced
   ½ t. salt
Pour into greased casserole.
Toss together:
   ¼ c. bread crumbs
   1 T. melted margarine
Sprinkle around border of casserole.
Bake at 350° for 30 minutes.

   Rosemary Moyer, North Newton, Kan.

123

•••••••••••••••••••••••••
Chicken-Cheese
Casserole

Serves 6
350°
45 min.

Cook and drain according to package
directions:
¾ lb. noodles
Sauté in a skillet:
5 T. margarine
1 small onion, chopped
3 T. chopped green pepper
½ c. sliced mushrooms (optional)
Add:
5 T. flour
Cook and stir until bubbly.
Add:
1½ c. chicken broth
1½ c. milk
½ t. dry mustard
salt and pepper to taste
Cook, stirring until thickened.
Combine:
white sauce
cooked noodles
3 c. cooked chicken or turkey
Put in greased casserole dish and top
with:
⅔ c. shredded cheese
buttered bread crumbs
Bake at 350° for 45 minutes.

Mona Sauder, Wauseon, Ohio
Marjorie Geissinger, Zionsville, Pa.

•••••••••••••••••••••••••
Anna Lou's
Broccoli-Tuna Casserole

Serves 6
350°
20-25 min.

Cook in boiling salted water until barely
tender:
2 lb. broccoli, cut in spears
Combine in saucepan:
1 9-oz. can tuna
1 10-oz. can mushroom soup or
equivalent sauce (see p. 118)
½ c. milk
½ c. grated cheese
Heat until almost boiling. Place layer of
cooked broccoli in shallow greased
casserole. Cover with layer of tuna
mixture. Repeat.
Sprinkle with:
⅓ c. grated cheese
Bake at 350° for 20-25 minutes.

Rosemary Moyer, North Newton, Kan.

In the short term, there is probably nothing anyone can do to forestall mass starvation in some rice-dependent areas. But the very least we can do is to take a symbolic stand and cook rice with reverence, taking care that each precious grain swells to its fullest but stays firm and separate from the rest. Perhaps we could even inaugurate our own rice ritual: a moment of silence for those who are not getting enough.
—Raymond Sokolov

How to cook perfect rice? So many North Americans who knew rice only as pudding during childhood ask this question.

The food industry tried to answer it by giving us minute rice. I have never understood the advantages of that food, which to me is expensive, takes more last-minute fiddling than ordinary rice, and is supremely tasteless. It takes exactly 25 minutes to prepare ordinary rice, and seldom can I manage to fix anything to serve with it and complete other meal preparations in less time than that. And during the last 20 minutes ordinary rice requires no attention at all—in fact, tampering with it is forbidden!

●●●●●●●●●●●●●●●●●●●●●●●●●
Basic Steamed Rice

Serves 6

Combine in heavy saucepan:
1½ c. rice
½ t. salt
Just enough water to rise above rice level to a depth of one inch; Asians measure using index finger from tip to middle of first knuckle.
Over high heat, bring to a full rolling boil. Stir through with a fork, loosening grains at the bottom of the pan. Reduce heat to simmer, cover with tight-fitting lid, and *do not stir or peek* for 20 minutes. (If electric burner stays too hot and causes rice to boil over, pull saucepan partially off the burner for first 5 minutes of cooking time.) After 20 minutes, turn off heat and let rice stand covered until ready to serve. Flake gently while transferring to serving dish. Yields a tender but slightly chewy dry rice with no gluey moisture at the bottom.

Options:
Measure 1⅔ c. water to 1 c. rice. Use cooking method above, but reduce water when cooking large quantities.
Use brown rice but increase cooking time to 45 minutes.
Omit salt if serving rice with salty or spicy side dishes.

Baked Rice
Preheat oven to 350°.
Combine in covered casserole:
2 c. hot water
1 c. rice
½ t. salt
1 T. margarine
Cover and bake 45 minutes or longer for large quantities.

Reheating Rice
Place rice in heavy saucepan and sprinkle with about 1 T. water per cup of cooked rice. Heat, covered, over very low heat 20-30 minutes. Stir lightly several times with a fork.

*Contributor says,
"Our children like this
with gravy made from broth
bought from the MCC meat
canner. Serve with a
tossed salad and/or vegetables
and homemade whole wheat
bread."*

*The sharper the cheese,
the tastier the loaf.*

●●●●●●●●●●●●●●●●●●●●●●●●●
Savory Rice

●●●●●●●●●●●●●●●●●●●●●●●●●
Savory Rice Loaf

T·S

Serves 6-8

Serves 6
350°
1 hr.

Combine in large heavy saucepan:
- **4 c. rice**
- **1 t. salt**
- **1 T. dry parsley and/or dried
  celery leaves**
- **2 t. whole thyme or 1 t. powdered
  thyme**
- **¼ t. coarse ground black pepper**
- **2 T. finely chopped onion**
- **2 T. finely chopped green pepper**
- **3 beef bouillon cubes, dissolved in
  7 c. water**

Bring to a boil; cover and reduce heat to
simmer. Cook 20-25 minutes without
stirring or peeking.

Dorothy Slagell, Hydro, Okla.

Grease loaf pan (9x5x3"). Line bottom
with waxed paper.
Toss together lightly in mixing bowl:
- **3 eggs, slightly beaten**
- **1½ c. cooked rice**
- **1½ c. grated cheese**
- **½ c. fine dry bread crumbs**
- **¼ c. chopped celery**
- **2 T. chopped onion**
- **2 T. chopped parsley**
- **2 T. chopped green pepper**
- **¾ t. salt**
- **1 c. milk**
- **¼ c. melted margarine**

Pour into loaf pan. Place pan in baking
dish which contains 1" hot water. Bake at
350° for 1 hour or until loaf is set in center.
Loosen loaf around edge with spatula;
turn out onto platter. Remove paper.
Serve with tomato or mushroom sauce
(see p. 118).

Lois Hess, Columbus, Ohio

To obtain coconut milk, whirl in blender chunks from one fresh coconut with coconut liquid and 2 c. hot water. Let cool to lukewarm. Strain and press out liquid for this recipe and use remaining grated coconut in baking.

Contributor says, "Liza, who came to us in 1966 from France through MCC's Exchange Visitor Program, introduced this family favorite."

●●●●●●●●●●●●●●●●●●●●●●●●●
Coconut Rice

●●●●●●●●●●●●●●●●●●●●●●●●●
Liza's Tomato Sauce, Rice and Eggs

T·S

Serves 4

Serves 6-8

Heat in heavy saucepan:
2 T. oil or margarine
Add:
½ c. chopped onion
2-3 whole cloves
2-3 cinnamon sticks
2-3 bay leaves
Fry until onions are lightly browned.
Add:
¼ t. ground saffron or tumeric
¼ t. salt
Fry a few seconds.
Add:
1 c. rice
2 c. coconut milk (see above)
Bring to a boil, reduce heat, cover, and cook 30 minutes. If desired, whole spices may be removed before serving and a few raisins, cashews, or walnuts added.

Doris Devadoss, Calcutta, India

Prepare:
hot cooked rice for 6-8 people
(see p. 125)
1 hard-boiled egg per person
Tomato sauce
Sauté in heavy saucepan:
3 T. margarine
1 onion, finely chopped
Blend in:
4 T. flour
Add:
4 c. tomato juice
1½ t. salt
2 t. sugar
chopped parsley
1 beef bouillon cube
dash pepper
Cook, stirring until thickened. Simmer 5 minutes. Serve over hot rice and garnish with sliced eggs.

Gladys Rutt, New Holland, Pa.

••••••••••••••••••••••••••
Broccoli Rice

Serves 4
350°
45 min.

Cook ½ c. rice (see p. 125), or have ready 1½-2 c. leftover rice.
Sauté in small skillet:
¼ c. margarine
1 onion, chopped
Add:
2 c. chopped broccoli, cooked and drained
⅔ c. grated cheese
½ c. milk
cooked rice
Bake in covered casserole at 350° for 45 minutes.

Becky Harder, Mt. Lake, Minn.

••••••••••••••••••••••••••
Brown Rice
Skillet

Serves 4-6

Heat in skillet to boiling:
3 c. water
1 T. instant chicken bouillon or 2 cubes
Stir in:
1 c. brown rice
Cover skillet, reduce heat to low, and simmer 45 minutes.
Hard-boil:
4-6 eggs
Sauté in small skillet:
2 T. margarine
½ c. sliced mushrooms
2-4 scallions, sliced
When rice is done, stir in:
hard-boiled eggs, chopped
1 c. water chestnuts, drained and sliced (optional)
sautéed vegetables
Heat through. Serve with soy sauce.

Bonnie Krehbiel, Madison, Wis.

••••••••••••••••••••••••••
Rice Guiso

T·S

Serves 3-4

Heat in heavy saucepan or covered skillet:
1 T. oil or trimmed meat fats
Add:
¼-½ lb. pork or beef, cut in small cubes
Brown well. Add:
1 onion, chopped
1 c. rice
1 t. salt
⅛ t. pepper
Sauté briefly. Add:
1¾ c. water
2 T. tomato paste (optional)
Cover, lower heat, and cook very slowly about 30 minutes or until rice is tender.

Myrtle Unruh, Filadelphia, Paraguay

*Meat and cottage cheese
together yield
a high-protein dish.*

●●●●●●●●●●●●●●●●●●●●●●●●
Pizza Rice
Casserole

Serves 6
325°
30 min.

Cook:
   **⅔ c. rice (see p. 125) or have
      ready 2 c. leftover rice**
Brown in large skillet:
   **¾ lb. ground beef
   1 onion, chopped**
Add:
   **2 c. tomato sauce
   ¼ t. garlic salt
   1 t. sugar
   1 t. salt
   dash pepper
   ¼ t. oregano
   1 t. parsley flakes**
Cover and simmer 15 minutes.
Combine:
   **1½ c. cottage cheese
   cooked rice**
Put ⅓ of rice mixture in a buttered 2 qt.
casserole. Top with ⅓ of meat-tomato
sauce. Continue to alternate layers,
ending with tomato sauce. Sprinkle with:
   ½ c. shredded cheese
Bake at 325° for 30 minutes, or until hot
and bubbly.

   Myrna Schmidt, Lakewood, Colo.

●●●●●●●●●●●●●●●●●●●●●●●●
Rice with Cheese
And Tomatoes

T·S

Serves 6

Cook:
   **1 c. rice (see p. 125) or have
      ready 3 c. leftover cooked rice**
Sauté:
   **3 T. fat or oil
   1 medium onion, chopped
   3 stalks celery, chopped
   1 green pepper, chopped**
Add:
   **2 c. cooked tomatoes
   cooked rice
   2 c. shredded cheese
   1 t. salt
   dash pepper**
Cover and simmer until cheese is
melted.

   Susan Holland, Hillsboro, Kan.

Use oven method for cooking rice when oven is already hot for other purposes. See p.125.

●●●●●●●●●●●●●●●●●●●●●●●●●
Vietnam
Fried Rice

T·S

Serves 4

Cook 1 c. rice (see p. 125) or have ready 3 c. leftover rice.
Heat in large skillet:
4 T. cooking oil
Add:
¼-½ lb. any cooked or raw meat, cut into thin strips
3 cloves garlic, minced
1 large onion, chopped coarsely
1 t. salt
1 t. pepper
1 t. sugar
1 T. soy sauce
Stir-fry until meat is tender and hot, about 1-2 minutes.
Add:
3 c. cooked rice
Stir-fry 5 minutes. Add:
1 c. leftover or frozen vegetables, such as peas, green beans, or carrots
Stir well into rice-meat mixture.
Just before serving, add:
2 eggs, beaten
Over medium heat, stir carefully through rice until eggs are cooked. Serve piping hot with salad of leaf lettuce, cucumbers, fresh mint and parsley.

Pat Hostetter Martin, Quang Ngai, Vietnam

●●●●●●●●●●●●●●●●●●●●●●●●●
Kay's
Japanese Rice

Serves 5-6

Cook according to directions on p. 125:
1½ c. rice
Prepare:
2-3 carrots, cut in long thin strips
2 onions, sliced very thin and separated into rings
½ lb. raw or cooked meat or seafood, cut in thin strips
When rice is nearly done, heat a skillet and add:
2 T. margarine or oil
meat, if raw
prepared vegetables
salt and pepper
Stir-fry quickly just until vegetables are crisp-tender and meat is cooked. If using cooked meat, add at the last minute just to heat through. Put mixture in serving dish. Keep warm.
To hot skillet, add:
1 T. margarine or oil
Beat together:
2 eggs
1 T. milk
½ t. salt
Pour egg mixture in skillet and allow to spread out. When partially firm, turn like a large pancake and cook briefly on second side. Remove from skillet, roll up, and cut into thin strips. Add egg strips and vegetable mixture to hot rice. Stir gently to combine and return to serving dish. Serve with soy sauce.

Option:
Add 1-2 c. bean sprouts with vegetables.

Marjorie Stucky, Murdock, Kan.

•••••••••••••••••••••••••
Nasi Goreng
(Indonesian Fried Rice)

Serves 10-12

Cook 4 c. rice without salt, according to directions on p. 125.
Heat in large skillet:
6 T. oil
Sauté until golden brown:
2 large onions, chopped
Add and sauté for 1 minute:
½ t. black or white pepper
1 t. paprika
1 t. garlic powder
1 t. ground coriander
1 t. cumin
1 t. tumeric
2 t. laos (Java galingale root)
½ t. sereh powder (lemon grass or citronella)
2½ t. salt
Tabasco, dried chili pepper flakes or fresh hot pepper to taste
While preparing the above, sauté in separate skillet:
1 lb. ground beef, cubed raw chicken, cubed raw pork or small shrimp
Add cooked rice and sautéed meat to spice mixture.
Sauté over low heat, stirring occasionally, to blend flavors (about 10 minutes).
Beat with fork in small bowl:
4 eggs
½ t. salt
dash pepper
Using skillet in which meat was fried, fry eggs in several thin layers, turning each layer once and rolling each as you take it from the skillet. Cut each roll into strips ⅛" wide.
Serve fried rice on a large platter. Put strips of egg on top and garnish with radishes, cucumber wedges, and parsley.

Option:

Sereh powder and laos can be omitted but the dish loses some of its Spice Island authenticity. Check availability in Chinese grocery stores.

Jean Miller, Akron, Pa.

It's just an easy hamburger curry— so quick and so good.

•••••••••••••••••••••••••
Pakistani Kima

T·S

Serves 5-6

Sauté in skillet:
3 T. butter or margarine
1 c. chopped onion
1 clove garlic, minced
Add:
1 lb. ground beef
Brown well. Stir in:
1 T. curry powder
1½ t. salt
dash pepper
dash *each* cinnamon, ginger, and tumeric
2 c. cooked tomatoes
2 potatoes, diced
2 c. frozen peas or green beans
Cover and simmer 25 minutes. Serve with rice.

Ann Naylor, Ames, Iowa

My mom discovered the recipe for Pakistani Kima was like one she'd been making, but with tastier seasonings. The one thing she liked better about her original recipe was that it called for garnishing with coconut before serving. She made the new, improved kima a few times, and I quickly decided it was one of my favorites. Our two teenage sons have grown up on Pakistani Kima, with plenty of coconut!
—Cynthia Linscheid, Newton, Kan.

●●●●●●●●●●●●●●●●●●●●●●●●
Pork Sausage
Casserole

Serves 6-8
350°
1 hr.

Brown in a skillet:
1 lb. bulk pork sausage
1 onion, chopped
Drain excess fat.
Add:
2 c. raw long-grain rice
1 c. chopped celery
½ c. chopped onion
½ t. poultry seasoning
chopped parsley
3½ c. boiling chicken broth
salt and pepper
Bake at 350° for 1 hour.

Elsie Epp, Marion, S.D.
Mary Lou Houser, Lancaster, Pa.

●●●●●●●●●●●●●●●●●●●●●●●●
Hamburger
Casserole

Serves 6
325°
2 hrs.

Combine in casserole with cover:
1 lb. hamburger
1 c. uncooked rice
1 c. diced carrots
1 c. onions, finely chopped
2 10-oz. cans tomato soup
OR equivalent sauce
(see p. 118)
1 t. salt
pepper to taste
2 c. boiling water
Cover and bake at 325° for 2 hours.

Options:

Substitute 1 qt. tomato juice for tomato soup and water.

Sprinkle with ⅓ c. grated cheese 10 minutes before removing from oven.

Verna Wagler, Baden, Ont.
Fran Sauder, Lancaster, Pa.

●●●●●●●●●●●●●●●●●●●●●●●●
Mandarin
Rice Bake

Serves 6
350°
1 hr., 15 min.

Place in greased 2 qt. casserole:
¾ c. raw rice
1½ c. boiling water
½ t. salt
Add over rice:
1½-2 c. cubed ham or other
leftover meat
1½ c. chopped celery
1 c. chopped onion
½ c. chopped green pepper
¼ c. chopped pimiento (optional)
Stir in:
1 can condensed cream of chicken
or mushroom soup OR
equivalent sauce, (see p. 118)
2 T. soy sauce
Cover; bake at 350° for 1 hour and 15 minutes.

Evelyn Bauer, Goshen, Ind.

*You'll stand over the stove,
but not for long;
the result has no comparison
in texture and flavor
with what comes from a can!*

●●●●●●●●●●●●●●●●●●●●●●●●●
Quick
Chop Suey

T·S

Serves 4-6

Cook rice according to directions on p. 125.
Sauté together:
**½ lb. ground beef
1 onion, sliced
¾ c. celery, sliced**
Add:
**2 c. canned (drain) or 3 c. fresh
bean sprouts
1 c. beef or chicken broth
½ c. sliced mushrooms (optional)**
Cover skillet. Simmer 5 minutes.
Combine:
**1 T. cornstarch
2 T. soy sauce**
Add to beef mixture, stirring constantly.
Cook until thickened and smooth.
Serve over hot rice.

Option:

Diced leftover beef, pork, or chicken may replace ground beef. Sauté onion and celery in 2 T. oil. Add meat during last 10 minutes just to heat through.

Helen Hiebert, Winkler, Man.

●●●●●●●●●●●●●●●●●●●●●●●●●
Chow Mein

Serves 6-8

Cook rice according to method on p. 125.
Prepare and have ready:
**1 lb. pork, beef, chicken, or
shrimp, cut in thin slices
3 c. celery, sliced diagonally
2 c. onions, sliced lengthwise
¾ c. mushrooms, fresh or canned
(drain)
3 c. fresh bean sprouts**
Combine in a small bowl and set aside:
**1 T. fresh ginger, chopped
OR ¼ t. powdered ginger
1 t. sugar
3 T. cornstarch
5 T. soy sauce
¾ c. soup stock or reconstituted
bouillon**
Heat in a large skillet:
1 T. oil
Add meat and stir-fry just until done. Remove from heat. In another skillet, stir-fry in 1 T. oil each vegetable just until slightly cooked. Add each vegetable to meat skillet after stir-frying. Just before serving, reheat meat mixture and add sauce. Cook just until sauce thickens and clears. Serve hot with rice.

LaVonne Platt, Newton, Kan.

Serves 7-8

Vegetarian Indian Meal

John Nyce, registrar at Goshen College, Goshen, Indiana, learned to cook Indian food while teaching at Woodstock School, Mussoorie, India. Here he presents menu and recipes for a complete Indian meal for 7-8 people. Although no meat is included, proteins in the split peas, rice, and cottage cheese or yogurt complement each other for an adequate supply.

Menu
Garden Vegetable Curry*
Curried Split Peas (Dhal)*
Long-Grain Rice
Tomato Chutney*
Small Curd Cottage Cheese or Yogurt
Fresh Fruit Tray
Hindustani Tea*
*Recipes included

The meal requires little last-minute fuss. Curried Split Peas, Tomato Chutney, and Hindustani Tea can be prepared 3-4 hours in advance. Garden Vegetable Curry should be started 1¼ hours before serving time, but needs minimal attention the last half hour. Thirty minutes before serving time cook 3-4 c. long-grain rice, according to directions on p. 125. One pound of cottage cheese or yogurt served as a side dish adds protein and provides a pleasant contrast to the hot spicy dhal and curry. Another curry (see p. 171) could be substituted for the one given here. Food purchase and preparation could easily be divided among several households and then put together for a feast with minimal time input for anyone.

Heat in 3-4 qt. saucepan on medium heat:
3 T. vegetable oil
Add and fry lightly for 4-5 minutes (do not brown):
2 medium onions, finely chopped
2 cloves minced garlic
Add:
2 T. curry powder
1 t. tumeric
1 t. whole cumin seed
Continue frying 3-4 minutes. Add:
1 c. chopped tomatoes
Cook briefly until a thick sauce results. Add:
1 medium head cabbage, chopped
3 medium carrots, diced
4-5 small potatoes, unpeeled and cut into ¾" cubes
3 c. green beans
Stir until all are covered by sauce. Add:
1 t. salt
Reduce heat and simmer 30-45 minutes. Add water any time sauce is below ⅔ depth on vegetables. 15 minutes before serving time, add:
1 T. lemon juice
additional salt if needed

Options:

Use canned or frozen green beans, but add 15 minutes before serving time.

Substitute 1 c. tomato sauce for fresh tomatoes.

Substitute 2 chopped zucchini squash and 3 chopped green tomatoes for cabbage and carrots. Experiment with adding peas, lima beans, eggplant, and cauliflower.

Top curry with halved hard-cooked eggs.

John Nyce, Goshen, Ind.
Lon and Kathryn Sherer, Goshen, Ind.

Tomato
Chutney

Combine in a bowl:
**2 c. chopped fresh or canned
    tomatoes
1 medium onion, chopped
3 T. lemon juice
2 T. vinegar
1 T. sugar
pinch of salt
pepper**
Garnish with fresh coriander, if
available. Serve as a side dish with rice
and curry.

John Nyce, Goshen, Ind.

Curried
Split Peas (Dhal)

Serves 7-8

Soak 3-4 hours or by quick method:
**1 c. dried split peas or mung beans
2½ c. water**
Add:
**1 t. tumeric
½ t. cayenne red pepper
1 t. salt**
Bring to boil, reduce heat, cover
partially, and simmer 20-30 minutes.
Peas should be tender and beginning to
disintegrate. Add additional water if
needed to maintain thick gravy
consistency.
Sauté in small frying pan:
**3 T. margarine or butter
1 large onion, thinly sliced
    lengthwise
1 t. whole cumin seed
10 whole cloves
5 whole black peppercorns**
Fry until onions are well browned (10-12
minutes). Add onion mixture to cooked
peas and set aside until near mealtime.
Reheat before serving. Serve as a sauce
to be placed over rice.

*John Nyce, Goshen, Ind.
Shirley Yoder, Pati, Java
Ruth Eitzen, Barto, Pa.*

Hindustani Tea
(Chai)

Serves 7-8

Heat together in a 3-4 qt. saucepan:
**6 c. water
7 t. loose tea**
Boil 10 minutes. Add:
6 c. milk
Heat to near boiling. Add to taste:
10-15 t. sugar
Tastes best when prepared 2 or more
hours in advance and set aside. Reheat
during meal and serve with fresh fruit for
dessert.

John Nyce, Goshen, Ind.

••••••••••••••••••••••••
Easy Curry

T·S

Serves 3-4

Brown in small amount of fat:
   **¼-½ lb. chicken or other meat
   (raw or cooked), finely cut**
Add:
   2-2½ c. water
Chop and add in order according to
cooking time needed:
   2 medium carrots
   3 stalks celery
   1 green pepper
   ½ medium onion
Add:
   1 t. salt
   ⅛ t. pepper
   1 T. curry powder
Blend together and add:
   1 c. tomato sauce
   ⅓ c. milk
   2 T. cornstarch
Simmer 45 minutes or until vegetables
are tender and sauce is thick and glossy.
Stir frequently. Serve over rice, noodles,
or biscuits.

Marie J. Frantz, North Newton, Kan.

••••••••••••••••••••••••
Cracked Wheat
or Bulgar Pilaf

T·S

Serves 6

Sauté in a skillet:
   1 T. oil
   1 small onion, chopped
   1 c. cracked wheat or bulgar
Stir over medium heat until onion is
transparent and wheat is glazed.
Add:
   ½ t. salt
   2 c. broth or stock
Reduce heat to low, cover and cook 25
minutes or until liquid is absorbed.

Option:

¼ lb. sliced mushrooms may be added
when sautéing onion; increase oil to 3 T.

Grace Whitehead, Kokomo, Ind.

••••••••••••••••••••••••
Beef-Barley
Skillet

T·S

Serves 6

Sauté in skillet:
   ¾ lb. ground beef
   ½ c. chopped onion
   ¼ c. chopped celery
   ¼ c. chopped green pepper
Drain off excess fat. Stir in:
   1¼ t. salt
   ⅛ t. pepper
   ½ t. marjoram
   1 t. sugar
   1 t. Worcestershire sauce
   ½ c. chili sauce
   2 c. canned tomatoes, broken up
   1½ c. water
   ¾ c. quick-cooking or pearl barley
Bring to a boil. Reduce heat to simmer,
cover, and cook about 35 minutes for
quick-cooking barley or 1 hour for pearl
barley.

Marjorie Stucky, Murdock, Kan.
Marjorie Ruth, Akron, Pa.

136

●●●●●●●●●●●●●●●●●●●●●●●●

Campfire
Pocket Stew

_____

Charcoal Fire
30 min.

Prepare a good bed of coals.
For each person to be served, wash and
slice thinly:
  1 potato
  1 carrot
  1 onion
  ¼ green pepper
  small handful fresh green beans
Add:
  several ½″ chunks of cheese
  salt and pepper
Wrap in:
  2 large cabbage leaves
Wrap all in aluminum foil, shiny side in,
and cook on the coals, 15 minutes on
each side.

Karen Kreider, Goshen, Ind.

●●●●●●●●●●●●●●●●●●●●●●●●

Six-Layer
Dish

_____

Serves 4
300°
2½-3 hrs.

Layer in order given in a 2 qt. greased
casserole, seasoning each layer with
salt and pepper:
  2 medium potatoes, sliced
  2 medium carrots, sliced
  ⅓ c. uncooked rice
  2 small onions, sliced
  1 lb. ground beef
  1 qt. canned tomatoes
Sprinkle over:
  1 T. brown sugar
Bake at 300° for 2½-3 hours.

Options:

Just before ground beef add 1 c. cooked
kidney beans, drained.

Substitute browned pork sausage for
ground beef.

Bonnie Zook, Leola, Pa.
Martha Buckwalter, Lancaster, Pa.
Fern Lehman, Kidron, Ohio

Garden
Supper Casserole

Serves 4
350°
30-35 min.

Mix:
2 c. cubed soft bread
½ c. shredded sharp cheese
2 T. margarine, melted
Spread half the mixture in greased 1 qt. casserole and top with:
1 c. cooked peas or
other vegetable
Sauté until tender:
3 T. margarine
2 T. chopped onion
Blend in:
3 T. flour
1 t. salt
⅛ t. pepper
Cook over low heat, stirring until mixture is bubbly.
Stir in:
1½ c. milk
Cook, stirring constantly, until thickened.
Stir in:
1 c. cooked beef, chicken or pork,
diced
Pour over peas. Arrange on top:
1 large tomato, sliced (optional)
Sprinkle with remaining bread mixture. Bake uncovered at 350° for 30-35 minutes.

Judy Classen, Akron, Pa.

Meat, Cheese, and Potato
Scallop

Serves 4-6
300°
1 hr., 15 min.

Make a cheese sauce:
2 T. butter or margarine
2 T. flour
¼ t. salt
1½ c. milk
¾ c. cheese
Combine in greased casserole:
1 medium onion, sliced
4 medium potatoes, sliced
2½ c. canned luncheon meat or
leftover ham, diced
Pour cheese sauce over meat and potatoes mixture. Cover and bake at 300° for 1 hour. Remove cover and bake 15 minutes longer.

Betty Lou Huber, Atmore, Ala.

El Burgos

Serves 8
350°
30 min.

Cook in small amount of water just until tender:
5 large potatoes, thinly sliced
Drain.
Sauté in skillet:
1 lb. ground beef
2 green peppers, chopped
1 large onion, diced
Combine in a bowl:
2 c. shredded cheddar cheese
1 t. salt
1 T. brown sugar
2 c. tomato sauce
Alternate layers of meat mixture and potatoes in greased 2 qt. casserole. Pour cheese-tomato mixture over all. Bake at 350° for 30 minutes.

Mary Ella Weaver, Lititz, Pa.

●●●●●●●●●●●●●●●●●●●●●●●●●●
Easy Moussaka (Greece)

T·S

Serves 6
350°
40 min.

Preheat oven to broil.
Cut into ½" slices:
1 large eggplant, unpared
Place slices on cookie sheet, brush with melted margarine, sprinkle with salt and pepper, and broil 5 minutes, or until golden. Turn slices, brush and season again and brown second side. Set oven at 350° when broiling is completed.
Meanwhile, fry together:
1 lb. ground beef
1 onion, chopped
1 clove garlic, minced
salt, pepper, and dash nutmeg
Add:
2 c. tomato sauce
⅓ c. tomato paste
½ t. oregano
1 T. chopped parsley
1 T. chopped mint (optional)
In 9x9" baking dish, layer half of eggplant slices and half of meat mixture; repeat with remaining ingredients.
Sprinkle with:
½-1 c. grated cheese
Bake 40 minutes.

Option:
Omit meat. Sauté onion and garlic in 2 T. oil and proceed with tomato sauce.
Combine separately:
1 egg, beaten
2 T. Parmesan cheese
1 c. cottage cheese
Place half of tomato sauce in casserole, add half of eggplant, all of cottage cheese mixture, remaining eggplant, remaining tomato sauce. Sprinkle layers and top with additional Parmesan. Omit last ½-1 c. grated cheese. Bake as directed.

Louise Claassen, Elkhart, Ind.
Elizabeth Yoder, Bluffton, Ohio

●●●●●●●●●●●●●●●●●●●●●●●●●●
Yaksoba (Japan)

T·S

Serves 4

Cook and drain according to package directions:
1 c. thin noodles
(Leftover noodles or spaghetti may be used.)
Slice as indicated and have ready:
½-¾ lb. round steak, sliced very thin
2 medium onions, cut in thin wedges
2 medium carrots, sliced very thin
¼ head cabbage, sliced in strips
2 c. fresh or 1 c. canned bean sprouts, drained
Heat in skillet:
2 T. oil
Brown meat. Add vegetables in order as given above, stir-frying each a few minutes, and adding salt and pepper with each addition. Add noodles last and cook just long enough to heat through. Vegetables should be crisp-tender. May be served on rice or alone. Pass soy sauce.

Betsey Zook, Leola, Pa.

Sausage-Sweet Potato Bake

Serves 4-6
375°
50-60 min.

Brown in skillet:
1 lb. bulk sausage
Break up large pieces and drain off excess fat.
Arrange in 2 qt. casserole:
2 medium raw sweet potatoes, peeled and sliced
3 medium apples, peeled and sliced
browned sausage
Combine and pour over:
2 T. sugar
1 T. flour
¼ t. ground cinnamon
¼ t. salt
½ c. water
Cover and bake at 375° for 50-60 minutes, or until potatoes and apples are tender.

Option:
Use cooked or canned sweet potatoes.

Esther Martin, Lancaster, Pa.

New Potatoes And Peas With Ham

Serves 4-6

Scrub and cook in boiling salted water until partially tender:
8-12 small whole new potatoes
Add:
3-4 green onions, chopped
2 c. fresh peas
Continue cooking until vegetables are tender. Drain, reserving liquid.
Make a white sauce:
2 T. margarine
2 T. flour
1½ c. vegetable liquid and milk
salt and pepper
Pour sauce over vegetables. Add:
1-2 c. cubed cooked ham
½ c. grated cheese
Heat through and serve.

Eunice Gerbrandt, Drake, Sask.

*In Newfoundland
Boiled Dinner is followed
by bread or muffins with jam
and tea for dessert.*

● ●

Newfoundland Boiled Dinner

Serves 4-6

Bring to boil in soup kettle:
  **1-2 lb. ham pieces, ham hocks
  or ham bone
  1 medium onion, cut in chunks
  water to cover**
Simmer until meat is tender. Remove
meat from bone and return to broth.
Taste broth and add salt if needed.
Cut vegetables in large pieces and add
in this order:
  **3-4 carrots
  3-4 yellow turnips
  3-4 potatoes
  4-6 small whole onions (optional)
  1 head cabbage, cut in large
  wedges**
Cover and cook until vegetables are
tender.
Serve from pot onto large plates.

*Ruth Detweiler, Akron, Pa.
Helen Coon, Quakertown, Pa.*

● ●

Turkey Apple Casserole

Serves 5-6
400°
20 min.

Sauté in skillet until soft, but not brown:
  **2 T. margarine
  3 T. minced onion**
Stir in:
  **½ t. garlic powder
  2 t. curry powder
  ¼ c. firmly packed brown sugar
  1¼ c. turkey broth
  2 c. pineapple juice**
Heat almost to boiling. Add:
  **2 c. soft bread crumbs
  3 c. diced unpeeled red apples
  3 c. cubed cooked turkey**
Remove from heat and turn into
casserole. Sprinkle with:
  ¼ c. buttered bread crumbs
Bake at 400° for 20 minutes.

Miriam B. Buckwalter, Salunga, Pa.

When the Mennonite
Voluntary Service unit at
Wiltwyck School for Boys,
north of New York City,
closed in 1975, I was trans-
ferred to Cincinnati, Ohio. To
treat my new housemates, I
searched More-with-Less
Cookbook for a Vareniky
recipe (p. 144). Several years
later, I got to know Susan
Duerksen from Killarney,
Man., who had submitted the
recipe. I married her daughter, Lynda, and have had the
good fortune of eating
vareniky at her table.
Voluntary Service enriched
my life in several ways: I
learned to know about
vareniky; I met Lynda; and
later I even got to know the
woman whose recipe helped
me make my first batch of
vareniky!
—David Brubacher,
Vineland, Ont.

141

●●●●●●●●●●●●●●●●●●●●●●●●●●
Cheese Pizza

*For a special flavor, add 1 t. dry basil
and 2 t. sesame seed to pizza dough
dry ingredients when mixing crust.
—Jocele Meyer, Fresno, Ohio*

●●●●●●●●●●●●●●●●●●●●●●●●
Colorado Pie

Serves 4-6
400°
25 min.

Prepare pastry for 2-crust pie, using 1 t.
onion salt in pastry if desired. Line 9″ pie
pan with half the pastry. Roll out top
crust.
Brown in skillet:
**1 lb. ground beef
½ c. chopped onion**
Stir in:
**1 T. sugar
¼ t. pepper
2 c. cooked green beans, drained
½ t. salt
⅛ t. oregano
1 10-oz. can tomato soup
OR equivalent sauce (see p. 118)**
Pour into pastry-lined pan, add top crust
and cut slits in it.
Bake at 400° for 25 minutes.

MCC Dining Hall, Akron, Pa.

*My husband, John, and I
lived in Kawimbe village,
Zambia, and cooked over a
charcoal brazier. I learned to
make Cheese Pizza in a skillet over the brazier. I put a flat
lid over the skillet and
heaped additional coals on
top to bake it. More-with-Less
has been a reminder that discipleship extends into all of
life, including the kitchen.
—Holly Blosser Yoder,
Wellman, Iowa*

Serves 4-6
450°
20-25 min.

Crust:
Combine in large bowl:
**1 c. warm water
1 pkg. yeast**
When dissolved, add:
**1 T. sugar
1½ t. salt
2 T. vegetable oil
1¼ c. flour**
Beat until smooth. Add:
**2 c. additional flour, or enough
to make stiff dough
(may use part whole wheat)**
Knead until elastic, about 5 minutes.
Place in greased bowl and let rise until
double, about 45 minutes. Form 2 balls.
Pat and stretch to fill 2 greased pizza
pans. Let rise 10 minutes.

Sauce:
Combine in saucepan:
**1 small onion, chopped
2½ c. canned tomatoes, OR 2 c.
tomato sauce, OR 3 c. fresh
tomatoes, chopped
1 bay leaf
1 t. salt
1 t. oregano
½ t. basil
dash pepper
1 clove garlic, minced**
Bring to boil, crushing whole tomatoes.
Cover and cook slowly for 30 minutes or
until sauce is slightly thick. Discard bay
leaf. Pour over crust.
Sprinkle on:
**2 T. chopped onion
1 finely chopped green pepper
2 t. oregano
1 t. basil
salt, pepper and garlic salt, to taste**
Arrange on top:
**½-1 lb. sliced cheese—mozzarella,
cheddar, and/or Swiss**
Bake at 450° for 20-25 minutes, or until
crust is golden brown.

*Kamala Platt, Newton, Kan.
Jocele Meyer, Brooklyn, Ohio*

Mini-Pizzas

T·S

Serves 6

Split and arrange on baking sheet:
6 English muffins
Combine in bowl:
**2 c. tomato sauce
1 t. salt
½ t. pepper
½ t. oregano
½ t. Italian seasoning
¼ t. garlic salt**
Coat muffins with tomato mixture.
Sprinkle on:
2 c. (½ lb.) grated cheese
Broil until cheese is bubbly. Remove and serve hot.

Options:

Add browned hamburger, sausage, chopped salami, green pepper, onion, or mushrooms.
Egg Salad Pizzas:
**4 hard-cooked eggs, chopped
½ c. shredded cheese
⅓ c. tomato paste
¼ c. mayonnaise or salad dressing
2 T. finely chopped onion
to taste: salt, pepper, basil,
    oregano, garlic powder**
Spread on 4 split muffins. Broil until heated through.

Joan Manolis, Upland, Calif.

When I was cook at Sojourners Daycare Center in Washington, D.C., I worked my way through More-with-Less Cookbook. *Ed Spivey said my Soybean Salad was the best "tuna salad" he ever ate. The kids loved the little pizzas made out of English muffins. I was fortunate to meet Doris Longacre shortly before she died. What a gift to the world!*
—*Laura Winnen, Portland, Ore.*

Ten-Minute All-In-One Meal

T·S

Preheat broiler.
For each person to be served, place side by side on a cookie sheet:
2 slices whole wheat bread
Layer on each slice of bread:
**1 slice from a large tomato
1 thin slice from a large onion
1 slice favorite hard cheese**
Broil until cheese melts and edges of bread are crusty.
Eat with fork or fingers.

Flo Harnish, Akron, Pa.

Serve with clear soup and green salad.

Tuna or Chicken Turnovers

Serves 5-6
400°
15 min.

Preheat oven to 400°.
Combine:
**1 c. tuna or diced cooked chicken
1 c. shredded cheese
¼ c. chopped celery
1 t. chives OR 1 t. onion,
    finely chopped
mayonnaise to moisten
salt and pepper**
Prepare:
1 recipe biscuit dough (see p. 72)
Roll dough ⅛-¼" thick and cut into four-inch rounds or squares. Place about 2½ T. filling on each; fold over and seal. Brush tops with melted margarine. Bake 15 minutes.

Ruth Heatwole, Charlottesville, Va.

•••••••••••••••••••••••
Bierrocks

"Vareniky schmaikt goat!"
say the Low Germans.
Try this satisfying meatless
dish from Russian Mennonite
tradition. Some cooks brown
vareniky briefly
in butter after taking
them from the boiling water.

Serves 10

350°

20-30 min.

•••••••••••••••••••••••
Vareniky

Prepare as for roll dough: (see page 64)
2 c. warm water
2 pkg. dry yeast
¼ c. sugar
1½ t. salt
1 egg
¼ c. margarine
6-6½ c. flour
Chill dough several hours.

Serves 6

Meat mixture:
Brown in skillet:
1½ lb. beef
½ c. onion
Add:
3 c. cabbage, finely cut
1½ t. salt
½ t. pepper
dash Tabasco sauce
Cover skillet and continue cooking over
low heat, stirring occasionally, until
cabbage is tender. Do not add liquid.
Cool slightly.
Roll out dough into thin sheets. Cut in 5"
squares. Place 2 T. meat mixture on each
square, pinch edges together, and place
pinched side down on greased cookie
sheet. Let rise 15 minutes. Bake at 350°
for 20-30 minutes.

Combine in a bowl:
1 lb. *dry curd* cottage cheese
1½ T. onions, finely chopped
(optional)
½ t. salt
3 egg yolks
Mix well with hands until cottage cheese
is in fine curds. Set aside.
Combine in separate bowl:
3 egg whites, lightly beaten
1 c. milk
2 t. salt
3-3½ c. flour
Mix together, adding flour as necessary
until dough is stiff enough to roll out. Turn
onto floured board. Roll out half of dough
⅛" thick, and cut into squares or circles
5" in diameter. Use large cookie cutter or
invert small bowl on dough and cut
around with knife. Place 1 rounded
tablespoon cottage cheese mixture on
each circle and fold over to form half
circle; pinch edges firmly. Repeat with
remaining dough and dough scraps.
In saucepan, heat 4-6 c. water to boiling.
Add 1 t. salt. Drop vareniky into boiling
water, several at a time. Cook five
minutes. Remove with slotted spoon and
drain. Keep hot.
Serve with *cream gravy.*
Sauté in a skillet:
2 T. margarine
1 small onion, finely chopped
(optional)
Add:
1 c. cream
salt and pepper to taste
Heat slowly, but do not boil.

Options:

Pizza-flavored filling: To browned beef
and onion, add:
¾ c. tomato paste
¼ c. water
2 t. sugar
1 t. oregano
1 t. salt
⅛ t. pepper
Cool slightly. Place several tablespoons
meat mixture on half of each square.
Sprinkle on each:
1-2 t. grated cheese
Bake as directed above.
Reduce amount of filling, use any roll
recipe, and make just enough for one
meal as a treat on baking day.

MCC Dining Hall, Akron, Pa.
Louise Claassen, Elkhart, Ind.

Susan Duerksen, Killarney, Man.
Ruby J. Wiebe, Hillsboro, Kan.

144

A variety of economical but delicious Mexican-American foods can be made from basic ingredients such as tortillas, chili sauce, and refried beans. Tortillas are usually cheap if available fresh or frozen; packaged dry varieties are expensive. See p. 84 for flour tortilla recipe, or look for masa harina flour mix for home preparation. Refried beans are available canned, but home-cooked beans are easy to make and far more economical. See p. 101.

Great for eating on the run, camping, or with small children.

●●●●●●●●●●●●●●●●●●●●●●●●●●
Burritos

Spoon refried beans or scrambled eggs onto heated tortilla.
Top with grated cheese.
Roll up, tucking in ends to keep filling from falling out.

Marianne Miller, Topeka, Kan.
Carol Friesen, Reedley, Calif.

●●●●●●●●●●●●●●●●●●●●●●●●
Quesadillas

Serves 4-6

Have ready:
1 can (7 oz.) California green chilies, seeds and pith removed
1 lb. Jack cheese, cut in sticks, 1x4x½″
12 corn or flour tortillas
margarine, lard or salad oil for frying (optional)
Place about half a chili and a thick stick of Jack cheese in the center of each tortilla. Fold tortilla over cheese and pin shut with a small toothpick.
Fry in shallow hot fat until crisp, turning occasionally. Drain on paper towels. Or heat and soften the tortilla on each side on a medium-hot ungreased griddle or frying pan, until cheese has melted. Chilies may be omitted.

Carol Friesen, Reedley, Calif.

●●●●●●●●●●●●●●●●●●●●●●●●●
Chili-Tomato Sauce

Makes about 3 cups

Sauté in heavy saucepan:
2 T. salad oil
1 medium-sized onion, minced
When onion is just yellow, not brown, add:
3½ c. tomato puree or sauce
2 cloves garlic, minced or mashed
1-2 T. chili powder
¼ t. dried oregano
1 t. salt
Cover and simmer at least 30 minutes, stirring frequently. Put through medium strainer. Use for tacos or enchiladas.

Carol Friesen, Reedley, Calif.

145

When using tortillas, in this and any recipe, it's not necessary to dip them in oil. If you need to soften them, heat for a few seconds in the microwave.
—Jocele Meyer, Fresno, Ohio

I bought my first More-with-Less Cookbook in college. I finally had to replace it when both covers fell off, soon after my third child was born. By then, most of the pages were stained and rumpled. Our two sons often request Navajo Tacos for their special birthday meal.
—Becky Horst, Goshen, Ind.

Enchiladas

Serves 6
350°
15-20 min.

Brown in skillet:
¾ lb. ground beef
1 medium onion, chopped
Stir in:
2 c. refried beans (see p. 101)
1 t. salt
⅛ t. garlic powder or 1 clove garlic, mashed
Heat until bubbly, cover, and keep warm.
Prepare:
12 tortillas
Dip, one at a time, in shallow hot oil to soften; drain quickly.
Heat chili-tomato sauce (see p. 145); pour about half into an ungreased, shallow 3 qt. baking dish. Place about ⅓ c. beef-bean filling on each tortilla, and roll to enclose filling. Place, flap side down, in the sauce in the bottom of the baking dish. Pour remaining sauce evenly over tortillas; cover with:
2 c. (½ lb.) shredded cheddar cheese
Bake uncovered at 350° for 15-20 minutes, or until thoroughly heated.

Options:

Bake immediately or assemble and refrigerate several hours or overnight.
Roll enchiladas as described above, or spread filling over tortillas and stack evenly. Cut stack in wedges to serve.
Omit meat. Sprinkle a little shredded cheese over refried beans before rolling up each tortilla.

Carol Friesen, Reedley, Calif.

Tacos

To prepare taco shells:
Fold warm tortillas in half and use as is with fillings below, or fry each tortilla briefly in shallow hot fat (about ¼"), turning once and then folding in half before tortilla becomes too crisp. Drain folded shells on absorbent paper and keep warm until ready to serve.
Fillings:
refried beans
browned ground beef
chopped cooked chicken
chopped onions, tomatoes,
radishes, avocado
finely shredded lettuce
grated cheese
hot chilies
chili-tomato sauce
Serve basket of taco shells with fillings in individual bowls, inviting guests to make their own. Refried beans, chopped onions, shredded lettuce, grated cheese, and chili-tomato sauce would provide enough variety for a delicious meal.

Anne Rogers, East Petersburg, Pa.
Sam, Lois, Jennie, and Sara Miller, Harrisburg, Pa.

Navajo Tacos

Spread **Navajo Fry Bread** (p. 83) with **Refried Beans** (p. 101)
Top with **shredded cheese** and broil until cheese melts.
Sprinkle generously with **shredded lettuce.**

Shirley Kauffman Sager, Arriba, Colo.

Gather Up the Fragments

●●●●●●●●●●●●●●●●●●●●●●●●
Empanadas
(Mexican Turnovers)

Serves 6-8
400°
15-20 min.

Sift together in bowl:
2 c. flour
2 t. baking powder
1 t. salt
Cut in:
½ c. shortening
Add:
⅓ c. cold milk
Stir into a ball, handling like pie crust.
Roll out thin and cut in 4″ rounds or
squares. Place a spoonful of filling on
one half of a round. Fold over, moisten
edges, and press firmly so they seal.
Deep fry, or bake 15-20 minutes at 400°.

Fillings:
— ground cooked chicken or beef,
   sautéed with onion, raisins, and
   blanched slivered almonds. Add ½
   t. cumin, 1 t. chili powder.
   1 beaten egg.
— refried beans, grated cheese, and
   chopped chili.
— tuna or salmon with mushrooms,
   chopped chives, and chili.
— for sweet turnovers, add 2 T. sugar
   to dry ingredients while making
   dough. Fill with 3 oz. cream cheese
   blended with 3 T. strawberry or
   apricot preserves, or simply with
   shredded cheese. Sprinkle fried
   empanadas with confectioners
   sugar.

Lois Deckert, North Newton, Kan.
Myrtle Unruh, Filadelfia, Paraguay
Geraldine Lehman Mumaw,
*   Santa Cruz, Bolivia*

1.
"Meat in spaghetti sauce doesn't have to
be only ground beef," says my
sister-in-law of Italian ancestry. She
accumulates odds and ends of any kind
of cooked meat, chops it finely, and uses
it in her sauce, which is outstanding.
—*Helen Peifer, Akron, Pa.*
2.
When reheating leftover casseroles,
make and pour over a little more of the
sauce used, whether tomato, cream
sauce, etc. Add a fresh sprinkling of
cheese or bread crumbs and bake.
Reheated look and dry texture is gone.
3.
Freeze leftover main dishes in small
casseroles to heat for one or two
persons—handy when parents are going
out but must feed children first, or for
spouse at home alone.
4.
Whirl small amounts of leftover main
dishes in the blender and incorporate
resulting sauce into another soup or
main dish. For example, leftover
macaroni and cheese goes into a cheese
sauce.
5.
Use dollops of leftover mashed potatoes
with cheese sprinkle to top a variety of
casseroles, not just Shepherd's Pie.
6.
Use leftover rice for fried rice (see
recipes, p. 130, 131). Stir-fry leftover
cooked noodles or spaghetti in the same
way with scallions or onions, bits of
meat, vegetables, and eggs. Eat with
soy sauce.
7.
Some recipes using leftover rice:
Creamed Chicken over
   Confetti Rice Squares, p. 187
Savory Rice Loaf, p. 126
Broccoli Rice, p. 128
Pizza Rice Casserole, p. 129
Vietnam Fried Rice, p. 130
Cheese-Rice Souffle, p. 156

147

eggs, milk, and cheese ....

Eggs are a complete protein food containing all the essential amino acids required by the human body. In fact, the amino acid pattern of eggs is closer to matching the ideal pattern than that of any other high-protein food, including meat.

Eggs rank low among animal proteins in amount of grain required in production. But, like other animal protein foods, eggs should be used carefully. An egg contains 7 grams of complete protein. If a meal includes an egg or more per person plus vegetable protein in breads or legumes, let that be enough. Adding deviled eggs or Pennsylvania Dutch red-beet eggs to a meal including meat is a waste of protein. Instead serve these egg specialties occasionally to replace meat.

Eggs team up naturally with milk and cheese. Combinations like scalloped eggs, soufflés, and quiches (cheesy main-dish custard pies) can be as high in protein per serving as several ounces of meat.

As a protein source, eggs have been cheap in recent years. Because eggs are sold by the dozen and not by the pound, price comparisons with meat are tricky. In Canada and the United States, eggs are sized as follows:

Size	Minimum Weight per Dozen
Jumbo	30 ounces
Extra Large	27 ounces
Large	24 ounces
Medium	21 ounces
Small	18 ounces
Peewee	15 ounces

If you buy large-sized eggs, keep in mind that two thirds of a dozen is at least one pound. If large eggs cost 89 cents per dozen, you are paying 59 cents per pound for an animal protein food.

Are small, medium, or large the best buy? A quick rule to remember when standing in front of an egg counter with a child tugging on your hand is this: if there is less than a 7-cent price spread per dozen between 2 adjoining sizes in the same grade, buy the larger size.

With eggs, the drawback is their high-cholesterol content. The American Heart Association recommends no more than 3 egg yolks a week, including those used in cooking, for persons on fat-controlled, low cholesterol diets. Any middle-aged man in a sedentary occupation would do well to aim for this limit. Egg whites present no cholesterol problem.

As with so many foods, the cheapest source of eggs is a friendly farmer. Be willing to take brown shells, odd sizes, and cracks, and you may find a protein source far cheaper than 59 cents per pound. Eggs keep well in the refrigerator, so if any driving distance is involved, buy enough to last a month. Eggs purchased in a supermarket may be much older.

Another reason for buying directly from a farm is that you can return the cartons. Throw-away styrofoam egg cartons are a gross source of pollution, and giving them to a kindergarten class to make flowers doesn't solve the problem. If you must throw them away, try to buy cardboard cartons.

Milk and Cheese

Principles that apply to using eggs responsibly also fit milk and cheese.

One glass of milk (8 oz.) has 8.5 grams of complete protein, more than 1 egg. A 1-inch cube of cheddar cheese has 7 grams protein, and ½ cup of cottage cheese has 15. Do we need cheese cubes on an appetizer tray, cottage cheese salad, and a glass of milk with a ham dinner? From menus like these come the figures that show North Americans eating 90-plus grams of protein per person daily.

Buying milk. Using nonfat dry milk is a hard-to-beat habit, both for economy and health's sake. Start with it in baking and cooking. To convert a household to drinking nonfat dry milk, mix it half and half with whole milk at first. Always mix it 5 to 8 hours in advance and serve thoroughly chilled. Brands vary in acceptability of taste.

Nonfat dry milk is low in cholesterol. Heart disease experts recommend getting children used to the taste of nonfat milk from early childhood.

Buying cheese. So many varieties and styles of cheese line the dairy case that a shopper can be thrown into total confusion. Two guidelines are worth remembering: 1) Always check *price per pound,* 2) know the difference between *natural* and *pasteurized process cheese.*

Cheese often comes packaged in odd sizes rather than in 1-pound chunks. Some wrappers show the number of slices in huge print but to read the ounces contained you must find a light and adjust your glasses. Thrifty shoppers find the price per pound no matter what other information is offered.

Sorting out the difference between natural and pasteurized process cheese takes more skill. *Natural cheese,* sometimes called hard cheese, is simply made from coagulating milk and separating curds from whey. Varieties of natural cheese resulting from different ripening processes include cheddar, longhorn, Jack, Swiss, Edam, colby, brick, Muenster, Parmesan, and on and on.

Pasteurized process cheese, often called American, is made from natural cheese by shredding, melting, pasteurizing, and adding an emulsifier. If the words *cheese food* or *cheese spread* appear on the label, even more liquids and stabilizers than are allowed in pasteurized process cheese have been added.

Pasteurized process cheese is understandably cheaper, because it contains more added liquids. Natural cheese, while a little more expensive, gives you more protein and calcium and fewer additives. Process cheese may be handy for certain recipes, such as Cheese Spread (p. 161). But for sandwiches and most recipes, you get as much for your money with natural cheese. Commercial cheese foods and cheese spreads are particularly poor buys.

Many recipes in this book do not identify which kind of cheese to use. This is intentional, encouraging you to look for best buys in your community and use what is on hand.

Both eggs and cheese respond best to short cooking time on low-medium heat. High heat and long cooking give tough, rubbery products. Be a gentle cook and save energy while you save the texture of your eggs and cheese.

Arrange halved hard-boiled eggs in a casserole and pour over mushroom soup or sauce. Bake until bubbly. Or make creamed eggs in mushroom sauce on the stove top.

Contributor says this was her mother's standby when unexpected guests stayed for Sunday evening supper.

●●●●●●●●●●●●●●●●●●●●●●●●●
Puffy Cheddar Omelet

●●●●●●●●●●●●●●●●●●●●●●●●●
Old-Fashioned Bread Omelet

Serves 3

Serves 4
325°
10 min.

Beat until soft peaks form:
4 egg whites
In separate small bowl, beat together:
4 egg yolks
¼ c. mayonnaise
3 T. water
½ t. salt
Carefully fold yolk mixture into whites. Heat in 10″ skillet:
2 T. margarine
Add egg mixture. Cook without stirring over low heat until egg is cooked through, about 15 minutes. Cover after 5 minutes to insure even cooking.
Sprinkle on:
1 c. finely shredded cheddar cheese
1-2 T. chopped herbs, such as parsley, chives, basil, or tarragon
Cover long enough to melt cheese. Fold omelet in half and slide onto warm plate.

Frances Lehman, Goshen, Ind.

Combine and soak 15 minutes:
1 c. bread cubes
½ c. milk
Preheat oven to 325°.
Combine in bowl:
4 eggs, beaten
¼ c. grated cheese
½ t. salt
bread and milk mixture
Heat in skillet:
1 T. margarine
Pour in egg mixture and cook over medium heat without stirring, about 5 minutes. When browned underneath, place pan in oven for 10 minutes to finish cooking on top. Turn out onto hot platter, folding omelet in half.

Adele Mowere, Phoenixville, Pa.

Heat oil in a skillet, and fry several cups shredded raw potato with chopped scallions. Season. When brown and crispy, pour several beaten eggs into skillet. Fry over low heat without stirring until almost set. Flip over to cook top; cut in wedges and serve. Leftover cooked potatoes can be used.

Cheese dinner rolls: Roll out yeast dough as for cinnamon rolls. Sprinkle with grated sharp cheese and paprika. Roll up, cut, and bake in greased muffin tins. Tastes delicious and cheese complements grain protein in the rolls.

●●●●●●●●●●●●●●●●●●●●●●●●●
Scrambled Eggs And Noodles

Serves 5

Cook and drain according to package directions:
2 c. wide noodles
Heat in a skillet:
3 T. margarine
Add noodles and stir-fry briefly.
Combine and pour over:
3 eggs, beaten
⅓ c. milk, cream or evaporated milk
salt and pepper to taste
Scramble until eggs are set.
Garnish with paprika, chopped parsley, and tomato wedges.

Option:
Sauté chopped scallions or onion in margarine before adding noodles.

Bobbie Wilcox, LaVeta, Colo.

●●●●●●●●●●●●●●●●●●●●●●●●●
Poached Egg Surprise

Serves 4

Make 1 c. Medium White Sauce (see p. 118).
Stir in:
2 T. chopped green pepper
Place on individual serving plates:
4 slices toast
Spread toast thickly with:
soft sharp cheese
Poach until firm:
4 eggs
Place an egg on each slice of toast and pour hot sauce over all.

Elvera Goering, Salina, Kan.

Pour 2 cups cheese sauce into shallow buttered casserole. Slip in 6 raw eggs—do not crowd. Top with grated cheese and parsley sprinkle; bake at 350° for 20 minutes.

Serve fresh fruit and cheese tray as dessert to round out a low-protein meal.

Make a thick tomato sauce seasoned with curry. Add halved hard-cooked eggs, heat through and serve on rice. Or add hard-cooked eggs to any curry to stretch meat.

Serve with green salad and corn muffins for supper or late-morning breakfast.

●●●●●●●●●●●●●●●●●●●●●●●●●
Huevos Rancheros (eggs poached in tomato sauce)

Serves 6

Sauté in skillet:
3 T. oil
1 green pepper, thinly sliced
1 large onion, chopped
2 cloves garlic, minced
Add:
2 large fresh tomatoes, finely chopped OR 2 c. stewed tomatoes, drained
½ c. tomato sauce
½ t. salt
1-2 T. chili powder
½ t. cumin
½ t. oregano
Cook over medium heat 20 minutes, occasionally mashing tomatoes. Break into hot sauce:
6 eggs
Cover eggs with:
6 slices mozzarella cheese
Cover skillet and poach eggs over low heat 3-5 minutes, or until as firm as desired.

Elizabeth Yoder, Bluffton, Ohio

●●●●●●●●●●●●●●●●●●●●●●●●●
Swiss Eggs

T·S

Serves 6
375°
25 min.

Preheat oven to 375°.
Cover bottom of shallow greased casserole with:
1 c. grated Swiss or cheddar cheese
Make 6 depressions in cheese. Slide an egg into each depression, using:
6 eggs
Sprinkle with:
¼ c. cream or evaporated milk
salt and pepper
chopped parsley
Top with:
½-1 c. additional grated cheese
Bake 25 minutes or until eggs are firm but not hard.

Ruth Eitzen, Barto, Pa.

With a crisp green salad,
cheese fondue
makes a hearty meal.

●●●●●●●●●●●●●●●●●●●●●●●●●●

Sunny
Scalloped Eggs

Serves 4-5
400°
15 min.

Sauté in heavy saucepan:
- **¼ c. margarine**
- **1 c. diced celery**
- **2 T. minced onion**

Blend in:
- **3 T. flour**

Cook and stir until bubbly. Add:
- **1 t. salt**
- **1½ c. milk**

Cook and stir until thick. Stir in:
- **2 T. chopped parsley**

Arrange in greased 5-c. casserole:
- **6 hard-cooked eggs, halved**

Pour sauce over eggs. Toss together:
- **2 T. melted margarine**
- **1 slice bread, cubed**

Place on top of casserole. Bake at 400°
for 15 minutes.

Options:

Stir ¾ c. shredded cheese into white
sauce.

Eggs Florentine: Cook ¾ lb. fresh or 2 c.
frozen spinach just until tender. Drain,
chop, and season. Place in bottom of 2
qt. casserole. Proceed with recipe as
given, placing eggs and sauce on top of
spinach. Top with grated cheese and
buttered crumbs. Serves 6.

Prepare as in Option 2, but substitute
broccoli for spinach. Chop broccoli or
leave in spears.

Helen June Martin, Ephrata, Pa.
Janice Wenger, Ephrata, Pa.

●●●●●●●●●●●●●●●●●●●●●●●●●●

Cheese
Fondue

Serves 6

Melt in fondue pot:
- **2 T. margarine**

Add:
- **3 T. flour**

Stir until blended. Add:
- **2½ c. milk**
- **1 t. caraway seeds, soaked in
  hot water for 15 minutes
  (optional)**
- **dash Worcestershire sauce**

Add gradually:
- **1 lb. Swiss or cheddar cheese,
  diced**

Stir until cheese melts. When it begins
bubbling, add:
- **1 t. salt**
- **1 T. lemon juice**
- **⅛ t. nutmeg**

Spear cubes of crusty French or rye
bread with fondue fork and dunk.

Options:

Make fondue in a heavy saucepan. Keep
warm over hot water.

Pour fondue over bread cubes for
individual servings.

Kamala Platt, Newton, Kan.
Annie Lind, Windsor, Vt.
Ruth Eitzen, Barto, Pa.

●●●●●●●●●●●●●●●●●●●●●●●●
Chili Con Queso
(a Mexican Fondue)

*Tester's five-year-old
says it tastes like
toasted cheese sandwiches.*

●●●●●●●●●●●●●●●●●●●●●●●●
Oven
Cheese Fondue

Serves 4

Serves 5
325°
30 min.

Heat in fondue pot:
**1 c. stewed tomatoes or
  tomato sauce
chilies or cayenne pepper to taste**
Add slice by slice:
24 slices American cheese
Serve with an assortment of dunkers:
**carrot strips
celery
cauliflower
corn chips
tortillas
breadsticks
bread cubes**

Kamala Platt, Newton, Kan.

Preheat oven to 325°.
Beat until lemon-colored:
5 eggs
Add and mix well:
**1 t. salt
dash pepper
2-3 c. grated cheese**
Add:
**2½ c. hot milk
1 qt. cubed bread**
Pour into greased 7x11″ baking pan.
Bake 30 minutes, or until set.
Top with chopped parsley just before
serving.

Florence Mellinger, Lancaster, Pa.
Erma Clemens, Chestertown, Md.

*One evening, our cell group
discussion centered on
simple living. A young, single
woman shared her story. She
gardened and preserved
much of her own food and
was committed to a simple
lifestyle. One day she saw a
copy of* More-with-Less
Cookbook. *She couldn't
believe there was a church
whose faith included concern
about the use of food! She
checked the church news in
her daily paper and found
Columbus (Ohio) Mennonite
Church. She attended and
found Christians who were
trying to live a simple
lifestyle and whose denomi-
nation had published* More-
with-Less Cookbook *as a wit-
ness to their faith.
—Viola Weidner,
Allentown, Pa.*

Give more color and flavor to an old standby by layering macaroni and cheese in a casserole with a cup or two of the Basic Spaghetti Sauce (p. 119). Top with shredded cheese and bake until bubbly.

●●●●●●●●●●●●●●●●●●●●●●●●●
Cheese Strata

Serves 6
350°
45 min.

Preheat oven to 350°.
Butter lightly:
  12 slices bread (can be stale)
Arrange 6 slices in bottom of 9x13" greased baking dish. Cover with:
  6 slices cheese or 2 c. shredded cheese
Top with remaining bread.
Beat together and pour over:
  2⅔ c. milk
  4 eggs
  ¾ t. salt
  ¼ t. dry mustard
Bake 45 minutes or until puffed and golden. May be prepared in advance and refrigerated before baking.

Option:
Add a layer of sautéed vegetables (onion, green pepper, mushrooms) or leftover cooked vegetables just before cheese.

Janet Landes, Phoenix, Ariz.
Ruth Magnusen, Glendale, Ariz.
Viola Wiebe, Hillsboro, Kan.

●●●●●●●●●●●●●●●●●●●●●●●●●
Basic Cheese Soufflé

Serves 4-6
350°
50-60 min.

Preheat oven to 350°.
Make 1 c. Thick White Sauce (see p. 118).
Add to hot white sauce:
  ⅛ t. pepper
  ¼ t. dry mustard
  3 egg yolks, slightly beaten (reserve whites)
  1 c. shredded sharp cheese
Stir until cheese melts. Remove from heat.
Beat until stiff but not dry:
  3 egg whites
  ¼ t. cream of tartar
Carefully fold egg whites into cheese sauce. Pour into ungreased 1½ qt. casserole and set in pan of hot water 1" deep. Bake 50-60 minutes, until puffed and golden. Serve immediately.

Options:
Corn Soufflé: Omit cheese. Fold 2 c. fresh grated or home frozen (thawed) corn into white sauce.

Broccoli or Spinach Soufflé: Cook ¾ lb. broccoli or spinach. Drain and chop finely (should yield 1½-2 c.). Omit cheese. Fold vegetable into white sauce.

Chicken Soufflé: Reduce cheese to ¼ c. Fold 1 c. finely chopped cooked chicken into white sauce.

Kitty Collier, Millersville, Pa.
Joann Smith, Goshen, Ind.
Chris Schmidt, Walton, Kan.

*Contributor's teenage son
requested this
for his birthday dinner.
Doris serves it
with green beans,
garlic bread,
and fresh fruit tray.*

●●●●●●●●●●●●●●●●●●●●●●●●●
Bread and Cheese Soufflé

●●●●●●●●●●●●●●●●●●●●●●●●●
Cheese and Rice Soufflé

Serves 4-5
350°
30-40 min.

Serves 5
350°
40 min.

Preheat oven to 350°.
Scald in a saucepan:
   1 c. milk
Add:
   1 c. soft bread crumbs
   1 c. shredded cheese
   1 T. margarine
   ½ t. salt
Stir until cheese melts, heating gently if necessary.
Separate:
   3 eggs
Add cheese mixture to beaten egg yolks; beat egg whites until stiff, but not dry and fold into cheese mixture. Pour into greased 1 qt. baking dish. Set in pan of hot water and bake 30-40 minutes, until puffed and golden.

Jean Horst, Lancaster, Pa.

Preheat oven to 350°.
Make a white sauce:
   2 T. margarine
   3 T. flour
   ¾ c. milk
Add:
   2 c. sharp cheese, shredded
Cook over low heat, stirring constantly, until cheese melts.
Add to cheese sauce:
   4 egg yolks, slightly beaten
   (reserve whites)
   ½ t. salt
   dash pepper
   1 c. cooked rice
Remove sauce from heat and pour into large bowl.
Beat until stiff, but not dry:
   4 egg whites
Gently fold whites into cheese mixture. Turn into greased soufflé dish. To form crown, with spoon make shallow path about 1″ in from edge all the way around. Bake 40 minutes and serve at once.

Doris Yoder, Newton, Kan.

156

•••••••••••••••••••••••••
Quiche Lorraine

Serves 8-10
375°
10 min./45-50 min.

Crust
Mix as for pie crust:
2 c. sifted flour
½ t. salt
¼ t. sugar
½ c. chilled margarine cut into
   ½″ bits
3 T. chilled vegetable shortening
5 T. cold water
Roll·out and fit into 2 9″ pie pans. Prick
pastry with fork. Bake at 400° for 10
minutes.

Quiche Filling (enough for 2 pies)
Beat until blended:
6 eggs
2 c. light cream or
   evaporated milk
2 c. milk
1 t. salt
dash pepper
dash nutmeg
Add:
2 c. grated Swiss cheese
Pour into pastry shells. Bake at 375° for
45-50 minutes. Cool 5 minutes before
serving.

Option:

Place in pie shells before pouring in egg
mixture:
— 1 chopped onion, sautéed
— 4 slices bacon, fried crisp
   and crumbled
   OR 1-2 c. cooked ham, finely
   chopped

Joann Smith, Goshen, Ind.
Eleanor Hiebert, Elkins Park, Pa.

•••••••••••••••••••••••••
Tomato Quiche

Serves 6
375°
10 min./40-45 min.

Preheat oven to 375°.
Prepare 1 9″ pie shell. Bake for 10
minutes.
Place in shell:
2 c. chopped or sliced tomatoes
Sprinkle with:
½ t. basil
1 t. salt
⅛ t. pepper
½ t. sugar
4 scallions, chopped
Spread over tomatoes:
½ c. grated Swiss cheese
½ c. grated cheddar cheese
Combine:
2 eggs, slightly beaten
2 T. flour
1 c. evaporated milk
Pour over cheese and bake at 375° for
40-45 minutes, or until set.
Cool 5 minutes before serving.

Mary Lou Houser, Lancaster, Pa.
Carry Dueck, Saskatoon, Sask.

Cornmeal
Quiche

Serves 6
425°/350°
40-45 min.

Crust:
Combine in bowl:
  ½ c. cornmeal
  ¾ c. sifted flour
  ½ t. salt
  ⅛ t. pepper
Cut in:
  ⅓ c. shortening, soft
Sprinkle over while tossing with a fork:
  3 T. cold water
Stir lightly until mixture will form a ball.
Roll out on lightly floured board. Fit
loosely into 9″ pie plate; fold edge under
and flute.
Preheat oven to 425°.

Filling:
Lay on bottom of unbaked crust:
  6 slices or 1¼ c. shredded cheese
Spread over cheese:
  2 c. whole kernel corn, well drained
Combine in a bowl:
  5 eggs
  ¾ c. light cream or evaporated milk
  1 t. salt
  ¼ t. cayenne
Beat until well blended. Pour over corn.
Place on bottom rack of oven. Bake for 15
minutes. Reduce temperature to 350°
and continue baking 25-30 minutes. Let
stand 10 minutes before cutting and
serving.

Eleanor Hiebert, Elkins Park, Pa.

*Attractive and delicious
with its crispy-brown
potato edging.*

Meat-Potato
Quiche

Serves 4-5
425°
15 min./30 min.

Preheat oven to 425°.
In 9″ pie pan, stir together:
  3 T. vegetable oil
  3 c. coarsely shredded raw potato
Press evenly into pie crust shape. Bake
at 425° for 15 minutes until just beginning
to brown. Remove from oven.
Layer on:
  **1 c. grated Swiss or
  cheddar cheese**
  **¾ c. cooked diced chicken,
  ham, or browned sausage**
  ¼ c. chopped onion
In a bowl, beat together:
  **1 c. evaporated or rich milk
  (part cream)**
  2 eggs
  ½ t. salt
  ⅛ t. pepper
Pour egg mixture onto other ingredients.
Sprinkle with:
  1 T. parsley flakes
Return to oven and bake at 425° about 30
minutes, or until lightly browned, and
knife inserted 1″ from edge comes out
clean. Allow to cool 5 minutes before
cutting into wedges.

Donna Koehn, Blaine, Wash.

Eggs Foo Yung
can be made
on an electric griddle
or frying pan at the table.

●●●●●●●●●●●●●●●●●●●●●●●●
Torta Pascualina
(Argentine Spinach Pie)

●●●●●●●●●●●●●●●●●●●●●●●●●
Eggs Foo Yung

Serves 4
350°
30-40 min.

Have ready:
**1 pie shell and crust for top,
unbaked**
Cook, drain, and chop finely:
1½ c. frozen or 2 qt. fresh spinach
Sauté until tender:
2 T. oil
1 onion, chopped
Combine:
spinach
sautéed onion
¼ t. nutmeg
1 t. oregano
½ t. salt
2 beaten eggs
1 c. grated Swiss cheese
Pour into pie shell. Arrange top crust and
seal. Bake at 350° for 30-40 minutes.
Serve hot in wedges.

Carol Byler, Montevideo, Uruguay
Jean Gerber Shank, Goshen, Ind.

Serves 6-8

Patties:
Brown in skillet:
½ lb. ground beef
Combine in bowl:
**¾ c. finely chopped onion
or scallions**
¼ c. finely diced celery
**1 c. canned (drain) or 2 c. fresh
bean sprouts**
6 eggs, well beaten
1 t. salt
Add beef to egg mixture. Heat in a skillet:
2 T. fat
Fry by ¼ cupfuls. Keep patties shaped
with pancake turner by pushing egg
back into the patties. When set and
brown on one side, turn and brown other
side. Serve hot with rice and sauce.

Sauce:
Combine in saucepan:
¼ c. soy sauce
1 T. cornstarch
2 t. sugar
2 t. vinegar
¾ c. water or chicken broth
Cook, stirring constantly, until sauce
clears. Keep hot.

Helen Hiebert, Winkler, Man.

Hominy,
a traditional Southern
United States favorite,
is dried corn
with the
hull and germ removed.

Very high in protein—
over 20 gr. per serving.
Homemade yogurt cuts cost.

●●●●●●●●●●●●●●●●●●●●●●●●●

Grits and Cheese Casserole

Serves 8
275°
1 hr.

Bring to boil in saucepan:
  4 c. water
Add:
  1 c. hominy grits
Cook over low heat 5 minutes, stirring occasionally. Remove from heat.
Add:
  ⅓ c. margarine
  2 c. shredded cheese
  1 t. Worcestershire sauce
  6 drops hot pepper sauce
  1 t. salt
  3 eggs, beaten
Turn into 2 qt. casserole. Sprinkle with paprika.
Bake at 275° for 1 hour.

Miriam Bowers, Grantham, Pa.

> In 1978, my husband, Lloyd, and I took off for a three-year MCC assignment in Brazil. More-with-Less *was practical and easy to use in a foreign land. It called for readily available, fresh foods, and MCCers used it heavily. When we visited others' homes, I would go home and write beside the recipe at whose house we first tasted that dish. Now, as I leaf through the pages, a flood of memories, sights, sounds, and smells instantly come to mind.*
> —Goldie Kuhns, Akron, Pa.

●●●●●●●●●●●●●●●●●●●●●●●●●

Creamy Egg and Noodle Bake

Serves 8
350°
25 min.

Cook and drain according to package directions:
  3 c. noodles
Sauté until tender:
  2 T. margarine
  ½ c. finely chopped onion
Combine:
  sautéed onion
  drained noodles
  8 hard-cooked eggs, chopped
Combine separately:
  2 c. small curd cottage cheese
  1 c. plain yogurt
  ⅓ c. Parmesan cheese
  2 t. poppy seed
  1 t. Worcestershire sauce
  ½ t. salt
  dash pepper
Fold into noodle mixture. Pour into greased casserole.
Combine and sprinkle over:
  ¾ c. soft bread crumbs
  1 T. melted margarine
Bake uncovered at 350° for 25 minutes.

Becky Mast, State College, Pa.

●●●●●●●●●●●●●●●●●●●●●●●●●
Sour Cream
Substitute

Makes 1¼ c.

Combine in blender container:
   ¼ c. water
   1 c. cottage cheese
Blend on high speed for 20 seconds,
until cottage cheese is liquified.
Add:
   1 t. lemon juice
   ½ t. salt
   ¾ t. garlic or onion salt
   chopped chives, or parsley
Use on salads, baked potatoes, or as a
dip with fresh vegetable sticks.

Virginia Birky, Salem, Ohio

●●●●●●●●●●●●●●●●●●●●●●●●●
Buttermilk
(from dry milk powder)

Makes 1 qt.

Pour into quart jar:
   3 c. water at room temperature
Add:
   1⅓ c. dry milk powder
Stir until dissolved. Add:
   ½ c. commercial buttermilk
   dash of salt if desired
Stir until blended. Let stand at room
temperature until thickened. Stir just until
smooth; refrigerate. Stir before using.
Save ½ c. buttermilk to use as the base
for next batch.

Rosemary Moyer, North Newton, Kan.

*A big saving
over commercial
cheese spreads!*

●●●●●●●●●●●●●●●●●●●●●●●●●
Cheese Spread

Makes 5 4-oz. jars

Combine in top of double boiler:
   1⅔ c. (1 can) evaporated milk
   **1 lb. pasteurized process
      (American) cheese, grated**
Heat and stir over hot water until cheese
melts. Remove from heat and add:
   2 T. vinegar
   ½ t. dry mustard
   ½ t. salt
   dash cayenne pepper
   flavoring (see options)
Stir occasionally as spread cools. Store
covered in refrigerator. Keeps several
weeks.

Options:
Flavor with crumbled bacon or
soybean-based bacon substitute,
crumbled blue cheese, chopped
pimiento, or onion and garlic salt.

After spread cools, form into ball or rolls.
Roll in chopped nuts or parsley. Serve
with crackers or celery.

Dorothy King, Dalton, Ohio

Drain the curd. Dip the curds into a cotton bag or cloth. Reserve the whey for cooking and baking. Wash curds with tepid, then very cold water.
Add:

1 t. salt

Mix gently. Hang bag up to drain until cheese has reached the consistency you prefer. Store in a covered container in the refrigerator. For creamed cottage cheese, add:

½ c. cream

Option:

Buttermilk: Prepare milk for fermentation as directed. When curd is set, stir it vigorously with a whisk. Save a starter for future batches.

Used by permission from The No Fad Good Food $5 a Week Cookbook, *by Caroline Ackerman. New York: Dodd, Mead & Co., 1974.*

Making Cheese

Basic directions for soft or hard cheese:

1.
Ripen the milk: Add 1 cup starter to 1 gallon fresh milk. Use buttermilk, yogurt, clabbered milk, or a commercial powdered cheese starter. Cover and set at room temperature overnight.

2.
Add rennet: Add ½ rennet tablet dissolved in ¼ c. cool water and stir thoroughly. Cover and leave 30-45 minutes, or until milk coagulates. This step can be omitted if, in ripening the milk, you let milk set 18-24 hours or until it separates.

3.
Cut the curd: When curd is firm and a little whey appears on the top, use a long sharp knife to cut into ½" strips lengthwise. Then slant the knife and cut crosswise in the opposite direction. Stir carefully with a wooden spoon.

4.
Heat the curd: Place the container of curds and whey into a larger container of water and heat slowly to 100°F. The temperature should rise 2 degrees every five minutes. Hold at this temperature until curd is of desired firmness. Gently squeeze a small handful of curds; curd is ready when it breaks easily and doesn't stick together. This should happen 1½ to 2½ hours after adding the rennet. For cream cheese, curd can be softer than for other types.

●●●●●●●●●●●●●●●●●●●●●●●●●●
Cottage Cheese

Makes 1⅓ lb. cheese

Scald with boiling water:
3-quart saucepan
measuring cup
whisk or slotted spoon
Measure into saucepan and mix:
10 c. warm water (110°)
4 c. dry milk solids
1 c. commercial buttermilk or
**   starter from previous batch**
Incubate at 90° constant heat for 11 hours, or until the milk has set to the consistency of custard. (A sharp knife will leave a clean cut.) If when you check the milk you find that the whey is separated, you will know that it has set too long. A good incubating place in most homes is the kitchen oven with *only* the light turned on.

Cut the curd. Dip out one cup of curd with a scalded dipper and put it into a scalded container. Stir. Cover tightly. Set in very cold place in back of refrigerator to keep for your next batch of cheese. With a sharp blade that reaches to the bottom of the pan, cut the curd in ¾" checkerboard squares. Slash crosswise with the knife to make uniform cubes. Let stand undisturbed 15 minutes.

Cook the curd. Pour hot water (120°) over the curds to a depth of 1 inch. Set pan in a large pot containing hot water (120°). Heat so gradually that the curd temperature rises 3 degrees every 10 minutes. Very gently rotate the curds, tumbling them over with a spoon, trying not to break them up. Repeat this every 10 minutes. At the end of 1¼ hours the curds should be shrunken quite separate from the whey.

5.

Remove the whey: Pour curds and whey into a colander or strainer lined with cheesecloth or a clean dish towel. Stir or work through with your hands until whey has drained off and curds have cooled to 90°F. Save whey.*

6.

Salt the curd: Sprinkle salt to taste throughout the curd and mix well. To make *cottage cheese*, pour curds into a bowl, add a little cream, chill and serve. To make *cream cheese*, put in a cheese press** for 5 minutes to form.

To make *hard cheese*, proceed as follows:

7.

Press the curd: Wrap curd in a circle of cheesecloth. Put in cheese press and insert follower. Start with a weight of 3 or 4 bricks for 10 minutes; drain off any whey, replace follower, and add 2 more bricks. Remove from press after 1 hour.

8.

For *mild cheese,* press the cheese: Remove cheesecloth; rinse the cheese in warm water; smooth any holes in the surface. (If the cheese is not firm do not wash.) Dry with a cloth and replace in press. Let set 18-24 hours. Cheese is now ready to eat.

9.

For *sharper cheese,* cure as follows: Wash and smooth cheese under warm water; put cheese on a shelf in a cool, dry place. Turn and wipe daily for 3 to 5 days, until a rind forms. Heat ¼ lb. paraffin to 210°F. Hold cheese in the paraffin for 10 seconds, covering the whole surface. Put cheese back on the shelf in a cool place and turn daily. Cheese can be cured any length of time up to five months, but taste from time to time to make sure it doesn't get stronger than you want. Each time you make cheese, results may be a little different. Don't let a failure deter you from trying again.

*

Use whey in baking or cooking to replace water. Whey may be recooked to make various kinds of cheese; look for instructions in more detailed cheese-making manuals.

**

Make cheese press from a plastic jug. Cut off both ends and cut two circular boards to fit tightly inside. Punch nail holes in the bottom board for drainage. Place bricks on top of the follower board to make weight.

Kamala Platt, Newton, Kan.

Gather Up the Fragments

1.

Moldy cheese: Just trim off mold and use remaining cheese—it's perfectly safe.

2.

Hard, dry cheese: Grate finely and sprinkle over spaghetti or other Italian dishes.

3.

Leftover egg yolks: Cover unbroken yolks with water to prevent drying out in the refrigerator.

— Two egg yolks will replace one whole egg in thickening power.

— Don't fret looking for special recipes calling for a few egg yolks; use them to enrich scrambled eggs, fried rice, breads, cakes, cookies, coffee cakes, sauces, puddings, and custards.

— Gently hard-cook unbroken egg yolks in small amount water. Grate over salads, sauces, or vegetables.

— To feed egg yolks to baby, break egg and drop yolk into gently boiling water to hard-cook. Collect whites in container in refrigerator or freezer. (To use whites, see below.)

— Mix one egg yolk with 1 T. water and brush over rolls and bread before baking—gives a lovely glaze.

— Use in these recipes:
  Mock Hollandaise Sauce, p. 223
  Cooked Mayonnaise, p. 245
  Pumpkin Ice Cream, p. 275

4.

Leftover egg whites:

— Use 1 or 2 whites with several whole eggs in scrambled eggs or omelets—recommended for low-cholesterol diets.

— Beat 1 or 2 extra whites until stiff and fold into waffle or cake batter. Yields a higher, lighter product.

— Make a cornstarch pudding without eggs; pour into baking dish. Beat egg whites into meringue, adding 2 T. sugar per egg white. Spread over pudding and brown in oven. Good for cholesterol-watchers.

— Use in these recipes:
  Jelly Frosting, p. 284
  Whipped Topping II, p. 281

meats and fish

Meat could be used more imaginatively in North America. There are ways of serving meat other than placing a three by six-inch slab on every dinner plate.

When our family set up housekeeping in Saigon, I watched our cook unpack her market basket. I could not believe anything special would result from the tiny piece of pork and the little handful of shrimp she unfolded from a banana leaf. In my terms, it was enough to serve one person, and we were having guests. But that little bit of meat flavored a whole array of Vietnamese dishes. Vegetables and meat both tasted more exciting than do the Western each-stewed-in-its-own-juices varieties. This is one reason Oriental cuisine has so many converts.

Most of the recipes in this chapter are for meats as such. Check also the way meats are used together with vegetables in Chapters 4 and 8. No wonder our children will not eat vegetables. We cook them limp and watery and serve them up plain, when they could be stir-fried half crisp, complemented Asian-style with bits of meat and a delicious sauce. Try the Japanese Yaksoba (on page 139), given me by a fourth-grade child who usually doesn't like her vegetables either.

In a beautiful way, using meat carefully and creatively also saves money and benefits health.

Buy straight meats
Check the table on Comparative Costs of Protein Sources, page 36. In almost every case, you pay less for 100 grams of protein by buying a chunk of raw fresh or frozen meat than you do by buying cold cuts, hot

dogs, canned meat spreads, breaded meat, or convenience foods containing meat. Exceptions are canned tuna and mackerel.

Note that in all-meat hot dogs, 100 grams of protein costs $1.50. In ground beef the same amount of protein costs $1.10. Canned pork luncheon meat costs $1.66 for 100 grams of protein, sliced boiled ham $2.88, but smoked picnic ham only $1.24.

You pay for anything food processors do to meat. If you want your meat turned into cold cuts, cooked and put in cans, breaded, batter-dipped, or stuffed into casings, you pay for the labor involved. You pay for special packaging, energy to cook and process, and just for a fancier product with an appealing name.

Very rarely are chicken parts a better buy than whole chickens. At the time the chart on protein costs (p. 36) was prepared, whole chicken at 47 cents per pound cost 82 cents for 100 grams of protein. The same amount of protein in the form of cut-up chicken cost 92 cents, breasts cost $1.46, and legs $1.86.

The United States Department of Agriculture says that when whole fryers cost 45 cents per pound, chicken parts are an equally good buy if breasts are 63 cents, drumsticks and thighs 58 cents, and wings 36 cents. Check your supermarket against this guide. Usually you pay heavily for leaving bony pieces in the store. Meaty chicken parts sold separately are priced so high that you could view it this way: When you want chicken breasts or legs, buy several whole chickens, cut them up yourself, and you get the bony pieces free. You gain a kettle of homemade chicken soup and meat for several casseroles.

Convenience products which have a long shelf life, such as luncheon meats and hot dogs, contain preservatives. Additives for color, flavor, and texture are also used liberally. These extended meat products may look cheap compared to raw fresh meat. Consider the cost of ingredients, however, to determine if you can do the same thing yourself for less.

Stir bread crumbs or ground soybeans into a meat loaf, and make enough for tomorrow's sandwiches. You pay less for both the meat and the filler than if you buy bologna. Get a sharp knife and slice your own cold cooked meat. Freeze ground cooked meat in convenient-sized containers for spreads. Rely on peanut butter, cheese, egg salad, and soybean spreads (see p. 114).

Bacon is not an economical protein source. Note on page 37 that it ranks at the top in price for 100 grams of protein. Nitrites used in processing bacon, hot dogs, and sandwich meats are increasingly suspected of causing cancer-related chemical reactions in the body. Furthermore, bacon is full of saturated fats. A little bacon really adds to the flavor of beans and other meatless dishes, but use it with a light touch if you use it at all. Soybean-based bacon substitutes are available but are fairly expensive.

Buy cheaper cuts
In the future as much grain as possible must be conserved for people to eat directly. This may mean slightly tougher meat calling for long, slow cooking, but also meat that is lower in price, cholesterol, and calories.

For tougher cuts, learn to make stews and curries. The Chinese Savory Beef (p. 170), is a dish I often made in Vietnam where some chunks of beef brought home from the market were dark red, utterly devoid of fat, and tough as shoe leather. I suspect this "beef" originated from the backsides of worn-out water buffaloes who had plowed many a paddy. Savory seasoning and 4-hour stewing turned the shoe leather into delicious tender dishes.

Eat less of it
Earlier chapters documented that North Americans overeat protein. Cut the meat in smaller portions and serve it less frequently.

The fun of experimenting with a new eating style comes through again and again in letters from our contributors. North Americans have such wide resources of food available that learning to eat less animal protein should not be a painful process.

Make up in quantity
and freeze patties
to save time later.

●●●●●●●●●●●●●●●●●●●●●●●●●
Soy, Cheese, and Meat Loaf

●●●●●●●●●●●●●●●●●●●●●●●●
Basic Burger Mix

Serves 5
375°
45 min.

Serves 6
350°
35 min.

Preheat oven to 375°.
Combine in mixing bowl:
- ½ lb. ground beef
- 2 oz. vegetable-protein meat extender with
- ¾ c. milk
  OR ¾ c. ground cooked soybeans, mashed
- 2 eggs
- ⅓ c. bread crumbs or rolled oats
- ½ c. grated cheese or cottage cheese
- 2 T. minced parsley
- 1 minced onion
- 1 t. salt
- pepper

Shape into loaf and spread with ketchup or tomato sauce, if desired. Bake 45 minutes. Let cool 5 minutes before slicing.
To mash soybeans easily, whirl in blender together with eggs and cottage cheese.

Christine Swartzendruber, Ft. Wayne, Ind.
Olive Schertz, Tiskilwa, Ill.

Put through food grinder in order given:
- 1 c. cooked soybeans, drained
- 1 c. any cooked meat OR raw ground beef (grinding not necessary)
- 1 onion, coarsely chopped
- 1 c. whole wheat bread pieces

Add:
- 2 T. parsley, chopped
- 2 eggs, beaten
- 1 t. salt
- ½ t. celery salt
- ½ t. garlic salt
- 2 t. Worcestershire sauce
- other seasonings to taste

Form into patties and coat with:
- ½ c. dry bread crumbs or wheat germ

Fry in oil, bake at 350° for 35 minutes, broil, or grill over charcoal. Serve in warm buns with lettuce and tomato.

Option:

Omit meat and add 1 c. cooked brown rice.

Lois Hess, Columbus, Ohio

●●●●●●●●●●●●●●●●●●●●●●●●●
**Five-Hour
Stew**

Serves 8
250°
5 hrs.

The evening before, brown in Dutch oven:
2 lbs. stew meat, dredged in flour
Add:
**favorite seasonings (salt, pepper,
    garlic, basil, parsley)
3 large potatoes, cut up
1 medium onion, cut up
4 carrots, cut in chunks
1 qt. stewed tomatoes
¼ c. tapioca, sprinkled over all**
Refrigerate overnight. Bake covered, for 5 hours at 250°.

Lois Zehr, Ft. Dodge, Iowa

●●●●●●●●●●●●●●●●●●●●●●●●●
**Poor Man's
Steak**

Serves 5-6
300°
1½ hr.

Combine and mix well:
**1½ lbs. ground beef
½ c. fine bread or cracker crumbs
½ c. water
2 t. salt
½ t. pepper**
Pat out about ¾" thick on cookie sheet. Refrigerate overnight. Cut into pieces, dip into flour, and brown in small amount hot fat.
Preheat oven to 300°.
Lay pieces in baking dish or roaster.
Pour over:
**1-2 c. mushroom or tomato sauce
    (see p. 118)**
Bake 1½ hours.

*Anna Petersheim, Kinzers, Pa.
Clara Yoder, Milford, Del.*

●●●●●●●●●●●●●●●●●●●●●●●●●
**Oven
Beef Stew**

Serves 4
350°
2 hrs.

Shake in a bag:
**2 T. flour
1 t. salt
dash of pepper
1 lb. beef cubes**
Heat in heavy skillet:
2 T. shortening
Brown beef cubes, then place in greased casserole dish.
Preheat oven to 350°.
Add:
**2 c. tomato juice
1½ c. chopped onion
½ t. dried basil**
Cover and bake 1 hour.
Add:
**4 medium potatoes, cubed
4 medium carrots, cut in 1" pieces**
Bake 1 hour longer, or until tender.

Bonnie Zook, Leola, Pa.

Making the most of stewing chicken: Wash chicken and remove as much fat as possible. Simmer slowly with water in large kettle or roast in slow oven until tender.

Remove meat from bones, reserving all skin and undesirable parts such as lungs and kidneys. Freeze meat and broth in separate containers for more flexibility in usage.

Chop fat into small pieces and render slowly in heavy pan, stirring occasionally to prevent sticking. Strain. Freeze in 1 pound cottage cheese boxes.

●●●●●●●●●●●●●●●●●●●●●●●●

Hamburger Stew

Serves 6

Brown in heavy kettle:
1 lb. ground beef
Drain excess fat and add:
2 c. tomato juice
½ c. chopped onion
1 c. diced potatoes
1 c. diced carrots
2 t. salt
Cover and simmer until vegetables are tender.
Make white sauce:
2 T. butter
2 T. flour
2 c. milk
Blend into first mixture and serve.

Option:

Add limas, soybeans, corn, green beans or other vegetables. Increase liquid as needed.

Sarah E. Campbell, Dayton, Va.

●●●●●●●●●●●●●●●●●●●●●●●●

Filled Round Steak

Serves 4-5
300°
2 hrs.

Prepare:
1-1½ lbs. round steak
If 1″ thick, cut through horizontally to make thin large steaks. Or pound a ¾″ steak to make it large and thin.
Combine for filling:
1 c. leftover mashed potatoes
⅓ c. dry bread crumbs
1 small onion, diced
1 egg
salt and pepper to taste
Spread filling over meat and roll up. Tie with string or secure with toothpicks. Place in baking pan. Baste with bacon drippings or margarine, cover, and bake at 300° for 2 hours, or until tender. Remove to platter and slice.
Serve with brown gravy:
Brown in 4 T. meat drippings:
2-3 T. flour
salt and pepper
pinch sugar
Add liquids from cooking vegetables. Cook and stir until thickened.

Susanna Vogt, Drake, Sask.

Use in baking to replace up to half of shortening.

Skin and other discarded parts make excellent dog food. Mix in a blender with oatmeal and/or dried bread and leftover vegetables. Freezes well.
—Esther Hostetter, Akron, Pa.

My husband began accompanying local hunters on his snowmobile (on Baffin Island in the Eastern Arctic). It is Inuit custom to share any kill or catch with the community, so he would return with huge hunks of caribou meat in plastic grocery bags. Caribou is mild, low in fat, and does not have the gamy taste associated with wild meat. It substitutes nicely for beef, pork, or lamb. As in any isolated community, food here becomes part of the entertainment. I have found numerous helpful hints in More-with-Less Cookbook, especially as I tried to make caribou stock for the first time.
—Jennifer Kennedy, Kimmirut, Nunavut

●●●●●●●●●●●●●●●●●●●●●●●●●
Hamburger–Onion Pie

Serves 6-8
400°
30 min.

Preheat oven to 400°.
Combine with fork:
  1 c. biscuit mix (see p. 69)
  ⅓ c. light cream or evaporated milk
Knead and roll dough to line 9″ pie pan.
Sauté:
  1 lb. ground beef
  2 medium onions, sliced
Add:
  1 t. salt
  ¼ t. pepper
  1 t. curry powder
  2 T. flour
Spread meat mixture in dough-lined pan.
Combine:
  2 eggs, slightly beaten
  1 c. small-curd cottage cheese
Pour over meat but *do not* mix. Sprinkle with paprika.
Bake 30 minutes.

Viola Wiebe, Hillsboro, Kan.

●●●●●●●●●●●●●●●●●●●●●●●●●
Fiesta Sloppy Joes

Serves 6

Brown in heavy skillet, keeping meat in chunks:
  1 lb. ground beef (may use part soy extender)
Drain off excess fat. Add:
  ¾ c. uncooked rice
  1 c. sliced onion
  ¼ c. chopped green pepper
  1 clove garlic, minced
  ½ t. sugar
  ¼ t. dry mustard
  ¼ t. celery seeds
  1 t. salt
  ¼ t. chili powder
  2 c. cooked tomatoes or
  1½ c. tomato juice
Bring to a boil. Reduce heat to low, cover, and cook 25 minutes without stirring. Stir and serve hot in buns.

Author's Recipe

●●●●●●●●●●●●●●●●●●●●●●●●●
Chinese
Savory Beef

Serves 8

Heat in heavy skillet or Dutch oven:
2 T. oil or minced fat from beef
Add and quick-fry until brown:
**2 lb. lean beef, cut in 1½″ squares
(may use very tough meat)**
Add and quick-fry a few minutes:
**3 scallions, chopped
OR 1 onion, chopped
2 cloves garlic, crushed
2 thin slices ginger (optional)**
Add:
**½ c. soy sauce
2 T. brown sugar
⅛ t. pepper
3 c. water**
Bring to a boil. Reduce heat, cover, and simmer 3 hours. Add more liquid if needed. Just before serving thicken with small amount flour if desired. Serve over rice or noodles.

Option:
20-30 minutes before serving add ½ lb. vegetables, such as green pepper, mushrooms, or carrots.

Author's Recipe

●●●●●●●●●●●●●●●●●●●●●●●●●
Chinese
Meatballs

Serves 8

Cook rice or noodles to serve 8.
Prepare and reserve ready to fry:
**1 cucumber, peeled and sliced
2 stalks celery, sliced
2 green peppers, sliced
1 large onion, sliced
1½ c. frozen peas
2 large tomatoes, cut in wedges
1½ c. pineapple chunks, drained
(reserve juice)**
Season, shape into small balls, and fry:
**1½ lb. ground beef (may use
part soybean extender)**
Combine and pour over meatballs:
**¾ c. brown sugar
¾ c. vinegar
3 T. soy sauce
½ t. ginger
juice from pineapple
2-3 T. cornstarch**
Allow sauce to thicken, then reduce heat and simmer 20 minutes.
In separate skillet, stir-fry vegetables in small amount of hot oil until crisp-tender, adding tomatoes and pineapple last. Serve on large platter with rice or noodles in center, meatballs around, vegetables over the rice, and sauce over all.

Erma Weaver, Manheim, Pa.

Serve with hot steamed rice and, if
desired, a selection of the following
condiments placed in small bowls:
Chop Salad, p. 250
Tomato Chutney, p. 135
peanuts
sunflower seeds
coconut
**chopped scallions, onions,
    tomatoes, green pepper**
pineapple tidbits
diced apples
raisins
banana slices
chopped hard-cooked eggs

See also p. 134
for Vegetable Curry
and side dish recipes.

●●●●●●●●●●●●●●●●●●●●●●●●●
Basic
Meat Curry

Serves 8

Sauté in heavy deep skillet or kettle:
2 T. fat, oil, or shortening
2 onions, finely chopped
1-2 cloves garlic, minced
Blend in small bowl:
2 T. lemon juice or vinegar
2-4 t. curry powder
Stir curry mixture into sautéed onions
and fry lightly 1-2 minutes. This
produces a relatively mild curry; if
desired, season with additional spices
as listed under Option 1 below.
Add *one* of the following:
**1 3-lb. chicken fryer, cut into
    12-15 small pieces**
2 lbs. beef, cut in 1" chunks
2 lbs. mutton, cut in 1" chunks
2 lbs. boneless fish, cut in chunks
**3 c. any leftover cooked
    diced meat**
2 lbs. meatballs, browned
Stir-fry briefly to coat meat with spices.
Add:
1 c. tomato juice or sauce
1 t. salt
1-2 c. broth or water
Bring to a boil, reduce heat, cover, and
simmer about 2-3 hours for beef and
mutton, 1½ hours for chicken, 20 minutes
for fish and cooked meats. Add more
liquid during cooking as needed for thin
stew consistency. Thicken slightly with
flour just before serving, if desired.

Options:
Ideally all curry powder should be added
at the beginning and fried briefly before
adding meat. But if later the curry tastes
bland, add more. Experience tells. Curry
is a blend of spices; among those used
are cardamom, cloves, cinnamon,
coriander, tumeric, ginger, cumin, and
cayenne. Season with these alone or use
in combination with curry powder.

About 20 minutes before serving add 2
medium potatoes, cubed.

Egg curry: Replace broth or water with
additional tomato sauce. Use 8-10
hard-cooked eggs, halved, to replace
meat. Heat through and serve.

Make curry ahead of time and reheat
before serving. Freezes well.

Author's Recipe

Five meals from a leg of lamb:
*Meal 1—Roasted leg of lamb
with gravy.
Meal 2—Sliced roast, served
cold, or heated in foil in oven.
Meal 3—Scrappy slices, served
with mushrooms in leftover
gravy on toast.*

●●●●●●●●●●●●●●●●●●●●●●●●

West African Groundnut Stew

Serves 8

In large heavy kettle, heat:
3 T. oil
Add:
**2 lbs. beef cubes, 1" or smaller,
rolled in flour**
While browning, add:
**½ t. nutmeg
1 T. chili powder**
When meat is browned, add:
**4 medium-sized onions, sliced
1 clove garlic, minced
¾ c. tomato paste
6 c. water
red pepper, if desired**
Simmer until meat is tender.
A half hour before serving, heat in small saucepan:
**½ c. chunky peanut butter
2 T. oil**
Stir over medium heat 5 minutes. Add peanut-butter mixture slowly to beef stew and simmer over low heat 20 minutes. Serve over rice. May be accompanied with small dishes of condiments. See curry condiments, p. 171.

Options:
Use chicken pieces in place of beef.
To use leftover cooked meat, begin by sautéing onion and garlic, then add meat with tomato paste and water.

*Grace Hostetter, Lagos, Nigeria
Alice and Willard Roth, Elkhart, Ind.
Vietta Nofziger, Barberton, Ohio*

●●●●●●●●●●●●●●●●●●●●●●●●

Genghis Khan

Serves 5-6

Heat in heavy skillet:
2 T. oil
Add and brown quickly:
1 lb. thinly sliced mutton or beef
Add:
**2 large onions, sliced
4 carrots, thinly sliced
2 green peppers, sliced
2 stalks celery, sliced**
Stir-fry briefly, then add:
**¼ c. Worcestershire sauce
⅓ c. soy sauce
1 T. sesame seeds**
Heat through until vegetables are crisp-tender. Serve over hot rice.

Ruth Zook; Toyoto, Japan

Soon after I was married, my husband, Mike, and I began as co-directors of Swan Lake Christian Camp in South Dakota. More-with-Less Cookbook became a cooking bible for our staff as we learned how to cook in a big way. Easy French Bread, Koinonia Granola, and Cheese Pizza appeared weekly, nourishing hundreds of hungry campers. When we had an international emphasis, Groundnut Stew and Vietnam Fried Rice were standards and stretched the palates of campers used to hamburgers and French fries.
*—Marlene Harder Bogard,
Newton, Kan.*

Meal 4—*Bits of meat trimmed from bone, ground and mixed with rice, seasonings, celery, onion, and any leftover gravy for casserole.*

Meal 5—*Cook the bone thoroughly for soup. Use at least 2 waters to get all the broth.*
—*Ruth Hershberger, Harper, Kan.*

●●●●●●●●●●●●●●●●●●●●●●●●●

Liver Fricassee

Serves 6

Pour boiling water over:
1 lb. sliced liver
Let stand 5 minutes. Drain, wipe dry and cut into strips.
Dredge with:
½ t. salt
⅛ t. pepper
¼ c. flour
Brown quickly in hot bacon or other fat.
Add:
½ t. poultry seasoning
½ t. celery salt
1 c. cooked tomatoes
1 onion, chopped
1 c. boiling water
Simmer 45 minutes. Serve with cooked noodles.

Elsie Epp, Marion, S.D.

●●●●●●●●●●●●●●●●●●●●●●●●●

Stir-Fried Liver

T·S

Serves 4

Cut in strips:
½ lb. partially frozen liver
Combine:
2 slices fresh ginger root, minced (optional)
2 t. cornstarch
2 t. cooking sherry (optional)
1 T. soy sauce
¼ t. sugar
Add to liver and toss to coat. Let stand 20 minutes.
Heat in skillet:
2 T. oil
Add:
2 scallions, chopped
1 clove garlic, minced
½ t. salt
approx. 2 c. of any of these vegetables, sliced: mushrooms, peas, green beans, celery, carrots, green pepper
Stir-fry just until vegetables are crisp-tender. Remove vegetables from skillet. Add liver and stir-fry 2-3 minutes. Return cooked vegetables to skillet and stir to reheat. Serve over rice.

Option:

Just before returning vegetables to skillet, add a sauce of 1 c. beef broth and 2 t. cornstarch.

Louise Lehman, Wapakoneta, Ohio
Lois Kauffman, West Point, Neb.

173

*This recipe, invented when
our children were small,
continues as a family favorite.
There's no meat to cut
at the table and
fingers are allowed.
I serve it with buttered corn
and green salad.
Seldom is even one stick
left for the cat!*

●●●●●●●●●●●●●●●●●●●●●●●●
Our-Children-Love
Liver

Serves 4-5

Cut into sticks about ½" wide and 2-3"
long:
**1 lb. partially frozen sliced
beef liver**
Place liver sticks on absorbent paper to
catch excess juice as meat thaws.
Fry in a large skillet:
2-4 slices bacon
When crisp, remove and set aside.
Combine in paper bag:
**¼ c. flour
1 t. salt or seasoned salt
dash pepper**
Shake liver sticks in the bag. Place one
by one in hot skillet and fry in bacon fat
over medium heat. Turn sticks
individually with sharp-tined fork as they
brown. Fry only until crisp and
golden—5-8 minutes. Remove to platter.

Add small amount oil to skillet if
necessary.
Add and fry briefly, stirring constantly:
**1 onion, sliced and separated
into rings**
Sprinkle with salt and pepper. When
onion rings just begin to wilt, transfer to
platter and arrange over liver sticks with
crisp bacon, broken into pieces. Eat as
finger food and pass ketchup for
dipping.

Author's Recipe

●●●●●●●●●●●●●●●●●●●●●●●●
Baked
Beef Heart

Serves 10-12
300°
2 hrs.

Prepare heart by removing as much fat
and tendon as possible. Salt freely with
seasoned salt. Fill with moist bread
stuffing.
Place heart in a covered roaster and
add about ½" water. Bake at 300° for 2
hours. Potatoes and green beans may be
added to the roaster, allowing 1 hour
cooking time.
Slice through heart and stuffing to
serve. Arrange slices on platter with
vegetables.

Vietta Nofziger, Barberton, Ohio

*"Venison, moose, elk, mutton,
goat, or economy cuts of beef
can be transformed
into company fare
with this method.
The aroma is wonderful!
Bake potatoes
and an apple dessert alongside,"
says contributor.*

●●●●●●●●●●●●●●●●●●●●●●●●●
Wild Game
Braise

Serves 12
325°
3-4 hrs.

Heat in heavy skillet or Dutch oven:
   cut-up fat or tallow from meat
When skillet is well-greased, remove
remaining fat pieces.
Brown in hot fat, a layer at a time:
   **3 lbs. meat, sliced ¾" thick
      (use less tender cuts)**
Season with:
   salt and pepper
Add:
   1 c. hot water
Sprinkle over in a layer:
   **2 large onions, sliced
   salt and pepper**
Bring to boiling point and cover.
Bake at 325° for 3-4 hours. Add more
water if necessary.
Make gravy from pan drippings.

   Martha Nafziger, LaCrete, Alta.

●●●●●●●●●●●●●●●●●●●●●●●●●
Ham Loaf

Serves 8
350°
1½-2 hrs.

Combine in bowl:
   1 lb. fresh pork, ground
   1 lb. cured ham, ground
   1 c. bread crumbs
   1 egg
   1 t. salt
   ⅛ t. pepper
   ¾-1 c. milk
Mix well. Shape into a loaf, dust with
flour, and place in baking pan.
Bake at 350° for 1½-2 hours.
At the end of 1 hour pour over the loaf
either
   1 c. tomato juice
or this sauce:
   ¾ c. brown sugar
   1 t. dry mustard
   ½ c. water
   ½ c. vinegar
Bring to boil before pouring over ham
loaf.

   Mennonite Community Cookbook, *used
   by permission.*

●●●●●●●●●●●●●●●●●●●●●●●●●

German Pork Chops

T·S

Serves 6
350°
1 hr.

Preheat oven to 350°.
Place in bottom of greased casserole dish:
   2-3 potatoes, pared and sliced
Sprinkle with:
   salt, pepper, and caraway seed to taste
Add:
   2 c. drained sauerkraut
Sprinkle with more caraway seed.
Top with:
   6 pork chops
   salt, pepper, and caraway seed
Pour over:
   ⅓ c. water
Bake, covered, 1 hour, or until done.
Uncover last 15 minutes to brown chops.

Danita Laskowski, Goshen, Ind.

●●●●●●●●●●●●●●●●●●●●●●●●●

Pork Hocks Pot Dinner

T·S

Serves 4
325°
4 hrs.

TS—needs time not attention

Preheat oven to 325°.
Place in large casserole with cover:
   4 pork hocks
Cover with:
   2-3 c. drained sauerkraut (reserve liquid)
   1 t. caraway or celery seed
   ¾ c. sliced onion
Pour over:
   reserved sauerkraut liquid plus water to make 2 c.
Cover and bake 3 hours.
Add to casserole:
   4 medium potatoes, pared and halved
   salt and pepper to taste
Cover and continue baking 1 hour or until meat and potatoes are tender.

Lois Kauffman, West Point, Neb.

Groats are hulled and crushed
or coarsely ground grains.
Buckwheat groats
(South Dakota Mennonites
say "gritz") are eaten in
Russia as kasha.
This old recipe from the
Freeman community probably
originated in Russia.

●●●●●●●●●●●●●●●●●●●●●●●●
Sweet and Sour
Pork

●●●●●●●●●●●●●●●●●●●●●●●●
Pork–Grits Sausage

Serves 5

Makes 3-4 lbs. sausage

Combine in bowl for marinade:
1 egg, beaten
1 T. sugar
1 t. salt
1 T. soy sauce
Add to marinade and let stand 20-30 minutes:
1 lb. lean pork, cubed
Prepare and set aside:
1 clove garlic, minced
4 slices ginger root, finely chopped (optional)
1 green pepper, cut in chunks
1 onion, cut in wedges
1 tomato, cut in wedges
¾ c. pineapple chunks, drained (reserve juice)
Combine and set aside:
3 T. vinegar
3 T. brown sugar
2 T. soy sauce
1 T. cornstarch
¾ c. pineapple juice
Heat in a wok or skillet:
4 T. oil
Dredge pork cubes in cornstarch. Fry on all sides until brown. Remove from skillet and keep warm. Pour off excess fat if necessary, leaving about 2 tablespoons. Stir-fry garlic, ginger, peppers, and onions 2-3 minutes. Add tomato chunks, pineapple chunks, and sauce ingredients. Cook just until sauce thickens and clears. Return pork to skillet, heat to bubbling, and serve immediately with hot rice. Onions and peppers should be partially crisp.

Jessie Hostetler, Portland, Ore.
Bonnie Zook, Leola, Pa.

Boil until well done:
3 lb. pork roast in
several cups water
Place in large bowl:
2 c. buckwheat groats (grits)
Pour boiling pork broth over groats. Set aside.
Sauté until clear, but not brown:
¼ c. fat
1 large onion, chopped
Grind the cooled pork. Combine:
groats (drain off some broth if necessary)
meat
onions
salt and pepper
Form into patties and freeze.
To serve brown in frypan or broil.

Adina Graber, Freeman, S.D.

177

*Delicious for lunch
or supper
as well as breakfast.*

●●●●●●●●●●●●●●●●●●●●●●●●
Grace's
Kitchen-Stove Scrapple

Serves 6-8

Brown in skillet:
**1 lb. bulk sausage or
hamburger-sausage mixture**
Drain off some fat, if necessary.
Add:
**1 small carrot, grated
¼ c. chopped celery
½ c. chopped green onion**
Sauté until tender. Season with salt,
pepper, onion, and garlic salt as
desired.

In large saucepan, bring to a boil:
3 c. water or stock
Combine and stir slowly into boiling
water:
**1 c. cold water
1 c. cornmeal**
Stir constantly over medium heat until
thick. Cover and cook 10 minutes longer,
stirring occasionally.

Add sausage-vegetable mixture to
cornmeal mixture. Rinse loaf pan in cold
water, then pour in scrapple. Cover and
refrigerate overnight. Slice ½" thick, dip
in flour, and fry until crisp. Serve with
syrup, apple butter, or ketchup.

Grace Whitehead, Kokomo, Ind.

●●●●●●●●●●●●●●●●●●●●●●●●
Cornmeal
Scrapple

Serves 6-8

In heavy saucepan, bring to boil:
3½ c. water, stock or broth
Combine in bowl:
**1½ c. cornmeal
⅓ c. flour
1½ t. salt
⅛ t. *each* savory, sage, and pepper
1½ c. cold water**
Slowly add cornmeal mixture to boiling
water, stirring constantly with wire whisk.
When thickened, add, bit by bit:
**¾ c. raw ground meat (beef
or pork)**
When well blended, turn into double
boiler and cook slowly over hot water for
2 hours. Pour into a loaf pan and chill at
least 12 hours. Slice ¼-½" thick, dust
with flour, and fry in shallow hot fat until
golden. Serve with syrup, jam,
applesauce, or apple butter.

Arlie Weaver, Chinle, Ariz.

Coating Mix
For Oven-Fried Chicken

T·S

Makes 2⅓ c. mix
350°
1 hr.

Combine in a bowl:
2 c. dry bread crumbs (see p. 85)
1½ t. salt
1½ t. paprika
1 t. celery salt
1 t. onion salt
¼ t. pepper
1 t. poultry seasoning (optional)
¼ c. vegetable oil
Blend ingredients with fork or pastry
blender until well mixed. Keeps
unrefrigerated in tightly covered
container.
When ready to use:
Preheat oven to 350°.

Put ½ c. coating mix in plastic or paper
bag. Moisten chicken pieces with water
or milk and shake one piece at a time in
bag. Add more mix as needed. Lay
chicken skin-side up in greased pan and
bake 1 hour or until tender. No turning
needed.

Option:

Use for fish fillets. Bake 30 min.

Grace Anders, Souderton, Pa.

Baked Herb
Chicken

T·S

Serves 6
325°
1¼ hrs.

Preheat oven to 325°.
Arrange in 9x13″ baking pan:
1 3-lb. fryer, cut up
Combine and pour over:
1¼ c. thick mushroom sauce
(see p. 118)
OR 1 can mushroom soup
1 t. grated lemon rind
2 T. lemon juice
½ t. salt
¼ t. basil
¼ t. oregano
Bake uncovered 1¼ hours. Serve with
hot cooked rice.

Option:

Bake at 250° for 2½-3 hours—makes a
good Sunday chicken dinner.

Carolyn Weaver, Lancaster, Pa.

●●●●●●●●●●●●●●●●●●●●●●●●●
Honey-Baked
Chicken

Serves 6
350°
1¼ hrs.

Preheat oven to 350°.
Arrange in shallow baking pan, skin-side up:
 1 3-lb. fryer, cut up
Combine and pour over:
 ⅓ c. margarine, melted
 ⅓ c. honey
 2 T. prepared mustard
 1 t. salt
 1 t. curry powder
Bake 1¼ hour, basting every 15 minutes, until chicken is tender and nicely browned. Good served with rice.

Jan Harmon, Upland, Calif.

My husband and I met in voluntary service with Mennonite Central Committee. That experience led us to buy a house with another couple in 1976. More-with-Less Cookbook was just coming out, and I received a copy for Christmas. The four of us began the wonderful adventure of exploring the contents of the cookbook. Twenty-five years later, my cookbook is minus its cover, has torn and spotted yellowed pages, and continues to be my most-used cookbook. More-with-Less has been much more than just a cookbook—it has been a valuable resource for learning about nutritious eating. It has challenged us and called us to live more responsibly.
—Sue Shantz, St. Jacobs, Ont.

●●●●●●●●●●●●●●●●●●●●●●●●●
Two Meals
For Four People
From a Three-Pound
Chicken

Meal 1: Chicken Stew
Combine in soup kettle:
 5 c. water
 4 chicken bouillon cubes
 ¼ c. wine vinegar
 celery leaves
 1 onion, chopped
 1 chicken, cut in pieces
 salt and pepper
Place in tea ball or spice bag and add:
 4 cloves
 4 peppercorns
 ½ bay leaf
Simmer until chicken is tender. Near end of cooking time, add desired vegetables, such as:
 4 medium potatoes, halved
 4-6 carrots, in large chunks
 1-2 c. fresh or frozen peas
  (add shortly before serving)
Remove spice ball. Remove to serving dish meaty chicken pieces and vegetables. Reserve some meat and most of broth for Meal II. Refrigerate or freeze.

Meal 2: Chicken Soup
Bring stock to boil. Add:
 ½ c. uncooked rice OR 1-2 c.
  leftover cooked rice
Sauté in small skillet:
 2 T. margarine or oil
 2 carrots, chopped
 2 stalks celery, chopped
 1 c. peas (optional)
Just before serving, add reserved meat and sautéed vegetables to stock and rice. Heat and serve.

Norma Fairfield, Singers Glen, Va.

Baked Chicken With Tomato–Rice Stuffing

T·S

Serves 4
350°
1 hr.

Brown in skillet:
2 lbs. chicken parts
Preheat oven to 350°.
While chicken fries, combine in bowl:
⅓ c. chopped celery
¼ c. chopped green pepper
⅓ c. chopped onion
⅔ c. uncooked rice
1 c. cooked tomatoes
½ c. water
¾ t. salt
dash pepper
¼ t. powdered sage
Turn into 12x7x2" baking dish.
Arrange chicken on top of rice. Sprinkle with additional salt, pepper, and paprika.
Cover; bake 1 hour, or until chicken is tender.

Linda Grasse, Chambersburg, Pa.

Chicken Pie

Serves 6
400°
20 min.

Place in large kettle:
1 3-lb. chicken
5 c. water
½ t. salt
Cook until chicken is tender. Drain, reserving broth. Remove meat from bones.
Cook in small amount salted water:
1 c. sliced celery
2 c. frozen mixed vegetables
or similar combination
Drain vegetables, reserving broth.
In saucepan combine:
5 T. flour
½ c. light cream or milk
2½ c. chicken and vegetable broth
1 t. salt
⅛ t. pepper
Cook over medium heat, stirring constantly, until thickened. Stir in vegetables. Place ⅓ of vegetable mixture in 2 qt. casserole. Add chicken meat, then remaining vegetable mixture. Bake at 400° until bubbly, about 20 minutes.

Meanwhile, prepare 1 recipe biscuits (see p. 72). Cut with doughnut cutter, if desired. Top casserole with biscuits and return to oven for 10-15 minutes until biscuits are golden.

Option:
Substitute canned tuna or leftover cooked beef for chicken. Use bouillon cubes to replace broth.

Arnetta Kaufman, Fonda, Iowa
Anna K. Hersh, Glenshaw, Pa.

*A traditional
Pennsylvania Dutch dish,
sometimes seasoned
with saffron.*

●●●●●●●●●●●●●●●●●●●●●●●●●
Chicken
Potpie

Serves 6-8

Cook in large kettle until tender:
**1 large chicken fryer or
stewing hen, cut in pieces
2-3 qt. water
salt and pepper**
Cook until tender. Remove chicken
pieces, cool, and remove meat from
bones.
Prepare vegetables:
**2-3 potatoes, cubed
1 onion, chopped
2 stalks celery, chopped
¼ c. parsley, chopped**
Prepare potpie dough:
Combine:
**2 c. flour
¼ t. salt**
Cut in:
1 T. lard or shortening
Add:
**¼ c. water
1 large egg, slightly beaten**
Mix to form a ball. Cover bowl and let
stand 15 minutes.
Add vegetables and chicken meat to
broth. Cook just until vegetables are
tender. On a floured surface, roll out
potpie dough as thin as possible, cut into
1½" squares, and drop into broth. Cook
5-10 minutes and serve.

Rhoda King, Cochranville, Pa.

●●●●●●●●●●●●●●●●●●●●●●●●●●
Chicken–Pineapple
Skillet

T·S

Serves 6

Bone and skin:
**2 or 3 chicken breasts
(cook bones and skin for broth
to use in another dish)**
Cut each breast half into 10-12 strips.
Assemble:
**1 onion, halved and sliced
1 c. celery, sliced diagonally
1 green pepper, cut in strips
2 c. pineapple chunks, drained
(reserve juice)**
Combine in bowl:
**pineapple juice
2 t. cornstarch
½ t. cinnamon
1½ t. soy sauce**
Heat in large skillet:
2 T. margarine or oil
Over high heat sauté strips of chicken.
Sprinkle with salt and stir constantly for 3
minutes. Add onion, celery and green
pepper and continue to cook, stirring
constantly 2 minutes. Add pineapple,
then juice mixture. Stir and bring to a
boil. Reduce heat and cook just until
clear. Serve over hot rice.

Option:

Use leftover cooked chicken; add to
sautéed vegetables just before adding
juice mixture.

*Rhoda Ehst, New York, N.Y.
Marjorie Ropp, Montreal, Que.*

*Contributor suggests
freezing leftover turkey
in 2-c. containers
for use in this recipe.*

*Contributor says,
"My grandmother brought
this recipe when she came
with other Mennonites
from Russia to the United States.
They stopped for some time
in Turkey
where they learned
to make pilau."*

●●●●●●●●●●●●●●●●●●●●●●●●●
Chicken Strata

●●●●●●●●●●●●●●●●●●●●●●●●●
Chicken Pilau I

Serves 6

325°

50 min.

Serves 8-10

Prepare:
8 slices day-old bread
Butter 2 slices bread, cut in ½" cubes
and set aside. Cut remaining bread in 1"
cubes and place half in bottom of 8x8x2"
baking dish.
Combine in a bowl:
2 c. diced cooked chicken or turkey
½ c. chopped onion
**½ c. chopped green pepper
(optional)**
½ c. finely chopped celery
½ c. mayonnaise
¾ t. salt
dash pepper
Spoon over bread cubes. Sprinkle
remaining unbuttered bread cubes over
chicken mixture.
Combine in bowl:
2 slightly beaten eggs
1½ c. milk
Pour over all. Cover and chill 1 hour or
overnight.
Preheat oven to 325°.
Spoon on top:
**1¼ c. white sauce made with
mushrooms or chicken broth
(see p. 118)**
**OR 1 can cream of mushroom
soup**
Sprinkle with buttered cubes. Bake 50
minutes, or until set.

Cook until tender:
1 stewing hen
5-6 c. water
salt and pepper
Remove chicken pieces and skim broth.
Combine in large saucepan:
4 c. broth
2 c. rice
¼ c. finely diced carrot
½ c. raisins
1-2 t. salt
dash pepper
Bring to boil, stir briefly, cover and cook
without stirring on very low heat until rice
is almost done. Place chicken pieces on
top and finish cooking.

Option:

For a spicier pilau, add onion, garlic, and
curry.

Elsie Epp, Marion, S.D.

Janice Wenger, Ephrata, Pa.

●●●●●●●●●●●●●●●●●●●●●●●●
Chicken Pilau II

Serves 8

Combine in large kettle:
1 3-4 lb. frying chicken, cut up
2 qts. water
1 clove garlic
1 t. salt
Sauté in small skillet:
3 T. oil
2 onions, minced
Add to chicken and bring to a boil. Cover and simmer 20 minutes.
Add:
2½ c. brown rice
Cover and simmer 40 minutes, or until chicken and rice are done.
Remove chicken to a platter.
Stir into rice:
1½ c. raisins
1½ T. curry powder
1 t. salt
1 T. honey
2 T. lime or lemon juice
Mound rice around chicken and garnish with:
½ c. slivered almonds (optional)
¼ c. chopped parsley

Cleta Gingerich, Colorado Springs, Colo.

●●●●●●●●●●●●●●●●●●●●●●●●
Chicken or Turkey Loaf

Serves 6
325°
1 hr.

Preheat oven to 325°.
Combine in large bowl:
1 c. chicken broth
2 slightly beaten eggs
1 c. soft bread crumbs
2 T. chicken fat or margarine
3 c. cooked chicken or turkey, ground or finely chopped
½ c. finely chopped celery
3 T. finely chopped onion
2 t. crushed sage
1 t. salt
¼ t. pepper
Mix thoroughly and place in greased loaf pan. Bake 1 hour, or until firm.

Miriam Byer, Upland, Calif.

When my husband returned to graduate school 20 years ago, I went back to work and he took over some home responsibilities, including cooking. He had little experience, and More-with-Less became one of his regular resources. Chicken Pilau II was a favorite with our family. When authorities recommended that families use a password for children to identify safe adults, our children chose "Chicken Pilau" as our password. To this day, we enjoy the dish every month or so.
—Mary Swartz, Chester, Va.

*Sometimes chicken wings
are available cheaply
by the pound—
or you can slowly accumulate
a bagful in the freezer.*

●●●●●●●●●●●●●●●●●●●●●●●●●
Chicken Wings
Hawaiian

Serves 5-6
350°
45 min.

Cut off tips from:
2 lbs. chicken wings
Cook tips in 1½ c. salted water to make
broth. Reserve for sauce below.
Cut remaining pieces in two. Arrange
side by side in shallow baking pan.
Combine in saucepan:
½ c. soy sauce
1 clove garlic, crushed
**½ c. finely chopped green onions
   (or 1 onion)**
¼ c. sugar
1 t. dry mustard
1 t. ground ginger
¼ c. margarine
¼ c. water
Bring to boil and cool. Pour over chicken,
refrigerate, and marinate several hours.
Turn pieces, then place in 350° oven
without removing sauce. Bake
uncovered 45 minutes, turning pieces
after 30 minutes.

Cook rice. Lift out chicken pieces and
arrange like spokes of a wheel on platter
of hot cooked rice. Garnish with parsley.

Skim fat from remaining sauce if
necessary and heat quickly with 1 c.
chicken broth. Thicken with:
2 t. cornstarch
2 T. water
Pass sauce.

Author's Recipe

*The chicken is the parent;
the egg, the child,
in this very standard
Japanese meal.
Serve with salty pickles
and green tea.*

●●●●●●●●●●●●●●●●●●●●●●●●●
Oyako Domburi
(Japanese
Parent–Child Dish)

Serves 4

Cook rice for 4 persons (see p. 125)
Cut into small servings:
**½ lb. raw chicken cut from bone
   (use 1 large breast)**
OR chicken leftovers
Beat in a bowl:
5 eggs
Dust chicken pieces with flour, dip in
beaten egg (reserve extra), and fry on
both sides in hot oil until brown.
Combine in saucepan:
1 c. water
3 dried mushrooms
Simmer 10 minutes, remove mushrooms,
and cut fine.
Drain any excess oil from skillet. Add to
skillet:
mushrooms and liquid
¼ c. sugar
⅓ c. Japanese-type soy sauce
Simmer 15 minutes. Add:
**2 scallions, cut diagonally,
   OR 1 onion, sliced**
Simmer 10 more minutes. Add:
2 c. chopped fresh spinach
While spinach is still bright green, add
reserved beaten eggs to skillet and
cover. Cook briefly, just until set. Ladle
over individual rice servings in bowls
and top with chopped parsley.

Mary Alene Miller, Obihiro, Japan

Indian Chicken

Serves 6
350°
1 hr.

Heat in large skillet:
2 T. margarine
2 T. vegetable oil
Flour and fry until browned:
1 3-lb. fryer, cut up
Remove from skillet and place in casserole.
Preheat oven to 350°.
In remaining fat, sauté until golden:
2 medium onions, chopped
Combine and add to onions; stirring to blend well:
3 T. flour
2 T. curry powder
1 t. ground ginger
2 t. salt
Combine and add to onion mixture:
⅓ c. honey
¼ c. soy sauce
3 c. chicken broth or bouillon
Cook over high heat, stirring, until sauce thickens. Pour sauce over chicken and bake, covered, about 1 hour.

Options:
Add 3-4 c. cooked drained chick-peas (garbonzos) to casserole before adding sauce.

Serve with rice.

Helen Peifer, Akron, Pa.

Creamed Chicken

T·S

Serves 6

Heat in skillet or heavy saucepan:
¼ c. margarine or chicken fat skimmed from broth
Add and sauté just until soft:
1 onion, chopped
½ green pepper, chopped (optional)
Add, stir, and cook until bubbly:
¼ c. flour
Add:
2 c. chicken broth
1 c. milk
salt and pepper to taste
Cook, stirring constantly, until smooth and thickened.
Add:
2-3 c. diced cooked chicken
1 T. chopped parsley
Heat through and serve over rice, noodles, mashed potatoes, waffles, or with one of the following recipes:
Confetti Rice Squares, p. 187
Cornbread Dressing, p. 187
Potpie Crackers, p. 188

Option:
Add 1 c. cooked or frozen peas.

Author's Recipe

Tester called it
"absolutely the most delicious
dressing I've ever eaten."
But don't bake corn bread
just for this—plan ahead
and serve meaty chicken pieces
on Monday, baked beans and
hot corn bread (double recipe)
on Tuesday, and this
finale on Wednesday.

●●●●●●●●●●●●●●●●●●●●●●●●●●

Creamed Chicken Over Confetti Rice Squares

Serves 8

325°

40 min.

Rice Squares:
Preheat oven to 325°.
Combine:

3 c. cooked rice
1 c. shredded cheese
½ c. chopped parsley
⅓ c. chopped onion
**⅓ c. chopped pimento or
sweet red pepper**
1 t. salt

Add:

3 eggs, beaten
1½ c. milk

Turn into 1½ qt. buttered baking dish. Bake 40 minutes or until knife inserted near center comes out clean. Cut into squares and serve with creamed chicken.

Gladys Longacre, Susquehanna, Pa.

●●●●●●●●●●●●●●●●●●●●●●●●●●

Creamed Chicken With Corn Bread Dressing

Serves 6

325°

40 min.

Combine in saucepan:

**About 2 lbs. giblets and bony
chicken pieces**
1 qt. water
seasonings as desired

Cook 1 hour or until meat is tender. Remove chicken and take meat from bones. Reserve meat and broth.

Dressing:
Combine in large bowl:

4 c. corn bread, crumbled
1¾ c. croutons (see p. 85)

Melt in skillet:

¼ c. margarine

Add:

4 stalks celery, sliced
1 large onion, chopped
⅓ c. chopped walnuts (optional)
1 t. celery seed
¼ c. minced parsley (optional)
2 t. poultry seasoning
salt and pepper

Sauté until tender and add to bread mixture.
Brown in skillet:

3 oz. pork sausage

Add to bread mixture along with 1 c. reserved chicken broth. Combine and turn into greased casserole. Sprinkle with sausage drippings. Bake at 325° for 40 minutes.
Use reserved chicken meat and broth to make creamed chicken. Serve over dressing.

Linda Albert, Visalia, Calif.

*Tiny crisp crackers
turn creamed chicken
into special fare.*

●●●●●●●●●●●●●●●●●●●●●●●●
Creamed Chicken
With Potpie Crackers

Serves 6-8
375°
10 min.

Combine in large bowl:
3 c. flour
½ t. salt
Cut in:
½ c. shortening or margarine
Add:
2 eggs, slightly beaten
¼ c. milk
Stir lightly with fork and form into ball.
Divide dough into three parts. Roll each
part out a little thinner than for pie dough.
Lay rolled out dough on greased cookie
sheets and cut into ½-1" squares. Bake at
375° for 10 minutes or until crackers are
lightly browned. Makes 2 qt. crackers.

Make creamed chicken seasoned
lightly with saffron. Place crackers in
serving dish and pour creamed chicken
over, or arrange on individual serving
plates. Garnish with parsley.

Crackers keep well in tightly covered
container and can be made in advance.

Option:
Dough may be used for patty shells; cut
into 5" circles, fit over upside-down
muffin tins, prick with fork, and bake until
golden.

Doris Brubaker, Mt. Joy, Pa.

●●●●●●●●●●●●●●●●●●●●●●●●
Baked Fish

T·S

Serves 6
350°
35 min.

Preheat oven to 350°.
Place in shallow greased baking dish:
**1½ lbs. fish fillets, cut in
serving pieces**
Sprinkle with:
¼ t. salt
dash pepper
1 T. lemon juice
Make 1¼ c. white sauce, adding 2 t. dry
mustard (see p. 118).
Pour over fish.
Sprinkle with:
⅓ c. buttered bread crumbs
1 T. minced parsley
Bake 35 minutes.

Options:
Add ½ c. grated cheese to white sauce.
TS
Easy, low-calorie baked fish: Simply
place whole cleaned or filleted fish on
greased pan; sprinkle with lemon juice
and seasonings. Bake at 350° about 25
minutes for 1 lb., 35-40 minutes for 2 lbs.
Thin people may add melted margarine.

*Karen Rix, Fonda, Iowa
Anna K. Hersh, Glenshaw, Pa.*

We bake seafood in scallop shells which adds to its attraction for children. Sauté chopped peppers in margarine. Stir in a little flour. Add 1 can cream of spinach or cream of mushroom soup and 1 large can tuna, drained. Put on oiled scallop shells. Sprinkle with parsley and Parmesan cheese. Garnish with pepper ring. Bake at 350° until bubbling and slightly brown.
—Ruth Eitzen, Barto, Pa.

●●●●●●●●●●●●●●●●●●●●●●●●●●
Fish Cakes

Serves 6-8

Combine in mixing bowl:
**2 c. shredded, cooked, salt codfish
OR 1 lb. canned mackerel
(use half of liquid)
2 c. mashed potatoes
⅛ t. pepper
1 beaten egg
1 onion, chopped (optional)**
Mash all ingredients together. Salt to taste if using unsalted fish. Shape into cakes and fry slowly in small amount hot fat.
Good served with tomato or cheese sauce.

Laura Dyck, Winkler, Man.
Ruth Weaver, Reading, Pa.

●●●●●●●●●●●●●●●●●●●●●●●●●●
Scalloped Mackerel

Serves 8
375°
40 min.

Preheat oven to 375°.
Place alternate layers into casserole or 9x5x3" loaf pan:
**1 lb. canned mackerel, flaked
2 c. cracker crumbs**
Combine in a bowl:
**2 eggs, beaten
2 c. hot milk
1 t. salt
dash pepper
poultry seasoning
¼ c. melted butter**
Pour over contents of casserole. Sprinkle with parsley or paprika.
Bake 40 minutes.

Option:
Substitute 6 oz. flaked tuna, or cooked salmon if available at low price.

Carolyn Yoder, Grantsville, Md.
Marian Zuercher, Wooster, Ohio

189

••••••••••••••••••••••••
Fancy Flounder
Roll-Ups

Serves 8
350°
20 min./15-20 min.

Cook and drain:
**1¼ lbs. fresh or frozen broccoli
   spears**
Place broccoli on:
8 fillet of flounder (2 lbs.)
Preheat oven to 350°.
Roll up; secure with toothpicks. Arrange
in 12x8x2" baking dish. Bake 20 minutes.

Combine:
**1¼ c. white sauce with celery
   (see p. 118)
OR 1 can cream of celery soup
¼ c. mayonnaise
1 T. lemon juice**
Pour over fish, stirring in liquid around
the sides. Bake 15-20 minutes.
Arrange roll-ups on a platter; stir sauce
and pour over.

Danita Laskowski, Goshen, Ind.

••••••••••••••••••••••••
Chinese Fish
And Vegetables

Serves 6

Clean and bone:
1 2-lb. fish
Cut against grain into steaks. Wipe dry;
dredge lightly in cornstarch.
Heat 2-3 T. oil in skillet and brown fish
quickly on both sides.
While fish browns, prepare:
**3 c. sliced vegetables—celery,
   cabbage, carrots (slice thinly),
   onions, mushrooms**
Mince finely:
**1 clove garlic
2 slices fresh ginger root (optional)
2 scallions**
Combine in bowl:
**1 c. broth or stock
2 T. soy sauce
1 T. cooking sherry (optional)
1½ t. brown sugar
½ t. salt
2 t. cornstarch**
Remove fish from skillet. Add 1 T. oil and
heat. Add minced vegetables, then
sliced vegetables and stir-fry about 1
minute. Add liquid and bring to boil.
Return fish to skillet. Simmer, covered,
about 5 minutes until fish is done and
vegetables crisp-tender. Serve over hot
rice.

Options:
Use frozen fish fillets.
Sweet-sour dish: add 2 T. vinegar to
liquids and increase brown sugar to 3 T.

Louise Lehman, Wapakoneta, Ohio

*Tuna, eggs, milk, and cheese
yield a very high
protein dish.
Omit meat the rest of the day.*

●●●●●●●●●●●●●●●●●●●●●●●●●

San Francisco
Fish Stew

T·S

Serves 5-6

Sauté in Dutch oven or large saucepan:
   1 T. oil
   1 clove garlic, chopped
   ½ c. chopped onion
   ⅓ c. chopped green pepper
Add:
   ¼ lb. mushrooms, sliced (optional)
   2 c. cooked tomatoes
   ¾ c. tomato paste
   1 c. chicken broth
   1 T. lemon juice
   1 small bay leaf
   ½ t. dried oregano
   1 t. sugar
   ¾ t. salt
   ⅛ t. pepper
Cook uncovered 20 minutes. Add:
   **1-1½ lbs. flounder or other white
      fish, cut into large pieces**
Cook 10-15 minutes, or until fish flakes
easily. Serve over rice or spaghetti.

   Catherine Kornweibel, Easton, Pa.

●●●●●●●●●●●●●●●●●●●●●●●●●

Tuna Soufflé
Sandwiches

T·S

Serves 4
375°
45 min.

TS—a make-ahead dish

Place in greased 9x13" baking pan:
   **4 slices bread, spread with
      mayonnaise**
Combine in bowl:
   1 7-oz. can tuna, flaked
   ¼ c. chopped celery
   ¼ c. chopped onion
   1 t. salt
   ½ t. paprika
Spread tuna mixture over bread slices.
Add:
   4 slices Swiss cheese
Top with:
   4 slices bread
Combine in bowl:
   3 eggs
   1½ c. milk
Pour over sandwiches. Refrigerate 2-12
hours.
Bake at 375° for 45 minutes.

   Option:
Use salmon, mackerel, or other canned
fish.

   Lena Hoover, Leola, Pa.
   Carolyn Weaver, Lancaster, Pa.

●●●●●●●●●●●●●●●●●●●●●●●●
Mock Lobster

T·S

Serves 3-4

Bring to a boil in a saucepan:
2 c. water
1 t. vinegar
1 t. seafood seasoning
Add:
**1 lb. haddock or other white fish,
left in large pieces**
Reduce heat, cover, and simmer about
10 minutes or just until fish is cooked. Cut
or break into bite-sized pieces. Serve
with melted margarine blended with
lemon juice if desired.

Bonnie Zook, Leola, Pa.

*Doris Janzen Longacre was a close
friend of mine. My husband,
Lawrence, and I served with Doris
and her husband, Paul, in Indonesia
under Mennonite Central
Committee. When her cookbook
came out, she sent a copy to me
inscribed: "To Shirlee with love and
good wishes—selamat makan (eat
well)!" More-with-Less Cookbook
became my food bible, not only for
its recipes, but also for its philosophy. To look at the hungry world
and decide to consume less of its
precious resources—that is truly
responsible Christian living! As our
three sons have moved out to live
on their own, I've sent a copy of
More-with-Less Cookbook along
with each of them. I see it as a
survival manual!*
*—Shirlee Kohler Yoder,
Harrisonburg, Va.*

●●●●●●●●●●●●●●●●●●●●●●●●
Poor Man's Lobster
Thermidor

Serves 4
425°
6-10 min.

Preheat oven to 425°.
Sauté:
2 T. chopped onion
½ c. sliced mushrooms (optional)
2 T. margarine
Stir in:
2 T. flour
½ t. salt
dash pepper
dash paprika
Cook until bubbly. Add:
½ c. milk
½ c. chicken broth
½ t. Worcestershire sauce
Cook and stir until thickened. Add:
1 egg yolk
**1 T. sherry flavoring or 2 T.
white cooking wine (optional)**
Add:
**2 c. cooked white fish pieces
(halibut, perch, dolphin,
flounder, etc.)**
Place in shallow casserole or individual
baking dishes.

Top with:
**buttered bread crumbs and/or
grated cheese**
Bake 6-10 minutes.

Loretta Leatherman, Akron, Pa.

*"A whiffle is a soufflé
that any fool can make."*
—Peg Bracken

●●●●●●●●●●●●●●●●●●●●●●●●
Clam
Whiffle

Serves 6
350°
40-45 min.

Preheat oven to 350°.
Combine in bowl:
   1 c. milk
   1¼ c. crumbled soda crackers
Let soak 5 minutes. Add:
   ¼ c. melted margarine
   **1 can (8 oz.) minced clams,
      drained and rinsed**
   2 T. finely chopped onion
   4 T. finely chopped green pepper
   ¼ t. salt
   dash pepper
   dash Worcestershire sauce
   2 eggs, well beaten
Pour into greased casserole and bake
40-45 minutes until puffy and golden.
Serve at once.

Evelyn Kreider, Goshen, Ind.

*Maria serves these
to in-and-out guests
on Christmas evening.
In Puerto Rico
bacalaitos are sold
at small food stands
along the beach
and at baseball games.*

●●●●●●●●●●●●●●●●●●●●●●●●
Bacalaitos

Serves 4-6

Bone and cut in small pieces:
   ½ lb. codfish
If using salted fish, wash and soak in
cold water to remove extra salt.
Combine in mixing bowl:
   2 c. flour
   ½ t. baking powder
   ½ t. salt (omit if using salted fish)
Add:
   cut up codfish
   **2 garlic cloves, minced, or
      ¼ t. garlic powder**
   white pepper to taste
Mix well. Add:
   1½ c. cold water
Set aside 10-15 minutes.
Heat oil for deep frying to 275°. Drop the
mixture by tablespoonfuls into hot oil.
Turn once or twice and fry until golden
brown. Serve hot.

*Maria Luisa Rivera de Snyder,
   Hesston, Kan.*

●●●●●●●●●●●●●●●●●●●●●●●●

Pia-Pia (Indonesian Shrimp Fritters)

Serves 4

Combine:
- **1 c. flour**
- **1 egg, beaten**
- **½ c. bean sprouts, fresh or canned, drained**
- **¼ c. chopped celery**
- **¼ c. finely chopped onion**
- **1 clove garlic, pressed**
- **½ t. salt**
- **pepper**
- **2 T. water**
- **½ c. small shrimp**

Heat in wok or small heavy saucepan:
- **2 c. oil**

Drop a soup spoonful of the mixture into hot oil, holding it down until it takes on a rounded shape. Turn and fry until golden. Several may be fried at once. Serve with rice and a mixture of sweet soy sauce and hot peppers for dipping.

Armini Djojodihardjo, Pati, Indonesia

●●●●●●●●●●●●●●●●●●●●●●●●

Lentil Burgers

Serves 6

Combine in a bowl:
- **2 c. cooked, cooled lentils, drained**
- **1 egg**
- **½ c. cracker crumbs**
- **1 small onion, minced**
- **tomato juice**
- **salt and pepper**

Mix all ingredients together using just enough tomato juice to hold mixture in shape when pattied. Fry like hamburgers in small amount hot oil, shortening or bacon fat.

Carolyn Yoder, Grantsville, Md.

●●●●●●●●●●●●●●●●●●●●●●●●

Grits Croquettes

Serves 6

Combine in a bowl:
- **2 c. cooked hominy grits**
- **2 c. ground cooked chicken or flaked fish**
- **2 T. chopped onion**
- **1 t. salt**
- **dash pepper**
- **1 t. Worcestershire sauce**
- **½ c. bread or cracker crumbs**
- **1 egg, beaten**

Chill, then shape into 12 croquettes. Roll in additional crumbs; dip in egg and roll again. Pan-fry until golden brown.

Rhoda Sauder, Spring Grove, Pa.

Gather Up
the Fragments

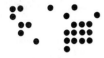

1.
Include skin when grinding cooked chicken for croquettes or sandwich spread.

2.
Save pieces of chicken fat in container in freezer. When enough is accumulated, melt down and return to refrigerator. Use in baking. (Or melt down immediately when cooking chickens.)

3.
Use fat from chicken, pork, or bacon in baking bread.

4.
Trim excess fat from meat, dice finely, and melt in skillet instead of using oil or shortening to fry the meat.

5.
Make a sandwich spread by mashing one or two cooked chicken livers and combining with chopped hard-cooked eggs and a little mayonnaise.

6.
Save all bones and meat scraps for making soup. See Soups.

7.
Chop and freeze leftover ham in small packages for adding to soups, salads, and casseroles.

8.
Sprinkle a chunk of leftover roast beef with a little water. Wrap tightly in foil and bake one hour at 250-300°. Slice and serve. Tastes like just-roasted beef.

9.
Recipes using leftover meats:

Beef and other meats
Vietnam Fried Rice, p. 130
Kay's Japanese Rice, p. 130
Mandarin Rice Bake, p. 132
Easy Curry, p. 136
Garden Supper Casserole, p. 138
Empanadas, p. 147
Meat-Potato Quiche, p. 158
Basic Burger Mix, p. 166
West African Groundnut Stew, p. 172
Zucchini Skillet Supper, p. 236

Chicken and Turkey
Chicken-Cheese Casserole, p. 124
Turkey-Apple Casserole, p. 141

Chicken Soufflé, p. 155
Chicken Pineapple Skillet, p. 182
Chicken Strata, p. 183
Chicken or Turkey Loaf, p. 184
Creamed Chicken, p. 186
Summer Night Salad, p. 252
Chinese Chicken-Cucumber Salad,
    p. 254

Ham Bones and Ham
Calico Baked Beans, p. 100
Easy Lentil Stew, p. 105
Newfoundland Boiled Dinner, p. 141
Quiche Lorraine, p. 157
Meat-Potato Quiche, p. 158
Bean Soup, p. 208
Blackbean Soup, p. 209
Hambone Dinner, p. 215
Hunter's Stew, p. 216
Summer Night Salad, p. 252

soups

"Gather Up the Fragments" fits better at the beginning of this chapter than at the end. Soup making is collecting the odds and ends—cleaning out the refrigerator, going through the cupboards, finishing off the garden. Leftover soup is generally no problem. It is reheated next day for two at lunch, served as a first course at dinner, or poured into someone's thermos. Most soups freeze well and many actually improve with reheating.

In compiling this book, we received far too much good advice on soup making to list much of it by contributor. According to the letters, trustworthy Mennonite cooks are still watching over the soup kettle to produce delicious, heart-and-stomach-warming meals that stretch meat and serve grains, legumes, and vegetables in a tasty way. Various resources feed into the kettle.

A Way with Bits, Bones, and Broths

I save all bones from poultry and meat in my freezer until I have enough for my largest kettle. This is my method: Crack the largest bones (with a cloth-covered hammer) to allow the marrow to escape. Barely cover the bones with water adding ¼ c. vinegar and 2 t. salt for each 2 qt. water. This aids dissolving calcium out of the bones into the stock. Cover the kettle and simmer 3 to 4 hours—or cook 30 minutes in a pressure cooker. (I have a wood range so use the slower method.) Add chopped parings

and vegetable leftovers, 4 peppercorns, and 1 crumbled bay leaf, and simmer it slowly.

Strain broth through colander, cool, and chill overnight. Discard bones and parings (but let the dog pass inspection on them first!). Remove the chilled fat on top and use stock as a base for delicious soups.
—Norma Fairfield, Singers Glen, Va.

A variation of Norma's method was unappetizingly called Garbage Soup by one newspaper clipping, but the results can surpass any canned consommé. You identify one kettle as the ongoing soup pot and fill it half full with water. Keep it in the refrigerator, but get it out every evening and place on the stove to cook for an hour or so while making and cleaning up from dinner. Into it go all bones (long cooking kills germs from dinner plates), clean vegetable parings, vegetable liquid, leftover vegetable salads (rinse away dressing), bits of gravy, and other odd things too small to save. If you cook meat but don't make gravy, add a little water to cooking pan, heat and swish, then pour into soup pot. Allow the kettle to cool until bedtime, then return it to the refrigerator. After a week or so strain out solids and broth is ready to use. Start over.

Although the butcher looks at me very strangely, I always ask to have all the bones saved when we have a quarter of beef cut and wrapped. I take them home, put them in my canner, cover with water, and boil 3 to 4 hours. I strain the broth and can it. It's ready anytime to start off

a wonderful soup, or to take to
sick people.
—*Evelyn Fisher, Akron, Pa.*

Get "dog-bones" free and
trimmed bones cheap. Cook
into broth, then feed bones to
the dog.
—*Carol Ann Maust,
Upland, Calif.*

Broth sometimes spoiled
before I used it all. Now I take
fresh broth and freeze in
ice-cube trays. Store cubes in
plastic bag in freezer. One cube
is about ¼ cup. It's easy to take
out the number you need for
any recipe.
—*Linda Albert, Visalia, Calif.*

Reserved Leftovers
Some people let leftovers die in the
back of the refrigerator in lovely
Tupperware caskets. Here's a better
way:

I keep a large plastic container
in the freezing compartment of
our refrigerator. Into it go
leftovers — vegetables,
noodles, broth, meat —
anything which might be good
in a vegetable soup. When the
container is full, I add water,
perhaps more broth and
seasonings and cook
everything together. We have
had some delicious soups made
this way and since each is just a
little different, it is always a
surprise (not another rerun of
Standard-Brand
Vegetable-Beef). Some
advantages; we seldom have to
eat leftovers and I rarely have to
throw food away which sat too
long in a corner of the
refrigerator.
—*Helen Peifer, Akron, Pa.*
—*Joann Smith, Goshen, Ind.*

Grains, Legumes, and Vegetables on Tap
You have the broth and leftover
vegetables from gathering
fragments. Now the soup needs
thickening and enriching if it's going
to hit the empty spot. Keep a row of
jars, maybe on top of the cupboard,
with rice, barley, dried peas, lentils,
and beans in them. Of these, the first
four need no presoaking. Toss in a
handful early in the process and
they will simmer to tenderness while
you're chopping vegetables and
herbs. Or base the soup entirely on
one of the legumes. A bean or lentil
soup eaten with whole-grain bread
provides cheap high-quality
protein. (See p. 32 on
complementary proteins.)

Blenders are a great aid to soup
making. Almost any leftover
vegetable, blended with a little milk,
forms the base of a cream soup.
Simply add more milk, heat, season,
and soup is ready. The blended
vegetable usually provides enough
thickening. If not, stir in a bit of white
sauce mix (p. 118).

The same trick can be used with
leftover casseroles. Whirl up a cup
of leftover chicken-noodle mixture
and you have a good stand-in for
cream of chicken soup. Leftover
macaroni and cheese blended
makes a thick, mild cheese sauce.
Leftover baked beans go into bean
soup.

A Back-Door Herb Garden

My mother planted parsley around the outside water faucet. Spills and drips kept the plants a luscious green through scorching Kansas summers. But most herbs grow fairly well in dry, poor soil. To the parsley add a clump of chives, some dill, and as space allows, a variety that can bring gourmet taste to the plainest soup. Dry herbs for the winter. Many of these plants fit windowsill pots if no outdoor space is available.

Dry celery leaves in a napkin-lined basket in a warm spot in the kitchen. When dry, crumble into a jar and keep on hand for soups.

And this last idea which may not be practical in many modern homes, but expresses how savory hot soup feeds our souls:

> *For this winter fare, it helps a lot if there's a space-heater in the living room where the soup can simmer from after breakfast until supper time. It smells good, and makes the room seem really a little warmer than it is.*
> **—Ruth Ressler, Sterling, Ohio**

Using the Recipes

For quick method for soaking and other information on beans, see p. 96. Precooked frozen or canned beans may also be used in bean soup recipes.

Whenever a recipe calls for broth, use home-cooked broth or stock, or substitute 1 c. water plus 1 bouillon cube (1 t. powdered bouillon) for each cup required. Commercially canned broths are expensive and waste containers.

●●●●●●●●●●●●●●●●●●●●●●●●●●

Cream of Tomato Soup

T·S

Serves 3-4

Sauté:
   2 T. margarine
   2 T. onion, chopped
Blend in:
   3 T. flour
   2 t. sugar
   1 t. salt
   ⅛ t. pepper
   dash of garlic salt, basil, oregano, thyme
Remove from heat. Gradually stir in:
   2 c. tomato juice
Bring to a boil, stirring constantly. Boil 1 min.
Stir hot tomato mixture into:
   2 c. cold milk
Heat almost to boiling and serve.

Option:

Thicken the soup with doodles:
Combine:
2 eggs, beaten
2 T. water
1 t. salt
flour to make very thick batter
Drop by teaspoonfuls into boiling soup, coating spoon with hot soup each time. Turn off heat and cover until serving time.

Ann Burkholder, Orrville, Ohio
Esther Lehman, Lowville, N.Y.

●●●●●●●●●●●●●●●●●●●●●●●●●
Good Friday Vegetable Soup

T·S

Serves 4-5

Heat in heavy kettle:
3 T. vegetable oil
Add:
3 medium carrots, sliced
2 medium onions, sliced
1 or 2 stalks celery, sliced
1 to 2 c. shredded cabbage
¼ c. chopped parsley
¼ t. salt
Cook over medium heat about 15 min., stirring occasionally.
Add:
4 c. chicken broth
2 c. fresh or frozen French-cut green beans
¼-½ t. caraway seed
Heat to boiling. Reduce heat to low, cover, and simmer 15 min. or until vegetables are tender.
Dice into soup bowls:
¼ lb. cheese
Ladle hot soup directly onto cheese to melt it slightly.

Rosemary Moyer, North Newton, Kan.

●●●●●●●●●●●●●●●●●●●●●●●●●
Timeless Vegetable-Beef Soup

Serves 8-10

Combine in a large kettle:
2-3 lbs. beef soup bones
3 qts. water or stock
1½ t. salt
¼ t. pepper
1 bay leaf
Cover and simmer 2-3 hours. Remove bones and skim fat if necessary. Cut off, chop, and reserve meat.
Add:
½ c. barley
Continue cooking about ½ hour.
Add:
1 c. diced carrots
1 c. diced potatoes
1 c. peas or green beans
1 c. diced celery and leaves
½ c. chopped onion
2 c. shredded cabbage
2 c. cooked tomatoes
herbs and seasonings to taste
reserved meat
Cook just until vegetables are tender. Add any leftover vegetables available. Heat through.

Options:

Add chili sauce or chili powder to taste
Stir in ½ c. sour cream just before serving.

Mary Ella Weaver, Lititz, Pa.
Helena Pauls, Inman, Kan.

Vegetable Chowder

T·S

Serves 6

Combine in kettle:
- **½ c. rice, uncooked**
- **3 chicken bouillon cubes**
- **5 c. water**
- **½ c. diced carrots**
- **1 c. diced potatoes**
- **1 minced onion**
- **½ c. finely cut celery**
- **1 c. canned tomatoes**
- **2 t. salt**
- **⅛ t. pepper**

Bring to boil and simmer 45 minutes.
Add when ready to serve:
- **1 c. milk**

Heat almost to boiling and serve immediately.

Mildred Langs, Cambridge-Preston, Ont.

German Potato Soup

T·S

Serves 4-6

Combine in saucepan:
- **4 medium potatoes, peeled and diced**
- **1 onion, sliced**
- **1 t. salt**
- **dash pepper**
- **3½ c. water**

Cook until potatoes are tender.
Heat in second saucepan:
- **1 T. butter**
- **1 T. flour**

Allow butter and flour to brown, stirring constantly.
Add:
- **3 c. liquid drained from potatoes**

Cook and stir until smooth. Add potatoes and onions and heat through. Sprinkle with parsley.

Martha Roggie, Lowville, N.Y.

Quick Corn Soup

T·S

Serves 4

Puree in blender:
- **2 c. corn, whole kernel or cream-style**
- **1 c. milk**

Pour into saucepan. Add:
- **2 c. milk**
- **½ t. salt**
- **pepper**
- **celery and onion salt to taste**

Heat through. Pureed corn serves as thickening.

Option:

Any leftover cooked vegetable may substitute for corn.

Sara Claassen, Beatrice, Neb.

Golden Potato Soup

T·S

Serves 4

Sauté slowly in saucepan until yellow:
- **2 T. oil or shortening**
- **⅓ c. finely cut onion**

Blend in:
- **1 T. flour**
- **1 t. salt**
- **dash pepper**

Add:
- **1 c. water**

Boil 2 min., stirring constantly. Add:
- **1 c. (or more) leftover mashed potatoes**
- **2½ c. milk**
- **½ c. grated cheese**

Heat slowly until cheese melts. Do not boil. Garnish with parsley or croutons.

Ruth Sommers, Kokomo, Ind.

Cream of Pea Soup

T·S

Serves 4

Combine in blender:
**1½ c. frozen green peas, thawed
2 chicken bouillon cubes
1 thin slice onion
2 T. flour
3 c. milk
dash pepper
dash mace**
Whirl until smooth. Pour into saucepan and heat slowly, stirring constantly. Additional milk may be added.

Option:
Leftover cooked vegetables may replace frozen peas.

Loretta Leatherman, Akron, Pa.

Susan serves the soup with traditional Roll Kuchen (see p. 83), for a favorite summer supper.

Green Bean Soup

T·S

Serves 6

Sauté in heavy kettle until golden:
**3 T. butter
1 large onion, diced**
Add:
**6 c. water or stock
1 c. carrots, shredded
1 c. potatoes, diced
4 c. fresh or frozen green beans, cut up
fresh parsley, chopped
1 bunch summer savory, tied for easy removal**
Cook until vegetables are tender. Just before serving, remove summer savory. Add:
**½ c. cream or evaporated milk
salt and pepper**
Heat through and ladle into bowls. Sprinkle over each serving:
diced hard-cooked eggs

Susan Duerksen, Killarney, Man.

*I served German Potato Soup to a dear woman who comes to our home each week selling eggs. I had added boiled and cut-up eggs to the recipe. The woman's stomach was hurting, and I asked if she was hungry. She was, so I heated up a bowl. She said it was delicious, and if I made it every day, I could buy more eggs from her!
—Carol Shenk Bornman, Senegal, West Africa*

Kidney Bean Soup

Serves 6

Combine in large kettle:
**1 lb. dry kidney beans
2 qts. water**
Soak overnight or by quick method. Add:
**1 c. sliced celery
2 c. sliced carrots
½ c. chopped onion
1 T. Worcestershire sauce
1 T. salt
1 bay leaf
⅛ t. ground cloves**
Over high heat, bring to boil. Reduce heat and simmer 1½ hours, stirring often.

Alice Lapp, Goshen, Ind.

•••••••••••••••••••••••••
Cheese and
Corn Chowder

T·S

Serves 4

Combine in saucepan:
½ c. water
2 c. diced potatoes
1 c. sliced carrots
1 c. chopped celery
1 t. salt
¼ t. pepper
Cover and simmer 10 minutes. Add:
2 c. cream-style corn
Simmer 5 minutes. Add:
1½ c. milk
⅔ c. grated cheese
Stir until cheese melts and chowder is heated through. Do not boil.

Option:
Use leftover whole kernel corn pureed in blender.

Jean Horst, Lancaster, Pa.
Elvera Goering, Salina, Kan.

•••••••••••••••••••••••••
Corn and Bean
Chowder

Serves 6-8

In a large soup pot, sauté:
¼ c. oil
2 c. sliced onions
2 cloves garlic, minced
Add:
3 c. corn (fresh or frozen)
4 c. stock or broth
¼ t. nutmeg
Bring mixture to a boil. Simmer until corn is tender.
Puree in a blender:
1 additional c. corn
Add to soup:
pureed corn
½ c. dry milk solids
1½ c. cooked kidney beans
½ t. salt
Bring soup almost to boiling, lower heat, and simmer a few minutes.

Option:
To make a thicker soup increase dry milk to 1 c. and add 1-2 cooked potatoes.

Virginia Birky, Salem, Ohio

> *I have used the* More-with-Less *philosophy to adapt all my cooking, by using less meat, more legumes and vegetables, and serving soup as a main dish. With an introduction to foods from other traditions, I have been motivated to try a greater variety of foods.*
> *—Jocele Meyer,*
> *Fresno, Ohio*

202

••••••••••••••••••••••••
Ham-Green Bean
Soup

Serves 6-8

Combine in 6 qt. saucepan:
2 lb. meaty ham bone
2 qt. water
Cook 1½ hrs. Remove meat from bone
and cut in chunks. Add to soup stock,
along with:
4 c. cut-up green beans
3 c. cubed potatoes
2 medium onions, sliced
¼ c. chopped parsley
4 sprigs summer savory, chopped
OR 1 t. dried savory
1 t. salt
¼ t. pepper
Bring to boil; reduce heat and simmer,
covered, 20 min., or until vegetables are
tender. Skim off excess fat. Just before
serving, stir in:
1 c. light cream or milk

Margaret Rich, Newton, Kan.

••••••••••••••••••••••••
Fresh Asparagus
Soup

Serves 4

Cook in covered saucepan:
1 lb. fresh asparagus, chopped
¼ c. chopped onion
1 c. chicken broth
When asparagus is just tender, if
desired, press through food mill or blend
until smooth.
Heat in saucepan:
2 T. margarine
2 T. flour
½ t. salt
dash pepper
Stir in:
1 additional cup chicken broth
Cook over medium heat, stirring
constantly, until mixture reaches boiling
point.
Stir in:
asparagus puree
1 c. milk
Stir a little hot mixture into:
½ c. sour cream or plain yogurt
Stir into hot mixture. Add:
1 t. fresh lemon juice
Heat just to serving temperature, stirring
frequently. Sprinkle with fresh chives.

Option:
Tough ends of asparagus may be
included if blender or food mill is used.

Rosemary Moyer, North Newton, Kan.

*Marcia calls this
"wonderful
for Christmas Eve-type
supper."*

●●●●●●●●●●●●●●●●●●●●●●●●
Barley–Cabbage
Soup

●●●●●●●●●●●●●●●●●●●●●●●●
Cream of Carrot–Cheddar
Soup

Serves 6

Combine in kettle:
  ¼ c. pearl barley
  4 c. meat or vegetable broth
  (may use bouillon)
Simmer, covered, for 2 hours.
Sauté in skillet:
  3 T. oil
  2 medium onions, chopped
  3-4 c. green cabbage, finely
  chopped
  ¼ c. parsley, chopped
Cook until soft, but do not brown.
Make a white sauce with:
  4 T. vegetable oil
  4 T. flour
  4 c. milk
  4 chicken bouillon cubes
  ½ t. celery salt
Add white sauce to barley and broth. Stir
in sautéed cabbage and onion.
Check seasonings. Serve sprinkled with
bacon bits, chopped ham, or croutons.

*Rosemary Moyer, North Newton, Kan.
Joann Smith, Goshen, Ind.*

Serves 6

Sauté in large kettle:
  2 T. butter or margarine
  ½ c. finely chopped onion
Add and simmer until vegetables are
tender:
  1 lb. carrots (8-10), shredded
  1 lb. potatoes (3-5), shredded
  6 c. chicken broth
  ½ t. dried thyme
  1 bay leaf
  ⅛ t. Tabasco sauce (or more
  to taste)
  ½ t. Worcestershire sauce
  ½ t. sugar
  salt and pepper to taste
Add, stirring until cheese is melted:
  1½ c. milk (may use part cream)
  1-2 c. cheddar cheese, shredded
Discard bay leaf. Serve hot with parsley
sprinkled over.

*Marcia Beachy, DeKalb, Ill.
Janet Landes, Phoenix, Ariz.*

Cream of Cauliflower Soup

Serves 6-8

Cook in salted water until soft:
 1 medium head cauliflower, chopped
Sauté in large saucepan until yellow:
 4 T. butter or margarine
 ¼ c. chopped onion
Blend in:
 ¼ c. flour
Add:
 3 c. chicken broth
 2 c. milk
 1 t. Worcestershire sauce
 cauliflower and cooking water
Cook until mixture thickens slightly. Add:
 1 c. shredded cheese
Stir to melt cheese and serve sprinkled with herbs.

Option:

Zucchini (use 2-3 medium) substitutes well for cauliflower. May be whirled in blender after cooking.

Miriam Witmer, Manheim, Pa.

French Onion Soup

Serves 6

Combine in skillet:
 ¼ c. margarine
 3 c. thinly sliced onions
Cover and cook slowly about 15 minutes.
Blend in:
 1½ t. salt
 2 T. flour
Add:
 4 c. beef broth or stock
Heat to boiling. Reduce heat and simmer about 1 hour.

Options:

Toast slices of French bread in slow oven until dry and crisp. Put one slice in each soup bowl. Sprinkle toast with grated cheese and ladle hot soup over.

Pour soup into casserole. Float enough toasted French bread on top to cover. Sprinkle liberally with grated Swiss cheese; finish with dash of Parmesan. Heat in 425° oven 10 minutes, or until cheese bubbles. Serve from casserole.

Annie Lind, Windsor, Vt.

●●●●●●●●●●●●●●●●●●●●●●●●
Spinach Soup

T·S

Serves 6

Fry in deep skillet:
4 slices bacon
Remove slices, drain, and reserve.
Add to bacon fat:
**2 large leeks, thinly sliced
(or green onions)
6 medium unpeeled potatoes,
diced
1 t. salt
3 c. boiling water**
Cover and simmer 15 min.
Melt in separate saucepan:
2 T. butter
Blend in:
**3 T. flour
1 t. vegetable broth powder**
Add:
**1½ c. dry milk solids, mixed with
3 c. water**
Cook and stir until thick. Then add to
cooked vegetables and heat.
Add:
1½ c. finely shredded spinach
Simmer 5 minutes. Sprinkle on dash of
pepper, nutmeg, and crumbled bacon.

Marian Franz, Washington, D.C.

*Don says,
"Buzz and I put this together
from memories of Brussels
and from our late-winter
mulch garden and root cellar."*

●●●●●●●●●●●●●●●●●●●●●●●●
Buzz and Don's
Leek Soup

Serves 6-8

Bring to boil:
**3 qts. water and
4 chicken bouillon cubes
OR 3 qts. chicken stock**
Chop and add:
**1½ lbs. fresh leeks, including
green tops
1½ lbs. potatoes
1½ lbs. carrots
1 stalk celery**
Simmer 1-2 hours or until vegetables are
soft.
Add:
**½ t. summer savory
½ t. marjoram
pinch of rosemary
1 T. parsley, chopped
salt to taste**
Simmer another half hour. Puree in
blender or put through a fine sieve or
food mill. Reheat before serving.

Don Ziegler, Lancaster, Pa.

Huge pots of mutton borsch
traditionally served
Russian Mennonite weddings.
The given combination
of herbs
is a must in real borsch.

●●●●●●●●●●●●●●●●●●●●●●●●●
Pumpkin Soup

●●●●●●●●●●●●●●●●●●●●●●●●●
Russian
Borsch

T·S

Serves 6

Melt in large heavy kettle:
2 T. margarine
Add:
¼ c. chopped green pepper
1 small onion, finely chopped
Sauté until vegetables are soft but not brown.
Blend in:
2 T. flour
1 t. salt
Add:
2 c. chicken stock or broth
2 c. pumpkin puree
2 c. milk
⅛ t. thyme
¼ t. nutmeg
1 t. chopped parsley
Cook, stirring constantly, until slightly thickened.

Option:

Add 1 c. cooked tomatoes.

Elvesta Hochstedler, Kalona, Iowa

Serves 8-10

Combine in large kettle:
2 lbs. mutton neck or lamb bones
2 qt. water
2 t. salt
1 T. vinegar
Simmer 2-3 hours. Remove bones from broth and set aside. Set kettle in cold place to harden fat. Remove fat. Measure out and return to soup kettle:
6 c. mutton broth
Add:
1 large onion, chopped
1 qt. cabbage, coarsely chopped
5 c. potatoes, diced
1 c. tomato sauce or 2 c. cooked tomatoes
2 sprigs parsley or parsley root
Secure in bag or tea strainer:
5 peppercorns
3 sprigs dill
1 dried red pepper
1 bay leaf
Drop spice bag into soup. Simmer until vegetables are tender. Cut meat from bones and add to soup. Simmer a few minutes longer to blend flavors. Remove spice bag before serving and add salt and pepper if needed.

Options:

Use beef or chicken.

Add beets or beet tops.

Add 1 c. sweet or sour cream just before serving, or pass cream.

Martha B. Nafziger, LaCrete, Alta.
Selma Martin, Corn, Okla.

Serve with corn bread
or graham muffins
to complement legume protein.

●●●●●●●●●●●●●●●●●●●●●●●●
Quick Beet
Borsch

T·S

Serves 4

Combine in saucepan:
  1 c. cabbage, finely chopped
  1 onion, finely chopped
  2 c. water
Cook 10 min. Add:
  2 c. stock or broth
  **2 medium beets, cooked and
    chopped**
  ½ c. beet juice
  ½ t. salt
  dash pepper
  1 T. lemon juice
Bring to a boil. Pour into soup bowls and
top each serving with:
  2 T. whipped sour cream
Serve with toasted rye bread.

Options:

Add diced carrots with cabbage.

Add tomatoes.

Mabel Hertzler, Mechanicsburg, Pa.
Ruth Ressler, Sterling, Ohio

●●●●●●●●●●●●●●●●●●●●●●●●
Bean Soup

Serves 8

Soak overnight or by quick method:
  2 c. navy or marrow (pea) beans
  2 qts. water
Add:
  **1 ham bone or several pork hocks
    (optional)**
  1 onion, chopped
  **3 stalks celery with leaves,
    chopped**
  3 carrots, sliced
  **1 qt. tomato juice or stewed
    tomatoes**
  salt and pepper to taste
Simmer 2 hours or more until beans are
tender. Add more liquid if necessary.
Remove meat from bones, chop, and
return to soup.

Ruth Ressler, Sterling, Ohio
Marcia Beachy, DeKalb, Ill.

*Doris J. Longacre introduced
the new* More-with-Less
Cookbook *with a two-day
workshop for 30-40 persons
from Kansas communities.
Lila Sisler and I came from
Lincoln, Nebraska. When we
returned, we held similar
workshops for three other
groups. Months later, a
governor's conference on
"Hunger in the World" was
part of a statewide meeting in
Lincoln for agriculture leaders, business leaders, and
nutritionists. We sold all 48
copies of the book before the
conference ended.
—Naomi E. Fast,
Newton, Kan.*

Poor Man's Soup

Serves 8

Combine in large kettle:
1 c. dried marrow or pea beans
3 qts. water
Soak overnight or by quick method.
Simmer beans 45 minutes.
Add:
2 c. tomato juice or cooked
**   tomatoes**
1 c. diced celery
1 carrot, cubed
1 potato, cubed
¼ c. uncooked rice
⅓ c. chopped onion
1 beef bouillon cube
1 T. salt
¼ t. pepper
pinch basil
Brown in skillet:
½ lb. ground beef
Bring soup to boil, add meat, cover and
simmer 1 hour.

Loretta Lapp, Kinzers, Pa.

Blackbean Soup

Serves 8

Soak overnight, or by quick method:
1 lb. dried black beans in water
**   to cover**
Drain and add water to make 6 c. liquid.
Add:
1 c. chopped onion
1 c. chopped green pepper
1 minced clove garlic
1 smoked ham bone
2 bay leaves
2 t. salt
¼ t. pepper
Cover and cook slowly for 2 or 3 hours, or
until beans begin to fall apart, adding
more water if necessary. Remove ham
bone, dice meat, and return to soup.
Add:
¼ c. wine vinegar or 2 T. cider
**   vinegar**
Ladle soup over a mound of rice in each
bowl and sprinkle with chopped parsley.
Pass lemon slices, chopped
hard-cooked eggs, and chopped onions.

Ruth Ressler, Sterling, Ohio

Minestrone Soup

Serves 8

Soak overnight or by quick method:
8 oz. pea or navy beans
Cover and cook 1½ hours. Drain,
reserving liquid.
Place in large heavy pan:
**8 oz. salt pork, skinned and
diced, or other diced pork**
Cover and sauté in its own fat until brown.
Drain off some fat.
Add:
**1 onion, chopped
2 cloves garlic, minced**
Sauté until soft. Add:
**10 c. liquid (reserved bean liquid
plus water)
4 beef bouillon cubes
2 carrots, thinly sliced
2 stalks celery, chopped
¼ cabbage, thinly shredded
2 tomatoes, peeled and chopped
(or ¾ c. cooked tomatoes)
salt and pepper**
Cover, bring to a boil, reduce heat and
simmer soup for 1½ hours.
Add:
**2 c. frozen peas or green beans
½ c. elbow macaroni**
Simmer for another 20 minutes.
Just before serving stir in:
3 T. chopped parsley
Serve hot, sprinkled with Parmesan
cheese.

Kay Gusler, Wise, Va.

Minute Minestrone

T·S

Serves 6

Stir together in saucepan:
**3 c. boiling water
1 envelope dry tomato-vegetable
or similar soup mix**
Add:
**1 medium onion, chopped
2 c. cooked kidney beans
2 c. cooked or frozen corn
1 c. tomato sauce
1 t. salt
⅛ t. pepper**
Cook 10 minutes. Add:
¼ c. chopped parsley

Option:
Hot broth plus extra vegetables and
herbs could substitute for water and
soup mix.

Janet Landes, Phoenix, Ariz.

Quick
Soybean Soup

T·S

Serves 4

TS—using precooked beans

Fry in large heavy saucepan:
3 strips bacon, chopped
Pour off excess drippings if necessary, leaving about 2 T.
Add and sauté briefly:
1 onion, chopped
1-2 cloves garlic, mashed
2 stalks celery, chopped
Add:
1 qt. cooked tomatoes or tomato juice
1 c. water, vegetable stock, or bean liquid
2 c. cooked soybeans
1½ t. chili powder
1 t. salt
½ t. pepper
½ t. basil
additional herbs and seasonings to taste
Bring to a boil, reduce heat, cover, and simmer 15-30 minutes to blend flavors.

Options:

Any cooked beans may replace soybeans.

Slow-simmered soup: Double recipe, using 1 lb. soaked uncooked soybeans. Cook slowly 3 hours. Add more liquid if necessary. Add sautéed bacon ½ hour before serving.

Louise Leatherman, Akron, Pa.

Savory Grain and
Bean Pot

Serves 8-10

Heat in large kettle:
2 T. olive oil or other oil
Add and sauté:
1 c. chopped onions
2 c. chopped vegetables (carrots, mushrooms, celery)
Add:
1 c. cooked soybeans
1 c. cooked tomatoes
2-3 peppercorns
pinch cayenne
¼ t. *each* basil, tarragon, oregano, celery seed, summer savory
pinch *each* thyme, rosemary, marjoram, sage
2 T. soy sauce
½ c. brown rice
⅓ c. bulgar or cracked wheat
6-8 c. vegetable stock or broth
Bring soup to a boil. Reduce heat and simmer 1-2 hours until grains are tender, or pressure cook 10-15 minutes.

Option:

Soup may be further enriched with 3 T. soy grits if available. Combine grits with a little liquid and add to soup with grains.

Elvera Goering, Salina, Kan.

Basic
Lentil Soup

T·S

Serves 6

Combine in kettle:
½ lb. lentils
6 c. water
Cook 30 minutes or until lentils are tender.
Add:
2 carrots, chopped or sliced
½ c. sliced green onions
1 clove garlic, crushed
1½ c. tomato juice
½ c. minced parsley
1 T. margarine
1½ t. salt
dash pepper
½ t. dried oregano
Bring to boil, reduce heat, and simmer just until carrots are tender.
Check seasonings and serve.

Options:

Add diced bacon or ham cubes.
Stir in 1 T. wine vinegar just before serving soup.
Use the whole pound of lentils in a double recipe and freeze half.

Twila Strickler
Alice Lapp, Goshen, Ind.

Hearty
Lentil–Sausage Soup

Serves 8

Brown in 5 qt. kettle:
1 lb. pork sausage, broken into
chunks
Remove meat and pour off all but ¼ c. drippings.
Add:
2 medium onions, chopped
1 garlic clove, minced
4 medium parsnips, cut in chunks
(optional)
Cook 5 minutes or until onions and garlic are tender.
Add:
2 c. lentils
1 T. salt
½ t. marjoram
2 c. cooked tomatoes or juice
2 qt. water
browned sausage
Simmer 30 minutes or until tender.
Cut in diagonal slices:
1 loaf Italian bread
To serve, place a bread slice in each soup bowl and spoon soup over bread. Pass Tabasco sauce.

Mabel Eshleman, Lancaster, Pa.

●●●●●●●●●●●●●●●●●●●●●●●●
Middle Eastern
Lentil Soup

T·S

Serves 4-6

Combine in soup kettle:
1 c. lentils
4 c. water
½ t. cumin
Cook until lentils are soft (30-45 minutes), adding water if necessary for good soup consistency.
Heat in skillet:
1 T. olive oil
Add and sauté just until yellow:
1 onion, chopped
1 clove garlic, minced
Blend in:
1 T. flour
Cook a few minutes. Then add sautéed ingredients to lentils and bring soup to boiling point, stirring occasionally. After soup boils, remove from heat and stir in:
2 T. lemon juice
salt and pepper to taste

Option:
Olive oil is expensive but worth the price to some who recognize Middle Eastern flavors. Others may substitute vegetable oil or margarine.

Louise Claassen, Elkhart, Ind.
Carolyn Yoder, Cairo, Egypt

●●●●●●●●●●●●●●●●●●●●●●●●
Spicy
Split Pea Soup

Serves 6

Combine in large saucepan:
5 c. chicken broth or bouillon
5 c. water
1 lb. dried split peas or lentils
Heat to boiling, turn off heat, cover, and let stand for 1 hour. (Omit this step if using lentils.) Reheat, and simmer over low heat for 45 minutes.
Sauté in skillet over medium heat:
2 T. butter or margarine
½ c. chopped onion
1 clove garlic, finely chopped
1 T. curry powder
1 t. crushed coriander seeds
¼ t. crushed red peppers
1 t. salt
Stir-fry about 7 minutes. Stir spice mixture into split peas, cover, and cook over low heat for 20 minutes. Cool slightly. Puree 2 c. of the soup in covered blender, holding lid partially ajar to let steam escape. Repeat until all has been pureed.
Stir in:
½ c. light cream or milk
Heat to serving temperature. If soup is too thick, thin with small amount of water or milk.

Option:
Soup can be served without blending. Substitute ¾ t. ground coriander for coriander seeds, and cayenne pepper for crushed peppers.

Evelyn Bauer, Goshen, Ind.

Gumbo is a favorite company meal with both contributors. "Make it with just the backs, wings, and ribs," says Francis.

Janet learned to make this soup from Vietnamese students attending Goshen College, Goshen, Ind. While it originates in a tropical climate, the peppery broth is equally good for warming up on cold nights. Make nothing else and eat two bowlfuls.

●●●●●●●●●●●●●●●●●●●●●●●●●

Vietnamese-Style Chicken Noodle Soup

Serves 6-8

In large kettle, cook until tender:
    1 chicken, or 2-3 lbs. bony pieces
    2½ qt. water
    ½ t. monosodium glutamate
    1-2 cloves garlic, crushed
    salt and pepper
Remove chicken; skin and bone it.
Return meat to broth and keep at simmer.
Cook separately until tender:
    1½ lbs. thin spaghetti
Drain.
To serve, fill individual soup bowls with spaghetti. Pour over hot broth with chicken. Sprinkle over each bowl:
    1-2 T. chopped scallions
Each person may add, to taste:
    chopped red pepper or Tabasco
    soy sauce
    freshly ground black pepper
Eat with chopsticks and soup spoon.

Janet Friesen, Seattle, Wash.

●●●●●●●●●●●●●●●●●●●●●●●●●

Spicy Chicken Gumbo

Serves 8

Sauté in large, heavy kettle:
    ¼ c. oil or margarine
    2 onions, sliced
    2 cloves garlic, minced
    1 green pepper, diced
Blend in:
    2 T. flour
Cook and stir over low heat until vegetables are tender.
Add:
    2½ c. cooked tomatoes
    2 c. cooked okra, or 1½ c. frozen
        whole okra
    ⅔ c. tomato paste
    3 c. broth or stock
    1½ T. salt
    ¼ t. pepper
    1½ T. Worcestershire sauce
    ⅛ t. ground cloves
    ½ t. chili powder
    pinch dried basil
    1 bay leaf
Simmer 1 hour. Prepare cooked rice (see p. 125).
Chop and reserve:
    ⅓ c. parsley
Add to gumbo:
    2-3 c. cooked chicken, diced
Simmer briefly. To serve, combine hot cooked rice with chopped parsley and mound rice in center of soup bowls, using ice-cream dipper or large spoon. Pour hot gumbo around.

Options:

Omit okra.

Add 1 T. gumbo file, if available.

Substitute cooked clams for chicken.

Pearl Zehr, New Wilmington, Pa.
Francis Griffin, Ft. Worth, Tex.

●●●●●●●●●●●●●●●●●●●●●●●●●
Ham Bone
Dinner

Serves 6-8

Combine in large kettle:
**2 c. dried yellow or green
   split peas
4 peppercorns
1 ham bone
salt to taste
water to cover**
Bring to boil, then simmer 2-3 hours until peas are done, adding water if necessary. Remove ham bone, cut off meat and chop finely.
Add to soup:
**ham bits
6 carrots, sliced
1 green pepper, chopped
2 onions, diced**
Cook until carrots are done, about 30 min. Check seasonings and serve.

Options:

Substitute chopped bacon or salt pork for the ham bone, or omit meat entirely and flavor with herbs.

Just before serving add several chopped hard-cooked eggs.

Add dumplings:
Combine:
**2 c. flour
½ t. salt
4 t. baking powder**
Rub in:
1 T. margarine
Gradually add:
1 c. water
Place on top of simmering soup in large spoonfuls. Cover and cook without peeking 15 min. Use dumplings when all the soup can be eaten at once—they do not reheat well.

*Martha B. Nafziger, LaCrete, Alta.
Laura Dyck, Winkler, Man.*

---

*Simple
but elegant version
of chicken-rice soup.*

●●●●●●●●●●●●●●●●●●●●●●●●●
Greek
Egg–Lemon Soup

Serves 4

Cook together:
**Bony pieces from 1 chicken
5 c. water
1 bay leaf
1 t. salt
dash pepper**
When chicken is tender, remove meat and discard bay leaf. Take meat from bones.
Add to broth and cook until tender:
⅓ c. rice
Return meat to soup. Adjust seasonings. Heat soup to boiling, then remove from heat.

In small bowl, beat until light:
1 egg
Stir into egg:
**several tablespoons hot soup
juice of ½ lemon**
Stir egg mixture into soup. Serve immediately with parsley sprinkle.

Louise Claassen, Elkhart, Ind.

*Meatball Soup (Sauer Klops)
is a traditional dish still found
on the table in
North American Mennonite
homes of Prussian ancestry.
Broth has a distinctive
spicy-sour flavor.*

*Martin Stew was named
by a youth group who were
often served this by
Elizabeth Martin,
who says she was never sure
what time they would arrive.
It can be made ahead
of time and holds well.*

●●●●●●●●●●●●●●●●●●●●●●●●●
Meatball
Soup

●●●●●●●●●●●●●●●●●●●●●●●●●
Martin
Stew

T·S

Serves 4

Combine in mixing bowl:
   ½ lb. lean ground beef
   ½ c. finely rolled cracker
      or bread crumbs
   ½ c. evaporated or whole milk
   ½ t. salt
   dash pepper
Form into balls 1½" in diameter, and set
aside.
Combine in 3 qt. saucepan:
   2 c. cubed potatoes
   1 small onion cut in half
   7 kernels allspice
   chopped parsley
   1 carrot, sliced
   2 c. water
   1 t. salt
   dash pepper
Bring ingredients to boiling point, then
add meatballs. Cook 6 minutes in
pressure pan, or 20-30 minutes by
regular method.
Add:
   ½ c. milk or cream
   2 t. vinegar
Skim fat off top, if necessary, before
serving.

Options:

Add 1 c. fresh or frozen peas shortly
before removing from heat.
Omit potatoes in soup. Boil unpeeled
new potatoes separately and serve along
with soup.
Thicken soup slightly with flour, if
desired.

Elsie Epp, Marion, S.D.

Serves 6-8

Bring to boil in large kettle:
   1½ qts. water
Add:
   2½ c. macaroni
Meanwhile, brown in skillet:
   1½ lbs. ground beef
   1 onion, chopped
When redness is gone, add meat to
macaroni kettle.
Add:
   1 qt. tomato juice
   1 T. salt
   pepper
Simmer ½ hour. Just before serving, add:
   2 c. frozen peas
Cook a few more minutes and serve in
soup bowls.

Elizabeth S. Martin, New Holland, Pa.

●●●●●●●●●●●●●●●●●●●●●●●●
Hunter's
Stew

Combine in large kettle:
   1 ham bone with leftover meat
   5 c. water
Boil until meat is very tender (1-2 hours).
Remove bone, chop meat, and return to
broth.
Add:
   1 c. fresh, frozen, or canned
      lima beans
   1 c. spaghetti, broken into pieces
   2 c. canned, frozen or fresh corn
   1 large onion, chopped
   1 qt. tomato juice
   salt and pepper to taste
Simmer 20-30 minutes to finish cooking
and blend flavors.

Elsie Mann, Fairbault, Minn.

●●●●●●●●●●●●●●●●●●●●●●●●●
Peanut Soup

Serves 3-4

Sauté in heavy saucepan:
2 T. margarine
1 medium onion, chopped
When onion is yellow, stir in:
1 T. flour
Mix in a small bowl:
½ c. chunky peanut butter
1 c. hot water
Add to onions, cooking over low heat and
stirring until smooth.
Add:
1 chicken bouillon cube
3 c. milk
Heat slowly, stirring often, until bouillon
dissolves and soup is hot.
Serve with croutons and garnish with
parsley.

Option:

Chicken broth may replace the hot water
and bouillon cube, plus part of the milk if
desired.

Beth Fry, Conestoga, Pa.
Helen and Adam Mueller,
Cape Girardeau, Mo.

> *I first heard of* More-with-
> Less Cookbook *when I was
> involved in missionary circles
> about 15 years ago. Several
> recipes have become my old
> standbys. I didn't realize*
> More-with-Less *was
> Mennonite until about a year
> ago when my husband and I
> started exploring the
> possibility of becoming
> Mennonites. When I found
> out, how could I consider
> NOT joining?!*
> —Amy Spencer,
> Riverside, Iowa

●●●●●●●●●●●●●●●●●●●●●●●●●
Pot-Of-Gold
Peanut Soup

Serves 6

Combine in large saucepan:
1 oz. dried mushrooms (optional)
8 c. water
Soak about 5 minutes or until mushrooms
are rehydrated; remove and reserve
mushrooms. Add to water:
3 T. instant chicken bouillon
1 dried red chili pepper
OR ¼ t. dried crushed
red pepper
Bring to boil. Stir in:
⅓ c. pearl barley
Cover and simmer 1 hour or until barley
is tender. Remove saucepan from heat
and blend in:
1 c. chunky peanut butter
Stir with wire whip until smooth. Return to
heat and continue stirring until soup is
thickened. Stir in:
2 c. frozen chopped broccoli,
thawed and drained
reserved mushrooms
Simmer 3-5 minutes. Remove from heat
and add:
2 T. fresh lemon juice
2 T. chopped parsley

Option:

When omitting dried mushrooms, begin
by cooking barley in water and bouillon
(or broth). Fresh mushrooms may be
sautéed briefly and added with broccoli.

Elma Esau, Akron, Pa.

vegetables

Possibilities for eating plants are vast, yet many cooks dish up the same dull round of boiled carrots, corn, and green beans every week. Eating vegetables is for adventuresome people—people who look at a new food the same way they look at a book that hasn't been read or a hill that wants climbing.

Menus can be full of new experiences with vegetables for very little money. Consider what happened to two teachers in Zambia:

I'm impressed with what Zambians eat that North Americans throw away. Mostly this pertains to vegetables and the lungs and intestines of chickens. Mark and I haven't taken to intestines yet, but we've learned to throw away less vegetable matter. We're eating beet tops, bean, broccoli, and pumpkin leaves. Wash the leaves, chop, and boil with salt and a handful of finely chopped peanuts. It makes a lovely vegetable in peanut gravy.
—*Darlene Keller,*
  Lusaka, Zambia

Our neighbor's cauliflower would not produce a head, and since they had no other vegetables, they decided to eat the leaves. The interesting thing is, the leaves taste like cauliflower.
—*Ruth Martin, Katete, Zambia*

For those with even a little space, gardening can provide cheap excitement on the table. A dirt-gardener friend is becoming a specialist in growing and tasting every possible variety of peas and beans. When I received the Puerto Rican recipe on page 102, I phoned him for information on pigeon peas. He had never heard of them either, but I caught a note of excitement in his voice. Two weeks later he came to me with a triumphant grin. He found pigeon peas in an obscure seed catalog, ordered some, and next fall they'll be ready to try.

No book can say which vegetables are cheapest for those who don't garden. Every locale has its specialties. In most of North America, potatoes, carrots and cabbage are still the cheapest high-nutrient vegetables. Potatoes contain helpful amounts of vitamins and minerals. Baking potatoes in the skin preserves more nutrients than any other cooking method. Home-cooked and mashed potatoes, though not as good as baked, have twice the vitamins and minerals of the instant mashed variety. Carrots provide carotene which our bodies use to make Vitamin A. Cabbage, especially raw, is an excellent source of Vitamin C.

Iceberg lettuce, now standard salad fare on many tables year-round, is not usually a valuable buy for the nutrients it yields. There is no magic in the fact that iceberg lettuce is raw and crunchy. Its pale color gives away all but the outer leaves as a relatively poor source of vitamins. Grow your own greens in summer. Let the family chew carrots and cabbage in winter. Any of the following contain more vitamins for the money than iceberg lettuce: leafy, dark-green lettuce such as romaine; raw or cooked greens like endive, spinach, chard, collard greens; dark yellow-orange vegetables like carrots, yellow squash, or sweet potatoes.

Most vegetables should be cooked briefly in small amounts of water. Vegetable steamers, which fit inside ordinary saucepans, are available in some department stores. These steamers do a lovely job of preserving taste and nutrients.

Another fast, tasty, and vitamin-saving way to prepare vegetables is to stir-fry Chinese-style. Cut the raw vegetables, often a combination, into attractive uniform shapes. Set aside, grouping each kind of vegetable separately. If the recipe calls for a sauce, combine those ingredients in a small bowl and set aside. Have everything ready. Heat a skillet, add one or two tablespoons of oil, and when quite hot, add garlic if specified, and then vegetables, longest-cooking varieties first. With a wooden spoon or chopsticks, stir almost constantly over medium-high heat. As vegetables turn bright in color and begin to tenderize a bit, add other faster-cooking vegetables. When vegetables are still partly crisp (crisp-tender is the word used in recipes), add sauce mixture all at once, cook just until sauce clears and coats vegetables, and serve immediately. If no sauce is used, season while frying. The cooking itself may only take three to five minutes. A little practice lets you know just how crisp you should leave it. A little practice will also have you forgetting recipes as you invent new combinations from what is on hand.

The attractive color and delicious flavor of stir-fried vegetables has to be experienced. Somehow,

half-cooked vegetables taste bad when done in water, but absolutely wonderful when stir-fried. Their fresh crunchiness makes salads unnecessary. Cutting and chopping can be done well in advance, but once the dish is hot and sauced, making it wait means sacrificing the perfect texture.

Sometimes I forget other details of the meal because it's so much fun to get right into assembling the stir-fry dish. Then my frantic alarm cries out to the rest of the family to finish setting the table because I can't leave the stove. But it's only the last five minutes that are hectic. The rewards are great. See Stir-fried Green Beans (p. 221, Zucchini (p. 235), and Broccoli (p. 224).

A delicious and versatile vegetable catching on with more and more gardeners is zucchini squash. Linda Grasse, Chambersburg, Pa., writes:

We found that the zucchini squash is very easy to grow, is a prolific producer, adapts to many soil conditions and continues to produce most of the summer. However, I've also discovered that most people are unfamiliar with this variety of squash and do not know how to use them.

Many contributors must have shared Linda's sentiments for we received more recipes for zucchini than any other vegetable. Try some zucchini seed and then the recipes beginning on page 235. Check the growing squash daily and pick while they are only six to eight inches long. Zucchini is also delicious raw.

219

Vegetables
Au Gratin

Serves 6-8
350°
20 min.

Preheat oven to 350°.
Prepare:
   **1½ lbs. or about 4 c. cooked
      vegetables (especially good
      are sliced carrots, cabbage,
      green beans, zucchini,
      broccoli, cauliflower, small
      onions, or a combination)**
Toss together:
   ½ c. crushed cornflakes
   1 T. oil or margarine
Set aside for topping.
Sauté in saucepan over low heat:
   3 T. oil or margarine
   ⅓ c. (or more) chopped onion
Stir in:
   3 T. flour
   1 t. salt
   ⅛ t. pepper
Cook, stirring, until bubbly. Add:
   **1½ c. milk (use vegetable stock
      and powdered milk)**
Cook and stir until smooth. Add:
   1 c. (4 oz.) grated cheese
Stir until melted; remove from heat. Add:
   cooked vegetables
   1 T. dried or fresh snipped parsley
Spread mixture in shallow 1½-qt. baking
pan. Sprinkle crumb mixture evenly over
top. Bake 20 minutes or until sauce is
heated and bubbly. Let stand 3-5
minutes before serving.

Options:
Omit cheese.

Substitute bread crumbs for cornflakes.

Use leftover vegetables in combination.

Prepare ahead of time and refrigerate
until ready to bake.

Add 1 c. slivered ham for main-dish
special.

Rosemary Moyer, North Newton, Kan.

*This old favorite
still dresses up any vegetable
and can serve as main dish
(milk-cheese protein)
if you make plenty.
Add salad and hot bread.
Nice for a buffet.*

*Contributor says,
"We eat greens this way
'most every day
and they are nutritious
and easily digested—
good for people who
can't eat lots of raw cold salad."*

Basic
Cooked Greens

T·S

Serves 3

Prepare 1 qt. washed finely chopped
greens:
   celery with leaves
   lettuce
   dandelion
   turnip greens
   kale
   beet greens
   spinach
   cabbage
   sauerkraut
   endive
   Swiss chard
Place in covered saucepan. Add
chopped onions if desired. Water
clinging to leaves from washing is
usually sufficient. Cook just enough to
wilt.
Beat together:
   1 c. milk
   2 T. flour
   1 egg
   **seasoning to taste—salt, pepper,
      vinegar, mustard, sugar**
Pour over hot greens and cook, stirring,
until mixture thickens. Serve at once.

Option:
Add chopped cooked meat or
hard-cooked eggs.

Naomi Coffman, Harrisonburg, Va.

Paper-thin slices are easy to cut from partially frozen meat. Freeze some meat in ¼ lb. packages for quick stir-fried dinners, which can usually be prepared in the 25 minutes it takes to cook rice.

●●●●●●●●●●●●●●●●●●●●●●●●●

Stir-Fried Green Beans

T·S

Serves 4

Combine in small bowl and set aside:
½ t. salt
1 t. sugar
1 t. cornstarch
1 T. soy sauce
½ c. water or soup stock
Heat in skillet:
2 T. cooking oil
Add:
¼ lb. raw beef chuck, thinly sliced in bite-sized pieces
2 cloves garlic, minced
½ c. onion, diced
Stir-fry over high heat until beef begins to change color. Remove beef, onions, and garlic from skillet and set aside. If necessary, add more oil and reheat skillet. Add:
1 lb. fresh French-cut green beans
Stir until beans become bright green. At once add reserved soy sauce mixture and cook, stirring, until clear. Cover skillet and cook over medium heat until beans are just crisp-tender. Return beef to skillet, stir well and remove from heat. Serve immediately with rice. Add salad or light soup to complete the menu.

Options:
Use 1 chicken breast or ¼ lb. pork in place of beef.
Frozen green beans may be used but will not have the tender-crisp texture of fresh beans. Increase cornstarch to 1 T.

Pat Hostetter Martin, Quang Ngai, Vietnam

●●●●●●●●●●●●●●●●●●●●●●●●●

Puffy Green Bean–Cheese Bake

Serves 4
350°
50-60 min.

Preheat oven to 350°.
Grease a 1½-qt. casserole. Break in:
2 large or 3 medium eggs
Beat with rotary beater. Add:
1 c. milk
¼ t. salt
½ c. fine cracker crumbs
1 T. finely chopped onion
1 c. cheddar cheese cubes
Stir well. Arrange on top:
1¼ c. fresh green beans, cut in small pieces or equal amount frozen or canned beans
Drizzle over:
1 T. melted margarine
Bake, uncovered, 50-60 minutes.
May be prepared in advance except for adding melted margarine.

Vera R. Buehler, Conestoga, On.

See p. 244 for method
for sprouting beans.

*Carolyn, a teacher at
Ramses College for Girls, says,
"This is our noon meal
nearly every day
and it grows on you."*

●●●●●●●●●●●●●●●●●●●●●●●●
Egyptian
Tabikh

T·S

Prepare for cooking:
Green beans
Zucchini squash
OR a vegetable mixture
Instead of cooking in water, cook in
tomato juice.
Thicken the juice with tomato paste, if
desired.
Add sautéed onion and seasonings, as
desired.
Serve over rice.

Option:
Cook small pieces of meat in the tomato
juice until tender. Add vegetables during
last 15-20 minutes.

Carolyn Yoder, Cairo, Egypt

●●●●●●●●●●●●●●●●●●●●●●●●
Stir-Fried
Bean Sprouts

T·S
Serves 4

Heat in wok or skillet until very hot:
2 T. oil
Add and stir-fry 2 minutes:
1 lb. fresh bean sprouts
2 green onions, cut in 1½" lengths
1½ t. salt
dash soy sauce
Serve with rice.

Jessie Hostetler, Portland, Ore.

Vegetable Discoveries ▶

*Cook chunks of peeled
pumpkin, onions, tomatoes,
and seasonings together. Stir in
half a cup ground peanuts, cook
10 more minutes and serve over
rice. Pumpkin can be stored 6
months or longer, so this could
be an economical dish most of
the year.*
—Nell Peters, Choma, Zambia

*A recipe used for years
in Olive Wyse's
foods classes
at Goshen College.*

Sweet–Sour Beets

T·S

Serves 4-6

Grate finely:
1 large or 2 medium raw beets, peeled
Melt in saucepan:
2 T. margarine
Add grated beets. Cover and cook slowly until beets are tender, stirring occasionally.
Add:

**salt and pepper
1 T. vinegar
3 T. sugar
2 t. cornstarch dissolved in
¼ c. water**
Cook stirring, until sauce clears. Serve hot.

Options:

Add 2 T. orange juice with water.
Simply add salt and pepper to sautéed beets and serve without sauce.

Minnie O. Good, Denver, Pa.

*Fry ¼ inch slices of young green squash in a batter of flour, egg, salt, and milk. This was "steak" in the early days of Mennonite colonies in Paraguay.
—Myrtle Unruh,
Filadelphia, Paraguay*

Fresh Broccoli With Mock Hollandaise

Serves 4-6

Note: Cooking sulfur-containing vegetables such as broccoli, brussel sprouts, cauliflower, or cabbage, in larger quantities of boiling water shortens cooking time and lessens the formation of undesirable sulfur compounds. Any of these vegetables can be used in the following recipe.

Bring to boil in a large saucepan:
**enough water to cover broccoli
2 t. salt for each quart water**
Wash 1 head broccoli. Split large stem into fourths, but do not cut through head. Submerge broccoli in boiling water. Over high heat, quickly return to boiling. Reduce heat and cook gently, uncovered, just until stems are tender (7-10 min.) Remove from hot water immediately. Cut into serving pieces and arrange in oblong dish with heads at each end and stems in the center. Pour mock hollandaise over stems.

Mock Hollandaise
Melt in saucepan:
2 T. margarine
Blend in:
**2 T. flour
1 T. sugar
¼ t. salt**
Stir in:
**1 c. water
2 T. vinegar**
Cook until thickened. Cool slightly. Add:
**2 egg yolks, beaten or
1 whole egg, beaten**
Blend. Heat briefly before pouring over vegetables, but do not boil.

Olive Wyse, Goshen, Ind.

*A good way to make
broccoli stems acceptable
and to use celery not
in first-class condition
for serving raw.*

●●●●●●●●●●●●●●●●●●●●●●●●●
Broccoli–Celery Hollandaise

Serves 4-6

Wash and prepare:
1 lb. fresh broccoli
Remove heads and set aside. Slice
stems diagonally into ½" pieces. Slice
diagonally in ½" pieces:
2-3 stalks celery
Bring to boil in large saucepan:
2 qts. water (approx.)
4 t. salt
Add celery and broccoli stems. Boil,
uncovered, about 8 minutes. Add
broccoli heads. Cover until water returns
to boiling. Uncover and cook gently for 5
min. Using some of the cooking water,
prepare Mock Hollandaise sauce (see p.
223). Drain vegetables well and arrange
broccoli heads in circle in serving dish.
Add broccoli stems and celery to sauce.
Combine thoroughly. Pour sauce in
center of serving bowl.

Olive Wyse, Goshen, Ind.

*Cut broccoli heads
in flowerets
and slice stems diagonally.*

●●●●●●●●●●●●●●●●●●●●●●●●●
Stir-Fried Broccoli

T·S

Serves 4-5

Combine and set aside:
½ c. chicken broth
1 t. cornstarch
2 T. soy sauce
1 t. sugar
Heat in skillet:
3 T. oil
Add:
½ medium onion, diced
Fry until golden.
Add:
**1 lb. broccoli,
cut in small pieces**
Stir-fry for three minutes. Add sauce
ingredients. Stir-fry for 1 minute until
sauce clears.

Option:

May be used for cauliflower cut into thin
fan-shaped slices or
broccoli-cauliflower combination (lovely
color contrast!).

Olive Wyse, Goshen, Ind.

*Peel and cut the neck part of
crook-neck pumpkin in ⅓ inch
slices. Flour and fry slowly on
both sides in small amount hot
fat. Salt and pepper. After
removing slices to serving plate
add a little milk or cream to
skillet to make gravy.
—Martha Kaufman, Atglen, Pa.*

*Cook separately: egg noodles,
broccoli, cheese sauce.
Arrange noodles in a ring on a
platter, place broccoli in the
center, pour cheese sauce over
all for an attractive high-protein
main dish.
—Elizabeth Yoder,
Bluffton, Ohio*

●●●●●●●●●●●●●●●●●●●●●●●●●
Broccoli
Stuffing Bake

Serves 6-8
325°
45 min.

Preheat oven to 325°.
Heat and stir in saucepan until blended:
  2 c. milk
  1 c. (4 oz.) shredded sharp cheese
Beat in mixing bowl:
  4 eggs
Gradually stir hot mixture into eggs.
Add:
  2½ c. herb-seasoned croutons
    (see p. 85)
  2 c. frozen chopped broccoli,
    thawed
  ¼ t. salt
Mix well. Turn into greased 1½-qt.
casserole. Bake 45 minutes.

Lois Beck, West Liberty, Ohio

**Place cooked cauliflower,
cooked spinach, white sauce,
and cubed cheese in alternate
layers in casserole. Top with
buttered crumbs and bake until
bubbly.
—Geraldine Mitsch,
  Aurora, Ore.**

●●●●●●●●●●●●●●●●●●●●●●●●●
Skillet
Cabbage

T·S

Serves 4

Heat in large skillet:
  2 T. butter or margarine
Add:
  ⅔ c. chopped onions
  1 clove garlic, minced
Stir-fry briefly. Add:
  3-4 c. finely sliced cabbage
  ½ c. coarsely shredded carrots
Stir-fry about 5 minutes over medium
heat, until vegetables are crisp-tender.
Add:
  ⅛ t. paprika
  1 t. salt
  dash freshly ground pepper
  2 t. soy sauce (optional)
Stir until thoroughly blended and serve
immediately.

Options:

Indonesian—When vegetables are
crisp-tender, season well and pour over
2 eggs, beaten. Cook a few more minutes
over low heat, stirring just enough to
allow eggs to become cooked. Serve as
a main dish with rice.

Vietnamese—Top with a generous
sprinkling of chopped roasted peanuts,
serve with rice, and pass soy sauce.
Slivers of meat may be added at the
beginning with onions.

Dorothy Liechty, Berne, Ind.

*Anna's not sure
the dish is recognized in Taiwan,
but it's been a family favorite
with this name.*

●●●●●●●●●●●●●●●●●●●●●●●●

Formosan
Fried Cabbage

T·S

Serves 4

Brown together in heavy saucepan or
large skillet:
   **4 strips bacon or ½ lb. sausage,
      chopped**
   ½ medium onion, chopped
Drain off some of the fat. Add:
   **½ medium cabbage, coarsely
      chopped**
Stir-fry over low heat until cabbage is
tender. Add:
   1 T. soy sauce
Serve over rice and pass additional soy
sauce.

Anna Juhnke, North Newton, Kan.

●●●●●●●●●●●●●●●●●●●●●●●●

Creamy
Cabbage

T·S

Serves 6

Cook about 7 minutes, just until
crisp-tender:
   6 c. shredded cabbage
   ¼ c. onion, chopped
   ⅓ c. water
   ⅛ t. salt
Drain. Add and toss lightly while hot:
   3 oz. cream cheese, cubed
   ½ t. celery seed
   2 T. butter or margarine
   paprika

Zona Galle, Madison, Wis.

*Cook overripe peas and add to
cooked rice with onions, garlic,
and curry seasonings.
—Kamala Misra,
   Bhubaneswar, India*

*Add cheese to creamed peas
(or any other creamed
vegetable) and serve on toast.
—Esther Lehman,
   Lowvile, N.Y.*

*Add home-dried tangerine peel
(see p. 303) to cooked beets.
—Evelyn Liechty, Berne, Ind.*

*Mash drained carrots easily
by whirling in blender
with eggs and milk.*

●●●●●●●●●●●●●●●●●●●●●●●●
Ginger-Glazed Carrots

Carrot–Cheddar Casserole

Serves 4

Serves 8
350°
30 min.

Boil in small amount of water:

8 small carrots (or equivalent carrot sticks)

When almost tender, drain well. (Reserve liquid for soup making.)

Heat in heavy skillet:

**1½ T. margarine
¼ t. ground ginger
1 T. honey or sugar**

Add carrots and stir carefully to coat. Cook over low heat until glazed, turning frequently.

Option:

Omit ginger. Add 1 T. prepared mustard. Sprinkle with chopped chives, mint, or parsley.

*Jean Edmonds, Sparta, Tenn.
Winifred Paul, Scottdale, Pa.*

Preheat oven to 350°.
Combine in mixing bowl:

**3 c. cooked, mashed carrots (about 1½ lb.)
3 beaten eggs
2 c. milk
1⅓ c. shredded cheddar cheese
1⅓ c. crushed crackers (reserve ¼ c. for topping)
2-3 T. softened butter
1⅓ t. salt
dash pepper
1 T. chopped parsley**

Mix well. Turn into greased casserole and sprinkle with reserved crumbs. Bake 30 minutes, or until knife inserted in center comes out clean.

Mary Lou Houser, Lancaster, Pa.

*Cut fresh green beans French-style. Stir-fry in hot skillet with 2 T. margarine for 5 minutes. Season, cover, and remove from heat. Let stand 5 minutes and serve.
—Helen Funk, Laird, Sask.*

*Shred raw carrots or beets on a grater. Cook slowly in small amount of margarine, stirring often. Season and serve.
—Martha Snader, New Holland, Pa.*

227

●●●●●●●●●●●●●●●●●●●●●●●●●
Golden Eggplant Casserole

●●●●●●●●●●●●●●●●●●●●●●●●●
Skillet Eggplant

T·S

Serves 4-6
350°
45 min.

Serves 4

Preheat oven to 350°.
Combine in a bowl:
15 soda crackers, crumbled
2 T. melted margarine
Toss. Take out and reserve ¼ c. for topping.
Add to remaining crumbs:
3 c. cubed eggplant (¾" cubes)
½ c. shredded sharp cheese
¼ c. chopped celery
½ t. salt
¼ t. pepper
1 c. evaporated milk
Turn into greased casserole. Top with reserved crumbs. Bake 45 minutes.

Author's Recipe

Heat in a skillet:
2 T. margarine
Add:
2 c. diced unpeeled eggplant
1 c. thinly sliced scallions, green tops included
1 large green pepper, cut in thin strips
1 large tomato, diced
¼ c. water
½ t. salt
¼ t. ground allspice
1 t. sugar (optional)
Mix well. Simmer, covered, until eggplant is tender, about 20 minutes. Add additional water if necessary.

Option:
Substitute ½-1 c. tomato sauce for fresh tomato and water.

Rosemary Moyer, North Newton, Kan.

*Nell Peters wrote
assuring us this is husband Ed's
original creation,
to be found nowhere else!*

*Lots of fuss
but yields a really elegant
meatless casserole.*

●●●●●●●●●●●●●●●●●●●●●●●●●

Eggplant Supreme

T·S

Serves 4

Prepare:
   **1 eggplant, peeled and sliced
   ¼" thick
   1 onion, finely chopped
   1 large green pepper, thinly sliced**
Heat in 10" skillet:
   1 T. margarine
Place 4 slices eggplant symmetrically in
skillet. Add some onion and green
pepper in spaces between eggplant.
Sprinkle with:
   **chili powder
   salt**
In bowl, beat until foamy:
   4-5 eggs
When eggplant softens, pour into skillet
some of beaten egg, just enough to cover
eggplant. Fry over low heat, without
stirring, until egg is cooked. Turn
"pancake" and brown other side.
Remove to platter and hold in warm oven.
Repeat, adding more margarine to
skillet, until eggplant and eggs are used.
One "pancake" serves one person as a
main dish.

Option:

Add chopped tomatoes.

Ed Peters, Choma, Zambia

●●●●●●●●●●●●●●●●●●●●●●●●●

Eggplant Parmesan

Serves 6
375°
10-15 min.

Preheat oven to 375°.
Cut in ½" slices:
   1 medium eggplant
Cover with hot water and let stand 5 min.
Dry slices. Fry in ⅓ c. oil until lightly
browned. Sprinkle with salt and pepper.
Put in bottom of 9 x 13" baking pan.
Mix together and sprinkle over the
eggplant:
   **1 c. bread crumbs
   ½ c. Parmesan cheese
   2 T. chopped parsley
   1 t. salt
   ⅛ t. pepper
   1 t. oregano**
Combine in saucepan:
   **6 tomatoes, chopped
   2 green peppers, chopped
   2 onions, chopped
   2 T. oil
   1 clove garlic, minced
   2 T. tomato paste (or thicken
      sauce with 1 T. flour)**
Simmer uncovered about 20 minutes,
then spread on top of crumb mixture. Top
with:
   **1-2 c. grated Swiss cheese
   ¼ c. additional Parmesan**
Bake 10-15 minutes. Can be made
ahead and refrigerated.

Options:

Broil eggplant instead of frying as in
Easy Moussaka, p. 139.

Substitute zucchini for eggplant.

Zona Galle, Madison, Wis.

Corn Cheese Bake

Serves 6
350°
40-45 min.

Preheat oven to 350°.
Combine and mix well:
  2 c. cooked corn, drained
  ⅔ c. milk
  2 eggs, beaten
  ½ t. salt
  dash pepper
  1 c. shredded cheese (4 oz.)
  2 T. minced onion (optional)
  2 T. minced green pepper (optional)
Pour into greased 1½-qt. casserole. Top with:
  ½ c. cracker crumbs
  2 T. melted margarine
Bake 40-45 minutes.

Jocele Meyer, Brooklyn, Ohio

Mashed Potato Casserole

Serves 6-8
400°
20 min.

Preheat oven to 400°.
Cook and mash:
  3-4 large potatoes
Add:
  ⅓ c. sour cream or yogurt
  1 t. salt
  dash pepper
  ½ t. sugar
  ¼ c. margarine
Add just enough milk to bring to proper consistency and beat until fluffy. Add:
  ⅛ t. dill seed
  2 t. chives, chopped
  1 c. cooked spinach, well drained and chopped
Place in greased casserole and top with:
  ½ c. grated cheddar cheese
Bake 20 minutes.
May be made a day or two ahead and refrigerated, or make a double recipe and freeze half to add to future oven meal.

Helen June Martin, Ephrata, Pa.

*Tester reported
leftovers made extra delicious
potato cakes.*

●●●●●●●●●●●●●●●●●●●●●●●●

Golden
Potato Bake

Serves 8
350°
25 min.

Cook together in salted water until
tender:

**2 lbs. potatoes (about 6 medium),
   peeled**
2 c. thinly sliced carrots

When done, preheat oven to 350°.
Drain vegetables, reserving liquid. Mash
with mixer on low speed.
Add: enough vegetable liquid for
mashed potato consistency.

⅓ c. dry milk powder

Beat until mixture is fluffy. Stir in:

1 T. margarine
salt and pepper to taste

Turn into 2-qt. greased casserole.
Dot with additional margarine if desired.
Bake 25 minutes.

Option:

For main dish, stir in 1 c. shredded
cheese before baking.

Miriam LeFever, East Petersburg, Pa.

●●●●●●●●●●●●●●●●●●●●●●●●

Barbecued Potatoes
And Carrots

Serves 7-8
375°
1¼ hrs./15 min.

Preheat oven to 375°.
Combine in a bowl:

**4 c. thinly sliced potatoes (may
   scrub and leave unpared)**
1 c. bias-sliced carrots
½ c. chopped celery
½ c. chopped onion
**½ c. (2 oz.) shredded
   sharp cheese**

Add to vegetables, tossing to coat:

3 T. all-purpose flour
1 t. salt
dash pepper

Turn into casserole. Blend together in a
bowl:

⅓ c. ketchup
⅛-¼ t. cayenne (optional)
1 t. Worcestershire sauce
½ t. garlic salt
2 c. milk

Pour over vegetables. Cover; bake 1¼
hours. Stir; bake, uncovered, 15 minutes
more. Garnish with parsley.

Lucy Weber, Mohnton, Pa.

*Reserve cooking water when
draining potatoes to mash.
Sprinkle dry milk powder over
potatoes, mash, then add
reserved cooking water and
other seasonings. Fast, cheap,
nutritious.
—Anna Ruth Banks,
   Smithville, Tenn.*

*For scalloped potatoes, leave
peels on and add plenty of
celery, onions, and parsley.
Makes a hearty dish with
delicious nutlike flavor.
—Miriam LeFever,
   East Petersburg, Pa.*

*A traditional dish
used specifically
for leftover
mashed potatoes.*

●●●●●●●●●●●●●●●●●●●●●●●●
German
Potato Noodles

●●●●●●●●●●●●●●●●●●●●●●●●
MCC-Brussels
French Fries

Serves 6

Serves 4

Combine in a bowl:
2 c. mashed potatoes
1 egg, beaten
¾ c. flour
1 t. salt
Mix to form a dough. On lightly floured board, roll out pieces into long strips ¼" thick, and cut into strips 1" wide. In skillet, heat fat (½" deep) and fry until brown. Serve hot.

Adele S. Mowere, Phoenixville, Pa.

Scrub but do not peel:
4-6 medium potatoes
Cut into lengthwise strips ¼ x ¼".
Fill deep fryer half full of oil or lard. (Lard is preferred for flavor.) Heat to 375°. Fill wire basket ¼ full of potato strips and immerse in hot oil. If bubbles spill over, raise basket several times till they subside.
As strips fry, stir gently with long fork to keep them from sticking together. Fry 5 minutes or until strips soften and bend under fork without breaking. Remove from oil, let drip, and spill out onto clean newspaper to absorb excess oil. Repeat with all strips.
Now shake strips all together. Fill basket half full. Fry again about 5 minutes or until golden brown, slightly soft inside and crispy outside.
Remove, let drip, and drain French fries onto dry newspaper. Agitate to dry excess oil. Repeat with remaining strips. Salt lightly. Serve hot.

Don Ziegler, Lancaster, Pa.

*Potato filling
isn't filled into anything
but hungry
Pennsylvania Dutch stomachs.
It's simply a tasty
make-ahead version
of mashed potatoes.*

●●●●●●●●●●●●●●●●●●●●●●●●
Potato
Filling

Serves 4-6
350°
1 hr.

Preheat oven to 350°
Sauté in skillet:
**¼ c. margarine
1 c. chopped celery
1 c. chopped onions**
Pare and boil in salted water:
4 medium-sized potatoes
When done, prepare as for mashed
potatoes.
Mix into potatoes:
**1 egg, slightly beaten
2 slices bread, torn in
small pieces
onions and celery**
Season with salt and pepper to taste. Put
into greased baking dish. Bake for 1
hour. Cover for first half hour, uncover for
remaining time.

*Mabel Stoltzfus, Harrington, Del.
Edna Longacre, Barto, Pa.*

●●●●●●●●●●●●●●●●●●●●●●●●●
Potato
Pancakes

Serves 4

Combine in a bowl:
**2½ c. grated raw potato
(about 3 medium)
1 t. salt
dash pepper
2 eggs
2 T. flour
1 T. finely chopped onion**
Drop by spoonfuls into a lightly oiled hot
skillet. Fry until brown on one side, then
turn and brown on other side. Good
served with syrup, ketchup, or cheese
sauce.

Option:
Add 1 cup finely chopped cooked turkey,
chicken, or ham. Good with cranberry
sauce.

*Anna Ediger, Drake, Sask.
Elvera Goering, Salina, Kan.
Nell Peters, Choma, Zambia*

●●●●●●●●●●●●●●●●●●●●●●●●
Sweet Potatoes
Recife

Serves 8
400°
30 min.

Preheat oven to 400°.
Combine in mixing bowl:
**4 c. cooked mashed sweet
potatoes
2 c. cooked crushed pineapple,
drained
6 T. margarine, melted
1 t. salt
3 T. brown sugar
¼ t. ground cloves**
Turn into ungreased casserole. Sprinkle
on:
½ c. bread crumbs
Bake 30 minutes.

Josefa Soares, Recife, Brazil

●●●●●●●●●●●●●●●●●●●●●●●
Spinach
Loaf

Serves 4-6
350°
35-40 min.

Preheat oven to 350°.
Cook briefly and drain well:
   2 c. frozen chopped spinach
      OR
   2 qt.-saucepan fresh spinach,
      heaping full
Make a white sauce:
   2 T. margarine
   3 T. flour
   ⅛ t. pepper
   1 t. salt
   1 c. milk
Combine:
   spinach
   white sauce
   2 eggs, slightly beaten
Pour into buttered casserole. Bake 35-40
minutes, until knife inserted comes out
clean.

Options:

Sauté 1 onion, chopped, in margarine
when making white sauce.

Add ¾ c. grated cheese to white sauce.

Mary Lou Houser, Lancaster, Pa.
Elvera Goering, Salina, Kan.

●●●●●●●●●●●●●●●●●●●●●●●
Corn–Squash
Bake

Serves 6
350°
40 min.

Preheat oven to 350°.
Cut in 1″ rounds:
   3-4 medium zucchini or other
      summer squash, unpeeled
Cook in small amount of boiling salted
water until tender. Drain and mash with
fork.
Sauté:
   1 T. margarine
   1 small onion, chopped
Combine:
   mashed zucchini
   sautéed onion
   2 c. corn, fresh cut, cooked or
      frozen (thawed)
   1 c. shredded Swiss cheese
   ½ t. salt
   2 beaten eggs
Turn into 1-qt. greased casserole.
Combine and sprinkle on top:
   ¼ c. dry bread crumbs
   2 T. grated Parmesan cheese
   1 T. melted margarine
Place casserole on baking sheet; bake
for 40 minutes, or until set. Let stand 5-10
minutes before serving.

Linda Grasse, Chambersburg, Pa.

••••••••••••••••••••••••••
Stir-Fry
Zucchini

T·S

Serves 4

Heat in large skillet over medium heat:
3 T. salad oil
Add:
**1 lb. zucchini, cut into
    strips about 3″ long**
1 c. onion, cut in large pieces
Cook uncovered, stirring frequently, until
crisp-tender (about 5-8 minutes). Stir in:
2 T. sesame seeds
1 T. soy sauce
½ t. salt
dash pepper

Option:
Cut zucchini and onion in rounds.

Evelyn Liechty, Berne, Ind.

••••••••••••••••••••••••••
Skillet
Italian Zucchini

T·S

Serves 4

Slice diagonally, ½″ thick:
8 small zucchini, unpeeled
Heat in skillet:
2 T. butter or margarine
Add and sauté about 5 minutes:
½ onion, chopped
sliced zucchini
Add:
**2 c. spaghetti sauce, tomato
    sauce, or canned tomatoes**
**2 T. grated Parmesan cheese
    (optional)**
1 t. salt
½ t. leaf thyme
½ t. oregano
½ t. basil
dash pepper
Cover and simmer just until crisp-tender.

Linda Grasse, Chambersburg, Pa.

••••••••••••••••••••••••••
Baked Italian
Zucchini

Serves 6
350°
45 min./10 min.

Preheat oven to 350°.
Place in casserole, adding seasoning to
each layer:
**2 medium or 3-4 small unpeeled
    zucchini, sliced ½″ thick**
1 onion, sliced
**1 whole tomato, sliced
    (optional)**
1 t. oregano
½ t. basil
salt and pepper
Pour over:
**1-2 c. tomato sauce, enough to
    barely cover vegetables**
Cover and bake 45 minutes.
Uncover and add:
**1 c. cubed buttered bread
    or ½ c. bread crumbs**
½ c. grated cheese
Bake an additional 10 minutes,
uncovered.

Option:
Use frozen sliced zucchini, but increase
first baking time to 1 hour.

Author's Recipe

Tester reported:
"Husband HATES zucchini
but liked this
and never knew
what he was eating
until told."

●●●●●●●●●●●●●●●●●●●●●●●

Zucchini
Skillet Supper

T·S

Serves 4-5

Sauté in skillet in small amount hot fat:
4 c. zucchini, thinly sliced
1 onion, sliced
Add:
2 c. canned tomatoes with juice
¾ c. canned mushrooms, drained
(optional)
salt, pepper, and oregano to taste
cubes of cooked chicken, beef,
ham, or browned ground beef
Simmer just until heated through. Serve
in soup bowls and sprinkle with
Parmesan cheese.

Options:
Use fresh sliced mushrooms and sauté
with zucchini.

Use fresh tomatoes in season. Add
tomato juice for liquid.

Omit meat and serve as vegetable.

Eat over noodles or rice.

Ruth Sherman, Goshen, Ind.

●●●●●●●●●●●●●●●●●●●●●●●

Zucchini
Omelet

T·S

Serves 4-5
350°
25-30 min.

Preheat oven to 350°.
Heat in skillet:
2 T. margarine
Sauté gently until fork-tender, 5-7
minutes:
1 medium onion, sliced thinly
1 clove garlic, minced
2 lbs. zucchini squash, coarsely
grated
Add:
1½ t. salt
¼ t. pepper
Put squash in baking dish.
Meanwhile, combine:
2 eggs
½ c. milk
3 T. flour
½ c. grated Parmesan or other
cheese
Pour over squash. Bake 25-30 minutes,
or until firm.

Option:
Add 2 beaten eggs and seasonings
directly to sautéed vegetables. Cook and
stir until eggs are set.

Barbara Longenecker, New Holland, Pa.

●●●●●●●●●●●●●●●●●●●●●●●●●
Zucchini
And Eggs

T·S

Serves 3

Prepare:
4 small zucchini, unpeeled
Cut squash in half, then split each half
into 4 pieces. Heat in skillet:
2 T. margarine
2 T. oil
Flour squash lightly and fry until brown.
Sprinkle with salt and pepper. Arrange
zucchini evenly in skillet. Combine and
pour over top:
2 eggs, lightly beaten
1 T. milk
Cook slowly until set. Sprinkle with:
grated Parmesan cheese

Option:
Sauté onion with zucchini and season
with garlic salt, parsley, and oregano.

Olive Wyse, Goshen, Ind.
Linda Grasse, Chambersburg, Pa.

> *I have struggled with
> monetary cost versus
> environmental cost.* More-
> with-Less Cookbook *empha-
> sizes buying low-cost foods.
> Often, though, the low-cost
> food is more cheaply
> produced, using more food
> additives, more pesticides,
> etc. So it's not the healthier
> choice. Organic food is more
> expensive, yet it should be
> the healthier alternative.*
> *—Judy Martens,
> Blumenort, Man.*

●●●●●●●●●●●●●●●●●●●●●●●●●
Zucchini
Egg Foo Yung

Serves 4

Grate coarsely:
4 medium unpeeled zucchini
Mix in:
3 eggs, beaten
¼ c. flour or ½ c. wheat germ
¼ t. garlic powder (optional)
1 t. salt
1 onion, grated
Fry by tablespoonfuls in hot oiled skillet,
turning once when golden brown.
Arrange on platter and top with sauce:
Combine in saucepan:
1 c. chicken broth
2 T. soy sauce
1 T. cornstarch
Cook and stir over low heat until
thickened. Serve with rice.

Options:
Add fresh bean sprouts with grated
zucchini.

Switch from Chinese to Italian meal by
topping with tomato sauce and
Parmesan cheese sprinkle. Serve with
spaghetti.

Evelyn Liechty, Berne, Ind.
Eleanor Hiebert, Elkins Park, Pa.

●●●●●●●●●●●●●●●●●●●●●●●●
Tomatoes
Stuffed with Spinach

Kale and Swiss chard
stay green in the garden
long after the first frost
and were a good
early winter source
of Vitamin A before freezers.

Serves 6

375°
---
20 min.

Preheat oven to 375°.
Prepare for stuffing:
6 firm tomatoes
Cut off tops and scoop out centers.
Combine:
2 c. cooked spinach
1 T. melted butter
½ t. salt
½ onion, minced
Pack into tomato shells. Place in greased casserole and bake about 20 minutes. Serve with creamed hard-cooked eggs as a main dish.

Grace Horning, Ephrata, Pa.

●●●●●●●●●●●●●●●●●●●●●●●●
Brown Tomato Gravy

T·S

Serves 3

Peel and slice:
2-3 firm, ripe tomatoes
Heat in skillet:
2 T. margarine or shortening
Roll tomato slices in flour and brown quickly on both sides.
Reduce heat.
Add to skillet:
2 T. sugar
1 t. salt
1 c. water
Simmer 30 minutes, stirring occasionally and breaking up tomato chunks. Serve with potatoes, rice, noodles, or on toast.

Edna Mast, Cochranville, Pa.

●●●●●●●●●●●●●●●●●●●●●●●●●
Prussian
Kale

T·S

Serves 3

Prepare:
1 qt. fresh kale, finely chopped
Cover with cold water and bring to a boil. After boiling 2 minutes, drain off water and discard.
Add:
1 c. fresh water
½ t. salt
dash pepper
¼ c. oatmeal
one of the following to flavor:
piece of boiled fresh pork
ham bits
several strips crisp bacon,
crumbled
2 T. bacon fat or margarine
Simmer about 10 min.

Option:

Use other greens such as Swiss chard, turnip or beet greens, collards, spinach. Parboiling results in some loss of vitamins but is necessary with kale to remove bitterness. Other greens may not require this step.

Helene Janzen, Elbing, Kan.

*Salsify is a white root vegetable.
The all-salsify version
of this dish
is called "mock oyster scallop"
in Pennsylvania Dutch country.*

●●●●●●●●●●●●●●●●●●●●●●●●●

Salsify-Carrot Casserole

Serves 6
350°
35-40 min.

Preheat oven to 350°.
Combine:
  **3 c. cooked mashed carrots
    and salsify**
  1 c. cracker crumbs
  2 c. milk
  2 T. grated onion
  3 T. melted margarine
  3 eggs, slightly beaten
  salt and pepper
Bake in casserole 35-40 min.

Option:

All carrots or all salsify may be used, but
the combination is delicious.

Ann Huber, Lancaster, Pa.

*Squash flowers are a delicacy
in many parts of the world
when blossoms are
plentiful enough to predict
an ample harvest.
Hopi, Pueblo, and Zuni Indians
enjoyed their crisp, light texture.*

●●●●●●●●●●●●●●●●●●●●●●●●

Fried Squash Blossoms

Serves 6

Wash carefully and drain:
  **12 large squash blossoms
    (pick when blossoms are just
    ready to open)**
Make batter:
  2 eggs, beaten
  **1 c. flour (may use ⅓ or more
    soy flour)**
  1 c. water
  1 t. salt
  ¼ t. cayenne
  ½ t. tumeric
Heat in heavy saucepan:
  ½-1 c. oil
Dip blossoms in batter until well coated,
then fry in hot fat (375°) until golden
brown. (Takes less than a minute for
each.) Drain on absorbent paper and
serve warm.

LaVonne Platt, Newton, Kan.

*Vegetables may be cooked
an hour or two in advance
and need not be kept hot.
In Indonesia
the dish is served
at room temperature.*

●●●●●●●●●●●●●●●●●●●●●●●●
Gado Gado
(Indonesian
vegetable platter)

Serves 8

Vegetables:
Cook or steam each vegetable
separately just until crisp-tender:
  ½ small head cabbage, cut up
  **½ lb. fresh green beans, cut or
  French-style**
  **1 small head cauliflower, cut into
  flowerets**
  1 can or 2 c. fresh bean sprouts
  4 carrots, cut in small strips
  **other vegetables may be added
  or substituted**
Drain vegetables, reserving stock for
peanut sauce.
Peel and quarter:
  4 hard-cooked eggs
Slice:
  2 cucumbers
  6-10 radishes

Peanut Sauce
Sauté in heavy saucepan:
  3 T. oil
  ½ c. finely chopped onions
  2 cloves garlic, minced
Stir-fry until onions are soft and
transparent, not brown.
Add:
  3½ c. hot water or vegetable stock
  **1 c. peanut butter (an additional
  2 T. if chunky peanut butter
  is used)**
  **2 t. fresh chopped hot peppers,
  or Tabasco sauce to taste**
  2 bay leaves
  **1 t. scraped, finely grated fresh
  ginger root**
  ▶

●●●●●●●●●●●●●●●●●●●●●●●●
Ratatouille

T·S

Serves 6-8

Combine in large saucepan:
  1 medium eggplant, pared, cubed
  2 small zucchini, cubed
  1 c. finely chopped green pepper
  **1 medium onion, finely chopped,
  about ½ c.**
  **4 medium tomatoes, peeled and
  quartered**
  ¼ c. salad oil
  1 clove garlic, crushed
  2 t. salt
  ¼ t. pepper
Cook and stir ingredients until heated
through. Cover, cook over medium heat,
stirring occasionally, about 10 minutes,
or until vegetables are crisp-tender.

  Mary Alderfer, Scottdale, Pa.
  Kathleen Kurtz, Richmond, Va.

  2 t. lemon juice
  grated rind of one lemon
  1 t. salt
Reduce heat and simmer for 15 minutes.
Taste for seasoning and set pan aside.
Group vegetables attractively on a large
platter or two, with a bowl of peanut
sauce in the center. Garnish platter with
eggs, radishes, and cucumbers. Serve
with hot rice.

  Jean Miller, Akron, Pa.

*Mahsi recipe came with raves
(especially for the grape leaves)
from all around
the Mediterranean.*

●●●●●●●●●●●●●●●●●●●●●●●●

Mahsi
(Middle Eastern
Stuffed Vegetables)

Serves 6
325°
1½ hrs.

Preheat oven to 325°.
Prepare a variety of vegetables for
stuffing:

**Tomatoes, bell peppers, zucchini,
small eggplant—**
Cut off tops, reserving lids. Clean out
center seedy portions, reserving tomato
pulp.
Leafy vegetables—
Cabbage and green grape leaves.
Parboil 3 minutes to soften. Use newer
grape leaves—old ones are tough.
Four-inch size is needed to stuff easily.
Prepare *stuffing*:
Brown in a skillet:
**½-1 lb. ground beef, pork,
or lamb
1 large onion, finely chopped
3 cloves garlic, minced (optional)**
Add:
**½ c. minced parsley
1 c. uncooked rice
3 T. margarine or olive oil
1 t. salt
dash pepper
2 c. tomato sauce plus any
reserved tomato pulp
fresh chopped mint and/or
dill to taste**
Taste to check seasonings. Fill
hollowed-out vegetables ⅔ full with rice
mixture, replacing "lids."
For leaf vegetables, place 1 T. stuffing
mix on each. Roll up loosely so rice can
expand, folding in sides. May be
fastened with toothpicks.
Place vegetables in baking dish, add
water to ¼" depth, and bake 1½ hours.

▶

●●●●●●●●●●●●●●●●●●●●●●●●

Gemüse Eintopf
(one-dish
vegetable meal)

T·S

Serves 8

Combine in large kettle:
**2 lbs. potatoes, cut up
2 lbs. turnips or carrots, cut up
OR 1 lb. cooked pumpkin,
mashed
2 onions, chopped
2 stalks celery, chopped
3 T. fresh or dried parsley
2 cloves garlic, minced
salt and pepper to taste**
Add:
**small amount of water
¼ c. margarine or other fat**
Cook slowly until vegetables are tender.
When almost done, add:
**1 T. powder bouillon or 3 cubes
(dissolve in ¼ c. hot water)**
Serve as is, or put through food mill to
form a thick puree.

Irene L. Bishop, Perkasie, Pa.

Options:

To cook on top of stove, place
vegetables in a well-buttered skillet, add
2 c. boiling water or thin tomato juice, 2 T.
lemon juice, and cover with a light-fitting
lid. Bring to boiling and reduce heat to
simmer. Cook 1 hour or until rice is
tender.

Omit meat and increase rice and tomato
sauce amounts.

*Carolyn Yoder, Cairo, Egypt
Louise Claassen, Elkhart, Ind. (Crete)
Esther Samuel Geladah, Atbara, Sudan
Gwen Peachey, Amman, Jordan*

Gather Up
the Fragments

1.
Collect bits of cooked vegetables in container in freezer, along with juices from cooking. Use to make soup. See p. 197.

2.
Whirl leftovers in blender and add to cream soup, gravy, stew, casseroles.

3.
Pour oil and vinegar dressing over cooked green beans, beets, carrots, broccoli, cauliflower, asparagus. Marinate in refrigerator and serve on lettuce or add to tossed salad.

4.
Heat leftover pickle juice and pour over leftover vegetables; chill and serve on pickle tray. See p. 258.

5.
Reheat several vegetables with onion, garlic, and tomato sauce. Add curry seasonings and serve on rice. Curry powder masks any leftover taste.

6.
Leftover corn does not reheat with much flavor; stir it into corn fritters, corn bread (pp. 78-79), or one of the corn soups (pp. 200-202).

7.
Using scorched vegetables: Remove from heat. Place in another saucepan. Add small amount of liquid, place slice of bread or toast on top to absorb burned taste from vegetable and resume cooking.
—*Mae Holty, Roxbury, Pa.*

8.
Recipes that take well to vegetable leftovers:
Vegetables Au Gratin, p. 220
German Potato Noodles, p. 232
Corn-Cheese Bake, p. 230
Corn-Squash Bake, p. 234
Puffy Green Bean-Cheese Bake, p. 221
Vietnam Fried Rice, p. 130
Many soup recipes

salads......

Good cooks don't need many salad recipes. The best salads are simple collections of raw vegetables with only a light touch of dressing. Once you know how to put together the vegetables at hand, keep them crisp, and stir up an easy dressing, you can almost go on to the next chapter.

Too many salad recipes read like dessert: 2 boxes flavored sugared gelatin, sweetened canned fruit, marshmallows, nuts, and a whipped topping folded in. The first economy move would be to omit nuts; actually they are the single nutritious ingredient listed. Name these concoctions for what they are—expensive sweets. Serve them as desserts if at all.

Raw vegetable salads are more nutritious. But people still manage to go wrong by drowning their greens in sugary, orange stuff called French dressing. (Reportedly the French never allow it across their borders.)

Bottled salad dressings are expensive and high in fats and sugars. They contain enough preservatives to last forever in the door of your refrigerator. The glass bottles that go to waste may be worth more than their contents.

Homemade dressings are cheaper. With imaginative use of herbs and seasonings, they taste better than anything you can buy.

But beware the salad dressing recipe with ½ to 1 cup of sugar. These formulas are everywhere, teaching people to expect a foretaste of dessert on their greens.

Develop gradually your household's taste for herbs, lemon, garlic, and the natural flavors of crisp raw vegetables.

Raw Vegetable Salads

1. If you raise nothing else edible, plant at least a salad garden. A double-bed-sized plot of scallions, herbs, greens, and tomato vines can keep salad on the table May through October.

2. Iceberg lettuce has few vitamins. Use other greens or mix it with endive, romaine, Boston Bibb, or raw spinach.

3. Wash greens, drain well, pat dry with a clean towel, and refrigerate in plastic bag or closed container. Excess water clinging to the leaves makes dressing turn watery and tasteless.

4. Tear greens into a salad bowl instead of cutting them. You can then make salad hours ahead of time, cover it with plastic, and refrigerate. Torn edges do not wilt and darken quickly.

5. Shake together a little oil and vinegar dressing (see p. 247).

6. Just before serving, add dressing, toss, and serve. Garnish salads with croutons, sliced hard-cooked eggs, sliced radishes or scallions, chopped parsley, peanuts, or toasted sunflower seeds. Use these touches rather than sweet dressing by the cupful to make salads appealing.

Sprouting Mung Beans

Across Asia tiny round green mung beans are a staple food. Baskets of slender white sprouted beans appear in vegetable markets from Japan to Indonesia, usually costing just pennies a crisp handful. North America knows this nutritious, delightful food only in its wilted and strong-flavored canned form, although now fresh bean sprouts are sold in some Western supermarkets.

Bean sprouts are easy to make at home without special equipment. Growing them makes an interesting project for a child. Results are quickly visible and harvest comes in four days.

Buy mung beans at a health food or Chinese grocery store. You'll pay more per pound than for other dry beans, but you need only ⅓ c. to yield a quart of sprouts.

Use fresh sprouts in green salads, in sandwiches, or add to any stir-fried vegetable. Sprouts take only one to two minutes stir-frying. Don't cook longer or they'll wilt completely and lose their crunchy fresh flavor. See recipes on pp. 139, 159, 222, 249.

Sprouting method

1. Soak ⅓ c. mung beans in water overnight.
2. Drain and place beans in a colander lined with a clean cloth (old dishtowel or pillowcase). Fold edges of the cloth down loosely over the beans and run warm water through everything.
3. Set colander in a pie pan to catch drips and place in a warm dark place. A cupboard over a stove or refrigerator, or a covered box near a radiator work well.
4. Three times a day for 3 to 4 days rinse several quarts tepid water through colander, cloth and all.
5. Sprouts are ready to eat on the fourth day, or sooner if they are 1¼ inches long. Remove them from the cloth and refrigerate in a covered container. Yields about 4 to 5 cups.
6. Green hulls are good to eat. If you prefer to remove them, swish sprouts repeatedly in cold water, lifting them out and discarding hulls as they sink to the bottom.

Alternate Method

Put 2 T. soaked beans in each of several quart-size canning jars. Cover tops with cheesecloth, then screw on rings. Place jars on their sides in a warm dark place. Three times a day, run water in, swish beans, and pour off water. Circles cut to fit from metal screen can replace cheesecloth.

Alfalfa Sprouts

Use canning jar method as for mung beans, but soak only 2 tablespoons untreated alfalfa seed and use one jar. In one or two days when seed has sprouted, set jar in sunny window to develop deep green color as sprouts lengthen. Rinse regularly. Refrigerate when sprouts reach desired length, after 3 to 4 days. Use in salads or sandwiches.

*Depending on cost
of oil and eggs,
this can run as high
as commercial mayonnaise.
Check prices.*

●●●●●●●●●●●●●●●●●●●●●●●●●
Blender
Mayonnaise

Makes 1 pint

Whirl in blender:
2 eggs
1½ t. salt
1 t. dry mustard
½ t. paprika
Clean down sides. Add:
2 T. lemon juice
Start blender, remove cover, and *very*
slowly pour in:
½ c. salad oil
Add:
2 T. vinegar
Slowly, with blender running, add:
1½ c. salad oil

Esther Hostetter, Akron, Pa.
Sharal Phinney, Elkton, Va.

●●●●●●●●●●●●●●●●●●●●●●●●●
Low-Cal
Mock Mayonnaise

Makes about 1 cup

Shake in covered jar until smooth:
¾ c. skim milk
2 T. flour
3 T. sugar
½ t. salt
½ t. dry mustard
Pour into saucepan and cook until
thickened, stirring constantly.
Add:
¼ c. vinegar
Use hot or cold as a substitute for
mayonnaise. Just before using, stir in
finely chopped onion and/or other herbs
and seasonings to taste.
Makes 1¼ c.

Mary Slabaugh, Harrisonburg, Va.

*Costs about two thirds
as much as
commercial mayonnaise.*

●●●●●●●●●●●●●●●●●●●●●●●●
Cooked
Mayonnaise

Makes 3 cups

Combine in saucepan:
⅓ c. flour
½ c. sugar
1 t. salt
Add:
¾ c. water
½ c. vinegar
Cook over low heat, stirring until
thickened. Remove from heat and pour
into small mixing bowl or blender. While
beating, add:
1 clove minced garlic (optional)
2 whole eggs or 4 yolks
Continue beating and slowly add:
⅔ c. salad oil
Chill before serving.

Katie Swartzendruber, Wellman, Iowa

*We served with Mennonite
Central Committee in Nigeria,
and More-with-Less Cookbook
was like my cooking bible. It
gave me so many ideas for
things to make with the
resources available there.
There were also recipes to
make things we buy in this
country, such as mayonnaise,
sauerkraut, maple syrup,
tortillas, and English muffins.
I have tried close to half the
recipes; no other cookbook on
my shelf even comes close to
that.
—Marge Kempf
Swartzendruber,
Shickley, Neb.*

245

Combine in saucepan:
   ¼ c. sugar
   ¼ c. flour
   2 t. salt
   2 t. dry mustard
Add:
   1½ c. milk
   ½ c. mild vinegar or lemon juice
Cook over low heat, stirring until
thickened.
Stir at least half of the mixture into:
   1 beaten egg
Return egg mixture to saucepan and
bring to boil. Boil 1 minute. Remove from
heat. Stir in:
   1 T. butter or margarine
Cool.

   Bonnie Zook, Leola, Pa.

••••••••••••••••••••••••
Salad Dressings
With Mayonnaise
Base

Thousand Island
Combine:
   1 c. mayonnaise
   ¼ c. chili sauce or ketchup
   2 hard-cooked eggs, chopped
   2 T. *each* finely chopped green
       pepper and onion
   2 T. pickle relish (optional)
   1 t. paprika
   ½ t. salt

Green Goddess
Combine:
   ½ c. mayonnaise
   ¼ c. sour cream or yogurt
   2 T. lemon juice or vinegar
   2 T. snipped chives
   2 T. snipped parsley
   ¼ t. salt
   freshly ground pepper

Blue Cheese
Combine:
   1 c. mayonnaise
   ¼ c. crumbled blue cheese
   2 T. milk
   dash cayenne pepper

Tangy sweet-sour flavor
without being sugary.
Use on tossed salads.

••••••••••••••••••••••••
Honey–Lemon
Dressing

Makes almost 1 cup

Shake together:
   2 T. honey
   ¼ c. lemon juice
   ½ c. oil
   salt, pepper and herbs to taste

   Twila Strickler

•••••••••••••••••••••••••••
Fresh Fruit
Salad Dressing

___
Makes about 1½ cups
___

Beat well:
    2 eggs
Pour into saucepan. Add:
    ½ c. sugar
    ⅔ c. pineapple juice
    1½ T. lemon juice
Cook over low heat, stirring constantly, until thick. Chill.

Marian Franz, Washington, D.C.

•••••••••••••••••••••••••••
Parsley
Dressing

___
Makes 2 cups
___

Whirl in blender:
    ½ c. parsley, packed into cup
    ⅓ c. salad oil
    ¼ c. water
    ¼ c. honey
    ¼ c. lemon juice
    2 t. basil
    salt
    ½ c. chopped avocado (optional)
Use on greens or Chop Salad, p. 250.

Twila Strickler

*The simplest
of all salad dressings–
make it anywhere,
anytime by remembering
equal parts
oil and vinegar.*

•••••••••••••••••••••••••••
Basic Oil and
Vinegar Dressing

___
Serves 6-8 on green salad
___

Shake together or combine in bottom of salad bowl:
    2 T. salad oil
    **2 T. vinegar or lemon juice or
        combination**
    ½ t. salt
    **dash each freshly ground pepper,
        dry mustard**
Add to taste:
pressed garlic	**poppy seeds**
minced onion	**celery seeds**
oregano	**ketchup**
basil	**honey**
chopped parsley	
chopped chives	

Winifred Paul, Scottdale, Pa.

*Contributor says,
"I haven't bought
any bottled dressing
since I found this recipe."*

•••••••••••••••••••••••••••
French
Dressing

___
Makes 1⅓ cups
___

Shake, beat, or whirl in blender:
    1 T. grated onion
    1 t. salt
    2 T. sugar
    2 T. vinegar
    ½ c. salad oil
    ½ c. ketchup
    2 T. lemon juice
    1 t. paprika
Keeps well in refrigerator.

Esther Hostetter, Akron, Pa.
Grace Whitehead, Kokomo, Ind.

●●●●●●●●●●●●●●●●●●●●●●●
Garden
Salad

Serves 6

Combine in salad bowl:
½ c. shredded carrots
1 c. diced cauliflower
1 c. frozen peas, thawed
OR 1 c. cooked chick-peas,
drained
1 c. chopped celery
3 c. tomatoes, chopped
1 c. cucumbers, chopped
1 c. lettuce, chopped
½ c. roasted sunflower seeds
Toss and serve with Honey-Lemon
Dressing, p. 246.

Twila Strickler

So simple,
and just right
with almost any main dish.
Contributor grew up
in France
and now lives in Indonesia.

●●●●●●●●●●●●●●●●●●●●●●●●
French-Style
Lettuce Salad

T·S

Serves 4-6

Wash, drain, and dry thoroughly:
½-1 head lettuce
Rub salad bowl with:
1 clove garlic, sliced
Add directly to salad bowl:
2 T. salad oil
1 T. wine vinegar
¼ t. salt
freshly ground pepper to taste
1-2 T. minced parsley
1 t. lemon juice (optional)
Mix well with salad spoon. Criscross
salad fork and spoon in salad bowl to
keep lettuce from dressing until ready to
serve. With hands, tear lettuce leaves
and place over top of salad fork and
spoon. Just before serving, toss
thoroughly.

Cathy Bowman, Kotabumi, Sumatra

●●●●●●●●●●●●●●●●●●●●●●●●
Greens
With Croutons

Serves 6

Sauté lightly or brown in the oven:
1½ c. cubed bread
2 T. oil or margarine
Set aside.
Add to the bottom of salad bowl:
2 cloves garlic, minced
½ t. salt
½ t. dry mustard
freshly ground pepper to taste
2 T. wine vinegar
¼ c. salad oil
Stir with back of spoon. Set bowl aside.
When ready to serve, add:
5-6 c. fresh torn greens, using
spinach, endive, leaf lettuce,
romaine, or others as available
toasted croutons
Toss and serve. Reserve a few croutons
for topping, and add a sprinkle of
Parmesan cheese if desired.

Eleanor Hiebert, Elkins Park, Pa.

••••••••••••••••••••••••
Corn and Cabbage
Slaw

Serves 6

Combine in salad bowl:
    4 c. shredded cabbage
    ½ c. chopped onion
    1-1½ c. cooked corn
    ½ c. diced sharp cheese
    2 T. sliced black olives (optional)
    2 T. chopped parsley (optional)
Combine for dressing:
    ⅓ c. cooked salad dressing or
        mayonnaise
    2 t. prepared mustard
    ¼ t. celery salt
Pour dressing over salad and toss.

Eleanor Kaufman, Newton, Kan.

••••••••••••••••••••••••
Cucumber
Salad

T·S

Serves 4

Place in a bowl:
    1 large cucumber, thinly sliced
    1-2 T. finely cut fresh dill (use
        feathery leaves, not seeds)
Combine in small bowl:
    2 T. mayonnaise or sour cream
    1 T. vinegar
    2 T. oil
    1 t. salt
    dash pepper
Mix and pour over cucumber slices. Chill
and serve.

Irmgard Hildenbrand,
Rusinga Island, Kenya

Guaranteed
to tempt spinach-haters,
old and young.

••••••••••••••••••••••••
Sprouts
Salad

Serves 6

Place in dry skillet:
    ½ c. sunflower seeds
Toast by stirring over medium heat for
about 3 minutes.
Combine in large salad bowl:
    1 c. alfalfa or bean sprouts,
        loosely packed
    3-4 c. salad greens, torn into
        bite-size pieces
    6 or 8 radishes, sliced
    ½ cucumber, sliced
    toasted sunflower seeds
Shake together for dressing:
    ¼ c. salad oil
    2 T. vinegar
    ⅛ t. salt
    freshly ground pepper
    ⅛ t. garlic powder
Pour over salad and toss. Garnish with:
    1 or 2 hard-boiled eggs, sliced

Eleanor Hiebert, Elkins Park, Pa.

••••••••••••••••••••••••
Fresh Spinach
Salad

Serves 6

Combine in large salad bowl:
    1 qt. chopped fresh spinach
    ½ c. chopped celery
    1 onion or 3 scallions, chopped
    ¾ c. small Swiss cheese cubes
    3 hard-cooked eggs, chopped
Combine in small bowl:
    ½ c. mayonnaise
    2 T. vinegar
    ½ t. salt
    ½ t. horseradish
    ½ t. Tabasco, or dash
        cayenne pepper
Just before serving, pour mayonnaise
mixture over salad bowl and toss.

Carolyn Blosser, Akron, Pa.

Good served with boiled potatoes in the jacket and apple crisp for dessert.

●●●●●●●●●●●●●●●●●●●●●●●●

Dandelion Salad

Serves 4-6

Gather dandelion very early in spring before buds develop. At this time of year other greens are expensive, so take advantage of it as a first fruit. With a small sharp knife gather entire plants; cut off leaves, wash carefully, drain, and chop into a bowl. Proceed as follows:
Hard-cook:
   2 eggs
Cool and shell.
Fry in skillet until crisp:
   2 slices chopped bacon
Remove bacon and drain. Leave 2 T. drippings in skillet.
Combine and add to skillet:
   4 T. flour
   1 t. salt
   3 T. sugar
   3 T. vinegar
   1½ c. water or milk
Cook, stirring constantly, until sauce is smooth and thick. Pour sauce over:
   4 c. chopped dandelion greens
Stir lightly to coat greens. Garnish with sliced hard-cooked eggs and bacon bits.

Options:
Add 1 egg, beaten, to dressing mixture before pouring into skillet. Increase liquid to 2 cups.

Replace dandelion with other chopped greens such as endive, spinach, oak-leaf lettuce.

Martha Nafziger, LaCrete, Alta.
Ruth Eitzen, Barto, Pa.

●●●●●●●●●●●●●●●●●●●●●●●●

Chop Salad

Serves 6-8

Combine in bowl:
   1 c. finely chopped celery
   1 c. chopped green pepper
   ½ c. sliced scallions or
      chopped onions
   1-2 c. diced tomatoes
   1 c. chopped cucumbers
   chopped chives (optional)
   chopped parsley (optional)
   2-3 T. vinegar or lemon juice
   1 t. sugar
   ½ t. salt
   dash freshly ground pepper
Stir thoroughly and chill. Serve as salad or as relish (chutney) with rice and curry.

Options:
Omit celery, green pepper, or cucumber if unavailable.

Omit last 4 ingredients and use Parsley Dressing, p. 247.

Twila Strickler

Here is an easy way to preserve cabbage when heads begin to split in the garden. A large quantity provides instant salad for weeks.

●●●●●●●●●●●●●●●●●●●●●●●●
Refrigerator Coleslaw

T·S

Makes about 3 qts.

Chop in blender, or shred and cut finely:
- **2 large or 3 medium heads cabbage**
- **2 stalks celery**
- **3-4 carrots**
- **1 onion**

Sprinkle generously with salt and set aside while making dressing. Before adding dressing, squeeze dry.

Dressing:
Combine in saucepan:
- **2 c. sugar**
- **1 t. salt**
- **1 c. vinegar**
- **⅛ t. pepper**
- **1-2 t. celery seed**

Bring to a boil. Remove from heat. When cool, add to cabbage. Mix well.
Can be made in large amounts and stored in refrigerator or freezer. Keeps in refrigerator several months. Store in tightly covered containers.

Loretta Leatherman, Akron, Pa.

> *I mixed thawed Refrigerator Coleslaw with a bit of cream or creamy dressing, and my family loved it. A new favorite was born! Now I devote whole cabbage heads to this instant wintertime salad. I use cabbage alone, and use a weaker dressing made by combining 1 c. sugar, ½ c. vinegar, ½ c. water.*
> *—Delphine Carter, Newton, Ont.*

●●●●●●●●●●●●●●●●●●●●●●●●
Deluxe Coleslaw

Serves 10

About 1½ hours before serving or early in day, remove and reserve 4-5 outer leaves from:
- **1 medium head cabbage**

Shred remaining cabbage to make 8 cups.
In large bowl toss gently:
- **shredded cabbage**
- **1 green pepper, thinly sliced**
- **⅔ c. diced celery**
- **⅔ c. finely shredded carrots**
- **½ c. sliced radishes**
- **2 T. minced onion**

Combine for dressing:
- **1 c. mayonnaise or cooked salad dressing**
- **2 T. milk**
- **2 T. vinegar or lemon juice**
- **1 t. sugar**
- **¾ t. salt**
- **¼ t. paprika**
- **¼ t. pepper**

Mix well. Pour over vegetables and toss gently. Cover and chill. When ready to serve, arrange coleslaw on reserved cabbage leaves.

Anne Weaver, Blue Ball, Pa.

Cauliflower Salad

Serves 6

Combine in bowl:
2 c. diced raw cauliflower
½ c. sliced scallions
1 carrot, sliced
¼ c. salad oil
1½ T. lemon juice
1½ T. wine vinegar
1 t. salt
½ t. sugar
dash pepper
Mix well. Chill before serving.

Option:
Add ¼ c. sliced black olives.

Esther Yoder, Topeka, Ind.

Contributor suggests using any of the following: cooked broccoli, cauliflower, asparagus, corn, peas, green beans, and lima beans.

Summer Night Salad

Dressing serves 6

Combine in bowl:
variety of leftover cooked vegetables
small amounts fresh garden vegetables, cooked separately just until crisp-tender
cooked diced chicken or ham and/or diced cheese
1 hard-cooked egg per person, diced
½ c. pecans, chopped
Use favorite salad dressing or the following:
¼ c. mayonnaise
¼ c. cream
1 T. vinegar
1 t. salt
1 t. sugar
Toss all ingredients lightly with dressing and chill several hours. Serve on lettuce garnished with colorful raw vegetables.

Rosa Mullet, Pantego, N.C.

Israeli Supper

T·S

Put on the table in a bowl:
cucumbers
tomatoes
onions
green peppers
hard-cooked eggs
Give each person:
salad bowl
scrap bowl
sharp knife
Each person peels and chops his own cucumber, tomato, and adds a bit of onion and green pepper, then peels and chops his hard-cooked egg over it. Add a bit of salad oil, salt and pepper, and stir it up. Eat with good homemade bread, butter and jam, and hot tea. White cheese and/or yogurt may also be served.

Elizabeth Yoder, Bluffton, Ohio

252

Taco Salad

Serves 6

Brown together in skillet:
1 lb. ground beef
1 onion, chopped
Remove from heat and stir in:
**2 c. cooked kidney beans,
    drained**
1 t. salt
½ t. pepper
Combine in large salad bowl:
1 head lettuce, torn up
2 large tomatoes, chopped
**3-4 tortillas, fried crisp and
    broken up**
meat-bean mixture
Toss together. Serve with Chili-Tomato
Sauce, p. 145, as a dressing.

Options:

Omit meat. Add raw chopped onion and
1-2 c. grated cheese.

Arrange ingredients separately in bowls.
Each person assembles their own salad.

A 5 oz. package corn or tortilla chips may
be substituted for fried tortillas but will
make the dish more expensive.

Esther Kniss, Arcadia, Fa.
Bonnie Zook, Leola, Pa.

Beet and Apple Salad

Serves 6

Mix together:
2 c. cooked beets, diced
2 c. raw apple, diced
2 hard-boiled eggs, diced
Add:
**½ c. cooked salad dressing or
    mayonnaise**
¼ c. nuts
Toss lightly. Serve on lettuce and garnish
with chopped nuts and parsley.

Lena Brown, Grantham, Pa.

Company Chicken Salad

Serves 12

Combine in large bowl:
4 c. cooked, diced chicken
4 c. grated carrots
4 c. finely chopped celery
1 medium onion, chopped
Toss with:
3 c. salad dressing or mayonnaise
Chill. Just before serving, stir in:
**2-3 c. shoestring potatoes
    (optional)**

Dorothy Yoder, Hartsville, Ohio

Green Bean And Sprout Salad

Serves 6

Cook just until crisp-tender:
3 c. fresh French-cut green beans
Drain and cool. Add:
1-2 c. fresh bean sprouts
⅓ c. green onions, sliced
½ c. celery, thinly sliced
1 sweet red pepper, sliced
Toss to mix. Combine separately:
¼ c. vegetable oil
2 T. vinegar
**salt, sugar, pepper, and herbs
    to taste**
Pour over vegetables, toss and chill 1-2
hours. Serve on lettuce, garnished with
tomato wedges.

Author's Recipe

●●●●●●●●●●●●●●●●●●●●●●●●●
Green Bean
Salad

Serves 6-8

Combine in salad bowl:
**3 c. cooked green beans, cut in
  1″ pieces
4 hard-cooked eggs, chopped
1 medium onion, diced
1 large dill pickle, chopped**
Combine and pour over:
**2 T. vinegar
1 t. salt
⅔ c. mayonnaise or cooked
  salad dressing**
Stir gently, chill and serve.

Anna Petersheim, Kinzers, Pa.

*Goes well as one of several
dishes in a Chinese dinner
menu. Add a stir-fried
vegetable-meat dish, soup, and rice.*

●●●●●●●●●●●●●●●●●●●●●●●●●●
Chinese
Chicken–Cucumber
Salad

T·S

Serves 4-6

Cut or shred:
1 c. cooked chicken
Peel:
2 cucumbers
Cut in half lengthwise and scoop out
seeds; cut in strips.
Arrange cucumber strips on flat plate;
top with chicken. Cover and chill until
mealtime.
Combine and pour over chicken:
**½ t. dry mustard
½ t. salt
2 T. vinegar**

Louise Lehman, Wapakoneta, Ohio

●●●●●●●●●●●●●●●●●●●●●●●●●
Basic
Three-Bean Salad

Serves 10-12

Use 2 c. *each* of three kinds of cooked,
drained beans. Choose an attractive
color combination.
**cut green beans
cut yellow wax beans
soy beans
red kidney beans
green lima beans
great northern or navy beans
chick-peas or garbanzos**
In large bowl, toss beans with:
**1 medium onion, finely chopped
1 medium green pepper, chopped**
Combine and pour over
**½ c. salad oil
½ c. vinegar
½ c. sugar
1 t. salt
¼ t. pepper**
Chill before serving. Improves with
marinating overnight or longer.

*Gladys Sweigart, Lancaster, Pa.
Karen Harvey, Leola, Pa.*

254

●●●●●●●●●●●●●●●●●●●●●●●●●
Tabouleh
(Middle East)

Serves 6-8

Pour 4 c. boiling water over:
**1¼ c. raw bulgur wheat or
cracked wheat**
Let stand 2 hours, or until wheat is fluffy.
Drain well. Mix with:
**1 c. cooked chick-peas
(garbanzos), drained
1¼ c. minced parsley
¾ c. minced mint
¾ c. minced scallions, or 1 onion,
finely chopped
3 tomatoes, chopped
¾ c. lemon juice
⅓ c. oil (preferably olive oil)
1 t. salt**
Chill at least 1 hour. Serve on lettuce.

*Alice and Willard Roth, Elkhart, Ind.
Helen King Stork, Ventura, Calif.*

●●●●●●●●●●●●●●●●●●●●●●●●●
Main-Dish
Tuna Salad

Serves 6-8

Cook and drain as directed on package:
**7 oz. noodles, spaghetti rings,
or macaroni**
Cook, drain, and cool noodles or
spaghetti.
Combine in large mixing bowl:
**cooked pasta
1 7-oz. can chunk tuna
1 c. chopped celery
½ c. finely chopped scallions
with greens
½ c. chopped sweet pickles
3 hard-boiled eggs, chopped
½ c. mayonnaise
2 T. sweet pickle juice
1 T. prepared mustard
½ t. salt
dash pepper**
Chill and serve on lettuce leaves.
Sprinkle with paprika.

Rosemary Moyer, North Newton, Kan.

●●●●●●●●●●●●●●●●●●●●●●●●●
Soybean Salad
Special

Serves 5

Combine in salad bowl:
**½ head lettuce, torn in bite-size
pieces
1½ c. cooked soybeans, drained
1 fresh orange, peeled and diced
2 T. chopped onion or scallion**
Combine in a jar and shake:
**¼ c. oil
1 T. lemon juice
1 T. vinegar
¼ t. dry mustard
1 T. honey
1 T. orange juice
½ t. sugar
¼ t. salt
½ t. paprika**
Pour dressing over salad ingredients
and toss lightly.

Option:

Mix dressing in advance and pour over
soybeans. Marinate several hours or
overnight. Then add lettuce, orange and
onion; toss and serve.

Mary Lou Houser, Lancaster, Pa.

255

A gorgeous summertime salad—
bring with crusty
fresh bread
to an outdoor table.

●●●●●●●●●●●●●●●●●●●●●●●●●●

Salade
Nicoise

Serves 5-6

Prepare in advance and chill in separate
containers:
   3 c. potato salad (omit
      hard-cooked eggs)
   3 c. fresh green beans, cooked
      exactly 5 minutes and drained
   3-4 tomatoes, quartered
   1 head Boston or other leaf lettuce,
      separated, washed and
      drained
   3 hard-cooked eggs, peeled and
      quartered
   1 c. Basic Oil and Vinegar dressing
      with herbs and garlic
   2-3 T. minced fresh herbs such as
      chives, parsley and dill
Also chill:
   1 7-oz. can tuna
Shortly before serving:
—Season green beans and tomatoes
with 2 T. each of prepared dressing.
—In salad bowl, toss lettuce with 2 T.
dressing, then arrange leaves around
bottom and outside of bowl.
—Place potato salad in bottom of the
bowl on lettuce. Arrange green beans,
tomatoes, eggs, and drained tuna in an
attractive design on top of potato salad.
Pour remaining dressing over all,
sprinkle with herbs, and serve
immediately.

Author's Recipe

●●●●●●●●●●●●●●●●●●●●●●●●●

Lettuce–Tomato
with Beef

T·S

Serves 4-6

Stir together and set aside:
   ¼ lb. beef, sliced paper thin
      (use chuck or round steak)
   ½ medium onion, grated or
      crushed
   2 cloves garlic, crushed
   ¼ t. salt
   dash pepper
   ½ t. sugar
   ¼ t. monosodium glutamate
Arrange on platter:
   1 head Boston Bibb lettuce leaves
   2 tomatoes, sliced
   1 cucumber, sliced
Place tomatoes and cucumbers on
lettuce leaves, leaving well in the center
for meat.
Combine dressing in bowl and set aside:
   ½ onion, chopped
   3 T. vinegar
   3 T. oil
   ½ t. salt
   dash pepper
   1½ T. sugar
Heat in skillet over high heat:
   1 T. oil
Add marinated beef and stir-fry quickly
just until beef loses red color (about 1
min.). Put beef in "well" on salad platter.
Add 1 T. water to skillet, swish, and pour
into dressing. Stir and pour over meat
and vegetables. Serve with rice.

Mary Martin, Saigon, Vietnam

Vietnamese cooks cut beautiful cabbage salads without a grater. Here's how: remove leaves from head one by one. Lay several together and roll up tightly. Lay roll on board and slice across as thinly as possible with very sharp knife. Surprisingly fast, and yields a dish completely different from the usual shredded affair.

Complete the meal with a light soup and whole grain bread.

●●●●●●●●●●●●●●●●●●●●●●●●
Cabbage and Pork Salad

●●●●●●●●●●●●●●●●●●●●●●●●
Greens, Peas'n' Cheese Salad

T·S

Serves 4

Serves 5-6

Mix together in large bowl:
½ head cabbage, cut in long, slender pieces (see above)
2 carrots, grated
Add:
¼-½ lb. pork, boiled and thinly sliced
several sprigs fresh dill and mint, chopped
Mix thoroughly.
Combine in small bowl:
1 T. soy sauce
3 T. sugar
3-4 T. vinegar
2 t. lemon or lime juice
Pour over salad mixture and toss well. Just before serving, sprinkle over the top of the salad:
¾ c. roasted peanuts, salted and chopped
Eat with hot rice or as a salad accompaniment to soup or stew.

Option:

To serve as main dish with rice, garnish with hard-cooked egg and tomato wedges.

Tran thi Kim Trinh, Quang Ngai, Vietnam

Have ready:
4-6 c. bite-size greens (lettuce, spinach, endive)
1 small onion, thinly sliced
2 c. cooked peas
4 oz. Swiss cheese, julienne strips
6 T. cooked salad dressing or mayonnaise
2 t. sugar
2 slices bacon, fried crisp and crumbled OR equivalent soybean-based bacon substitute
In large salad bowl, place half the greens, onions, peas, cheese; sprinkle with 1 t. sugar. Dot with 3 T. mayonnaise. Repeat layers. Cover and refrigerate 2 hours. Add bacon and toss just before serving.

Mary Lou Houser, Lancaster, Pa.

Dilled
Onions

Makes 2 cups

Place in bowl:
**6 white onions, sliced into
    thin rings**
Combine in saucepan and heat:
**½ c. sugar
2 t. salt
¾ t. dill seed
½ c. white vinegar
¼ c. water**
Bring mixture to a rolling boil. Remove from heat and pour over onions. Let stand until cool. Store in refrigerator.

Miriam E. Shenk, Migori, Kenya

*If dill pickles
disappear at your house,
so will these
interesting additions
to a relish tray.*

Dilled
Carrot Sticks

Makes 2 cups

Simmer until not quite tender:
**6-8 carrots, cut in sticks
small amount salted water**
Drain carrots. Pour over:
**leftover brine from 1 qt. dill
    pickles**
Heat just to boiling. Cool. Keeps in refrigerator several weeks.

Iona Weaver, Collegeville, Pa.

Dried
Apple–Cranberry
Relish

Makes 6 cups

Combine in saucepan:
**8 oz. dried apple slices
2½ c. water**
Bring to boil, reduce heat, and simmer covered 10 minutes. Pour into bowl.
Combine in same saucepan:
**2 c. fresh cranberries
¾ c. light brown sugar or honey
1¼ c. water**
Bring to boil and cook until cranberries have popped. Add cooked apples and simmer 10 minutes, stirring occasionally. Chill.

Catherine Mack, Ardmore, Pa.

Gazpacho

Serves 4

Combine in bowl:
**1 c. peeled tomatoes,
    finely chopped
½ c. finely chopped green pepper
½ c. chopped celery
½ c. chopped cucumber
¼ c. chopped onion
2 t. snipped parsley
1 t. snipped chives
1 small clove garlic, minced
3 T. wine vinegar
2 T. salad oil
1 t. salt
¼ t. freshly ground pepper
½ t. Worcestershire sauce
3 c. tomato juice**
Chill. Serve as an appetizer or cold soup.

Option:

Gazpacho relish: omit tomato juice.

*Marian Franz, Washington, D.C.
Beverly Ehst, Ambler, Pa.*

Rhubarb Salad

Serves 8

Cook together:
- **3 c. finely cut rhubarb**
- **½ c. sugar**
- **¼ t. salt**
- **⅓ c. water**

Add:
- **2 3-oz. pkgs. strawberry gelatin**
- **1 c. finely chopped celery**
- **2¼ c. water**
- **1 T. lemon juice**
- **½ c. chopped nuts**

Chill until firm.

Virginia Ebersole, Landisville, Pa.
Mona Sauder, Wauseon, Ohio

Soybean Salad

Serves 4

Combine in bowl:
- **1½ c. cooked soybeans, drained**
- **½ c. diced celery**
- **½ c. diced carrots**
- **1 t. minced onion**
- **½ c. diced cheese**
- **2 hard-cooked eggs, diced**
- **¼ c. chopped sweet pickles**

Cover and chill thoroughly.
Combine by stirring French dressing slowly into mayonnaise:
- **½ c. French dressing (see p. 247)**
- **1 T. mayonnaise**

Pour over salad, toss, and chill 1 more hour or longer.

Clara Breneman, Waynesfield, Ohio

Use frozen cranberries and the salad will congeal quickly.

Blender Cranberry Salad

T·S

Serves 6

Combine in small saucepan:
- **1 envelope unflavored gelatin**
- **1 c. cold water**

Warm over low heat until gelatin dissolves.
Combine in blender container:
- **2 c. cranberries**
- **1 unpeeled orange, seeded and quartered**
- **1 apple, cored and quartered**
- **½-¾ c. sugar or honey**

Pour dissolved gelatin into blender.
Blend only until orange peels are well chopped. Add:
- **¼ c. nuts (optional)**

Chill until firm.

Options:

Omit gelatin and water and serve as a relish.

Use food grinder in place of blender to chop fruits.

Patricia Franke, Welcottville, Ind.

Tangy Carrot–Pineapple Mold

Serves 6

Drain, reserving juice:
- **1 c. crushed pineapple**

Dissolve and chill until slightly thickened:
- **1 3-oz. pkg. orange gelatin**
- **1 c. boiling water (include reserved pineapple juice)**

Fold in:
- **1 c. plain yogurt**
- **crushed pineapple**
- **1 c. grated carrots**
- **1 t. lemon juice**

Pour into mold and chill until firm.
Unmold and serve on bed of lettuce.

Option:

Replace orange gelatin with lime; replace pineapple and carrots with canned grapefruit sections.

Rosemary Moyer, North Newton, Kan.

259

desserts, cakes, and cookies......

Our biggest area of doing with less is desserts—we have them only occasionally.
—Janet Landes, Phoenix, Ariz.

I use less sugar in my cookies and coffee cakes than the recipes call for. I cut the amount of sugar by ¼ to ½. My children don't even notice the change. Cookies don't last any longer.
—Marianne Miller, Topeka, Kan.

I have been using ⅓ less sugar in all ice cream, cookies, brownies, pudding, and pie recipes and haven't ruined anything yet.
—Pauline Wyse, Mt. Pleasant, Iowa

Traveling in India we could toss banana peels out of the bus window without concern for littering. Momentarily a goat or a cow would wander past and dispose of the peel in a single gulp.

One day two small children retrieved the banana peels our family discarded. The girl, about eight years old, wore a ragged saree. Her little brother of four or five was clad only in an oversize shirt. They were not beggars but watched for banana peels because they saw me coming from the fruit stand. As four peelings landed on the dusty road the children pounced.

The girl brushed dirt from the peels. She handed all the peelings to her brother, pulled a grimy square cloth from the folds of her saree and smoothed it out carefully beside the road. She and the boy sat down.

Meticulously, the girl pulled the soft portion of each banana peel away from the outer skin and placed it on the cloth. The outer tough portions she tossed aside. She gave half to her brother. They began to eat.

Whoever says that hungry people eat like animals when they have the chance did not see that Indian girl serve banana peels to her brother.
—LaVonne Platt, Newton, Kan.

Sugar never was good for us. This fact seems to be rediscovered whenever the price goes up. We've long been aware of sugar's role in tooth decay, diabetes, and obesity. Recent research adds that excessive use of sugar can lead to premature atherosclerosis.

North Americans have each been eating 100-plus pounds of sugar yearly since the 1930s, except for a sharp decline during war-shortage sugar rationing in the early 40s. But back in 1880, 30 pounds a year was average. In those days white sugar was a luxury item brought out only for company, according to Laura Ingalls Wilder's *Little House* books. In *Farmer Boy*, Mother's parting call to her children as she leaves for a week to visit relatives is, "Don't use up all the sugar!"

One cannot condone some of the interests which send up the price of sugar. We reap certain blessings, however, when its cost is high in comparison to other foods. When sugar is cheap, it replaces more costly and nutritious ingredients in processed foods. Manufacturers are loathe to divulge to the public how much sugar is added to their products.

Much land now devoted to sugar should be used for other crops yielding proteins, vitamins, and minerals. Eating less sugar is one way of conserving world food resources.

A dessert is (almost by definition) a food containing sugar. But before getting into dessert recipes, let's remind ourselves that not all meals require a sweet ending. The daily dessert habit is firmly entrenched in North America, but not with most other peoples. In many countries sweets are used for celebrations only, not to top off everyday meals.

Mary Alene Miller, Obihiro, Japan, writes, "We usually eat fresh fruit after the evening meal. About once a week we have desserts—when guests are here or for other special occasions." Ann Zook, Americus, Ga., says, "I have grown to appreciate a much simpler way of cooking and have reached a point of preparing a guest meal without a dessert."

Fruit, with its natural sweetener, is the perfect dessert. People protest that fresh fruit is too expensive. This is true in certain seasons and localities. But if good oranges, for example, are a dollar a dozen, it will cost fifty cents to serve six people an orange each for dessert. You can hardly bake a cake or buy ice cream for six for that price. Any dessert concocted of gelatin, whipped topping, fruit, and graham cracker crumbs will run closer to a dollar. Add up the cost of a favorite snack or dessert recipe before concluding that fresh fruit is out of reach.

What is an economical dessert?

I read somewhere that economical cooking means nutritious cooking. Therefore fresh fruit or a dessert with milk and eggs is most economical since it provides the most nutrition.
—Elsie Epp, Marion, S.D.

What will this food do for us? is the question to ask. If dessert only adds more calories, better to be old-fashioned and tell everyone to have another slice of bread. It's cheaper and more nutritious.

Use milk, egg, and cheese desserts to good advantage with low-protein meals. For example, vegetable soup made with a bone or two doesn't really have much protein. Finish the meal with cheesecake, a rich dessert high in complete protein that goes well with a light meal. But you don't need cheesecake after roast beef, gravy, mashed potatoes, and corn.

Puddings, traditional fruit moos, cobblers, and crisps are good to round out light lunches and suppers. Yogurt and fruit is a perfect high-nutrient, low-calorie dessert. Made at home, yogurt is also economical.

What about the mixes?

Cake mixes are usually as cheap as home-baked cakes, unless you get your staples in quantity at a good price. If a cake-mix type cake is what you like, costwise they're acceptable. At our house we prefer not to have cake very often. With some patience my husband has convinced me that mix-made cakes are dusty—his description—and fairly worthless as a food. When we have cake we enjoy a moist, home-baked product that includes applesauce, dates, nuts, rolled oats, carrots, coconut, or some other texture and flavor in addition to just sweetness.

Most other dessert mixes are grossly overpriced. Stick to simple desserts and stir up your own.

Honey, corn syrup, and molasses

Honey is the only natural sweetener not refined with chemicals. It is high in calories, but doesn't yield most of the other harmful effects associated with refined sugar. The problem with honey is that it is too expensive to replace a heavy sugar habit unless you keep bees yourself. Better economy is cutting down on all sweets.

Keep some honey on hand for subtle sweetening on cereal, breakfast toast, or in salad dressings. Use it in desserts such as custards or cheesecakes which call for small quantities of sweetener. Baking cakes or cookies with honey, however, becomes very expensive. Since these products depend on sugar for structural qualities, you need specially developed recipes or the results will be heavy. If you are lucky enough to have a cheap source of honey and would like to experiment, see Appendix III, Substitutions.

Cup for cup, corn syrup and molasses will not yield as sweet a product as honey. Corn syrup has little nutritional advantage over sugar. Dark molasses contributes usable amounts of iron and calcium. Too often molasses is more expensive than sugar, when actually the reverse ought to be true because molasses takes less refining than sugar.

More with less sugar

Use less sugar and you will notice subtle sweetening qualities in other foods. Last Christmas I discovered that the filling in date bars needs no added sugar—flavor is enhanced without it! Canned and frozen fruits need some sugar for texture and preservation, but cut down on the amounts and learn to enjoy the tart fruit flavor. Unsweetened canned pineapple is now on grocery shelves and is a taste delight compared to the typical syrupy canned fruits we have come to expect.

Be forwarned! The recipes in this chapter are not very sweet. Many came in with reduced sugar amounts and some we reduced further. But our testers still gave them good ratings. Typical comment was, "Recipe calls for ¾ cup sugar. I made it a second time with only ⅔ cup and it still disappeared quickly. Half a cup would be enough." With sugar, when half a cup is enough, you get more with less.

Making Yogurt

Yogurt is simply milk jelled to a pudding consistency by certain acid-forming bacteria growing in it.

Yogurt is made from sweet milk, not sour, but has a characteristic sour taste that blends lusciously with the natural sugar of fruit. Mary Kathryn Stucky, a yogurt enthusiast who makes a gallon at a time for a family of four, writes, "Yogurt is something a person has to learn to like. Once you develop the taste for it, you will hate to be without." Yogurt is for people who enjoy tart flavors.

Yogurt is a dairy dessert without the added fats, sugars, and calories of ice cream. Essentially it contains the same calories, proteins, minerals, and other nutrients as milk. It may be made from whole or skim milk. Yogurt bacteria is friendly to the digestive tract, and leaves you with a good feeling of having eaten something light, tasty, and satisfying.

Yogurt is almost as cheap as milk if you make your own, but more expensive than ice cream if you buy it. Since it's easy to make, the advantages are all with home production.

Here is a method:

1. *Scald utensils* to be used with boiling water.

2. *Prepare the milk.* Start with 1 quart. Use raw, pasteurized-homogenized, dry, or evaporated milk, or follow recipe on page 264. Fresh milk should be brought up to 180°. Use a candy thermometer and watch closely so it doesn't boil over. Cool milk to 110°. If using dry or evaporated milk, reconstitute with warm water. If using skim or nonfat dry milk, add at least a little whole milk for a thicker culture.

3. *Add the starter.* Buy one container of plain commercial yogurt. Stir ¼ to ⅓ cup yogurt into 1 cup prepared milk, then add this to remaining warm milk and stir or shake briskly. Or buy yogurt starter at a health food store and follow directions. Pour milk into scalded jars and fasten lids loosely.

4. *Incubate the mixture* at 110-120° by any of these methods:
—Use a yogurt maker.
—Set jars into styrofoam ice chest. Fill chest with warm water (110-120°) to top of jars; cover. Add warm water as needed within next few hours to keep temperature up.

—Set jars into warm oven and turn off heat. Leaving oven light on may be exactly the right temperature. Check with thermometer.
—Set jars on rack in large pan of warm water on the stove; occasionally turn heat on briefly. Or set pan over pilot light.
—Set jars in pan of warm water, cover, and wrap all in a blanket.
—Set jar under tea cozy near radiator or heater.

5. *Check consistency.* Yogurt should not be moved while it is setting. Check in 2 to 3 hours, and every half hour after that. Usually 3 to 6 hours is needed for junket-like consistency. Refrigerate. Save ¼ cup to start next batch. Yogurt stays tasty in the refrigerator 1 to 2 weeks.

6. Serve yogurt
—with any fresh, frozen or canned fruits
—blended with frozen orange, grape, or pineapple concentrate (see Yogurt Popsicles, p. 313)
—with honey or molasses
—sprinkled with wheat germ or granola
—as a low-calorie sour cream substitute in salads, salad dressings, casseroles, or on baked potatoes
—accompanying hot, spicy dishes, especially curries

Always add fruit, sugar, or honey to yogurt with a folding motion. Stirring or beating breaks down the gel.

When introducing yogurt for the first time, be a little generous with the sweetener. Once people have acquired a taste for it, they will enjoy the tangy flavor for its own sake.

When you spoon yogurt out of its container, there is often some watery separation. This does not affect the taste, but to avoid it entirely, stir one envelope unflavored gelatin into ¼ c. cold water, warm to dissolve, and stir well into 1 qt. yogurt. Chill. Use this method to salvage a batch that won't thicken properly.

*See pp. 262
for detailed method.*

●●●●●●●●●●●●●●●●●●●●●●●
Yogurt

Makes 2 qts.

Combine in large bowl:
 3 c. powdered milk
 6 c. warm water
Stir well. Add:
 1 can evaporated milk OR
  1⅔ c. scalded whole milk
Combine separately:
 ¼-½ c. yogurt
 1 c. milk from the bowl
Blend until smooth and return to
remaining milk. Mix well. Pour into clean
jars. Incubate at 110-120° until set.
Refrigerate.

*Mary Lou Houser, Lancaster, Pa.
Mary Kathryn Stucky, Burrton, Kan.
Marcia Beachy, DeKalb, Ill.*

●●●●●●●●●●●●●●●●●●●●●●●
Quick
Chocolate Pudding

T·S

Serves 4-6

Combine in heavy saucepan:
 ⅓ c. sugar or honey
 2 T. cornstarch
 2 T. cocoa
 2 c. milk
Cook over low heat until thickened,
stirring constantly.
Add:
 1 t. vanilla
 1 T. margarine (optional)
Serve warm or cold.

Option:
Stir in ¼ c. peanut butter. Omit
margarine.

Grace Whitehead, Kokomo, Ind.

Fluffy
Vanilla Pudding

T·S

Serves 4-6

Combine in heavy saucepan:
   ⅔ c. dry milk solids
   ¼ c. water
Add:
   1½ c. hot water
Place saucepan over low heat.
In small bowl, beat together with fork or
wire whisk:
   ¼ c. sugar
   2½ T. cornstarch
   ¼ t. salt
   2 egg yolks (reserve whites)
   ¼ c. water
Pour egg mixture into hot milk, stirring
constantly until thickened. Cook 2
minutes over low heat. Remove from heat
and add:
   1 t. vanilla
   1 T. margarine (optional)
Cool pudding 10 minutes.
Fold in:
   2 stiffly beaten egg whites

Options:

Use 5 T. flour to replace cornstarch.
Make pudding in double boiler; takes
longer but doesn't require constant
stirring.
Serve with fruit.
Use for cream pies; instead of folding in
egg whites, reserve for meringue.
Serve with waffles and fruit.
Layer into serving dish with graham
cracker crumbs and sliced bananas.
Add 3 T. cocoa to egg yolk mixture;
increase sugar to ⅓ c.

Margot Fieguth, Mississauga, Ont.
Mary Kathryn Yoder, Garden City, Mo.
Carol Smith, Mechanicsburg, Pa.

Company
Pudding

Serves 6-8
425°
10 min.

Prepare one recipe Fluffy Vanilla
Pudding, increasing cornstarch to 3 T.
Preheat oven to 425°.
Crumble together in a bowl:
   ⅓ c. brown sugar
   ½ c. whole wheat or white flour
   ½ c. rolled oats
   ½ t. cinnamon
   ⅓ c. soft margarine
Press two thirds of the mixture into a
7x11" baking pan. Place remaining
crumbs on a pie pan. Bake both pans
5-10 minutes, or until brown. Cool.
On top of crust in 7x11" pan, spread thin
layer of *one* of these:
   applesauce
   chopped dates cooked in small
      amount water until thick
   drained peaches
   sliced bananas
Top with pudding. Sprinkle over
remaining toasted crumbs.
Chill at least 3 hours before serving.

Margot Fieguth, Mississauga, Ont.

265

*The humble breakfast cereal
makes a lovely dessert.
Grandmother unmolded this
pudding into a shallow serving
bowl and surrounded it with
cooked raspberries or
homemade grape juice.*

*Traditionally, moos
is served with fried ham
and potatoes,
or as a dessert;
it also makes
a good light meal
accompanied simply
by fresh bread
and butter.*

●●●●●●●●●●●●●●●●●●●●●●●●●

Cream of Wheat Pudding

Serves 6

Bring to boil in heavy saucepan:
2 c. milk
Add slowly, stirring constantly:
⅓-½ c. cream of wheat
Cook until thickened, about 5 minutes.
Combine and beat until light:
2 egg yolks (reserve whites)
⅓ c. sugar
pinch salt
Add slowly to cream of wheat, stirring
constantly. Cook 2 minutes. Remove
from heat and add flavoring:
**1 t. vanilla, vanilla and lemon
extract blended, or almond
and lemon**
Beat until stiff:
2 egg whites
Fold into pudding. Pour into serving bowl
or mold. Chill thoroughly. Serve with
strawberries or raspberries.

Helen E. Regier, Newton, Kan.

●●●●●●●●●●●●●●●●●●●●●●●●●

Fruit Moos

Serves 6

Moos, a Russian Mennonite dish, is a
fruit soup made from fresh, canned,
frozen, or dried fruits. Traditional *plume
moos* uses raisins and prunes. Tart,
flavorful fruits are best; try fresh or
canned sour cherries, apricots,
peaches, rhubarb, apple-blackberry, or
gooseberry. Dried fruits should be
covered with boiling water and allowed
to soak overnight.
Heat in heavy kettle:
1 qt. fruit in syrup
**3 c. additional water and/or milk
(if available, use 1 c. cream)**
½ c. honey or sugar
Cook slowly until fruit is soft. Combine in
small bowl:
4-5 T. flour
**additional honey or sugar if
needed (check sweetness
of fruit)**
1 c. milk or cream
Mix to a smooth paste. Dip out some hot
fruit and stir into the paste; then slowly
pour mixture back into the fruit, stirring
constantly. Continue cooking over low
heat until thickened. Serve warm or cold.
For large quantity, use ½ c. flour to 1 gal.
liquid.

Stein Goering, Gillingham, Wis.

Baked Custard

Serves 4
325°
50 min.

Preheat oven to 325°
Mix together:
⅔ c. dry milk solids
**¼ c. sugar or honey (add honey
after dry milk and water
are combined)**
few grains salt
Add slowly and stir until smooth:
2 c. water
Mix in:
2 eggs, slightly beaten
1 t. vanilla
Pour into 4 custard cups. Sprinkle with
nutmeg. Set in flat pan containing 1" hot
water. Bake 50 minutes or until knife
inserted near edge of custard comes out
clean.

Options:

Add 1½-2 c. cooked rice and ½ c. raisins
before baking. Serves 6-8.

Add ⅔ c. coconut before baking.

Miriam LeFever, East Petersburg, Pa.

Pumpkin Custard

Serves 4-6
350°
45 min.

Preheat oven to 350°.
Combine in mixing bowl:
1½ c. cooked, strained pumpkin
⅔ c. brown sugar
3 eggs, beaten
1½ c. scalded milk
1 T. cornstarch
1 t. cinnamon
½ t. ginger
**¼ t. *each* ground cloves and
nutmeg**
Pour into buttered baking dish. Bake 45
minutes.

Nora Bohn, Goshen, Ind.
Linda Yoder, Hartville, Ohio

●●●●●●●●●●●●●●●●●●●●●●●●

Creamy
Rice Pudding

Serves 6

Combine in top of double boiler:
¼ c. rice
2 c. milk
Cook uncovered 45 minutes or until rice is tender.
Beat together:
2 egg yolks (reserve whites)
¼ c. sugar
¼ t. salt
Stir some of rice mixture into beaten yolks; add yolks to hot rice mixture and cook 3-4 minutes, stirring constantly. Remove from heat and add:
1 t. vanilla
Beat until frothy:
2 egg whites
Add:
2 T. sugar
Beat until stiff. Fold egg whites into pudding. Chill and serve.

Options:

Place pudding in a baking dish. Spread beaten whites on top and brown delicately in the oven.

Add ½ c. raisins to pudding.

Special orange pudding: Add whites along with egg yolks. Stir in 1 t. grated orange rind. When chilled, blend in ½ c. cottage cheese.

Carolyn Yoder, Grantsville, Md., in
Mennonite Community Cookbook

●●●●●●●●●●●●●●●●●●●●●●●●

Rice
Pudding

Serves 6
275°
2-2½ hrs.

Preheat oven to 275°.
Combine in buttered baking dish:
4 c. milk, scalded
⅓ c. rice
⅓ c. sugar
¼ t. salt
dash nutmeg, cinnamon, or dried orange peel
Bake 2-2½ hours, until rice is tender and milk is creamy. Stir occasionally during first half of baking time. Pudding thickens as it cools. Serve warm or cold.

Option:

One-half hour before removing from oven, add ⅓ c. raisins.

Edna Longacre, Barto, Pa.
Florence Ressler, Dalton, Ohio
Ella May Miller, Harrisonburg, Va.

●●●●●●●●●●●●●●●●●●●●●●●●●

Applesauce
Bread Pudding

Serves 8
350°
55-60 min.

Preheat oven to 350°.
Arrange in bottom of greased 9″ square
pan:
   4 slices dry bread
Combine:
   2 c. applesauce
   ½ c. raisins
   ¼ c. brown sugar
   ½ t. ground cinnamon
Spread over bread. Top with:
   4 additional slices dry bread
Beat together:
   2 eggs
   2 c. milk
   ½ c. brown sugar
   ½ t. vanilla
   ¼ t. salt
   dash ground nutmeg
Pour over bread. Top with:
   ½ c. applesauce
   sprinkle of cinnamon-sugar
Bake 55-60 minutes. Serve warm or cold.

Miriam LeFever, East Petersburg, Pa.

●●●●●●●●●●●●●●●●●●●●●●●●●

Jamaican
Baked Bananas

Serves 4-6
350°
25-30 min.

Preheat oven to 350°.
Peel and arrange in casserole:
   4-6 bananas, sliced if desired
In saucepan, combine:
   2 T. margarine
   2 T. sugar
   1 c. orange juice
Cook and stir about 1 minute. Combine:
   2 T. cornstarch
   ¼ c. cold orange juice
Add to hot mixture and cook until clear
and thickened.
If desired, add:
   ¼-½ c. raisins
Pour over bananas. Top with grated
coconut. Bake 25-30 minutes at 350°.
Serve warm with custard sauce.

Option:

Simple baked bananas: Place 4 bananas
in shallow buttered casserole. Drizzle
over: 2 T. melted margarine, 2 T. honey,
and ⅓ c. apple or orange juice. Sprinkle
with cinnamon-sugar. Bake 20 min. at
350°. Serve warm.

Sarah Eby, Akron, Pa.

In Africa we seldom saw brown sugar. Missionaries gave me this recipe: To each cup of white granulated sugar, add 2 T. old-fashioned molasses. Stir well and store in airtight container. Excellent flavor in cookies or cake toppings, or on oatmeal. I make it since we're back because it's much cheaper and we like the flavor better.
—*Evelyn Fisher, Akron, Pa.*

Desserts

Banana Special: Peel a banana and cut in half lengthwise. Spread with peanut butter and press together. Place in dessert dish, sprinkle with cinnamon, and pour over slightly beaten evaporated milk.
—*Adele Mowere,*
 Phoenixville, Pa.

● ●
Fruit Dumplings

Serves 8
350°
45 min.

Prepare 2-3 c. finely chopped fresh fruit. Use apples, peaches, rhubarb, etc. Set aside.
Preheat oven to 350°.
Prepare 1 recipe biscuit dough, p. 72. Roll dough into large rectangle on floured board. Cover thickly with fruit. Sprinkle with cinnamon. Roll up like jelly roll and cut into 1" rings. Place in greased 9x13" baking pan.
Combine in saucepan:
  1 c. sugar
  1 T. flour
  1 c. cold water
Let come to a boil and pour over dumplings. Bake 45 minutes. Serve warm with milk.

Phoebe Coffman, Dayton, Va.

● ●
Apple Crisp

Serves 6
375°
35 min.

Preheat oven to 375°.
Combine and put in greased casserole:
  3 c. sliced or chopped apples
  1 T. flour
  ¼ c. sugar
  1 t. cinnamon
  ⅛ t. salt
  1 T. water
Cut together with pastry blender:
  ½ c. rolled oats
  ¼ t. salt
  ¼ c. margarine
  ⅓ c. brown sugar
Sprinkle on top of casserole mixture. Bake 35 minutes.

Option:
Add ¼ c. peanut butter to rolled oats mixture. Reduce margarine to 2 T.

Verna Wagler, Baden, Ont.
Ruth Weaver, Reading, Pa.

Scalloped Rhubarb: Combine 3 c. cubed stale bread, ½ c. melted margarine, 2 c. diced rhubarb, and 1 c. sugar. Put 1 T. water in each corner of baking dish. Bake at 325° for 45 min.
—Judy Classen, Akron, Pa.

When a gelatin dessert or salad calls for 2 packages flavored gelatin, use one envelope unflavored gelatin for the second package. Fold in fruits or vegetables as usual. End product is less sweet and less expensive, but just as tasty.
—Iona S. Weaver,
  Collegeville, Pa.

Baked Apples: Fill centers of cored apples with raisins or dates. Drizzle with honey and sprinkle with cinnamon and nutmeg. Add ½ inch water. Bake until tender, basting occasionally. To save fuel, cover and cook slowly on top of stove.
—F. Mabel Hensel,
  Harrisburg, Pa.

●●●●●●●●●●●●●●●●●●●●●●●●●
Granola Apple Crisp

Serves 6
350°
25-30 min.

Preheat oven to 350°.
Place in greased 9" square baking pan:
**5 medium cooking apples,
    peeled and sliced**
Combine:
**⅓ c. flour
1 t. cinnamon
½ c. firmly packed brown sugar
1½ c. granola
⅓ c. margarine, melted**
Sprinkle granola mixture over apples. Bake 25-30 minutes. Serve warm or cold with milk.

Option:
Peach Crisp: Substitute 4 c. fresh or canned (drained) peach slices for apples.

Author's Recipe

●●●●●●●●●●●●●●●●●●●●●●●●●
Grandmother's Brown Betty

Serves 8
350°
45-50 min.

Combine in large bowl:
**8 tart apples, sliced
½ c. raisins
½ c. honey
½ c. apple juice or water
¼ c. brown sugar
3 T. flour
1 t. cinnamon**
Turn into greased 7x11" baking pan.
Combine in bowl:
**½ c. quick-cooking rolled oats
½ c. whole wheat flour
½ c. wheat germ
½ c. shelled sunflower seeds
¼ c. honey
4 T. margarine**
Mix well. Spread over apple mixture. Bake at 350° for 45-50 minutes.

Anne Braun, Liberal, Kan.

Applesauce Pudding: Combine cookie or graham cracker crumbs with a little sugar and cinnamon. Layer alternately with applesauce into a glass serving bowl. Chill before serving.
—Ruth Gish, Mt. Joy, Pa.

When my mother moved into a small apartment, she gave away many household items, including a stack of cookbooks. Her children and grandchildren were invited to choose things. When I passed the list on to my daughter in college, she wrote back, "There's only one thing I'm really interested in—the More-with-Less Cookbook."
—Mary C. Meyer, Scottdale, Pa.

●●●●●●●●●●●●●●●●●●●●●●●●●
Fruit Crumble

Serves 6
375°
25 min.

Preheat oven to 375°.
Place in buttered 8x8" baking dish:
2½ c. fruit—cherries, or pared and sliced apples or peaches
Combine in bowl and mix to form crumbs:
1 c. flour
1 egg
dash salt
½ t. cinnamon
½ c. sugar
1 t. baking powder
Sprinkle over fruit. Drizzle over:
¼ c. melted margarine
Bake 25 minutes.

Adele Mowere, Phoenixville, Pa.

●●●●●●●●●●●●●●●●●●●●●●●●●
Applesauce Crunch

Serves 4-6
375°
15/30 min.

Preheat oven to 375°.
Mix together:
2 c. applesauce
⅓ c. brown sugar
¼ c. raisins
½ t. cinnamon
Pour into 9x9" baking pan. Heat in oven 15 minutes.
Combine:
1 c. biscuit mix (see p. 68)
¼ c. sugar
Cut in:
3 T. cold solid margarine
Add:
¼ c. chopped nuts
Sprinkle over applesauce mixture and bake until nicely browned.

Sharol Phinney, Elkton, Va.

Birchermüsli: Blend 2 c. yogurt, ½ c. raisins, ½ c. chopped nuts, 1 c. oatmeal, ½ c. sugar, 2 T. orange juice, 1 c. sliced fresh peaches, 1 c. sliced apples, 2 sliced bananas, ½ c. blueberries. Vary fruits according to availability.
—Elaine Sommers Rich in Mennonite Weekly Review

Yogurt Chutney: Blend 2 c. chilled yogurt; ¾ c. grated coconut, preferably fresh; 1 T. sugar or sweetened condensed milk; a few raisins, cashews, or walnuts. Serve as side dish or dessert with curry meal.
—Doris Devadoss, Calcutta, India

Crust begins on the bottom and ends on top. Consistency of cobbler varies depending on variety of fruit and amount of juice, but still tastes delicious.

●●●●●●●●●●●●●●●●●●●●●●●●●
Quick Fruit Cobbler

Serves 6

350°

40 min.

Preheat oven to 350°.
Combine in bowl:
½ c. sugar
½ c. flour
½ c. milk
1 t. baking powder
¼ t. salt
Pour into 9x9″ greased baking pan.
Add:
2 c. fruit—fresh, frozen, or canned
Bake for 40 minutes.

Jocele Meyer, Brooklyn, Ohio

●●●●●●●●●●●●●●●●●●●●●●●●●
Essie's Cobbler

Serves 6-8

350°

45-50 min.

Preheat oven to 350°.
Cream together in bowl:
¼ c. soft shortening
½ c. sugar
Combine separately.
1 c. flour
2 t. baking powder
¼ t. salt
½ t. cinnamon (optional)
Add dry ingredients to creamed mixture alternately with:
½ c. milk
Mix until smooth. Pour batter into greased 10x5″ or 9x9″ baking pan.
Spoon over:
2 c. drained fruit (reserve juice) use peaches, berries, or cherries
Sprinkle with:
2-4 T. sugar
Pour over:
1 c. fruit juice
Bake 45-50 minutes. Serve warm with cold milk, whipped topping, or ice cream.

Esther Hostetter, Akron, Pa.

●●●●●●●●●●●●●●●●●●●●●●●
Frozen
Lemon Cream

Serves 9

Beat until stiff:
**1 can (1⅔ c.) evaporated milk,
    thoroughly chilled**
Slowly add:
¾ c. sugar
Then add:
**3 T. lemon juice
    grated rind of 1 lemon**
Beat until very stiff.
Roll into crumbs:
12 graham crackers
Put half of crumbs in bottom of 9x9" pan.
Pour in cream. Add remaining crumbs on
top. Cover tightly and freeze until ready
to serve.

Elmira Fry, Elizabethtown, Pa.

●●●●●●●●●●●●●●●●●●●●●●●
Lemonade
Sherbet

Serves 6

Pour into a freezer tray:
1 can (1⅔ c.) evaporated milk
Freeze until ice crystals form around the
edges.
While milk is in freezer, chill mixing bowl
and rotary beater.
Pour chilled milk into bowl. Add:
**1 (7 oz.) can frozen lemonade,
    thawed**
Beat until fluffy. While beating, add
gradually:
3-4 T. sugar
Pour into freezer tray and freeze 2 hours,
or until firm. Serve within 24 hours.

Ruth Magnuson, Glendale, Ariz.

●●●●●●●●●●●●●●●●●●●●●●●
Homemade
Ice Cream

Serves 12

Combine in 1-gallon freezer:
**1 qt. thick vanilla pudding
2 qts. milk
1 can sweetened condensed milk
1 T. vanilla**
Turn freezer until ice cream is stiff.

Options:

Substitute 1 qt. cream, if available, for
sweetened condensed milk. Reduce
milk to 6 c. Add ½ c. additional sugar to
pudding.

Chocolate: Make chocolate pudding and
add ⅔ c. chocolate syrup.

Fruit: Substitute 3 c. strawberries,
peaches, blueberries, or pineapple for 3
c. milk.

Butternut: Make butterscotch pudding,
using brown sugar. Add 1 c. toasted
nuts.

Annie Lind, Windsor, Vt.

●●●●●●●●●●●●●●●●●●●●●●●
Snow
Ice Cream

Serves 8 children

Stir together lightly:
**2½ qts. clean snow
½ c. milk or cream
1 t. vanilla
1 c. sugar**
Eat right away.

Betsey Zook, Leola, Pa.

*An old recipe
with origins
in the Wellman, Iowa,
community.*

●●●●●●●●●●●●●●●●●●●●●●●●●●
Pumpkin Ice Cream

Serves 10

Scald in double boiler:
  2 c. milk
Combine in bowl:
  4 egg yolks or 2 eggs, beaten
  1 c. sugar
  ⅛ t. salt
  2 c. mashed cooked pumpkin
  2 t. cinnamon
  1 t. nutmeg
  ½ t. allspice
  ¼ t. ginger
  ½ t. vanilla
Add to hot milk and cook 4 minutes longer. Cool.
Add:
  1 c. cream
  1 c. pecans or other nuts (optional)
Pour into freezer container. Crank until stiff.

Irene L. Bishop, Perkasie, Pa.

●●●●●●●●●●●●●●●●●●●●●●●●●
Lime Frost

T·S

Serves 6

Prepare as directed on package:
  1 pkg. lime gelatin
Chill until nearly firm. Combine in blender:
  lime gelatin
  1 pt. slightly softened vanilla ice cream
  1 T. lime juice
Blend until mixture begins to hold shape. Pour into 6 sherbet glasses and chill. Serve with whipped topping and a lime slice for garnish.

Options:

Use other flavors of gelatin.
Prepare gelatin with 1 envelope unflavored gelatin, ½ c. frozen orange juice concentrate, and 1½ c. water. Dissolve according to package directions.

Lon and Kathryn Sherer, Goshen, Ind.

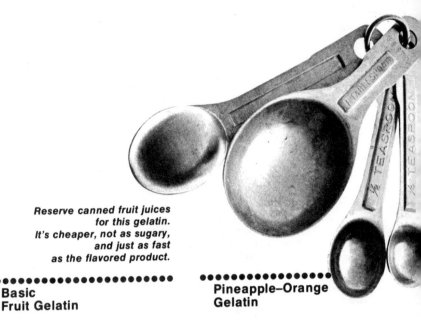

*Reserve canned fruit juices
for this gelatin.
It's cheaper, not as sugary,
and just as fast
as the flavored product.*

●●●●●●●●●●●●●●●●●●●●●●●●●

Basic
Fruit Gelatin

Serves 4-6

Combine in saucepan:
  **1 c. fruit juice, drained from
    canned fruit
  1 envelope unflavored gelatin**
Stir to begin dissolving gelatin. Then
heat almost to boiling point until liquid is
clear. Remove from heat and add:
  **1 c. cold fruit juice or water
  1 T. lemon juice
  1 T. frozen orange juice
    concentrate**
Chill until set.

Options:

When partially set, fold in fresh or
drained canned fruits as desired.

If using fresh unsweetened fruits and tart
juice, add 2-4 T. sugar to hot gelatin
mixture.

When partially set, fold in 1 c. whipped
cream or cottage cheese.

Replace second cup fruit juice with 1 c.
chilled yogurt.

Omit lemon juice and/or orange
concentrate if using strong-flavored fruit
juices.

Dorothy King, Dalton, Ohio

●●●●●●●●●●●●●●●●●●●

Pineapple–Orange
Gelatin

Serves 6

Combine in small saucepan:
  **1 envelope unflavored gelatin
  1 c. cold water**
Add:
  3 T. honey or sugar
Warm mixture just until gelatin dissolves.
Add:
  **2 T. frozen orange juice
    concentrate
  juice drained from unsweetened
    pineapple chunks plus water
    to make 1¼ c.**
Chill until syrupy. Fold in:
  **1 c. drained pineapple chunks
  2 oranges, peeled and diced
  1 banana, sliced**
Chill until set.

Ruth Gish, Mt. Joy, Pa.

●●●●●●●●●●●●●●●●●●●●●●●●●
Cheesecake

Serves 6
375°
30 min.

Preheat oven to 375°.
Prepare 1 8" unbaked graham cracker
pie shell.
Combine in bowl or blender:
  2 eggs
  **8 oz. cream cheese or cottage
    cheese, or a mixture**
  ⅓ c. honey or sugar
  ¼ c. dry milk solids
  2 t. vanilla
  1-2 T. lemon juice
Pour into crust and bake 30 minutes.
Cool 1 hour.
Add topping, if desired, and chill.

Options:
Add one of these to cheese mixture:
—1 t. almond extract (omit vanilla)
—¼ c. chopped almonds or walnuts
—1 small can crushed pineapple
—1½ t. grated lemon peel to both crust
  and filling
—2 T. cheddar cheese, finely shredded
—¼ c. yogurt

Use one of these as topping:
—Combine 1 c. yogurt or sour cream,
  2 T. sugar, 1 T. vanilla, 1 t. cinnamon,
  and/or ¼ t. nutmeg
—Add drained strawberries, pineapple,
  peaches, cherries, blueberries, or
  nuts to yogurt or sour cream topping.
—Thicken any of above fruits with
  cornstarch and use as topping.

Double recipe for larger cheesecake
made in springform pan.

LaVonne Platt, Newton, Kan.
Danita Laskowski, Goshen, Ind.

●●●●●●●●●●●●●●●●●●●●●●●●●
Graham Cracker Crust

T·S

Makes 1 pie crust
375°
8 min.

Combine and press into 9" pie pan:
  1⅓ c. graham cracker crumbs
  ¼ c. sugar
  ¼ c. melted margarine
  ¼ t. nutmeg
Bake at 375° for 8 minutes.

LaVonne Platt, Newton, Kan.

A low-calorie,
high-protein dessert
perfect for finishing off
a high-carbohydrate,
low-protein meal.

*Contributor is a Mennonite
grandmother who says, "Our
cookery has rated among the
best for years but there are
aspects to it that disturb me–so
many recipes are high in fats
and sugars." Her recipe passes
the test as a nutritious dessert.*

●●●●●●●●●●●●●●●●●●●●●●●●●

Refrigerator Cheesecake

T·S

Serves 6

Prepare graham cracker crust, or line 9"
pie pan or 8x8" baking pan with graham
cracker crumbs.
Combine in saucepan:
  1 pkg. unflavored gelatin
  ½ c. cold water
Warm over low heat until dissolved.
Combine in blender:
  dissolved gelatin
  1¼ c. water
  2 c. (1 lb.) cottage cheese
  1½ c. dry milk solids
  ½ c. sugar
  ⅛ t. salt
Whirl until liquified. Add:
  ¼ c. lemon juice
Blend until well mixed. Pour into crumb
crust. Chill until set.

Options:

Use any toppings suggested for
Cheesecake, p. 277.

Use just a few cracker crumbs for
low-calorie version.

Helen Burkholder, St. Catherines, Ont.

●●●●●●●●●●●●●●●●●●●●●●●●●

Yogurt–Cheese Pie

T·S

Serves 6

Prepare and cool:
  9" graham cracker pie shell
  (see p. 277)
Combine in small saucepan:
  ⅓ c. milk
  1 envelope unflavored gelatin
Stir to soften gelatin. Warm over low heat,
stirring constantly, until gelatin
dissolves.
Combine in blender or mixing bowl:
  1 c. cottage cheese
  1½ c. plain yogurt
  ¼ c. sugar or 3 T. honey
  dissolved gelatin mixture
Whirl or whip briefly. Chill mixture 20-30
minutes until it begins to set. Pour into
pie shell and chill.

Options:

Sprinkle with nutmeg.

Put 1-2 c. fresh berries or sliced bananas
into pie shell before pouring in yogurt
mixture. Chill and serve within 8 hours.

After filling sets, top with any thickened
fruit.

Instead of pouring filling into pie shell,
layer with fruit into parfait glasses.

Iona Weaver, Collegeville, Pa.

Milk Flitch (an old Pennsylvania Dutch pie with a variety of odd names, made for children from leftover pie crust): Into pie crust sprinkle brown sugar and flour. Dot with butter. Almost cover mixture with milk. Bake until brown and bubbling. Some like it dry, some like it runny—not measuring assures it will never be monotonous.
—Ruth Eitzen, Barto, Pa.

Quick Pie Crusts: If you make pies often, save time by cutting a quantity of fat and flour together in advance at a ratio of ¼ to ⅓ c. fat to 1 c. flour. Add salt. Store crumbs in tightly covered container in refrigerator or cool cellar. To make 2 crusts, measure out 2 c. crumbs and toss with 4 to 5 T. water.
—Edna Longacre, Barto, Pa.

I save pie crust scraps by using them to line a tart pan kept in the freezer. I make tarts when the pan is full.
—Karin Hackman, Hatfield, Pa.

●●●●●●●●●●●●●●●●●●●●●●●●
Cottage Cheese Pie

Serves 6-8
350°
1 hr.

Preheat oven to 350°.
Have ready 1 unbaked 9″ pastry or graham cracker pie shell.
Combine with mixer or blender:
2 egg yolks (reserve whites)
1½ c. cream-style cottage cheese
⅓ c. sugar or honey
2 T. flour
¼ t. salt
¼ t. cinnamon
1 c. milk
2 T. lemon juice
grated lemon rind
Beat until stiff but not dry:
2 egg whites
Fold into cheese mixture. Pour into unbaked pie shell and sprinkle top with:
1 T. sugar
½ t. cinnamon
Bake 1 hour, or until filling is almost firm in center. A slightly soft center will set as pie cools. Top with a fruit sauce if desired.

Rosemary Moyer, North Newton, Kan.

●●●●●●●●●●●●●●●●●●●●●●●●
Coconut–Custard Pie

T·S

Serves 8
350°
50-60 min.

Preheat oven to 350°.
Combine in blender:
4 eggs
6 T. margarine
½ c. flour
2 c. milk
¾ c. sugar
1 t. vanilla
Add:
1 c. coconut
Blend several seconds. Pour into a greased and floured 10″ pie pan, or two 8″ pans. Bake 50-60 minutes. Pie forms its own crust.

Lois Zehr, Ft. Dodge, Iowa

*Here's a good recipe
from the Orie Miller home
for the famed
Pennsylvania Dutch specialty.
Rich, yes—but also cheap!
Delicious served warm
with cold milk to drink.*

●●●●●●●●●●●●●●●●●●●●●●●●

Shoofly Pie

Serves 6
375°
35 min.

Preheat oven to 375°.
Prepare 1 unbaked 9" pie shell.
Cut together with pastry blender:

**1 c. flour
½ c. brown sugar
2 T. shortening or margarine**

Reserve ½ c. crumbs for topping.
Combine in mixing bowl:

**1 c. molasses
1 egg, slightly beaten
¾ c. cold water
1 t. soda in
¼ c. hot water**

Add crumb mixture and beat together.
Pour into unbaked pie shell. Sprinkle
reserved ½ c. crumbs on top. Bake 35
minutes.

Elta Miller, Lititz, Pa.

●●●●●●●●●●●●●●●●●●●●●●●●

Peach Kuchen

Serves 6
400°
15/30 min.

Preheat oven to 400°.
Combine in bowl:

**1⅓ c. sifted flour
¼ t. baking powder
½ t. salt
2 T. sugar**

Cut in:

⅓ c. margarine

Pat mixture over bottom and sides of a 9"
pie pan or skillet.
Arrange in pastry:

8-12 peach halves, canned or fresh

Sprinkle over:

**¼ c. sugar combined with
1 t. cinnamon**

Bake 15 minutes.
Combine:

**1 egg, beaten
1 c. sour cream, sour milk, yogurt,
or combination**

Pour over peaches and bake 30 minutes
longer.

Options:
Drizzle peaches with honey instead of sugar.
Use 2 c. fresh diced rhubarb. Increase sugar over fruit to ½ c.

Hilda Janzen, Newton, Kan.

Pumpkin Pie

Serves 6
425°/375°
10/30 min.

Preheat oven to 425°.
Have ready 1 9″ unbaked pie shell.
Combine in blender or mixing bowl:
  1 c. cooked, sieved pumpkin
  ½ c. sugar
  1 t. cinnamon
  ¼ t. ginger
  ¼ t. nutmeg
  ¼ t. cloves
  1 t. vanilla
  1 c. milk
  2 egg yolks
Beat until stiff:
  2 egg whites
Fold egg whites into pie filling. Pour into unbaked pie shell. Bake 10 minutes, then reset oven to 375° and bake about 30 minutes or until filling is set.

Options:

Substitute yellow squash, sweet potatoes or carrots for pumpkin. No need to mash vegetable first if using blender—just drain well. Spicy flavor sells any kind as pumpkin.

If using frozen pumpkin which may be watery, decrease milk to ¾ c.

Elizabeth Showalter, Waynesboro, Va.
Ruth Hershberger, Harper, Kan.

Whipped Topping—I

T·S

Makes about 2½ cups

Chill small mixer bowl and beaters several hours before using.
Put into bowl:
  ½ c. ice water (may be chilled in bowl)
  ½ c. dry milk solids
Beat at high speed until peaks form, about 5 minutes.
Add:
  3 T. lemon juice
Beat in gradually:
  3 T. sugar
Chill 1 hour.

Miriam LeFever, East Petersburg, Pa.

Whipped Topping—II

T·S

Makes about 2 cups

Shortly before serving, mash until smooth:
  1 medium ripe banana
Beat to stiff froth:
  1 egg white
Add banana to egg white 1 teaspoon at a time, beating constantly.
Add:
  1 t. sugar
Beat until light. Serve on fruit or puddings.

Viola Dorsch, Musoma, Tanzania

▼ Cakes

Cake Toppings

Use a thin glaze drizzled on the cake instead of thick icing.

Before baking, sprinkle a 9x13″ cake or 2 dozen cupcakes with a mixture of ¼ c. finely chopped nuts and ⅓ c. brown sugar. Add coconut if desired.

A light cake using almost no fat.

●●●●●●●●●●●●●●●●●●●●●●●
Grandma Witmer's Crumb Cake

Serves 12-15
350°
40 min.

Preheat oven to 350°.
Combine in large bowl:
4 c. flour
½ t. salt
2 c. sugar
Cut in to make crumbs:
1 c. shortening (may use part margarine)
Reserve ⅔ c. crumbs and set aside.
In separate bowl, stir together:
1 t. soda
1 t. cream of tartar
1 c. buttermilk or sour milk
Add:
2 beaten eggs
Add liquid mixture to crumbs. Mix together and pour into greased and floured 9x13″ pan. Sprinkle reserved crumbs on top, plus a dash nutmeg. Bake 40 minutes.

Ellen Longacre, Bally, Pa.

●●●●●●●●●●●●●●●●●●●●●●●
Carla's Hot Milk Sponge Cake

Serves 9-10
325°
30-35 min.

Preheat oven to 325°.
In mixing bowl, beat well:
2 eggs
Add:
1 c. sugar
1 t. vanilla
Beat until light. Combine separately:
1 c. flour
1 t. baking powder
¼ t. salt
By hand, fold dry ingredients into egg mixture.
Bring to boil in small saucepan:
½ c. milk
1 t. margarine
Add slowly to batter, stirring gently. Pour into well-greased and floured 7x12″ or 9x9″ cake pan. Bake 30-35 minutes.

Option:
When cake is partially cool, spread with ½ recipe Coconut Topping, p. 285. Broil as directed.

Carla L. Funk, Laird, Sask.

Sprinkle cakes or cupcakes with granola before baking.

Granola topping for coffee cake: ¼ c. granola, 2 T. brown sugar, 1 T. melted margarine.

Broiled coconut icing uses less sugar than other icings. See Oatmeal Cake, page 285.

●●●●●●●●●●●●●●●●●●●●●●●●●●
Roman Apple Cake

Serves 12-16
350°
35-40 min.

Preheat oven to 350°.
Combine in mixing bowl:
  1 c. sugar
  2¼ c. flour
  ¼ t. salt
  ⅜ t. baking powder
  1½ t. soda
  ½ t. cloves
  1 t. cinnamon
Beat in:
  ⅔ c. shortening
  2 eggs
  ⅔ c. milk
  1½ t. vanilla
Add:
  3 c. raw apples, pared and chopped
Mix well. Pour into greased and floured 9x13" pan.
Cover with *topping*:
Crumble together:
  1 T. melted margarine
  2 t. cinnamon
  ⅓ c. brown sugar
  2 t. flour
  ½ c. chopped nuts or coconut (optional)
  ¼ c. rolled oats
Bake 35-40 minutes.

Miriam LeFever, East Petersburg, Pa.

Combine 3-4 dried fruits: apples, apricots, figs, peaches, pears, dates, and golden or dark raisins. Snip larger fruits into small pieces.

●●●●●●●●●●●●●●●●●●●●●●●●●
Everyday Fruitcake

2 small loaves
325°
1 hr.

Preheat oven to 325°.
Combine in bowl:
  1 c. whole wheat flour
  ½ c. brown sugar
  1 t. baking powder
  ½ t. salt
Mix ¼ c. of this mixture with:
  2 c. dried fruit assortment (see above)
  ¾ c. walnuts or pecans, chopped
Set aside.
Stir together in large bowl:
  3 eggs, beaten
  ¼ c. honey
  ½ t. vanilla
  2 T. frozen orange juice concentrate
Add dry ingredients. Mix well. Fold in fruits and nuts. Spoon mixture into 2 3x6" or 1 4x8" loaf pan, well greased and bottoms lined with waxed paper. Bake 1 hour or until well browned. Cool on rack 10 minutes, then turn out loaves and remove waxed paper.

Evelyn Liechty, Berne, Ind.

*In Roman Apple Cake, substitute cooking oil for margarine. 1/3 cup of shortening is adequate, rather than 2/3 cup. The apples keep the cake moist.
—Jocele Meyer, Fresno, Ohio*

Split a cake and fill with pudding or custard. Add sliced bananas if desired.

Jelly Frosting: Combine in top of double boiler ½ c. tart jelly, 1 unbeaten egg white, and dash of salt. Beat while cooking until jelly disappears. Remove from heat and continue beating until frosting stands in peaks. Lovely to look at as well as eat!
—Geraldine Mitsch,
    Aurora, Ore.

Dust cakes with confectioners sugar. Pretty on a chocolate cake: Cover cake with paper doily, dust with confectioners sugar, carefully remove doily.

Serve freshly baked cake warm and unfrosted. Serve leftover cake a day later with fruit sauce or whipped topping.

Marvelous flavor—
a reward for patient people
who pick up, dry,
and shell black walnuts.

Black Walnut–Banana Cake

Serves 10-12
350°
45-50 min.

Preheat oven to 350°.
Cream together:
    1½ c. sugar
    ½ c. margarine or shortening
Beat in:
    2 eggs
    1 c. thinly sliced bananas
    1 t. vanilla
    ¾ c. sour milk, combined with
    1 t. soda
Sift together and beat in:
    2 c. flour
    1 t. baking powder
Add:
    1 c. black walnuts, ground or
        finely chopped
Pour into greased and floured 9x9″ cake pan. Bake 45-50 minutes.

Ruth Hynicker, Elizabethtown, Pa.

Gingerbread With Wheat Germ

Serves 9
350°
45-50 min.

Preheat oven to 350°.
Combine in mixing bowl:
    2 c. unsifted flour
    1 t. baking soda
    ¾ t. salt
    1½ t. cinnamon
    1 t. ginger
    ¼ t. cloves
    ¼ c. sugar
    ½ c. wheat germ
Add:
    1 c. buttermilk or sour milk
    ¾ c. molasses
    ⅓ c. oil or melted margarine
    2 eggs, beaten
Beat just until batter is smooth. Turn into well-greased 9x9″ cake pan. Bake 45-50 minutes or until tests done. Serve hot with applesauce blended with yogurt or a whipped topping (p. 281).

Rosemary Moyer, North Newton, Kan.
Elizabeth Showalter, Waynesboro, Va.

Contributor likes to cook
with a friend.
Invite a child
to help with this recipe.

●●●●●●●●●●●●●●●●●●●●●●●●●●
Applesauce–Nut Cake
(cooperative method)

Serves 10
350°
35-40 min.

Preheat oven to 350°.

Person 1:
Combine and set aside:
   1 c. sweetened applesauce
   1 t. lemon juice
Measure and mix together:
   2 c. flour (may use ¼ whole wheat)
   1 t. soda
   1 t. cinnamon
   ½ t. ground cloves
   ½ t. salt
Chop and set aside:
   ½ c. dates

Person 2:
Cream together:
   ½ c. margarine
   1 c. brown sugar
Add:
   2 eggs
Beat well. Measure:
   1 c. walnuts, chopped OR
      sunflower seeds
   ½ c. raisins
Grease and flour 8x12″ pan.

Now get together:
Add applesauce and dry ingredients
alternately to creamed mixture.
Beat well. Stir in nuts, dates, and raisins.
Pour batter into pan.
Bake 35-40 minutes.

   Jane Short, Elkhart, Ind.

---

*A rich, moist cake;
serve in small pieces.*

●●●●●●●●●●●●●●●●●●●●●●●●
Oatmeal
Cake

Serves 16-18
350°
35 min.

Preheat oven to 350°.
Combine and let stand 20 minutes.
   1 c. quick oatmeal
   1¼ c. boiling water
Cream together until fluffy:
   ½ c. shortening
   1 c. brown sugar
   1 c. white sugar
   2 eggs
   1 t. vanilla
Add oatmeal mixture. Beat well.
Sift together:
   1½ c. flour
   1 t. soda
   1 t. baking powder
   ½ t. salt
   1 t. cinnamon
Add to creamed mixture and beat well.
Pour into greased and floured 9x13″ cake
pan. Bake 35 minutes or until tests done.
Coconut Topping:
Combine:
   ½ c. brown sugar
   ⅓ c. margarine
   ¼ c. cream or milk
   ½ c. chopped nuts
   1 c. coconut
Spread on hot cake and broil 2-4 minutes
until brown. Watch closely.

   Ruth B. Hess, Akron, Pa.

●●●●●●●●●●●●●●●●●●●●●●●●●
Oatmeal Cookie Mix

	1 gal.	2 gal.

Put through a
coarse sieve:

white sugar	1½ c.	3 c.
brown sugar	1½ c.	3 c.
sifted flour	3 c.	6 c.
salt	2 t.	4 t.
soda	2 t.	4 t.
baking powder	1 t.	2 t.

Cut in:

shortening	2 c.	4 c.

Add:

rolled oats	6 c.	12 c.

Mix well. Store in cool place.

Makes 4 doz.
350°
12 min.

Oatmeal Cookies:
Combine in bowl:
2 eggs, beaten
2 t. vanilla
4 c. oatmeal cookie mix
Mix well. Drop teaspoonfuls onto
greased baking sheet, flatten with fork,
and bake at 350° about 12 minutes.

Options:
Add chopped nuts, raisins, coconut,
chocolate chips, or sunflower seeds.

Add 1 t. cinnamon to egg mixture.

Put 2 cookies together with a blend of
peanut butter and honey or jelly.

Hilda Janzen, Newton, Kan.

●●●●●●●●●●●●●●●●●●●●●●●●●
Date Oatmeal Cookies

Makes 6 doz.
350°
10-12 min.

Cream together:
½ c. margarine
1 c. sugar
3 eggs
Beat well. Sift together:
1½ c. flour
1 t. baking powder
½ t. salt
1 t. soda
1 t. cinnamon
½ t. allspice
Add to creamed mixture alternately with:
½ c. milk
Stir in:
2 c. rolled oats
1 c. chopped dates
½ c. coconut
½ c. nuts (optional)
Drop by teaspoonfuls on greased cookie
sheet. Bake at 350° for 10-12 minutes.

Lena Brown, Grantham, Pa.

Chocolate Chip Oatmeal Cookies

Makes 6-8 doz.
375°
10 min.

Cream together:
  1 c. shortening (may use half
    margarine and half lard)
  ¼ c. peanut butter
  ½ c. sugar
  ½ c. brown sugar
  2 eggs
  1 t. vanilla
Add:
  1½ c. flour
  1 t. soda
  ½ t. salt
  2 c. rolled oats
  1-2 c. chocolate chips
  1 c. chopped nuts (optional)
Mix well. Drop by teaspoonfuls on
greased cookie sheet. Bake at 375° for
about 10 minutes.

Elsie Epp, Marion, S.D.
Miriam LeFever, East Petersburg, Pa.

Chocolate Chip Cookies

Makes 5-6 doz.
375°
8-10 min.

Cream together:
  1 c. margarine or shortening
  1 c. brown sugar
  1 c. granulated sugar
Add:
  2 eggs
  2 T. hot water
  2 t. vanilla
Beat until fluffy. Sift together and add:
  1 c. white flour
  1½ c. whole wheat flour
  ⅔ c. soy flour
  1 t. salt
  1 t. soda
Add:
  2 c. or 12 oz. chocolate chips
  1 c. chopped nuts (optional)
Drop by teaspoonfuls on greased cookie
sheet. Bake at 375° for 8-10 minutes or
until light brown.

Priscilla Ziegler, Lancaster, Pa.

Crunchy Drop Cookies

Makes 6 doz.
350°
10-12 min.

Cream together:
  1 c. shortening
  1⅔ c. brown sugar
  2 eggs
  2 t. vanilla
  6 T. milk
Combine and add:
  2½ c. flour
  1 t. baking soda
  ½ t. salt
Stir in:
  4 c. granola
Drop by teaspoonfuls onto greased
cookie sheets. 350° for 10-12 minutes.

MCC Dining Hall, Akron, Pa.

No-Bake Cereal Cookies

Makes 2-3 doz.

Combine in saucepan and heat to
boiling:
  ½ c. brown sugar
  ⅓ c. light corn syrup
Stir in:
  1 t. vanilla
  ¾ c. peanut butter
Mix until smooth. Stir in:
  3 c. ready-to-eat cereal flakes
  1 c. flaked coconut (optional)
Drop by teaspoonfuls onto waxed paper.

Rosemary Moyer, North Newton, Kan.

Oatmeal Cookies With a Purpose

Makes 5-6 doz.
325°
10-15 min.

Purpose:
Constructive fun for children

Requirements:
1. Cookie dough
Cream together:
   1 c. margarine or shortening
   1 c. brown sugar
Add:
   2 c. rolled oats
   1 c. dry milk solids
   ½ c. water
Beat well. Sift together:
   2¼-2½ c. flour
   3 t. baking powder
   1 t. salt
Fold into creamed mixture and mix well.
Divide into small portions and chill.
2. Clean kitchen table.
3. Pie plates and cookie pans.
4. Rolling pins from toy bake sets or small round bottles.
5. Animal cookie cutters.
6. Aprons or old towels to protect children's clothing.
7. Children of either sex, ages 2 and up, with clean hands.

Extra Requirements (for parent, neighbor or grandparent):
1. Patience.
2. Loving-kindness.
3. Smiles.
4. Praise, given out liberally.
5. Wisdom, to help children share tools.
6. Pretend dark glasses.

Method:
1. Sprinkle flour on table for each child.
2. Distribute pieces of dough.
3. Demonstrate how to roll dough to ¼" thickness, cut out cookies, and transfer them to baking pans.
4. Preheat oven to 325°.
5. Wear pretend dark glasses to avoid seeing trail of flour from table to floor, or path of dough from fingers to mouth.
6. Pop pans into oven as soon as filled. Bake 10-15 minutes.
7. Put each child's cookies in separate container.
8. When all dough is baked, present each child with his or her container.

Results:
1. Sparkling eyes.
2. Happy faces.
3. Grimy hands.
4. Bulging cheeks.
5. Sweet voices saying, "Mm, good, it's yummy yummy in my tummy."
6. Spontaneous hugs from flour-covered arms.
7. A few cookies.

   Helen Bergmann, Virgil, Ont.

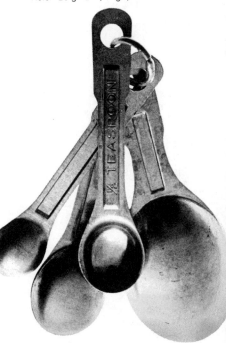

●●●●●●●●●●●●●●●●●●●●●●●●
High-Protein
Peanut-Butter
Cookies

Makes 6-7 doz.
375°
8-10 min.

Cream together until fluffy:
   1½ c. shortening
   ½ c. granulated sugar
   ½ c. brown sugar
   ½ c. honey
   1 c. peanut butter
   3 eggs
   1 t. vanilla
Sift together and add:
   2½ c. whole wheat flour
   1 c. dry milk solids
   ½ c. soy flour
   1 t. salt
   1 t. baking powder
   2 t. baking soda
Chill dough. Roll into 1″ balls and place on greased cookie sheets. Flatten with fork dipped in flour. Bake at 375° for 8-10 minutes.

Priscilla Ziegler, Lancaster, Pa.

●●●●●●●●●●●●●●●●●●●●●●●●
Whole Wheat
Peanut-Butter
Cookies

Makes 5 doz.
375°
8-10 min.

Cream together:
   ½ c. shortening
   1 c. peanut butter
   1½ c. sugar
   1 egg
Add to creamed mixture:
   1 c. wheat germ
   2 t. vanilla
   6 T. water
Combine and add:
   1½ c. whole wheat flour
   1 c. dry milk solids
   ½ t. salt
   1 t. baking powder
   2 t. baking soda
Roll into 1″ balls. Place on greased cookie sheet and flatten with fork dipped in flour. Bake at 375° for 8-10 minutes.

Marcia Beachy, DeKalb, Ill.

●●●●●●●●●●●●●●●●●●●●●●●●●
Dietetic
Date Cookies

Makes 5 doz.
350°
10-12 min.

Combine in saucepan:
  1 c. raisins
  ½ c. snipped dates
  1 c. water
Boil 3 minutes, stirring constantly. Cool.
Cream together:
  2 eggs
  ½ c. margarine
  3 t. liquid sweetener
  1 t. vanilla
Sift together:
  ¼ t. cinnamon
  1 c. flour
  1 t. soda
Add dry ingredients to creamed mixture
alternately with date mixture. Beat well.
Chill several hours. Drop from teaspoon
onto greased baking pan. Bake at 350°
for 10-12 minutes.

Geraldine Roth, Morton, Ill.

●●●●●●●●●●●●●●●●●●●●●●●●●
New Zealand
Whole Wheat
Crisps

Makes 3 doz.
350°
10-12 min.

Combine:
  ½ c. melted margarine
  1 T. corn syrup
  ⅔ c. sugar
Add:
  1 c. whole wheat flour
  ⅛ t. salt
  1 t. soda dissolved in
  2 T. water
Mix well. Stir in:
  ⅔ c. coconut
  ⅔ c. chopped nuts
Drop by level tablespoonfuls 2″ apart on
ungreased cookie sheet. Bake at 350° for
10-12 minutes.

Ruth Hunsberger, Doylestown, Pa.

●●●●●●●●●●●●●●●●●●●●●●●●●
Molasses
Crinkles

Makes 4 doz.
350°
12-15 min.

Cream together:
  ¾ c. shortening
  1 c. brown sugar
  1 egg
  ¼ c. dark molasses
Sift together and add:
  2¼ c. flour
  ½ t. salt
  2 t. soda
  1 t. cinnamon
  1 t. ginger
  ½ t. ground cloves
Mix thoroughly. Chill dough several
hours. Shape dough into balls 1″ in
diameter. Roll in granulated sugar and
place 2″ apart on greased baking sheet.
Bake at 350° for 12-15 minutes.

*Used by permission from Mennonite
Community Cookbook.*

Tester's husband says,
"They're good!
You make them
and I'll eat them."
A fair exchange of energies?

Wheat Germ Balls

Makes 3½ doz.
350°
12-15 min.

Combine in mixing bowl:
2 c. flour
1 c. toasted wheat germ
1 c. shortening
¾ c. sugar
1 egg
1 t. grated orange rind
1 t. vanilla
½ t. salt
Beat at low speed until well mixed. Chill dough. Roll into 1" balls. Roll in ¾ c. wheat germ. Place on cookie sheet and bake at 350° for 12-15 minutes.

Mary Lou Houser, Lancaster, Pa.

Use mild molasses
or combination of
dark molasses and corn syrup.

Gingerbread Treats

Makes 4 doz.
350°
10-12 min.

Mix together:
1 c. hot water
1 c. molasses
Combine separately and add:
3 c. flour
½ t. baking soda
1 t. baking powder
1½ t. ginger
½ t. salt
Add:
¼ c. melted shortening or oil
1 c. raisins
Mix well. Drop by teaspoonfuls onto greased baking sheet. Bake at 350° for 10-12 minutes.

Eleanor Hiebert, Elkins Park, Pa.

Peanut Bars

Makes 2 doz.
350°
30 min.

Cream together:
½ c. margarine
½ c. brown sugar
½ c. granulated sugar
1 egg
½ t. vanilla

Add:
1½ c. quick-cooking rolled oats
¾ c. whole wheat flour
½ t. baking soda
¼ t. salt
Stir in:
1 c. peanuts, coarsely chopped
½ c. seedless raisins
Pat mixture evenly into a greased 9" baking pan. Bake at 350° for 30 minutes. Cool in pan. Cut into bars.

Option:
Substitute other nuts as available.

Carolyn Blosser, Akron, Pa.

Raisin or Date Bars

Makes 3 doz.
400°
25-30 min.

Combine in saucepan:
   2½ c. raisins
   ¾ c. water
   ¼ c. sugar
   3 T. lemon juice
   2 T. cornstarch
      OR
   3 c. chopped dates
   1½ c. water
Cook over low heat until thick. Cool.
Combine in bowl:
   ¾ c. margarine
   ¾ c. brown sugar
   1 t. salt
   ½ t. baking soda
   1¾ c. flour
   1½ c. rolled oats
Mix well until crumbly. Firmly press half of crumb mixture into 9x13" greased pan. Spread cooled filling over top and cover with remaining crumb mixture, patting down lightly. Bake at 400° for 25-30 minutes. Cut into bars while warm.

Mary Lou Houser, Lancaster, Pa.

Butterscotch Brownies

Makes 2 doz.
350°
30 min.

Preheat oven to 350°.
Melt:
   ¼ c. margarine
Add:
   1 T. dark molasses
   ¾ c. sugar
   2 eggs, beaten
   2 t. vanilla
Stir well. Sift in:
   ½ c. plus 2 T. dry milk powder
   ½ t. baking powder
   ¼ t. salt
Add:
   1 c. wheat germ
   ½ c. walnuts or pecans, chopped
Stir only enough to blend, using no more than 20 strokes. Spread in greased 8x8" pan. Bake 30 minutes.

Lena Brown, Grantham, Pa.

Good
sugarless lunchbox sweet
or Christmas candy.

Coconut–Date Balls

Makes 3 doz.

Combine and cook over low heat, stirring constantly:
   2 eggs, beaten
   ½ c. margarine
   ½ lb. dates, finely cut
Boil 2 minutes. Remove from heat and add:
   1½ c. crisp rice cereal
   ½ c. nuts, chopped
   1 t. vanilla
Cool; shape into little balls. Roll in coconut.

Barbara Longenecker, New Holland, Pa.

Peppernuts

Old-Fashioned Sugar Cookies

400 °
10 min.

Makes 10 doz.
375°
10-12 min.

Cream together in large mixing bowl:
- 2 c. honey
- ½ c. margarine
- 1 egg

Add:
- ¾ c. hot water
- ½ c. finely chopped nuts or sunflower seeds
- 1 t. cinnamon
- ½ t. ginger
- ¼ t. cloves
- 1½ t. baking powder
- ½ t. soda
- 4 c. sifted whole wheat flour
- 4 c. unbleached white flour

Roll into long pencil-like sticks ¾" in diameter and freeze overnight between layers of waxed paper or dish towels. The next day, slice ⅜" thick and place on greased baking sheets so they do not touch each other. Bake at 400° for 10 minutes. Peppernuts will be hard after they cool. Spicy taste ripens by storing in a closed container several days.

Option:

Substitute corn syrup and molasses if honey is unavailable or too expensive.

Lois Barrett, Wichita, Kan.

Cream together:
- 1⅔ c. sugar
- 1 c. lard, margarine, or shortening
- 2 eggs
- 1 c. sour cream

Stir in:
- 2 t. baking powder
- 8-8½ c. flour
- 1 t. lemon extract (optional)
- 1 t. vanilla

Chill dough. Roll out, sprinkle with a little sugar, and roll over again lightly. Cut into small rounds. Bake at 375° for 10-12 minutes.

Martha Wiebe, Whitewater, Kan.

gardening and preserving
······················

The best place to learn how to raise food and put it up is in a community where people are doing it. In our small town the phone rings on August mornings with questions like these: Do you process your dill pickles in boiling water, or just pour in the brine and seal them? Are you canning tomatoes today? I have a half bushel to get rid of—we're leaving on vacation. Do you think it's too late to plant endive? I often place a call in return to learn where to find the best buys in corn or ask for a ketchup recipe.

We know the corner grocery store sells canned goods all winter, and even fresh produce flown in from warmer climates. Mass-oriented food production and distribution will provide anything we want—for a given price and taste. But in late summer our community still seems knit together by the common need to lay in food for the winter.

The lore of stocking up is not lost. It grows in little groups of sun-browned women gathered outside rural churches on a summer Sunday, in daylong visits to Mom to freeze corn, in struggles of a newly married couple making strawberry jam on an apartment stove, in a child given the job of fitting slippery peach halves down into Mason jars because his hand is small enough to go in.

"I think of a luxury in the sturdiness and grace of necessary things, not frivolity. That would heal the earth, and heal men," says Wendell Berry in *Farming: A Hand Book*. Don't begin gardening and preserving only out of duty to your budget and the world's hungry, although it helps. Begin it for joy, for healing. Begin it to receive the gift God gave when He placed us in a garden and said, "Behold, I have given you every plant yielding seed which is upon the face of all the earth, and every tree with seed in its fruit; you shall have them for food" (Genesis 1:29).

Space does not allow this book to become a manual on the necessary arts. Bookstores offer solid works on any aspect of stocking up food, and friends will teach. Here is a sampling of ideas shared by persons who grow and store their own.

Gardening and Preserving Discoveries

Gardening

Kidney beans are very easy to grow. Let them hang on the bush until pods begin to dry. Shell and wash in cold water. Spread them out on paper to dry for a few days, until they split when hit with a hammer. I put them in a big plastic bag in my freezer to help keep them fresh, and just scoop out what I need. Before kidney bean pods become dry on the stalk, we pick some and cook as a vegetable like lima beans. The shells are slightly yellow at this point and the beans a deep pink. To prepare, cook in water and add chopped onion and cream if desired. When creamed, they go nicely over potatoes instead of gravy.
—Kate Kooker, Ardmore, Pa.

We haven't found a fast way to shell out dry beans, so we work on them when we're sitting and talking with friends. We put the shelled beans we plan to eat (not those to be used for seed) in a 200° oven for several hours to keep them from getting weevils in storage.
—Don and Priscilla Ziegler, Lancaster, Pa.

Growing your own soybeans has several advantages over purchasing them in a health-food store. It is more economical, soybeans provide nutrients for your soil and you can harvest some while they are green. The taste difference between green (or fresh-frozen) and dried soybeans is reason enough to warrant growing your own.
—LaVonne Platt, Newton, Kan.

To harvest green soybeans: When pods are plump but still green, clip off plants at ground level. Leave roots to enrich the soil. Pile the plants under a tree and strip off the pods. Wash pods; drop into boiling water and cook 3 to 5 minutes, or until beans will pop out easily. Cool pods and shell out beans. Freeze without further blanching. To serve, cook ten minutes and season with butter, salt, and pepper.
—Rod and Mary Lou Houser, Lancaster, Pa.

Sunflower seeds, a traditional Russian Mennonite snack food, are easy to grow and fun to eat. To shell for use in cereals, cookies, or salads, try this: Put ¼ to ½ cup seeds in the blender; whirl at lowest speed for ten seconds. If all the seeds aren't shelled, repeat for a few more seconds. Stir cracked seeds into a bowl of water. Repeat the process until several cups of seeds have been cracked. Then let seeds and water set until kernels settle. Strain off the shells which float. (Use this as birdseed, since all may not be cracked.) Pour off the water. Spread the seeds out onto a cookie sheet. When dry, sort and clean the kernels. Store in cool, dry place, until ready to use in recipes.
—Kamala Platt, Newton, Kan.

Raise green leafy vegetables such as collards, kale, mustard, rape, spinach, and Swiss chard in a lavishly enriched portion of soil. Keep it well watered. Greens grown fast in ideal conditions in a cool season have a delicious flavor not to be compared to the taste of greens grown indifferently in hot dry soil. Plant greens very early in the spring and late in August for a fall crop.
—Rosa Mullet, Pantego, N.C.

Kale and Swiss chard will not freeze until temperatures go down to about 15°. My parents raised them in fall for an early winter vegetable.
—Helene Janzen, Elbing, Kan.

If it is possible in your climate to mulch with bales of hay so that the ground does not freeze hard, you can have fresh root vegetables all winter. Plant leeks, carrots, salsify, parsnips, beets, and turnips in July so that they reach ideal size by the time frost kills the tops. Vegetables will remain in delicious condition below the ground.
—Rosa Mullet, Pantego, N.C.

Canning

A true more-with-less pickle—cheap, fast, sugarless, crisp, and flavorful, and all ingredients except salt and vinegar can be home-grown.

●●●●●●●●●●●●●●●●●●●●●●●●●
Dill
Pickles

●●●●●●●●●●●●●●●●●●●●●●●●●
Bread and Butter
Pickles

Makes 10-12 qts.

Makes 12 pts.

Fill each of 10-12 sterilized quart jars with the following:
   **small whole cucumbers or larger
      cucumbers cut in spears**
   1 grape leaf
   1 sprig fresh dill
   ¼ onion
   1 clove garlic (optional)
   1 small red pepper
   **OR ¼ t. dried red pepper
   flakes (optional)**
Heat a canner half full of water.
Combine in saucepan:
   13 c. water
   6 c. vinegar
   1 c. salt
Bring to boil and pour brine into filled jars. Seal. Process jars for 5 minutes in boiling water. Ready to eat in 2 weeks.

Zelma Martin, Lancaster, Pa.

Cut into thin rings:
   **30 medium unpared cucumbers
      (1 gallon sliced)**
   8 medium onions
Cut in fine strips:
   2 large red or green peppers
Place vegetables in large bowl or kettle.
Dissolve in ice water and pour over:
   ½ c. salt
Let stand 3 hours. Drain.
Combine in large kettle:
   5 c. sugar
   5 c. vinegar
   2 T. mustard seed
   1 t. turmeric
   1 t. whole cloves
Bring to boil. Add drained vegetables and heat to boiling point. Do not boil. Pack into sterilized jars and seal.

Mennonite Community Cookbook, *used by permission.*

Canning fruit in just boiling water, or ½ apple juice and ½ boiling water, is a great way of making more with less. I have done this with both peaches and pears. With just water, the fruit must be very ripe when canned, then left for several months to allow the natural juices to sweeten it. Even then it tastes "unsweetened." The half-and-half version suited our palates better.
—Judy Martens, Blumenort, Man.

To can tomato sauce without cooking it down: Cook tomatoes as for tomato juice. Pour tomatoes into food mill and let juice run through without turning handle. Transfer food mill to another container and press through pulp for a thick sauce. Can thin juice for drinking or use in soups, pulp for tomato sauce to use in spaghetti sauce or casseroles.
—Anna Mary Brubacher,
   St. Jacobs, Ont.

Fast preparation for tomatoes: Wash tomatoes, core, and cut away bad spots. Leave skins on and cut in pieces. Puree in blender. This is good in chili, spaghetti sauce, and soups, and may be canned or frozen for future use.
—Wanda Hook, Hesston, Kan.

●●●●●●●●●●●●●●●●●●●●●●●●●
End-of-the-Garden Pickle

Makes 18 pts.

Soak several hours in brine of ½ c. salt and 2 qts. water:
   2 qts. small whole cucumbers
Cook separately in salted water just until crisp-tender:
   1 pt. pickling onions
   2 qts. carrot slices
   **1 qt. celery, sliced
      in ½" pieces**
   1 qt. cauliflowerets
   1 qt. yellow wax beans
   1 qt. lima beans
   4 sweet red peppers, cut in strips
Drain vegetables. Rinse and drain cucumbers. Place all vegetables in large enamel dishpan.
Combine in very large kettle:
   1½ qts. water
   1½ qts. vinegar
   6 c. sugar
   ¼ c. pickling spices tied in a bag
Bring to a boil and simmer 5 minutes. Remove spice bag. Add vegetables to hot syrup. Bring quickly to boiling temperature. Pack into hot jars and seal.

Option:
For a Pennsylvania Dutch Chow-Chow, add 1 qt. cut corn and 2-3 c. cooked kidney beans.

Olive Wyse, Goshen, Ind.
Nora Bohn, Goshen, Ind.

●●●●●●●●●●●●●●●●●●●●●●●●
Cucumber Relish

Makes 6-7 pts.

Grind through food chopper:
   12-14 cucumbers
   1 bunch celery
   2 onions
   2 green peppers
   2 sweet red peppers
Let stand overnight.
Drain and add:
   2 T. salt
Mix well.
Bring to boil in large kettle:
   3 c. sugar
   3 c. vinegar
   1 t. celery seed
   ½ t. tumeric
   1 t. mustard seed
Add vegetables and cook 30 minutes. Fill into jars and seal.

Judy Classen, Akron, Pa.

Canning beef: Cut meat in 2-to-3-inch squares. Pack into jars, not too tightly. Add 1 teaspoon salt to each jar. Don't add water. Seal and process in pressure cooker at 10 pounds for 90 minutes. Save tallow and render by frying to make soap.
—Irene P. Chrisinger,
Mt. Pleasant, Iowa

I must live on a sugar-free diet and enjoy canning my own grapefruit. Peel the grapefruit and pull sections apart. Use kitchen shears to cut off edge along the core, then gently peel back the skin. Drop sections into pint jars, fill with water and a little liquid sweetener if desired, then seal and process 10 minutes in boiling water bath. It does take time, but I have more time than money. When I buy grapefruit on sale it costs me 10 cents a pint to can.
—Lela Miller, Albany, Ore.

●●●●●●●●●●●●●●●●●●●●●●●●
Creole Sauce

Makes about 3 cups

Heat in large skillet:
  2 T. oil
Cook until soft, but not brown:
  1 c. onion, chopped
  ½ c. celery, chopped
  1 clove garlic, mashed
Add:
  **2 c. cooked or fresh Italian
      plum tomatoes, chopped**
  1 bay leaf
  pinch dried thyme
  ½ t. basil
  ¼ t. oregano
  ⅛ t. celery seed
  1 T. chopped parsley
  1 t. salt
  dash sugar
  freshly ground pepper
Cook uncovered over low heat about 1½ hours, or until sauce is reduced by half. Stir occasionally. During last 20 minutes of cooking time, add:
  1 large sweet pepper, diced
Store in refrigerator until ready to use. Serve with rice, chicken, beef, pork, or seafood. Make in large quantities to can or freeze when tomatoes are in season.

Evelyn Liechty, Berne, Ind.

●●●●●●●●●●●●●●●●●●●●●●●●
Chili Sauce

Makes 10-12 pts.

Cook until soft:
  1 gal. tomatoes, cut up
  2 medium onions, cut up
Press through collander to remove skins and seeds.
Add:
  1 c. sugar
  ½-1 c. vinegar
  5 t. salt
  1 t. cinnamon
  1 t. dry mustard
  ½ t. curry powder
  ½ t. nutmeg
  Cayenne or chili powder to taste
Cook down to desired consistency. Pour into pint jars, seal and process in hot water bath for 5 minutes.

Helena Pauls, Inman, Kan.

Raise Italian Plum tomatoes for tomato sauce. This variety contains little water and when cooked and pureed yields a nice thick sauce.
—Bonnie Zook, Leola, Pa.

Often when I want to use beans I don't have them soaked and ready, so I can 7 quarts at a time in my pressure canner. Soak 5 pounds navy beans overnight. In the morning divide the beans into 7 quart jars, add 1 teaspoon salt to each jar, and fill to the neck with water. Process in pressure canner for 1 hour at 10 pounds. Beans are ready for soup, baked beans, or whatever you want.
—Ada Beachy, Goshen, Ind.

Using blender yields a smoother ketchup.

●●●●●●●●●●●●●●●●●●●●●●●●●
Tomato Ketchup

Makes 8 pts.

Prepare by one of two methods:
4 qts. tomato pulp seasoned with 4-5 large onions
1. Pour boiling water over tomatoes; peel, quarter, and squeeze out some juice with hands (reserve to drink). Process tomatoes and onions in blender.
2. Quarter and cook tomatoes with onions. Pour into food mill, allowing thin juice to run off. Then transfer food mill to another bowl and press out thick pulp. Measure pulp. Combine in large kettle:
4 qts. tomato pulp
2 T. celery salt
4 t. salt
3 c. sugar
2 c. vinegar
¼ t. red pepper (optional)
4 t. mixed pickling spices tied in bag
Bring to boil. Reduce heat and cook slowly 1-1½ hours, stirring occasionally. Remove spice bag.
Combine in small bowl:
5 T. cornstarch
¼ c. water
Stir into boiling tomato mixture. Boil 5 more minutes. Seal in hot sterile jars.

Karen Rix, Fonda, Iowa

●●●●●●●●●●●●●●●●●●●●●●●●●
Spaghetti Sauce For Canning

Makes 12 qts.

Cut all in pieces:
¾ bu. tomatoes, unpeeled
3 large sweet potatoes, peeled
2 bunches celery
3 sweet red peppers
1 hot pepper
8 medium onions
3 cloves garlic
Cook together in large kettles for 2½ hours. Put through a food mill.
Add:
1½ c. sugar
2 T. salt
1 c. oil
Heat again to boiling. Pour into jars and seal. Process in boiling water bath ¾ hour.

Ada Beachey, Goshen, Ind.

*"I like this for Sunday dinner.
Set frozen box out when you
leave for church. When you get
back it heats in a hurry and you
have a well-balanced meal. I
learned this as a widow. You
don't make a large variety when
you're alone."*

●●●●●●●●●●●●●●●●●●●●●●●
Freezer
Vegetable Soup

Makes about 10 qts.

Brown in large heavy kettle:
  4 lbs. ground beef
Add:
  1 qt. corn
  1 qt. green or yellow string beans
  1 qt. peas
  1 stalk celery, finely chopped
  ½ head cabbage, finely chopped
  6 onions, finely chopped
  2 c. white or red cooked beans,
  ** or both**
  6 carrots, finely chopped
  6 sprigs parsley, chopped
  salt, pepper, and herbs to taste
  water or stock to cover
Cook until vegetables are tender. Divide
into containers and freeze.

Option:
Children enjoy alphabet noodles added
to this soup.

Minnie O. Good, Denver, Pa.

●●●●●●●●●●●●●●●●●●●●●●●
Easy
Sauerkraut

1. Sterilize quart jars. You will need 2 lbs.
of cabbage or a medium-sized head for
each quart.
2. Shred each head of fresh cabbage in
dime-thin pieces after removing outer
leaves. Use cores and outer leaves in
stock pot.
3. Sprinkle 4 t. salt over each shredded
head. Mix well with hands.
4. Pack tightly into jars until juice forms
and reaches top. Screw lids on loosely.
Set jars in a pan to catch juice as
cabbage ferments.
5. After 7-10 days the brine level will drop
suddenly, indicating kraut is done. Keep
in refrigerator a few weeks, or for longer
storage press kraut down with a wooden
spoon to remove the gas bubbles and
add more brine made of 4 t. salt to 1 qt.
water to fill jars.
6. Set jars in canner with warm water.
Bring all to boiling, cover, and boil 30
minutes; seal. This is a mild,
fresh-flavored kraut.

Alice W. Lapp, Goshen, Ind.

*Easy Sauerkraut is great—a
good way to preserve cabbage
from the garden. I have never
used the outer leaves in the
stockpot as suggested, but a
few years ago decided to try
using them in Refrigerator
Coleslaw (p. 251), which
I stored in the freezer.
—Delphine Carter,
Newton, Ont.*

●●●●●●●●●●●●●●●●●●●●●●●●●
Quick
Strawberry Jam

Makes about 4 cups

Mix well and let stand 4 hours or
overnight:
**2-3c. mashed strawberries
(depending on desired
thickness)
3 c. sugar**
Bring to a hard boil. Reduce heat to
medium. Boil 10 minutes.
Add:
**1 3-oz. package strawberry
gelatin**
Mix until well dissolved and bring to
boiling point again. Remove from heat
and let set a few minutes. Stir again. Put
in jars and keep in refrigerator or freezer.

Options:

Strawberries with pineapple gelatin.

Raspberries with raspberry gelatin.

Grapes with grape gelatin.

Peaches with peach, lemon, or
pineapple gelatin.

5 c. rhubarb, chopped, with raspberry or
strawberry gelatin.

Ellen Burkholder, Pembroke, Ont.
Helen Burkholder, St. Catharines, Ont.

●●●●●●●●●●●●●●●●●●●●●●●●●
Oven
Apple Butter

Makes 6 qts.
350°
3 hrs.

Combine in large greased roast pan:
**5 qts. applesauce, unsweetened
10 c. sugar
1 c. vinegar
2 t. cinnamon
1 t. cloves**
Bake at 350° for 3 hours, or until thick. Stir
every 20 minutes. Pour into jars and seal.

Edna M. Reed, New Cumberland, Pa.

●●●●●●●●●●●●●●●●●●●●●●●●●
Apple-Honey
Butter
(oven method)

Makes 10-12 pts.
300°
3 hrs.

Core, cut and cook until soft:
7 lbs. apples
Press through food mill to make 1 gallon
applesauce.
Combine in large enamel roaster:
**applesauce
1½ lbs. honey
1 c. cider or vinegar
1 c. crushed pineapple**
Bake at 300° for 3 hours, stirring
occasionally. Pour into jars and seal.

Ruth Gish, Mt. Joy, Pa.

Freezing

When onions are inexpensive, buy in quantity, chop, and freeze in small portions. When green peppers are plentiful, cut in strips or dice and freeze on cookie sheets. When frozen, scoop into containers, and return to freezer. Handy for casseroles.
—Miriam LeFever,
East Petersburg, Pa.

Chop a quantity of parsley and pack into several peanut-butter jars. Keep in freezing compartment of refrigerator. A tablespoonful flakes off easily anytime you want it.
—Edna Longacre, Barto, Pa.

We always seem to have one overripe banana left from each bunch. I freeze these right in the peel. When several have accumulated I use them in baking cake or breads.
—Esther Martin, Neffsville, Pa.

Freezing pumpkin: Cut pumpkins in half, take out seeds, turn upside down on cookie sheets and bake until soft. If you have enough pumpkins, fill your oven to save heat. When tender, scoop out pumpkin and blend till smooth with as little water as possible. Freeze.
—Patricia Franke,
Wolcottville, Ind.

Freezing apples for pie: Peel, quarter, and slice a few apples at a time. Drop immediately into cold salted water. Place in freezer container. Salt water prevents apples from darkening.
—Anna Ruth Banks,
Smithville, Tenn.

Freezing corn on the cob: Clean ears by trimming ends and removing silk. Do not wash or use water on them. Freeze in plastic bags. To serve, drop ears into boiling water. Cook 6 to 8 minutes after water returns to boiling. Tastes like fresh corn.
—Sarah Claassen,
Beatrice, Neb.

Freezing beet tops, spinach, and other greens: Cut off leaves, wash, blanch, cool immediately in ice water, drain, and freeze. To serve, cook with just a little water. Add salt and butter or a cream sauce.
—Esta M. Eby, Mohnton, Pa.

Near the end of the summer, collect odds and ends from the garden and freeze mixed vegetables for soup. Slightly overripe vegetables will be acceptable used this way.
—Dorothy Miller, Barto, Pa.

If you don't want to make your own ketchup, you can still save about one third by buying it in a number 10 can. Open the can and pour the ketchup into quart-size square plastic containers and freeze. Keep one container in the refrigerator. From it you can easily fill a plastic ketchup dispenser to use on the table or carry to picnics. Plastic dispensers are easier for children to control than glass bottles.

Drying

Dry apples for a snack food. Put peeled, cut-up apples in the sun with a screened cover. Or dry in the oven at very low heat for 4 to 6 hours. Old adjustable window screens make perfect oven racks and enable apples to dry on both sides at once.
—Phyllis Leaman,
Lancaster, Pa.
—Janice Pauls,
MacPherson, Kan.

I often dry bananas. My local produce market sells me a case of darkened bananas which are still beautiful inside for ⅓ the retail price. I peel the bananas, cut them lengthwise in quarters, and then crosswise in half. I place them on two old oven racks and dry in oven on very low heat for 24 to 48 hours. A pilot light or light bulb hung in the oven on an extension cord is enough heat– if it's too hot juices come out of the fruit and it's not as tasty. Eat as snack food.
—Kathy Histand,
   Sellersville, Pa.

Dry mint leaves in the shade on screen or newspaper and pack into jars. A dozen or more mint varieties are available, each with particular flavor.
   Plants are available from friends or herb nursery houses. Plant several around faucet beside the house for hardy perennial availability. Best flavor is in the newly formed leaves and growing tips at the end of the stalks. Pinch these off for tea. Lateral buds will push out to multiply your crop.
—Don Ziegler, Lancaster, Pa.

When tangerines are in season, wash skins well and air them several days until completely dry. Then break into pieces, or powder by processing in blender. If you want them thinly sliced, cut before drying. Store in attractive jars. Dried peels improve with age and keep well for years. Murcot Honey is a good variety of tangerine to use. Add dried peel to foods such as mincemeat, fruit cakes, puddings, pickles and red beets.
—Evelyn Liechty, Berne, Ind.

Wild Foods

While Euell Gibbons is often ridiculed as a nature nut, his suggestions on uses of wild foods may move from novelty to necessity. His intimate knowledge of plants is based on countless field studies and painstaking research. Try Stalking the Good Life, Stalking the Healthful Herbs, or Stalking the Wild Asparagus, published by David McKay Co., New York.
—Paul G. Jantzen,
   Hillsboro, Kan.

The combination of a Euell Gibbons' book and a 12-year-old who likes the outdoors is bound to produce some interesting menus and flavorful, nutritious new foods. Some favorites that are easy to find and identify are dandelions (see Dandelion Salad, p. 250), poppy mallow, polkweed, Jerusalem artichoke, pigweed, lamb's-quarters, sheep-sour, prickly pear, elderberries, wild raspberries, huckleberries, and wild plums. The only rules are to know that you've identified the plant properly, that it is an edible plant in that season of the year, and that it hasn't been sprayed with insecticides if you're eating leaves or berries.
—LaVonne Platt, Newton, Kan.

A favorite of the Russians was "Cossack asparagus," or the common cattail. Gather from young tender plants about two feet tall. Grasp inner leaves and pull; the inner core will break away from the root. Trim off the tough end as you would asparagus. Steam for a few minutes and serve with white or cheese sauce for a mild, novel vegetable.
—Martha B. Nafziger,
   LaCrete, Alta.

Take your children on a fall hike and pick up hickory nuts (shellbarks) and black walnuts from roadsides and woods where they're going to waste. Dry hickory nuts on the attic floor. Knock outer hulls off black walnuts with a hammer. Dump walnuts in a tub of water; discard those that float. Dry a month or two, then crack the nuts while visiting with friends.
—Paul Longacre, Akron, Pa.

snacks and miscellaneous

North American snack habits take criticism from all directions. Instead of spending more time denouncing the products we already recognize as wasteful, let's work positively toward a list of good snacks:

apples
bananas
bread or toast, whole grain
carrot sticks
celery,
   as is or spread with
   cheese or peanut butter
cheese
cherry tomatoes
cookies,
   made with whole grains
   and minimal sugar
crackers, whole grain
dates
dried apples
fruits and real fruit juices
fruit and nut breads
granola
honey on bread
milk
nuts
oranges
peanut butter
peanuts
popcorn
popsicles,
   homemade with minimal sugar
pretzels
puddings,
   homemade with minimal sugar
raisins
sunflower seeds
roasted soybeans
yogurt

Most of the above go well in lunch boxes or on car trips. Last summer our family took a week's trip with another family in a station wagon. The most popular snack in the car, while it lasted, was a huge plastic container of carrot and celery sticks and other raw vegetables. No one got sticky, thirsty, or irritable with a half-upset stomach. Apples, had they been in season, would have been as good.

It's easiest for me to encourage our children in wholesome after-school snacks if I have a bowl of fruit or the makings of sandwiches out on the table when they walk in. I like to take a break myself and sit down to cut apples or spread toast while we talk. If I ignore their hunger, they begin going through the cupboards themselves. Then they're likely to come up with chocolate chips I was saving or declare that nothing but ice cream will satisfy. You can discourage eating poor snack foods by simply not having them on hand, but it's also important to have good things invitingly displayed.

Roasted Soybeans—
I

Soak beans overnight. Cook 1 hour in salted water.
Preheat oven to 350°.
Dry beans in a towel, rubbing briskly to remove outer covering and split beans in half. Single-layer the beans in shallow pans. Bake 30 minutes, turning once or twice. Sprinkle with salt while warm.

Mabel Kreider, Lancaster, Pa.

Roasted Soybeans—
II

Soak soybeans overnight. Next morning put beans in a towel and dry thoroughly. Put beans in heated heavy skillet and stir until golden brown. Just before removing from skillet, add 1 T. margarine or peanut oil and sprinkle with ½ t. salt. Drain on paper.

Miriam LeFever, East Petersburg, Pa.

Roasted Soybeans—
III

Soak beans overnight. Place in a kettle with celery stalks and leaves, chopped onions, and salt. Cook over low heat 3-4 hours. Drain well.
Spread on a cookie sheet with 1-2 T. oil. Roast in 200° oven 4-8 hours until nutlike in flavor and texture. You can use the warm broiler of a gas stove while other baking is being done.

Marianne Miller, Topeka, Kan.

Roasted Wheat Berries (from Ethiopia)

Heat a small amount of oil in skillet.
Add wheat berries (whole wheat) and pop like popcorn.
They don't actually pop, but will puff up.
Serve hot with salt.

Catherine Kornweibel, Easton, Pa.

Seed Snacks—
I

Save squash and pumpkin seeds. Boil in water 5-10 minutes. Drain well.
For each cup of seeds, combine and sprinkle over:
   1 T. melted margarine
   1 t. Worcestershire sauce
Sprinkle with salt or seasoned salt. Bake at 350° for 30 minutes or until nearly dry.

Kathryn Leatherman, Goshen, Ind.

Seed Snacks—
II

Sprinkle squash or pumpkin seeds with turmeric, cumin, coriander, cayenne, and salt. Fry in small amount of oil.

Kamala Misra, Bhubaneswar, India

Roasted Chestnuts

To avoid chestnuts exploding, make a small cut on side of each nut with a paring knife. Place nuts in single layer on cookie sheet. Roast at 400° for about ½ hour. Shake pan occasionally. Different sizes require different time; sample before taking out.
You can also roast chestnuts in the fireplace, or boil in salted water for several hours.

Doris Hamman, Lansdale, Pa.

Take these on a car trip, pack little bagfuls in lunch boxes, and hide some in a high cupboard to sprinkle on salads. But calorie watchers, beware—once you start, it's hard to stop!

●●●●●●●●●●●●●●●●●●●●●●●●●
Roasted
Sunflower Seeds

Makes 2 cups
325°
30 min.

Combine in shallow baking pan:
2 c. hulled sunflower seeds
1 T. oil or melted margarine
1 t. Worcestershire sauce
¼ t. salt
garlic and onion salt to taste
Mix well. Toast at 325° about 30 minutes, stirring occasionally, until seeds are golden and crunchy.

Option:
Combine all in heavy skillet and toast over low heat, stirring often.

Author's Recipe

●●●●●●●●●●●●●●●●●●●●●●
Peanut-Butter
Popcorn

Pop enough corn to make 2 quarts. Cook to a rolling boil:
½ c. sugar
½ c. light corn syrup or honey
Remove from heat and add:
½ c. chunky peanut butter
½ t. vanilla
Pour over popcorn, stirring to coat.

Janet Landes, Phoenix, Ariz.

●●●●●●●●●●●●●●●●●●●●●●●●●
Raw Vegetable Dip

T·S

Makes 1¼ cups

Mix well and chill:
1 c. mayonnaise
1 t. horseradish
1 t. dry mustard
1 t. curry powder
dash lemon juice
2 T. sour cream
Serve with fresh unpeeled zucchini rounds or sticks plus other raw vegetables such as carrots, celery, cucumber, or cauliflower.

Options:
Add yogurt and/or blended cottage cheese.
Vary flavor with chopped herbs in season.

Ruth Heatwole, Charlottesville, Va.

●●●●●●●●●●●●●●●●●●●●●●●●
Apple Snack

Peel, core, and halve:
2 qts. apples
Shred apples coarsely and put on buttered cookie sheet. Bake at 225° until dry. Remove from cookie sheet with pancake turner; break into pieces. Store in air-tight container.

Lina Gerber, Dalton, Ohio

*"This method
captures the full
nose-tingling essence
of mint,"
says Don.*

●●●●●●●●●●●●●●●●●●●●●●●●●
Mint Tea

Makes 2 qts. concentrate

Stuff a 2-qt. jar until full with:
clean mint leaves
Add:
1 c. sugar
Run hot water over outside of jar to
prevent breakage, then pour in:
boiling water to fill
Agitate jar to dissolve sugar. Cover
loosely and let stand several hours or
overnight. Strain contents. Use resulting
concentrate by pouring into ice-filled tall
glasses. Concentrate may be frozen.

Don Ziegler, Lancaster, Pa.

●●●●●●●●●●●●●●●●●●●●●●●●●
Fresh Meadow
Tea

Makes 1 gal.

Bring to boil:
2 c. sugar
4 c. water
Pour over:
2 c. mint leaves, packed
2 sliced lemons
Let stand overnight. Strain off
concentrate and store in refrigerator.
When ready to serve, pour into a gallon
container and fill with water and ice.

Marilyn S. Dombach, Mt. Joy, Pa.

*Quick high-nutrient breakfast:
Orange Ice Delight
and a slice
of whole wheat toast.*

●●●●●●●●●●●●●●●●●●●●●●●●●
Orange
Ice Delight

Makes 1 pt.

Whirl in blender:
1 egg
⅓ c. concentrated orange juice
1 c. milk
4-6 ice cubes, partially crushed
1-2 t. sugar or honey (optional)
Makes 1 pint.

Option:
Substitute for orange concentrate: 1
banana plus ½ t. vanilla, or ½ c. sliced
strawberries.

*Virginia Birky, Salem, Ohio
Minnie Good, Denver, Pa.*

Cottage Cheese Dip

T·S

Makes 2 cups

Combine in blender:
1 lb. creamed cottage cheese
1 t. onion juice or minced onion
salt, pepper and paprika to taste
Whirl until smooth. Vary flavors and serve with crackers or vegetables as suggested in Raw Vegetable Dip, p. 306.

Lorraine Kroeker, Lexington, Neb.

Cheese Ball

Makes 1¾ lbs.

Have cheeses at room temperature. Combine in bowl:
8 oz. cream cheese
1 lb. sharp yellow cheese, shredded
¼ t. garlic salt
2 T. finely minced onion
½ t. salt
½ c. finely chopped black walnuts or other nuts
Form into balls or logs. Sprinkle with chili powder or roll in chopped parsley or nuts. Chill. Serve with crackers.

Elizabeth Showalter, Waynesboro, Va.

Nippy Garbanzo Spread

Makes 2 cups

Sauté:
2 T. margarine or olive oil
1 onion, finely chopped
Combine in saucepan:
1½ c. cooked chick peas (garbanzos), mashed or ground
sautéed onion
2 beaten eggs
Heat, stirring until thickened and dry. Add to taste:
salt
cayenne pepper
mayonnaise
Spread on bread or crackers.

Joan Gingrich, Lancaster, Pa.

Fancy Tea Crackers

T·S

Makes 2-3 doz.
375°
3-5 min.

Combine with fork:
1 egg white
¼ c. sugar
¼ c. chopped cashews or other nuts
Arrange soda crackers on baking sheet. Pile a little nut mixture on each cracker. Bake a few minutes at 375° until lightly browned. Serve with hot tea.

Viola Wiebe, Hillsboro, Kan.

●●●●●●●●●●●●●●●●●●●●●●●●
Soft
Margarine

Soften 1 lb. margarine to room
temperature. Whip with ½ c. milk; return
to refrigerator. Use on sandwiches or
wherever soft margarine is desired.
Makes it easy for children to spread their
own bread.

June Suderman, Hillsboro, Kan.

●●●●●●●●●●●●●●●●●●●●●●●●
Wheat
Crackers

Makes about 1¼ lbs.
425°
7-10 min.

Combine in bowl:
   3 c. white flour
   1 c. whole wheat flour
   1 t. baking powder
   ½ t. salt
Cut in:
   ¾ c. margarine or
      lard-margarine combination
Beat lightly:
   1 egg
Pour egg into 1 c. measure. Add:
   enough milk to make 1 c. liquid
Mix to form a ball. Knead lightly, about 20
strokes.
Preheat oven to 425°.
Divide dough into 4 parts, roll out thinly
on floured board and place on greased
cookie sheets. Cut with pie crimper or
pizza cutter to desired cracker size.
Prick dough all over. Sprinkle
generously with salt. Bake 7-10 minutes
or until lightly browned. Store in airtight
container.

Options:
Increase proportion of whole wheat flour
to white.

Add ¼ c. wheat germ.

Margaret Ingold, Goshen, Ind.

●●●●●●●●●●●●●●●●●●●●●●●●
Soda
Crackers

Makes about ½ lb.
375°
10-12 min.

Preheat oven to 375°.
Combine in bowl:
   2 c. flour
   1 t. salt
   ½ t. soda
Cut in:
   2 T. margarine
Stir in:
   ⅔ c. sour milk or buttermilk
Round dough into a ball and knead a few
strokes. Divide dough into several
pieces and roll out very thin on a floured
board. Lay sheets of dough on
ungreased flat baking pans. Sprinkle
with salt and prick with fork. Cut into 1½"
squares with sharp knife or pizza cutter.
Bake 10-12 minutes, or until lightly
browned.

Option:
Add 1 c. shredded cheese for cheese
crackers.

Viola Dorsch, Musoma, Tanzania

309

*Try these with the
soybean spreads
on p. 114.*

●●●●●●●●●●●●●●●●●●●●●●●●●
Wheat Thins

Makes ⅔ lb.
350°
10 min.

Preheat oven to 350°.
Combine in mixing bowl:
  2 c. whole wheat flour
  2 T. wheat germ
  1 t. salt
  1 t. baking powder
  2 T. brown sugar
  2 T. dry milk solids
Cut in with pastry blender:
  6 T. margarine
Combine separately and stir in:
  ½ c. water
  1 T. molasses
Knead a little until smooth. Grease two
cookie sheets (10x15″) and sprinkle
each with cornmeal. Divide dough in
half. Roll out half of dough directly onto
cookie sheet with floured rolling pin,
rolling dime-thin. Sprinkle lightly with
paprika, garlic, onion, or seasoned salt.
Run rolling pin over once more. Prick
with fork. Cut in squares or triangles.
Bake 10 minutes or until lightly browned.

Donna Koehn, Blaine, Wash.

●●●●●●●●●●●●●●●●●●●●●●●●●
Corn Chips

Makes ½ lb.
350°
10 min.

Preheat oven to 350°.
Combine in mixing bowl:
  1 c. yellow cornmeal
  ⅔ c. flour
  1 t. salt
  1 t. baking powder
  2 T. dry milk solids
Stir together in separate bowl:
  ½ c. water
  ¼ c. oil
  ½ t. Worcestershire sauce
  ⅛ t. Tabasco sauce
Add liquids to dry mixture and stir with
fork. Knead a little until smooth. Grease
two cookie sheets (10x15″) and sprinkle
each with cornmeal. Divide dough in
half. Roll out each half directly onto
cookie sheet with floured rolling pin,
rolling dime-thin. Sprinkle lightly with
paprika, garlic, onion, or seasoned salt.
Run rolling pin over once more. Prick
with fork. Cut in squares or triangles.
Bake 10 minutes or until lightly browned.

Donna Koehn, Blaine, Wash.
Miriam LeFever, East Petersburg, Pa.

*A nourishing lunch-box
or after-school snack.
Excellent keeping quality.*

●●●●●●●●●●●●●●●●●●●●●●●●●
Cheese Sticks

●●●●●●●●●●●●●●●●●●●●●●●●●
Hinkelsteins
(oat sticks)

Makes ⅔ lb.

375°
---
10 min.

Combine:
  1 c. grated sharp cheese
  ½ t. salt and dash pepper
  1¼ c. flour
Cut in with pastry blender:
  ⅓ c. margarine
Sprinkle with:
  3 T. milk
Toss with fork. Form into ball. Preheat
oven to 375°.
Turn dough onto floured board and roll
out ⅛" thick. Sprinkle liberally with
sesame seeds. Run rolling pin over
again. Prick dough with fork all over. Cut
into 1x2" sticks, or 2" squares and then
into triangles. Place on ungreased
cookie sheet. Bake 10 minutes or until
golden.

Miriam LeFever, East Petersburg, Pa.

Makes 100 sticks

375°

15-20 min.

Preheat oven to 375°.
Combine in large bowl:
  3 c. whole wheat flour
  **2½ c. oat flour (process rolled
    oats in a blender)**
  ½ c. soy flour
  2 t. salt
  2 c. chopped dates
  ¾ c. coconut
  ½ c. sesame seeds
  ½ c. sunflower seeds
  ½ c. chopped nuts
Stir thoroughly, making sure dates are
coated with flour mixture.
Add:
  ½ c. oil
  4½ T. honey
  OR 5 T. molasses
  1⅛ c. milk
Mix well. Divide into two greased 10x15"
jelly roll pans. Pat firmly and evenly. Cut
into 1x3" pieces with pizza cutter. Bake
15-20 minutes or until browned. Remove
sticks around the edges if they brown
before center is done.

Ruth Hollinger, Goshen, Ind.

Many of the famous sweets
of India
are made from fresh
milk curd, a high source
of protein.
One of the simplest
is Sandesh.

●●●●●●●●●●●●●●●●●●●●●●●●●

Sandesh

●●●●●●●●●●●●●●●●●●●●●●●●

Honey
Milk Balls

T·S

Makes 2-3 doz.

Makes 2 doz.

Bring to a boil:
2 qts. milk
4 T. lemon juice
OR 1½ c. whey from
cheese-making
Stir as milk begins to boil.
When milk separates into curds and
whey, remove from heat. (If milk does not
separate, add small amounts of lemon
juice and continue boiling until it does.)
Strain mixture through muslin-lined
colander. Place curds in saucepan.
Add:
⅓ c. sugar
Cook over low heat, stirring constantly,
until mixture is thick (10-15 minutes).
Pour onto buttered platter and spread to
¼" thickness. Top with podded whole or
crushed cardamon seed. Cool and cut
into diamond shapes.

LaVonne Platt, Newton, Kan.

Combine in bowl:
½ c. honey or corn syrup
½ c. peanut butter
1 c. dry milk solids
1 c. uncooked rolled oats
OR 1½ c. graham cracker
crumbs
Mix well, then knead by hand until
blended. Shape into small balls.
Makes 2 dozen.

Options:

Mold dough into a long roll and slice.
For each ball, shape dough around a nut.
Roll in coconut.

Marie Harnish, Akron, Pa.
Vi Nofziger, Barberton, Ohio

More-with-Less *joined our fam-*
ily when my husband, Jon, and
I, with our two small children,
Chad and Alicia, were MCCers
in Nigeria. It was a lifesaver, as
the recipes are adaptable to
environments where certain
ingredients are nonexistent.
Some ingredients can be
exchanged for others or left
out—an essential for recipes
we used then. In this way,
"less" often became "more"!
When the power was on strong
enough for the freezer to oper-
ate, Fudgsicles were a favorite
for the children. Currently the
Basic Meat Curry page is a
study in brown stains, and the
book resides on the shelf per-
manently opened to Koinonia
Granola.
—Violet Dutcher,
Cleveland, Ohio

Applesauce Candy

Combine in saucepan:
- **1 c. applesauce**
- **1 c. sugar**

Bring to a boil and cook 2 minutes.
Dissolve in applesauce:
- **1 pkg. fruit gelatin**

Add:
- **¾ c. nuts, finely chopped**

Pour into 8x8" pan. After 24 hours, cut into 1" squares and roll in sugar. Roll in sugar the second time 24 hours later and it's ready to eat.

Options:

Cinnamon Candy: Add 1 T. cinnamon and use raspberry gelatin.

Lime Squares: Add ¾ t. peppermint extract and use lime gelatin.

Lemon Candies: Add finely grated rind of one lemon and use lemon gelatin.

Florence Mellinger, Lancaster, Pa.

Orange Eggnog Popsicles

T·S

Makes 12 popsicles

In large mixer bowl or blender beat together:
- **1 pt. vanilla ice cream**
- **1 6-oz. can (¾ c.) frozen orange juice concentrate, thawed**
- **1 egg**

Gradually beat in:
- **1½ c. milk**

Freeze as directed in Yogurt Popsicles.

Option:

Subsitiute frozen grape or pineapple concentrate.

Virginia Birky, Salem, Ohio

Yogurt Popsicles

T·S

Makes 6-8 popsicles

Stir together:
- **1 pt. plain yogurt**
- **6 T. (½ small can) frozen orange juice concentrate**
- **1 t. vanilla (optional)**

Freeze in popsicle molds or small waxed paper cups. Insert sticks into paper cup molds when partially frozen. To serve, peel off paper cup.

Option:

Substitute frozen grape or pineapple concentrate.

Mary Lou Cummings, Quakertown, Pa.

Fudgsicles

T·S

Makes 8-10 popsicles

Make Quick Chocolate Pudding, p. 264. Increase milk to 2½ c., cocoa to 3 T., and sugar to ½ c.
Cool.
Freeze as directed in Yogurt Popsicles.

Option:

Use 1 box chocolate pudding mix (not instant) prepared with 3 c. milk.

Donna Kroeker, Lexington, Neb.

Soap takes 2-3 weeks to dry, but it can be used immediately. If lumps of soap are too large to dissolve easily during the cycle of washing, put them in a small amount of hot water first to soften them before adding the soap to washer.

●●●●●●●●●●●●●●●●●●●●●●●●●
Homemade Laundry Soap

Makes 9 lbs. soap

Clean grease, using either method:
1. Boil grease in an equal volume of water. Remove from heat; chill by adding 1 qt. cold water for each gallon of liquid. Remove firm fat from top.
2. Melt fat and strain through muslin. Place in iron, enamel, or stoneware container (never use aluminum):
   5 c. cold water
Slowly add to cold water:
   1 can lye
Stir to dissolve and allow to cool (may take several hours). Melt grease; allow lye solution and grease to come to correct temperatures:
—sweet lard or soft fat at 85° with lye solution 75°
—half lard, half tallow at 110°, with lye solution 85°
—all tallow at 130°, with lye solution 95°
Pour lye solution into melted fat in a thin stream with slow, even stirring. Too rapid pouring or stirring causes separation. Stir slowly 10-20 minutes until mixture is thick as honey. Pour into wood or cardboard box lined with damp cotton cloth. Cover with old blanket or rug to retain heat. Let stand 24 hours. Remove soap, cut into bars, and store where air can reach it. Dry in even temperature 2 weeks to age.
To use in automatic washer, you must have soft water. Shred soap finely on a grater, or cut in pieces, and melt in small amount of hot water before adding to washer.

Ada Beachy, Goshen, Ind.
Gladys Stoesz, Akron, Pa.

●●●●●●●●●●●●●●●●●●●●●●●●●
Granulated Soap

Makes 13 lbs.

Preparing grease:
Heat together accumulated fat and drippings. Strain. If fat contains meat juices or lots of dark particles, allow to cool and then use fat which rises to the top. Discard dark particles which settle to the bottom.
In a large iron or stainless steel kettle (do not use glass, or aluminum), mix together:
   1 can lye
   1 c. pure borax
   3 qts. cold water
Slowly add:
   4½ lbs. warm melted grease.
Stir, stir, stir, frequently throughout the day with a wooden spoon. When the mix becomes firm and can no longer be stirred easily, wear gloves and crumble the soap. A pastry blender can also be used to break up particles.
Do not double recipe. Use about ½ c. to a washer load of clothes.

Mary E. Groh, Albany, Ore.

••••••••••••••••••••••••••
**Paste for
Children's Play**

_____
Makes 5 cups
_____
_____
_____

Combine in top of double boiler:
**1 c. sugar
1 c. flour
1 qt. cold water**
Cook until thickened, stirring often.
Add to preserve:
**1 T. alum
½ t. oil of cloves**
Seal into jars. Paste will set to stiffer
consistency. Lasts indefinitely if kept
sealed.

*Nora Bohn, Goshen, Ind.
Herta Janzen, Calcutta, India*

••••••••••••••••••••••••••
Play-Dough

Mix together in bowl:
**2 c. flour
2 T. alum**
Heat to boiling:
**1½ c. water
½ c. salt
1 T. oil
food coloring**
Stir liquids into dry ingredients. Knead
until smooth. Store in airtight container.

Ada Beachey, Goshen, Ind.

Don't look to men for help;
  Their greatest leaders fail;
    For every man must die.

His breathing stops, life ends,
  And in a moment
    all he planned for himself is ended.

But happy is the man
Who has the God of Jacob as his helper,
whose hope is in the Lord his God—
the God who made both earth
and heaven, the seas and everything in them.

He is the God who keeps every promise,
and gives justice
to the poor and oppressed,
and food to the hungry.
—Psalm 146:3-7
  Living Bible

Index to Introductory Chapters

Index to Recipes

●●●●●●●●●●●●●●●●●●●●●●●●●

328